Jesus in a New Age, Dalai Lama World

Defending and Sharing Christ with Buddhists

Jesus in a New Age, Dalai Lama World

Defending and Sharing Christ with Buddhists

M. Tsering

We want to hear from you. Please send your comments about this book to us in care of the address below. Thank you.

P.O. Box 418
Upper Darby, PA 19082 USA
www.interserveusa.org

To Pa la and Ama la

without whom this book
could not have been written

Contents

A Note to the Reader

This book is a practical guide to sharing Christ with anyone whose religion is the Tibetan form of Buddhism: the American college student who is "into *dharma*," the Tibetan refugee in Canada, the Mongolian nomad, or the Sherpa trekking guide in the Himalayas. All of these people have been influenced by the beliefs and values of Tibet's unique form of Buddhism. From its beginnings in a remote corner of Inner Asia, Tibetan Buddhism has spread across the globe to become a worldwide religion.

Since the first edition of this book appeared in 1988, astonishing changes have taken place in the Tibetan Buddhist world. The Soviet Union gave way to Russia, Mongolia became a democracy, and China abandoned Maoism for capitalism. Governments formerly hostile to outside influences invited aid and development workers to enter their countries. Churches appeared where none existed before. A wide variety of people from the international Christian community now live and serve in Inner Asia. Conversely, more people from Inner Asia are moving to international destinations. Christians in Korea, Japan, Canada, Australia, the US, and the UK are getting new neighbors from Mongolia, Tibet, and Nepal.

Jesus in A New Age, Dalai Lama World: Defending and Sharing Christ with Buddhists (formerly published as *Sharing Christ in the Tibetan Buddhist World*) reflects these changes. The text has been completely revised and updated, and new material on the origins of shamanism and Tibetan Buddhism has been added. The Tibet-centered focus of the first two editions has been broadened to include Mongolia and the wider Tibetan Buddhist world. The author hopes that these new features (and a Korean translation of the second edition) will make the book useful to anyone who is working or preparing to work among Tibetan Buddhists wherever they may be found.

Because the rapid pace of political change in Asia will no doubt continue into the future, certain alterations have been made in the text. To protect local Christians from possible harm, some names have been changed, the details of various incidents altered, and details of church growth in recent decades in certain parts of Inner Asia has not been discussed. Likewise, some characters appearing in this book are composite figures, but everything that is said about them is drawn from the lives and experiences of real people.

Readers unfamiliar with Tibetan or Chinese terms will find the glossary helpful. Standard transliterations of Tibetan words appear in the glossary. Chinese terms are translated using the official Pinyin system, in which the letter Q is pronounced as "ch," X is pronounced as "sh," and ZH is pronounced as "j." Thus "Qinghai" is pronounced Chinghai; "Xining" is pronounced She-ning; and "Lanzhou" is pronounced Lan-jo. Many place names in China and Tibet have changed since 1949. For the convenience of the reader I have used modern place names only, except where historical context makes the older name more appropriate (e.g. Peking).

M. Tsering

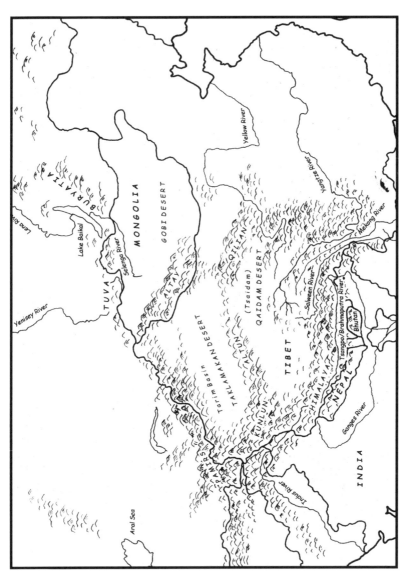

Buddhist Inner Asia

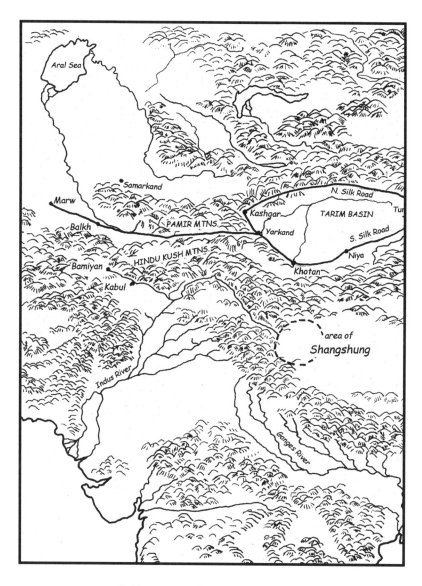

The Kushan Empire

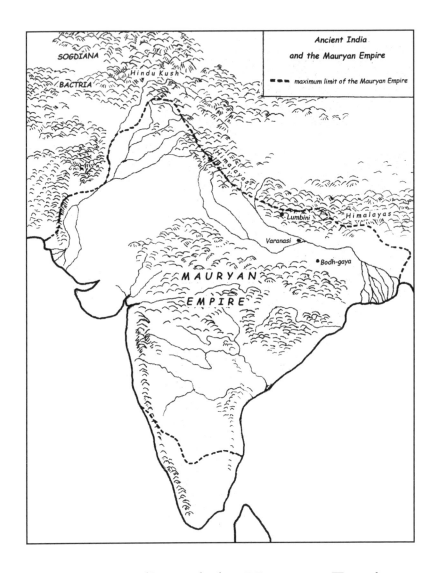

Ancient India and the Mauryan Empire

Buddhism Spreads Across Asia

1   Spread of Early Buddhism to Sri Lanka
2   Hinayana Buddhism to Southeast Asia
3   Mahayana Buddhism to Bactria
4   Mahayana Buddhism to China

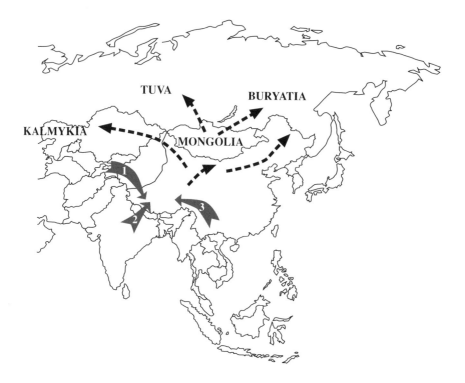

Buddhism Spreads Across Inner Asia

1 Tantric Buddhism Spreads to Western Tibet
(Shangshung)

2 Tantric Buddhism Spreads to Central Tibet
from India

3 Mahayana Buddhism Spreads to Central Tibet
from China

▬ ▬ ▬ Spread of Tibetan Buddhism 17th-20th Centuries

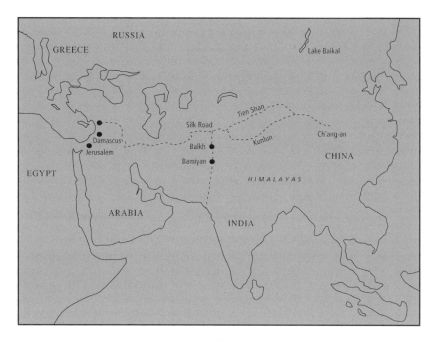

The Silk Road

CHAPTER 1

Out of This World

On the last night of July 1949, the American journalist Lowell Thomas and his son Lowell, Jr. set out on the adventure of a lifetime. Starting from Calcutta, India, they embarked on a month-long journey by train, truck, and mule north across the Himalaya mountains to the forbidden city of Lhasa, the capital of Tibet. Their expedition began at a time when Tibet's traditional government faced imminent destruction by an advancing Maoist revolution. Faced with a rapidly deteriorating political situation, the country's leaders hoped that the Thomas' visit and subsequent radio broadcasts would focus international attention on the Tibet and its unique form of Buddhism. The traditional government had invited the two Americans to visit some of the country's largest monasteries, each one of which housed thousands of red-robed, shaven-headed monks, one of whom was about to begin a spiritual pilgrimage that would lead him to faith in Jesus Christ. The story of his journey, and that of the Thomases, brings together the three forces that contended for the hearts and minds of Inner Asia[1] in the mid-twentieth century: Tibetan Buddhism, Christianity, and Marxism-Leninism. But this anticipates the situation in that tense summer of 1949, when the forces of violent change lay waiting at Tibet's door.

Two Journeys

Long closed to foreigners, Tibet was then an exotic and mysterious land that for centuries had been the goal of travelers, mystics, and scholars. The country's spiritual head, the Dalai Lama, was a priest-king ruling a people who seemed to be totally absorbed in the pursuit of their religion (known as

1

Tibetan Buddhism or Lamaism). The signs of this all-pervading faith were everywhere: in the monasteries perched above every Tibetan town, in the heaps of sacred stones at the tops of the mountain passes, and at the great shrines called *chortens,* where the Tibetans walked in circles for hours, gaining the religious merit on which their next life depended. During the Middle Ages, the Tibetans had used shrewd alliances and adroit political maneuvering to spread their faith across most of Central Asia, converting the Mongols and other Asian peoples in the process. By the end of the seventeenth century, dozens of people groups from the Himalayas to Siberia, and from China to the banks of Russia's Volga River, had adopted the Tibetan form of Buddhism. All of these diverse peoples looked to Tibet as their holy land, and to Lhasa as their holy city, the center of the Tibetan Buddhist world.[2]

By the late eighteenth century, Tibetan Buddhism had stopped expanding and turned inward. With the rise of British power in neighboring India in the late 1700s, the Tibetans grew suspicious of foreign motives and closed their country to outsiders. Tibet remained securely aloof from the rest of the world during the nineteenth century, but with the dawn of the twentieth, its shell of isolation began to crack. In 1904 the British launched a military expedition that briefly occupied Lhasa. The British force (known as the Younghusband Expedition after its chief political officer[3]) negotiated a treaty and withdrew after only two months in the capital. In 1910 the Chinese sent their own military expedition,[4] forcing the Dalai Lama to seek temporary refuge in India. Two years later the Chinese force withdrew, allowing the hapless Dalai Lama to return to his capital. Both the Chinese and the British expeditions brought home to the Tibetans the fact that just because they were not interested in the outside world, the reverse was not necessarily true.

By 1949 the situation on Tibet's frontiers had changed ominously. To the east, Tibet's giant neighbor China was in the throes of a civil war. Complete Communist victory seemed imminent, and no one in Tibet knew where, or if, the triumphant Maoist armies would come to a halt. True, Tibet was protected by some of the world's highest mountains and an arm of the Gobi desert, but the country's small, ill-equipped army was completely unprepared to meet the battle-hardened Chinese. With the military threat looming in the east, Tibet's rulers decided that their country needed foreign friends, and soon. Tibet would have to make its plight clear to the outside world. In a break with all past tradition, the government invited its first foreign press correspondents to visit Lhasa.

As a noted author, radio commentator, and explorer who had made his reputation in travel journalism,[5] the 57-year-old Lowell Thomas Sr. was only too happy to oblige. Tibet was one of the few exotic places he had not visited, and he was anxious to see the land that had been the unreached goal of so many other travelers. By the fifth of August, 1949, Thomas and his son had left from Gangtok, Sikkim, on the Indian side of the border, with a train of nine pack mules and six porters. Within a week they had crossed the 4,000 meter Natu La pass between Tibet and Sikkim, and begun to make their way across the high Tibetan plateau. Following the same route that Younghusband had taken to Lhasa in 1904, they reached the holy city 28 days after leaving the steamy Indian plains.

In the midst of the interviews, broadcasts, and receptions that followed, the two Americans set aside some time for sightseeing. They were particularly anxious to see the city's great monasteries. Tibetan Buddhism is a monastic religion, and at that time almost a quarter of the male population of Tibet lived in monasteries of one sort or another.[6] The greatest of these monasteries were in the city of Lhasa, and the largest of the Lhasa monasteries was called Drepung (the name means "rice heap" in Tibetan). At the time of the Thomases' visit, over 7,000 monks lived in its whitewashed cloisters.[7] The two Americans were received by the monastery's head abbot, Lobsang Tashi, and a delegation of senior monks who held positions of

Route of the Thomas Party
Summer 1949

influence with the government. With their odd-looking Western clothes and bulky boxes of recording equipment, Thomas and his son must have made a strange sight to the assembled monks. Questions about America followed, and Lobsang Tashi expressed his wish that the United States would eventually become a home to Tibetan Buddhism.[8] Through a strange chain of circumstances, his wish would be fulfilled sooner than he knew.

When the interview was finished, the Thomases made their way out of Drepung to finish their round of meetings in Lhasa. In mid-September they left, carrying their notes and photographs with them over the high passes to India. On their return to the United States, Lowell Jr. wrote a book about their journey. So alien had Tibet seemed to him that he entitled his record of their travels *Out of This World*.

Unknown to the Thomases, one of Drepung's thousands of monks had watched their movements with special interest. Tsering was born in south-central Tibet in 1917.[9] When he was six, his parents sent him to the local monastery to be trained as a monk. Tsering did well in his studies, and by the time of the Thomas' visit he had been admitted to the great monastery of Drepung. He hadn't recalled seeing any foreigners before, but the sight of the Thomases must have stirred his nimble mind to wonder what lay outside his native land. In 1951, he decided to see for himself. With a friend he set out down the great Chumbi Valley on his way to India, using the same route that the Thomases had taken two years before. Along the way Tsering and his friend decided to visit Bhutan, a remote kingdom that straddles the Himalayas along the east side of the valley. In this devoutly Tibetan Buddhist land the two monk friends found a warm welcome. They went from house to house begging their food, reading the Buddhist scriptures, and performing various rituals to make religious merit for the people they met.

In July of each year there is a traditional Tibetan festival that celebrates the preaching of the Buddha's first sermon.[10]

Tsering and his friend joined other monks for the festival, which, like many social occasions in Tibetan Buddhist lands, involved drinking *chang*, the local beer. In the course of this festival, the monks became drunk, and Tsering became sexually involved with a girl. Realizing that he had violated his monk's vows of celibacy, he left the Buddhist priesthood and continued on his journey to India. Like the disillusioned youth of a later generation, Tsering wandered among the Buddhist holy places of north India with no money and no possessions. He became seriously ill with malaria, and at this lowest point of his life he decided to return to Tibet.

The route back to Tibet lay near the city of Darjeeling, long famous for the tea it exports from the surrounding hills. As Tsering entered the Darjeeling market, he met a tall Englishman who invited him to stay in his home and become his Tibetan teacher. Tsering agreed, and it was there that he found a large book, printed in Tibetan, that told of a God who made the world and was not worshipped by making offerings to images. As Tsering read the book, this God seemed to speak to him directly:

> Forget the former things; do not dwell on the past.
> See, I am doing a new thing!
> Now it springs up; do you not perceive it?
> I am making a way in the desert
>   and streams in the wasteland.[11]

As Tsering read this and other Bible passages, his heart was changed, and he believed in the God who had made him. He did not understand everything about his new faith at once. Years of experience as a Tibetan Buddhist monk had not prepared him to understand what he read in his new Bible. Many things were very different from the way Tibetan Buddhists understood them. Yet as he read the Scriptures day by day, his understanding grew, and in 1955 he was baptized.

As Tsering's spiritual journey was beginning, events in his native land were about to bring radical changes to Tibet and its people. Shortly after the Thomases returned from their trip to Lhasa, the Chinese Communist Party gained complete control of China and proclaimed a Peoples Republic on October 1, 1949. Within months, Chinese armies arrived on Tibet's eastern borders.[12] By 1951 the Chinese asserted central government control over Tibet, provoking its people to armed resistance. Sporadic guerilla warfare eventually exploded in a full scale revolt against Chinese rule in the spring of 1959. In the fighting that followed, the Dalai Lama and thousands of his followers fled to India, where they began to rebuild their shattered lives and to create a focus of Tibetan culture and religion outside their homeland.

In Tibet itself, the short-lived revolt was crushed. The militantly antireligious communists began a campaign of terror against Tibetan Buddhism. Hundreds of monasteries were destroyed and their inhabitants shot or sent to labor camps. Ruthless political indoctrination and forced collectivization of farmland followed, bringing famine to Tibet by the 1960s. The Tibetan people entered a long night of suffering from which they would not emerge for many years. Though Buddhism had suffered a nearly mortal blow in Tibet, it began to flourish anew in the Tibetan refugee camps of India. Monks taught in newly established monasteries, set up schools, and translated Tibetan religious texts into English and other European languages. Selected monks went abroad to study and spread their faith among a generation of youth increasingly alienated from Western materialism.[13] In the mid-1960s the so-called hippies and other disillusioned young people from Europe and America began to drift into India in search of new mystical experiences. What many of them discovered was the Tibetan form of Buddhism. Within ten years this restless generation and its spiritual descendants successfully transplanted Tibetan Buddhism from the Indian subcontinent to the West. On college campuses, in training seminars, and at newly opened Tibetan Buddhist study centers and monasteries in Canada, the United States, and western Europe, thousands of young people came face to face with what until then had been an obscure Asian religion.[14]

Tibetan Buddhism found ample room for growth in the climate of religious experimentation that flourished in Western countries in the closing decades of the twentieth century. Reliable figures are hard to find, but it seems likely that tens of thousands of Europeans and Americans began to follow some form of Tibetan Buddhism during this period, and the number continued to grow thanks to a network of Tibetan Buddhist study centers. In common with the so-called "New Age" movement of which it was loosely a part, Tibetan Buddhism proposed a new spiritual agenda for the West: an agenda that in its understanding and worldview stood radically opposed to the Gospel. The wish that Lobsang Tashi made to the Thomases in 1949 had come true in just three decades.

The forces that brought Tibet into contact with the West also brought changes to the other peoples of the Tibetan Buddhist world. Tibetan Buddhists in Russia (then the Soviet Union), China, and Mongolia found their faith vigorously suppressed by Marxist-Leninist governments. As revolutionary fervor subsided, Marxism and Tibetan Buddhism reached an uneasy truce. A handful of monks were allowed to return to state supervised monasteries. Damaged temples were repaired, and a limited amount of worship grudgingly permitted. To the south, the Himalayan states of Nepal and Bhutan (perhaps mindful of what happened to the politically isolated Tibetans) opened their doors to the outside world. Diplomatic and aid missions were welcomed. Education brought new ideas and improved living conditions to previously underdeveloped areas. Finally, international tourism brought camera-wielding tourists to places only explorers had visited before. This wave of social change was compounded by the events of the last two decades of the century. The advent of religious liberty in the former Soviet Union and Mongolia stimulated Tuvan, Kalmyk, Buryat, and Mongolian Buddhists to revive their traditional culture and religion. Monasteries were rebuilt, young men trained as monks, and contacts established with Tibetan Buddhists abroad.

The opening of Tibetan Buddhist lands came at a time when Christians in many countries were awakening to the needs of cultures (or "people groups") which lacked an indigenous Christian presence. These people groups were often called "unreached" because they lacked a national church which could live out the life of Christ within that culture. For example, advocates of the people group approach pointed out that a group like the Yugurs[15] of China's Gansu province had no known fellowships of Christian believers. If the Yugurs were to hear about Christ, then someone from outside their culture would have to enter their world and live the Christian life in a way that was meaningful to them. The same was true of other peoples as well. From the Buryats of Siberia to the Sherpas of the Himalayas, millions of Tibetan Buddhists were seen as living on one of the last great frontiers of world mission.

The forces that shook the Tibetan Buddhist world in the last half of the twentieth century brought new opportunities for Christians from many countries to enter the long-forbidden lands of Inner Asia. Travel became easier as railroads and airports were built in remote areas. Tourism opened previously closed countries. The push for economic development created a demand for technical experts who could live and work among Tibetan Buddhist peoples. Because of these changes, the Tibetan Buddhist world became more accessible to the Church than at any time in recent history. A wave of late twentieth-century Christians responded to this new situation, but when they arrived, many of them found that their task was not as simple as they had thought.

The Case of the Baffled Lama

Take the case of John and Vivian, who were Christian workers in a certain city of Inner Asia. They wanted to talk about their faith with a Tibetan priest or *lama* who lived in their neighborhood. After greeting the lama with a suitable present, John and Vivian told him the story of a personal God who made the world and everything in it. They spoke of man's bondage to sin and death, and told the lama how God sent his Son to suffer and die for man's redemption. John explained that everyone who turns from sin and believes in Christ can receive God's salvation as a free gift. Saved by the blood of Christ, the sinner can enjoy eternal life in fellowship with God. The lama is baffled and offended by such a message, and only his monastic detachment keeps his annoyance from showing. As he explains it to his followers later, the foreign visitors made some extremely strange statements.

First, they spoke of Buddha, his body, and his word creating the world. This made no sense, since Buddha taught that the world had no beginning and was not made by anybody. (Actually, Vivian and John had used a Tibetan word for "God" which usually refers to the Buddha, his monks, and his teachings. They forgot to explain what they meant by it.) Second, these strange visitors said that all men were sinners, which is plainly not so, since Tibetan lamas have no sin. (The lama is right. In his thinking, he canceled all his sins long ago through the merit of his religious practices. John and Vivian had used the Tibetan word for sin, which means something that is a moral fault, but has nothing to do with offense against a holy and righteous God.) Thirdly, John and Vivian spoke of God having a Son, which the lama was completely unable to understand. Perhaps they meant that God came to earth in a mystical body, much as all lamas do. Or maybe he was a kind of reincarnated saint called a *boddhisattva*. But in that case, why had this Son of God suffered so much? Had he committed great sins in his previous lives? How could he believe in a religion that was based upon such suffering?

The foreigners spoke of "salvation" as a free gift. But why follow this strange path when anyone can earn liberation through the practice of religion? Clearly, the lama thought, the end of the Buddhist path and the end of the Christian path are one and the same. (Vivian and John had spoken of salvation without explaining what they meant. To a Tibetan Buddhist, this word meant liberation from rebirth. In effect they had told the lama that he could be delivered from rebirth by believing in Christ.) As Vivian and John left the lama, they gave him a copy of the Tibetan Bible, which they urged him to read. When he did so, he was shocked to find detailed instructions about the killing of animals,[16] commands for God's chosen people to go to war,[17] and a God who was described as "angry"[18] and "jealous."[19] When the lama read about the life of Jesus, he found that it was the head lamas who condemned Jesus to death.[20] (The version of the Tibetan Bible used by John and Vivian translated the crucifixion narrative using the term "head lama" for "chief priest.")

As the lama read the Gospels, he realized that the Christians based their religion on a blood sacrifice,[21] which he found primitive and unworthy of belief. The shedding of blood for religious purposes had ended long ago in the Tibetan Buddhist world. The lama decided that he could never follow such a strange religion, and closed his new Bible for the last time. His two Christian visitors later heard of his comments, and urged their friends to pray for the lama's "hardness of heart." While the lama's heart may have been hard, clearly he did not have a fair chance to understand the message that Vivian and John tried so hard to present. Nor had he seen it lived out among his people. The message of God's love in Christ ran afoul of double meanings and cultural taboos that made nonsense of the Gospel.[22] The result was miscommunication.

Summary

By the middle of the twentieth century, progress in trade, travel, and communications had made the world an increasingly interconnected place. Like other theocratic regimes before and since, the traditional Tibetan government tried to isolate its people from the social and political changes taking place all around them. When this effort failed, many Tibetans took their beliefs and practices with them into a diaspora which spread Tibetan Buddhism worldwide. At the same time, many in the international Christian community became aware of the physical and spiritual needs of peoples who lacked any opportunity either to hear of Christ or to see his life lived out in locally meaningful terms. As ongoing political and social changes in

Asia opened previously closed doors, Christians from many countries came to Asia with hopes of seeing the Church thrive in places where it had long been dormant or nonexistent. Though there were some exceptions, this effort was generally less successful than hoped, as John and Vivian discovered.

Yet this need not be the case. When it is rightly lived and appropriately presented, the Gospel is good news in every culture. With the right kind of preparation and training, Christians of the twenty-first century can learn how to live out the life of Christ in ways that Tibetan Buddhists can understand and appreciate. Learning how to do this effectively, however, requires a deeper understanding of Tibetan Buddhist life and worldview than John and Vivian had. The best way to gain such an understanding is to make a journey into the distant past, which we will begin in the next chapter.

CHAPTER 2

Why Inner Asia Became Buddhist: Part I

Crouching behind some low bushes, Dorj fixed his eyes on the trees at the far side of the valley, waiting for the slight movement that would betray the presence of his quarry. For three weeks he and his companions had waited here, watching intently for the first signs of the migrating reindeer. But now, for the first time in Dorj's 34 years, the reindeer had not come, and he did not know why. The last edible plants in the forest had withered with the first frost, the end of the carefully stored food was near, and the women of his tribe were beginning to peel bark from the trees in hopes of getting enough food for the children. As the group's oldest and most experienced hunter, Dorj knew that their survival depended on what he did next. Tightening his grip on his short spear, he inspected the stone blade that had taken so many weeks to sharpen. "If there is a tool to kill animals," he wondered, "then why isn't there a tool to make them come to our tribe?" He shivered inside his reindeer-hide cloak as the snowflakes fell indifferently around him.

The Story of Inner Asia

Dorj and his tribe of Ice Age hunters lived near what is now called Lake Baikal,[23] at the northern edge of a region which we will call Inner Asia. In geographical terms, Inner Asia includes the part of Siberia roughly 500 kilometers on either side of Lake Baikal, all of Mongolia, an immense swath of northern and western China, and the Himalayan portions of India, Nepal, and Bhutan.[24] Defined in this way, Inner Asia is a roughly figure-8 shaped area, oriented northeast-southwest, with its lower

Inner and Outer Asia

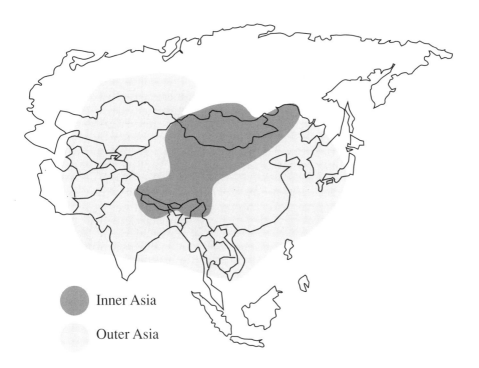

Inner Asia

Outer Asia

loop resting on the Himalayas, its slender waist at western China's Gansu Province, and its vast upper loop enclosing much of the Gobi Desert, the Mongolian steppes, and the southern fringe of Siberia. This part of Asia is distinct because of its high altitude, dry climate, poor soils, and distinct ecology.[25] These physical factors played a major role in the region's spiritual destiny, so before our story begins, it is worth taking a moment to understand them.

In the far-distant past, the subcontinent of India was an island in its namesake ocean. Pushed irresistibly northward by forces deep within the earth, India collided with the mainland of Asia, raising a range of low mountains. When mammoths and saber-toothed tigers walked the earth, the entire area was thrust skywards yet again, lifting the Himalayas higher than any other mountain range on earth. The intensity of this ongoing collision and uplift raised still other highlands, plateaus, and mountains deep within Asia, surrounding the thousand-kilometer-wide Tibetan plateau with mighty mountains: the Himalayas to the south, the Kunlun, Altun, and Qilian mountains to the north and west, and a set of incredibly rugged ranges to the east. On its north side the Tibetan Plateau drops away to two great deserts, the Taklamakan and the Gobi. The Gobi is a highland desert fringed with low mountains and scoured by ceaseless winds; in the north it merges with the grasslands of the Central Asian steppe. To the north of the steppe, the land rises to a complex of low, forested mountains, near the center of which lies 1,600 meter-deep Lake Baikal. From the Baikal region, the whole of Inner Asia stretches about 3,000 kilometers southwest to the central Himalayas.

Inner Asia lies far from the sea, and what little moisture reaches it[26] is drained away by great rivers. In Siberia and northern Mongolia, tributaries of the Lena and the Yenisey drain precious moisture away to the Arctic Ocean. The ever-rising Himalayas shed their melted snows toward the Indian Ocean (via the Indus, the Ganges, and the Brahmaputra rivers) and block life-giving heat and moisture that would otherwise come from the sea. Tibet's eastern mountains drain away to the Pacific across China (via the Yellow and Yangtze rivers) and Southeast Asia (via the Mekong). In the course of geologic time, the land has grown higher, drier, and colder. Lakes retreated into basins, turned salty, or evaporated altogether, leaving only naked rock or freezing dust. The few rivers that lie entirely within Inner Asia end in desert basins or languish in salt lakes.[27]

The dryness of Inner Asia is complemented by its cold. Winters are harsh: Mongolia and Tibet have air temperatures below freezing for as much as six months each year,[28] and even their average *annual* temperatures are slightly below freezing.[29] The northerly position of much of the area,[30] its great distance from the sea, and its high average altitude[31] keep the entire region colder than other places at the same latitude.[32] These high and dry conditions isolate Inner Asia from its neighbors, and bar easy access to it from almost every direction. The Gobi and Taklamakan deserts guard Tibet from the northwest and Mongolia from the south. In the north, the hardships and sheer distances of Siberian travel have protected Inner Asia from outside influences for most of history.

Inner and Outer Asia

The arid cold and salty soils of Inner Asia make it difficult for plants to grow. In most places, only a few salt-tolerant grasses and other hardy vegetation cling to the soil, blasted by bitter winds and freeze-dried by earth-cracking cold. With a few very important exceptions (such as the Yarlung Valley in Tibet) much of Inner Asia is unsuitable for farming.[33] For early human bands such as Dorj's, this left two alternatives: either hunt wild animals and gather native plants, or domesticate[34] certain animals and keep them in herds. Hunting wild animals and gathering wild plants as a sole source of food is difficult, unpredictable, and dangerous; this lifeway was almost extinct in Inner Asia by 1000 B.C.[35] Herding domesticated animals is a much easier option[36] and eventually became the dominant lifeway of Inner Asia. However, since the entire region is ecologically underproductive, herding animals requires a constant search for water and fresh pastureland. Such a lifestyle cannot support many families per square kilometer of available grazing land, so the human population of Inner Asia remained dispersed and its population density very low.[37] This had very important effects on Tibetan Buddhism, as we shall see later.

Fortunately for Dorj's early band of humans, some animals thrived in the difficult environment of Inner Asia, and their interaction with man plays a vital role in our story. In the Tibetan highlands roamed the large and ferocious wild yak.[38] Crossed with domestic cattle to produce the relatively mild-mannered domestic yak, these versatile animals furnished their nomadic owners with milk, meat, skins, transport, and fuel. The horse (first domesticated around 4000 B.C.[39] in the area north of the Black Sea) played a similar role in steppe areas. Cattle, sheep, goats, and asses (the ancestor of the domestic donkey) were first domesticated in the Middle East, but brought to Inner Asia at a very early date. Sheep provided Inner Asian nomads with wool, felt, and clothing. Within the great coniferous forests of Siberia, reindeer were the major domesticated animals, and they supported the lifeways of many Siberian peoples. The forests also held essential fur-bearing creatures such as ermine, sable, lynx, and bear. The bane of the nomads' existence was the wolf (a stock character in many folktales) and in Tibet, the beautiful snow leopard.

The animals in our story changed human history because they made life possible in an otherwise hopeless environment. Used as plow-pullers, the versatile domestic yak enabled the people of Tibet's Yarlung Valley to build an agriculture-based civilization that would later dominate its immediate neighbors and even threaten distant China.[40] Used as pack animals in trade caravans, yaks helped to forge a group of warlike tribes into a single people called the Tibetans. In the hands of the Mongols, the horse became the most feared military vehicle in history. The two-humped Bactrian camel (first domesticated around 2500 B.C.[41]) was a beast of long-distance trade. Local faiths became world religions by riding on its back. In the far north, the reindeer sustained the life and culture of the Siberian peoples who will appear later in this story.

The Story of Outer Asia

Almost surrounding the impoverished highland of Inner Asia was its gifted sister, Outer Asia. Here lay the great arc of rich and innovative cultures from which Buddhism would one day enter the heart of the Asian continent. To the west lay the ancient kingdoms of Bactria, Sogdia, and Kushan (now in the "stan" countries of Central Asia). Here were melting pots where ideas from China and India mixed with those from Mesopotamia and the Mediterranean. To the south lay India, a prodigious exporter of religions, and the original home of Buddhism. In the east was China, an enduring military foe of Inner Asian peoples: sometimes as their victim, and sometimes as their conqueror. Far to the northwest lay Russia, historically late to the game in Inner Asia, but a dominant player for the past 300 years. Inner Asia lay within these surrounding cultures like an egg in a cup.

Like unequally gifted sisters, Outer Asia seemed to have everything that Inner Asia lacked: proximity to the sea, temperate climates, abundant rain, good soils, and nutritious crops. In ancient India, the rivers pouring out of the Himalayas watered a magnificent subtropical jungle — a land of abundance where food and game were to be had for the taking. The fertile Indus Valley (now in Pakistan) and China's Yellow River valley became early centers of agriculture. The crops[42] raised in such places could be stored and used to feed people who did not themselves produce food: merchants, craftsmen, soldiers, and government officials. These specialists in turn supported well-fed sedentary populations who knew large-scale political organization,[43] writing,[44] and metalworking[45] from a very early period in history. The Indus Valley, Ganges, and Yellow River cultures became centers of population[46] and technological innovation[47] for the entire Asian continent.[48]

The contrast between the cultures of Inner and Outer Asia drives much of the story told in this book.[49] Inner Asia's cold, arid, and ecologically underproductive environment lay isolated behind vast mountains and deserts. As we have seen, conditions were unfavorable for agriculture, so the inhabitants herded domesticated animals that required frequent changes of pasture, meaning that their owners had to become wide-ranging nomads.[50] In marginally productive lands like those of Inner Asia, this sparked competition for limited grassland resources, which meant that Inner Asian peoples had to develop military skills from an early age,[51] a fact of great significance to China through much of its history, and to India and Europe during the rise of Genghis Khan. Inner and Outer Asia exchanged armies, religions, and ideas on their mutual borderlands, roughly defined by the Himalayas, the Great Wall in China, and by the

Silk Road in the Tarim Basin. Here lay the great oasis cities of the past — Kashgar, Khotan, Niya, Yarkand, Turfan, Dunhuang — which depended on the nomads' herds for food and raw materials. The nomads in turn depended on the oasis cities for manufactured goods and trade items. The trade between the nomads and the oasis cities created a camel-powered network for economic, cultural, and religious exchange along which Buddhism and Nestorian Christianity entered China.

The Way of the Shaman

As small bands of Stone-Age humans learned how to use the resources of Inner Asia, they left behind them traces of their activities which can still be seen today. They fashioned bone needles to make tailored clothing from animal hides. They made stone tools and wore necklaces carved from stones or animal bones. They created a series of remarkable paintings and rock carvings which have been found from Mongolia to the borders of Tibet.[52] Despite these technical and artistic achievements, the arid cold of Inner Asia forced most of them to live at the very edges of a bleak and mean existence. There were harsh conditions for survival: clothing had to be thicker, shelter warmer, and hunting more efficient than in Outer Asia. Bad weather, a poor hunting season, or a change in animal migration patterns could mean starvation for an entire tribe. Few individuals lived much past the age of thirty; sudden death from hunting accidents, disease, and warfare with other groups must have been very common. The first Inner Asians were forced to exploit every possible physical, psychological, and spiritual strategy for survival.

When Dorj, our discouraged hunter, returned empty-handed to his tribe, he and his companions collapsed exhausted around the campfire. Their women poked listlessly at the fire and their children wailed pitifully for food. Dorj knew that if he did not find those reindeer soon, he and his people faced a long, slow death from starvation. Chewing a piece of buckskin to keep the hunger pangs at bay, Dorj returned to the question he had pondered as he lay in wait for the reindeer: "If there is a tool to kill animals, why isn't there a tool to bring them to our tribe?"

Among Dorj's people was a man they called the Dreamer. Strange of dress and wild of eye, Dorj and his men found him useless on the hunt and the women warned their children to stay away from him lest he snatch them off in the night. Behind his back, they gossiped about his vivid dreams and his long days outside the camp, watching the animals as if trying to understand their ways. While Dorj and his companions lay listlessly around the fire after their hunt, the Dreamer sat by himself in his tent until he fell into a deep sleep. About midnight, he saw a vision of reindeer migrating through a nearby valley. The next morning he told the others about his dream, but they just laughed at him. Dorj took no animals in the hunt that day, or for the next several days, and the tribe grew still weaker. Realizing that the Dreamer's vision was their only hope of survival, the tribe used their remaining strength to reach the valley he had seen. Silent joy filled them as they saw with their own eyes the animals of the Dreamer's vision, just where he said they would be. There was meat that night, and the hunters honored the Dreamer with a portion of the food. A few seasons later, these events were repeated, and the Dreamer's place among his tribe was secure. From then on, they called him "he who knows," or in the language of Siberia's Tungus[53] people, *shaman*. Dorj had found his tool at last.

The true origins of the shaman are of course lost in prehistory, but the first shamans almost certainly lived in a society like Dorj's.[54] Inner Asia's Stone-Age hunter-gatherers almost certainly lived in a structured spiritual world since they first pushed east of Eden. In their sky lived a single and powerful creator god[55] whose once-close relationship to humans was now only a distant memory. In the lower heavens closer to the human world lived several of this god's sons or "messengers." These godlings were more interested in people's affairs than their parent-god, and far more susceptible to human influence through prayers, gifts, threats, and simple bribery.[56] To reach these heavenly beings, the shaman had to make an ascent, perhaps by means of a special tree or a sacred mountain.[57] Where these were lacking, the shaman simply made a symbolic ascent of a convenient pole, during which he might see visions of animal spirits, good hunting locations, or the godling who had caused one among his people to fall sick.

Beneath the heavens lay the world of people. Each human was believed to have at least three and as many as seven souls.[58] At death, one soul remained in the grave, one ascended to the sky, and one descended to the underworld to be greeted by the god of the dead. Sickness or misfortune might cause one of the souls to become "lost" or to be captured by a spirit being. Once in a trance, the shaman might send one of his own souls in search of the "lost" soul; if he recovered it, his patient was cured. If the soul were held hostage, it might be ransomed. But this was hazardous work, for the shaman could lose his own soul along the way, bringing certain death. Humans shared their world with the spirits of rocks, trees, and animals who were just as indifferent to human activities as the natural forces they represented. Beneath the human world lay an anti-heaven, or underworld, ruled over by an anti-god, or lord of the dead.[59] Here were the souls of the sick, snatched away by angry or jealous gods, and the souls of the dead. The gods of the underworld were much like their heavenly relatives: neither good nor evil (or sometimes both good and evil) and quite susceptible to manipulation by any shaman with enough spiritual power.

The shamanic vocation was not voluntary, for the shamans were always chosen by the spirits. The electing spirits might send a bird to descend upon an unwitting prospective shaman and announce his or her vocation. Then other spirits might use sickness, nightmarish dreams, or horrifying visions to harass or even torture the candidate shaman for months, or even years. When the victim finally agreed to become a shaman, the tortures ceased and an initiatory vision was granted. In a typical vision, demons might slice the novice shaman apart with knives, cook and eat her, then reassemble her body and "resurrect" her with supernatural abilities. While the details varied with the particular culture, the featured themes of almost all Inner Asian shamanic initiations were death, dismemberment, and a "resurrection" of the shaman's body with transcendent powers.[60]

After the initiation, the spirits continued to appear to the shaman in animal form. One spirit might become the shaman's helper, or teaching-spirit, or even his cosmic wife. Other spirits were hostile beings whom the shaman had to defeat in battle and compel to become his protectors.[61] And shamans needed protectors, because spirits, ghosts, and wandering souls filled the land, inhabiting every rock, tree, and body of water. There were sky spirits,[62] directional spirits (of east, west, etc.), water spirits, evil spirits, nature spirits, mountain spirits, and ancestor spirits. Sometimes the shaman would catch or trap a spirit in a spirit house.[63] These were put in sacred places and "fed" with offerings of blood, milk, fat, or fermented beverages. Spirits could be forced to live in certain animals, or even in the clothing, drum, or cap of the shaman. All the spirits were virtually human in their language, character, and motivations, and were susceptible to manipulation by various forms of magic.

Connecting the sky, the world of humans, and the underworld was a great mystical axis.[64] Some peoples thought of this axis as a great tree (the World Tree), some as a great mountain (e.g. Mount Tise or Kailash in Tibet), some as a tent pole, a rope, or even a chain of flying arrows. For the shaman, the world axis was a highway for trance-journeys to the upper and lower worlds. The repetitive beating of his drum[65] allowed the shaman to enter his trance. The drum itself served both as a dwelling for helper spirits and as a symbolic vehicle for crossing the skies and rivers of other worlds. A horse made of sticks carried the shaman skywards or down into the earth. Feathers symbolized the shaman's power to ascend to the upper world and his link to the eagle, a sacred bird believed to play a crucial role in the mythic origins of shamanism. Bones suggested the symbolic "death" and later "resurrection" on the shaman's return from the transcendental world. Masks[66] announced the possession of the shaman by an animal spirit, mythical ancestor, or god, for the entranced shaman could assume any of these forms at will. Shamanic drums, feathers, bones, masks, and cloth-ing gave the shaman magical power by serving as spirit dwell-ings during the dance which acted out the journey to the upper or lower world.

The trip to the transcendental world was often described as "flight" on a mystical bird or "riding" on a mystic horse.[67] On such a journey, the shaman could cover great distances in a single moment, assume any size, act in the past, present, or future, foresee changes in the weather, find game, and enter into close magical relationships with animals. On a journey to the under-world, the shaman could see the fate of the dead: the gossip nailed to a post by her ear, the slanderer by his tongue; the glutton surrounded by the choicest dishes yet being unable to reach them.[68] On these journeys the shamans used certain places (mountains, trees, stone piles, and spirit-houses) and people (newborns, shamans, and the recently dead) as portals to the upper, lower, and human worlds. Proper behavior around these places and people was governed by a set of rituals and taboos.

From linguistic and archaeological evidence we know that the peoples of prehistoric Inner Asia engaged in long-range mi-grations which spread customs and ideas across vast distances.[69] Under these mixing influences, shamanism gradually developed a more elaborate set of beliefs and practices. Later shamanism became very concerned with good fortune, personal energy, and psychic power.[70] Doing bad things depleted this power, while making offerings or burning incense to the sky god, the earth, or one's ancestors increased it.[71] Much of the shaman's work consisted in restoring imbalances in personal spiritual power.

Though technologically in the Stone Age, the early peoples of Inner Asia possessed the complex set of beliefs, feelings, and values that characterize modern human societies. The shaman was at the center of their world, for only he (or she) had the power to force the spirits to give people the health, safety, and security that they could not get by other means. Shamanism used magic to manipulate spiritual forces for human benefit, and in this sense it was a technology that put man at the center of its existence. As a technology, it was not concerned with questions of ultimate truth, morality, or philosophy, but with power, and the ultimate criterion of its success was whether the shaman's tribe survived when others perished. By this measure, the shamans were undoubtedly successful. Not only did they preserve their vocation and beliefs across the millennia, they spread shamanism widely across Inner and Northeast Asia[72] and even to the Americas. Indeed, the shaman is one of the few unchanging figures in this story. His beliefs and practices entered Tibetan Buddhism virtually intact, and he can still be met today in the forests of Siberia and the monasteries of the Himalayas.[73]

The First Tibetans

As the centuries passed, different groups of peoples wandered across Inner Asia seeking refuge or conquest. In their physical appearance, some of these peoples probably looked more like the Mongols, while others looked more like the Turks. At some point in prehistory, a large group of peoples migrated from the Inner Asian steppes south and west onto the Tibetan plateau, deep into the northern part of what is now Nepal, Sikkim, and Bhutan. Other groups, such as ancestors of the Dards, the Mons, and other Indian peoples, filtered northwards across the Himalayas. These prehistoric migrations made the people of the Tibetan plateau an ethnically and racially mixed group from a very early date.[74] From archaeological evidence it appears that they lived much as their ancestors had, carving tools of stone and bone, making simple pottery, and creating occasional rock paintings.[75] When these early migrations were finished, the ancestors of the Tibetans occupied a mountain-girt natural fortress some 2 million square kilometers in extent, splendid in its isolation from the surrounding world. Here they were free to develop their own ways of surviving in a high, dry, and very cold environment.

A fortunate few settled in "lowland" (3,000 m. above sea level) river valleys, where they used domestic yaks to cultivate wheat and barley. Those not so fortunate lived as nomads on the windswept, high-altitude (4,000 m.) grasslands, much as their ancestors had done for millennia on the Inner Asian steppes. Some nomads spent their summers at salt pans, scraping up the salt and loading it on yaks for trade with other Tibetans. Farmers, nomads, and the traders who connected them seem to have been present in Tibetan society from an early date. Since most of the Tibetan plateau only grudgingly supports life, the early Tibetans found themselves quite thinly scattered over a very wide area. Isolated from each other, they developed different ways of speaking, some of which were not mutually intelligible.

The early Tibetans lived in small, mutually antagonistic tribal groups or confederacies. Ancient Tibetan sources suggest that there were at least four such groups, called the Se, the Tong, the Dong, and the Mu. The Mu tribes seem to have controlled a land called Shangshung (in what is now western Tibet) which extended to the borders of the Hindu Kush and the Tarim Basin. The people of Shangshung lived and moved in a world familiar to the shamans of ages past. In the stunningly blue skies of Shangshung lay the multilayered heavens of the peaceful *lha* , *dud*, and *mu* spirits. Here too the *khyung* bird (like the eagle, a symbolic ancestor of all shamans) stood ready to carry the shamans on their mystic journeys.[76] Below them, in the human world, lived men and spirits. The Shangshung people believed that each person had a so-called "breath" or "life" soul (called a *srog*) and a "shadow soul" (called a *bla*). Some regarded these souls as gods which lived in a person, while others considered them as personal spiritual beings. Physical life resided in the "breath soul," and to lose it was to die; the *bla* soul could go on shamanic journeys or be lost in an accident or bad fright; in these cases the shaman had either to recover it or to coerce it into an animal or place. Besides these "souls" were the spirits who attached themselves to people: gender spirits (male and female), locality spirits, and life spirits (the outer manifestation of the life soul or *srog*), closely linked to which was one's personal energy or *rlung rta*.

In the surrounding environment a host of moody and easily-offended spirit beings lurked in the mountains, glaciers, springs, and rocks of the human world. The land was positively alive with fire spirits or *thab lha*, locality spirits called *yul lha*, man-eating demons called *sin po*, vampire demons called *nodjin*,[77] evil spirits called *'dre*,[78] the spirits of the dead or *dong dre*,[79] and the bloodthirsty *shi dag* gods, who were propitiated with human sacrifice. Some of these beings were personified natural forces associated with the weather, or with earthquakes. Beneath the earth lived the water-dwelling *lu* and the locality spirits called *sa dag*, as well as the spirits of the dead. When they troubled the people, powerful shamans could force these spirits into a rock, a spirit trap, an amulet, a shaman mask, or other ritual object, where they could do no more harm.

For the people of Shangshung and indeed all of Inner Asia, the spirit world was no less real than the human world. The next valley and the land of the dead and the heavens of the gods were entirely and equally real. So too were the spirits, demons, gods, and animals who inhabited these places. Everything was part of the same seamless whole, linked by the great mystical axis anchored into the landscape at 6,714 m. Mount Tise (Kailash), one of the most prominent mountains of western Tibet. Like Eden, it lay at the headwaters of four major rivers (the Sutlej, the Indus, the Karnali, and the Brahmaputra), hinting at inherent spiritual power. Shamanic traffic to the upper world along this axis rode the mythical *khyung* bird; shamans visiting the lower realms sought the assistance of water-loving *lu*[80] spirits. The shamans of Shangshung performed much the same services as shamans always had: healing the sick, controlling the weather, foretelling the future, and restoring the balance between humans and spirits. Their rites helped to preserve belief in the spirit realms of the upper, middle, and lower worlds; the spirits, gods and demons who lived there; the shamanic initiation, dance, costume, and journey along the cosmic axis; the use of helper spirits; the rituals for controlling and manipulating spirits and personified natural forces; the belief in multiple souls; and the belief in life-energy and personal spiritual power.[81] All of these beliefs would become a part of Tibetan Buddhism.

Raiders of the Steppe

Beside the Tibetans, three other groups of people will play major roles in our story: the Mongols, the Kushans, and a group of Indo-European[82] speaking peoples known as the Aryans. The Aryans were descended from a large group of Indo-European speaking nomads who originally roamed the area north of the Black Sea. Sometime around the year 2500 B.C., this large group split into two parts, one migrating from the Inner Asian steppes into Europe, and the other into what is now Iran. About 2000 B.C. the latter group, by then known as the Aryans, pushed their way into northern India[83] to settle in the Indus and Ganges basins. The Aryans worshipped sky gods and fire spirits with complex rituals of animal sacrifice performed by priests called *brahmins.* From about 1400 to 400 B.C., the brahmins collected their ritual praise songs and invocations in a set of Sanskrit language scriptures called the *Vedas.*[84] Sometime in the first half of the first millennium B.C., they turned their attention from songs and rituals to philosophical questions. In a set of scriptures known as the *Upanishads* (compiled about 700-500 B.C.) they speculated on the nature of reality. It is in the thought-world of the Upanishads that Indian (and ultimately Tibetan) Buddhism found its beginnings, as we shall see in the next chapter.[85]

Another Indo-European speaking group is known to history by its Chinese name, the so-called the Yueh Chih. In the second century B.C., the powerful Xiongnu Empire pushed the Yueh Chih out of their Inner Asian strongholds back upon the northwest frontiers of India (to areas which are now part of Tajikistan, Afghanistan, and northern Pakistan). Here they founded a state known as the Kushan Empire. Sitting astride the famed Silk Road, the Kushans grew wealthy by controlling the rich trade between China, India, and the Roman Empire. The Kushan state was amazingly cosmopolitan, blending cultural and religious influences from Greece, India, Iran, China, Rome, and Egypt.[86] By the second century B.C., the Kushans had become ardent patrons of Buddhism, and their monks enjoyed access to religious ideas from all these ancient cultures. During this period, all the major towns in what is now northern Afghanistan, Kashmir, and the Tarim Basin had large Buddhist monasteries.[87] These towns, or their connecting trade routes, bordered directly on the grasslands of western Tibet.[88] It is here that Buddhism probably first mixed with local shamanist beliefs to form a syncretic religion later called *Bon*. In later centuries, the Kushan Empire played a decisive role in the expansion of Buddhism into Inner Asia and China.[89]

Meanwhile, far away from India and its borderlands, the nomadic tribes of Inner Asia found themselves increasingly at war with each other, for reasons still disputed by historians.[90] Powerful groups such as the Scythians,[91] Xiongnu,[92] and Yueh Chih[93] terrorized the steppes and put heavy military pressure on China. A Xiongnu raid in the third century B.C. forced the Chinese emperor to construct the Great Wall to keep them out. Further Xiongnu raids caused the rulers of the Han dynasty (206 B.C.-221 A.D.) to pacify the region by settling ethnic Chinese in border areas occupied by minority peoples.[94] For a thousand years, battles raged between the rising and falling empires of the Turks, Uighurs, Kirghiz, Qidan, and other groups. Among these peoples were some shamanist tribes who wandered the forest and steppe between Lake Baikal and the Gobi Desert. They were often at war among themselves and with others. At the time we are considering, there was little to suggest that these people had any future other than the constant internecine warfare of their past. But once united under a charismatic leader, this situation would change dramatically. From that time onwards, they would be known to history as the Mongols.

Summary

Like people, cultures have *histories* that explain why they are the way we find them. Such histories happen when any group of human beings interacts physically and spiritually with the rocks, soils, plants, animals, and climate of their surroundings. To understand a people means to know how all these elements have made them who they are. In a purely mechanistic sense, it was the primal forces of the earth which set the stage for Tibetan Buddhism, for these forces caused the continents to drift, India to collide with Asia, the Himalayas and the Tibetan Plateau to rise, and the Gobi Desert and its mountains to appear. These events dried and cooled the climate of Inner Asia, producing the scant rainfall, salty soils, and high mountains that made for poor farming. This in turn forced people either to hunt or to become nomadic herders in order to survive on ecologically marginal lands. Nomadism kept population densities low, cultures isolated, languages fragmented, and military skills sharp. The harsh climate also forced the earliest inhabitants of Inner Asia to use every possible spiritual resource for survival, leading to shamanism, while the more productive environment of Outer Asia gave the Indo-European speaking peoples leisure for long-lasting philosophical inquiry into the nature of reality. This gave rise to the later forms of Vedism, and to its spiritual successor, Buddhism. Yet as important as these physical factors were, it was the primal forces of the human heart which really determined the spiritual destiny of the peoples of Inner Asia.

In the Biblical story of the Garden of Eden, God created a pristine and beautiful world for the archetypal human couple. But as the story unfolds, Adam and Eve discover that what they really want is not a relationship with a perfect God, but the moral knowledge with which they can replace Him, control the course of their lives, and transcend death. When their attempt to gain this knowledge ends in disaster, the couple are alienated from God, banished from his presence, and subjected to suffering and death. In this chapter we have seen humanity set in an equally pristine (if considerably colder) environment. Alienated from a distantly-remembered creator God, these people tried to manipulate the supernatural world for their own benefit by serving lesser, more accessible spirits who could be bribed, coerced, or deceived by the shaman — a tragic figure who lived in bondage to the very spirits he tried to control. Lost in a search for power over the spirits, the shaman offered no higher philosophy, no guiding moral principles, no ultimate revelations. But it was his genius to persist through the millennia, and his destiny to influence the lives of millions in the Tibetan Buddhist world.

CHAPTER 3

Why Inner Asia Became Buddhist: Part 2

Afamous Tibetan tale tells the story of a man who liked to go fishing. Each day he went to a pool behind his house and caught some fish. When his net was full, he brought the fish home, and his doting wife and young son would help prepare them for supper. After some time, the man died. Because he had killed and eaten these living things, he was reborn as a fish in the very pond where he had gone fishing. His loving wife also died, and because of her strong attachment to their son, she was reborn as the family dog. Then the family's main enemy died, and he was reborn as the fisherman's grandson. When all this had happened, the son became hungry and decided to go fishing. He caught his father who had been reborn as a fish, and cooked and ate him. When his dog (who was previously his mother) tried to eat the fish bones, he beat her. Then he took upon his lap his infant son, who was really the family enemy. A disciple of the Buddha passed by and saw all of this with his supernatural insight. He said, "A father's flesh is eaten and a mother beaten, a mortal enemy carried on the lap, a wife gnaws her husband's bones; the law of the round of rebirth draws a laugh."[95]

The Age of the Vedas

The Tibetan Buddhist belief in rebirth has its origins in the scriptures of the ancient Indo-European speaking peoples. As the Aryans pushed eastward to settle in the lush Gangetic Plain, an abundant food supply and a congenial climate gave them leisure to turn their attention from survival to philosophy. Sometime during the 7th century B.C., this philosophical speculation turned to the question of whether or not the world around

them had any kind of underlying unity. The Aryan philosophers proposed that a sort of "universal soul" called *brahma* lay
at the basis of all existence.[96] Impersonal and amoral,[97] yet superior to the Vedic gods,[98] brahma was not separate from the
universe, but an entity from which all individual things and
people derive their being and into which they will all one day
merge, much as raindrops fall into rivers that become one with
the sea.[99]

The Vedic philosophers pointed out that if brahma is the
basis of everything that exists, then there must be a little bit of
brahma in everything (and in everybody).[100] In other words, if
everything borrows its existence from brahma and everything
returns to it, then everything is ultimately one.[101] A person is
essentially no different from a star, or a flower, or an insect. In
the same way, moral concepts such as good and evil, or hate
and love, have no ultimate meaning, because all such pairs of
opposites are actually just part of the same underlying reality.[102]
Brahma is all there is.[103] There is nothing else. This idea, called
monism (because it held that everything is ultimately one) spread
widely in ancient India and laid the intellectual foundations for
Hinduism and Buddhism.[104]

If everything is ultimately the same as everything else, then
man's sense that things exist independently from himself is an
error.[105] In other words, if a supreme form of existence or brahma
is "god," then there is no difference between man and "god."
Man *is* "god." [106] So is everything else. The apparent existence
of a world of independently existing objects outside each person is just an illusion. In this view, every human being is trapped
in the delusion that he or she is an autonomously existing person.[107] Ignorance of this fact is man's basic problem. The only
way to escape its effects is to realize that individual humans and
ultimate reality are really just two sides of the same coin. Simply thinking about this ultimate unity is not enough — each
individual must realize this through a direct meditative experience.[108]

During the Vedic age, the idea of rebirth became popular.[109] In this theory of human destiny, a kind of impersonal

"life force" passes from an individual after death and is reborn into another being in an endless cycle of death and rebirth. The life force has no personal characteristics, and so it is not an "I" that is reborn (which is how rebirth differs from reincarnation).[110] In the scheme of rebirth, each individual alive today has had uncounted millions of past lives and will have uncounted multitudes of future lives as well. Most of these lives are lived as gods,[111] ghosts, hell-beings, or animals, for only rarely is one born as a human being. Which rebirth one receives depends on another Upanishadic idea[112] that shaped both Buddhism and Hinduism, the concept of *karma*.

The theory behind karma is that every action has a consequence. Good actions have good consequences and accumulate religious merit. Bad actions have bad consequences and accumulate demerit. When a person dies, the balance of merit ("good deeds") and demerit ("bad deeds") determines how one will be reborn. For example, a person leading a good life by being kind, giving money to brahmin priests, and not killing animals may be reborn as a wealthy merchant or even a god. A person who does evil may be reborn as a deformed baby, a beggar, or a hell-being. According to this view, people suffer in this life because they have done evil in past lives. The poor, the sick, and the unfortunate have brought their suffering on themselves,[113] while the rich and powerful are only reaping the rewards of virtuous actions in past lives. No god is needed to mediate these rewards and punishments; karma functions as an inescapable natural law,[114] like gravity (and with just as much room for forgiveness).[115]

Late Vedism and early Hinduism assumed a teeming spirit world. At the top of the cosmos were gods, the fortunate few whose great merit had carried them far beyond the plane of human existence. Beneath them were titans, jealous beings who fought the gods for a higher place in the universe. Humans were next on the scale, followed by animals. Below the animals were beings known as *pretas*, or ghosts. Pretas lived in a kind of purgatory where they were tantalized by unfulfilled desires. (To this day pretas are feared by night travelers in the Himalayas.)

At the very bottom of the system were the hell beings, fearfully tormented through many lifetimes for the evil done during other births. All these beings, from gods to those suffering in hell, were subject to death and rebirth. [116] While it was possible to move up the scale (from a preta to a god, for example), this did not happen very often. Rebirth into the lower realms (as pretas and the various kinds of hell beings) was much more likely, unless one's demerits could be offset by merit-making acts.

By the middle of the sixth century B.C., monism, rebirth, and karma were firmly entrenched among the intellectual cornerstones of Indian civilization. By making merit, people could hope for a better life the next time around, perhaps even as a god, but this offered little ultimate consolation. Even the gods died eventually, and then they faced rebirth just like anyone else. The cycle of rebirth was without beginning or end, so the human condition was basically fixed and unalterable. Ancient India's religious philosophers began to seek a way of breaking out of the cycle altogether. Some of them took the time-honored path of withdrawal from the world to practice severe austerities, such as eating only one grain of rice a day.[117] Others became hermits, forsaking family and possessions to meditate in the forest. If a hermit reached his mystic goal, others might become his disciples. If those disciples were both numerous and persuasive, a new school of philosophy might be born. By the middle of the fifth century B.C., one such school was about to spread across all of India. Its founder was named Siddhartha Gautama, later known as the Buddha (or "enlightened one").

Siddartha Gautama and the Gospel of Self Reliance

Despite the great influence of Siddartha's life, we know very little about him. The story of his life and teaching was passed down orally for at least 300 years before it was recorded in writing.[118] During this time, myths, legends, and voluminous commentaries obscured and ultimately overwhelmed the original oral tradition. About 563 B.C.[119] a son named Siddartha was born to King Shudhodanna and Queen Maya Devi, monarchs of a petty state on the north Indian plains. Mindful of a prophecy that his son would renounce his royal heritage, King Shudhodana was anxious to make his little son's life in the palace as attractive as possible. The child lacked nothing as he grew up, and his father made every effort to shield his little prince from suffering. One account relates that before Prince Siddartha left the palace for an outing, his father ordered all unclean and unsightly things removed from the roads. Even the aged and ill were to remain indoors while Prince Siddartha was traveling. Of course, such efforts were bound to fail, and eventually the young prince discovered that the people of his kingdom were subject to all the ills common to humanity.

Siddartha brooded over the sufferings of his future subjects. Even the pain of animals and the death of small insects is said to have touched him. Deeply moved by the suffering he saw all around him, the young prince resolved to find a way to deliver mankind from its bondage to pain, illness, and death. After meeting a wandering monk on the road, he decided to leave his father's palace and seek this way of deliverance through religion. Legend offers a touching picture of the 29 year old Siddartha, his mind set on a life of renunciation, getting up in the middle of the night to kiss his sleeping wife and infant son goodbye before disappearing into the forest to follow the life of an ascetic. Siddartha eventually found five other men who were also seeking a way of escape from suffering. With them he practiced severe austerities for six years (537-532 B.C. by some chronologies). Common ascetic practices at that time included starvation dieting, wearing no clothing, saying nothing for years at a time, and meditating in bizarre and uncomfortable positions.[120] Siddartha almost certainly did some of these things, with what effects on his mind and body can only be imagined. It is no wonder that at the end of the six years he was said to be hardly more than a skeleton. Yet he still had not found his way of escape from suffering.

In one legend, Siddartha was meditating when a wandering musician and his student passed by. The musician told his student that if an instrument's strings were made too tight, they would snap, but if they were too loose, the strings would not play. Overhearing this, Siddartha realized that the path he was sought lay neither in the luxuries of his father's palace nor in the austere life of a hermit. Deciding that his course lay between these two extremes, he left the forest, washed, ate, and set out for the city of Bodh Gaya, where he sat down under a *pipal* tree to meditate on his experiences. According to tradition, the 35-year-old Siddartha resolved not to get up until he had found the secret of release from suffering. As he reviewed his spiritual progress, he thought about the common belief that the human spirit was continually living, dying, and being reborn in other forms. He thought that he could see himself undergoing cyclic rebirths over countless past ages, finding escape from suffering through death, only to be reborn and suffer again. The only hope of release seemed to lie in the ancient Vedic belief that the world and man's personal existence in it were just mistaken perceptions. If one could somehow shatter this illusion of personal existence, then one could escape from the cycle of rebirth and enter *nirvana*, a metaphysical state so rarefied that even Siddartha never found the words to describe it. But entering nirvana was a difficult process. It was so hard that Siddartha realized that it could only be achieved through thousands of lifetimes of accumulated religious merit. No god could do this for a person. It was entirely a matter of self effort, achieved by meditation, good works, and mystical practices. Siddartha called this realization enlightenment, and ever afterwards he was known by the title *Buddha,* or "enlightened one."[121]

Siddartha emerged from this experience a changed man.[122] He gathered a group of disciples, urging them to follow his teaching. He taught them to take nothing on faith, but to test everything for themselves.[123] Self reliance was a key Buddhist doctrine from the very beginning, for like the Vedic priests before him, Siddhartha taught that ultimate truth can never be learned from man or revealed by a god, only realized directly by the meditative experience of each individual. If man was to be enlightened, it could only be by his own effort. Others could teach him to meditate, or help him realize his hopeless situation, but in the end everything depended on the individual himself. As Siddartha was to tell his disciples in later life: "Do not look for refuge to anyone besides yourselves."[124]

Tradition has it that after a month at Bodh-Gaya, Siddartha left for the city of Varanasi (Benares) where he began to preach his new doctrine around 528 B.C. As we have seen, Siddartha's teaching (or *dharma* as it was called in Sanskrit) was founded on the religious ideas current in India just as Vedism was giving way to its successor, early Hinduism. These ideas included monism, karma, illusion (the view that the visible world was incorrectly perceived), and deliverance from suffering through meditation. In keeping with the doctrine of impersonal rebirth, Siddartha vigorously denied that man possessed anything resembling a personal, immortal soul. Instead, he taught that man's personality was only an illusion, and until he rid himself of this illusion, man was doomed to suffering and rebirth.

Siddartha put these ideas into a new diagnosis of mankind's central problem: a formula either he or his later commentators termed "The Four Noble Truths." They are:

I. All is Suffering In its Buddhist sense, suffering means not only physical and mental pain, but virtually any unpleasant sensation. Examples of suffering include fear, hunger, illness, loneliness, grief, or just a philosophical sense of incompleteness. The young sage believed that all beings, from the lowest hell-beings up to animals, man, and gods, suffer throughout their lives.

II. Suffering Arises From Desire For the Buddhist, desire means a longing for independent, personal existence. It may also mean a sense of attachment (such as love) towards things or people. These emotions imprison man in the cycle of suffering and rebirth, and in one sense they occupy the same place in Buddhist thinking that sin does in Christian thinking. Desire, like sin, is what binds man to suffering and death. Another meaning of desire is selfishness, such as that of a man who is greedy for money, and whose greed leads him to steal.

To be paid back for his theft, he is reborn (through the action of karma) as a worm, which must suffer the attacks of birds and crawl through the soil all its life. In this example, the desire for money led to suffering as a worm. Conversely, the worm's suffering is due to its greed for money in a previous life.

III. Suffering is Destroyed by Eliminating Desire If a person has no attachments to anything or anybody, desires nothing, and realizes through meditation that neither he nor anything else has a soul, that person will cease to be reborn, and pass beyond existence to enter a state called *nirvana*. The word nirvana comes from a Sanskrit word meaning to go out, or to be extinguished. [125] The idea behind it is that once desire is extinguished, one is no longer bound to the cycle of rebirth, and so transcends personal existence into a metaphysical state whose essence cannot be expressed in words. [126]

IV. Desire is Eliminated by Following the Eightfold Path The eightfold path is a series of steps which, followed over many lifetimes, leads at last to nirvana. The eight steps are: 1) having an understanding of the basic principles of Buddhism; 2) having pure motives; 3) speaking in a truthful, helpful, and considerate manner; 4) obeying the five commandments of Buddhism: namely abstinence from killing any person, animal, or insect; avoiding stealing, sensuality, lying, and using alcohol or drugs; 5) following a trade compatible with the first four commandments (for example, one should not be a butcher); 6) making the moral effort required to remove all evil from one's mind and prevent new evil from entering, as well as developing one's good qualities; 7) mind control; and lastly 8) a mystical state in which one realizes intuitively the emptiness of all things. The last stage also involves mastery of occult powers, such as mind travel, being able to assume any shape, or controlling natural laws according to one's own will.[127] (Powers familiar to any shaman.)

The path that Siddartha laid out for his disciples was a rigorous one, involving self denial and long hours of meditation. These austerities were difficult for people in ordinary walks of life, so Siddartha's disciples organized themselves into communities of monks (collectively known as the monk body or *sangha*). The sangha accepted food and other donations from the lay people, while the lay people received religious teaching from the sangha.[128] The early monks lived together in an informal fellowship. In accordance with Siddartha's principle of self reliance, they had no central authority or fixed method of gaining enlightenment. Each monk or nun was free to choose their own path to nirvana, as seemed best to them. This lack of doctrinal authority encouraged many new Buddhist schools[129] to spring into existence, encouraged by the seemingly limitless fertility of the Indian religious imagination.

By the time of Siddartha Gautama's death (about 483 B.C.) his message had been preached across much of north India. His gospel of self reliance was good news to a people burdened by the expensive rituals of the brahmin priests. In place of these rituals, Siddartha offered a religious path with no castes, no rituals, no priests, and no restrictions on who might seek salvation. It is little wonder that the new teaching began to spread across India. Early Buddhist missionaries brought their teachings to south India, and probably to Sri Lanka as well, from which they spread by sea to Southeast Asia. Here Buddhism flourished among the Burmese, Thai, Khmer (Cambodian), and other peoples, and influenced great architectural monuments like Borobodur in Indonesia and Angkor Wat in Cambodia.[130]

The Rise of Mahayana

As we have seen, Siddartha's Eightfold Path did not set out an actual technique of gaining enlightenment, but only a general guide to the process. It was not long before different interpretations of the Buddhist path appeared, and their proponents organized themselves into different schools of practice. Some were more conservative, while others opened themselves to the vast panorama of Indian religious thought. One of the more liberal schools became prominent around the first century A.D., when new texts (such as the *Lotus Sutra* and the

Perfection of Wisdom Sutra) began to circulate among Buddhists in India. These texts claimed that the traditional story of Prince Siddartha was basically a fiction, a teaching method for less adept disciples. The real Buddha had never had an actual human body. He had not really been born as an Indian prince, had never practiced austerities, had never meditated, and he had never been enlightened. Instead, the historical Buddha was the emanation of a sort of eternal Buddha principle - a mystical figure who had been enlightened billions of ages ago.[131] Acceptance of these views caused profound changes in the way that Buddhists understood the person and work of their founder, the nature of the world around them, and the philosophy, techniques, and goals of their religious practice.

The new texts taught that one could postpone one's own entry into nirvana[132] while working to liberate others. The Buddhist saints who did this were known as *boddhisattvas*.[133] These semi-divine beings were believed to become "sons" or "daughters" of the Buddha; worthy of the worship of gods and men, possessors of eternal happiness, and immune from any kind of harm.[134] While in such a blessed state, the boddhisattvas work to liberate themselves and all other beings from suffering and rebirth. Of course, this idea was at odds with Siddartha's original teaching that each person could find enlightenment only for him or herself. Karma was not transferable, and in no sense could an incipient Buddha give away his merit to someone else. But doctrinal objections aside, the ideal of compassionate saints and saviors capable of liberating every being in the entire universe held a wide popular appeal.[135] Its proponents called it *Mahayana*, or "Great Vehicle" Buddhism, for it claimed to offer enlightenment to many more people than could be liberated by classical (also called *Hinayana* or "Small Vehicle") Buddhism.[136]

Just as the Mahayanists taught that there is more than one Buddha,[137] so they taught that there is more than one universe. In fact, they propounded the existence of innumerable other universes (called "pure lands" or "Buddha fields") each of which was little different from a paradise. Each universe had its own Buddha or Buddha-reflection. By the end of the first century

A.D. there were Buddhas of the past, present, and future, and an essentially infinite number of metaphysical Buddhas, many of whom were thinly disguised Hindu gods. Entire mythologies grew up around these new Buddhas,[138] and soon the Mahayanists had constructed a spiritual world as complex as that of its Hindu predecessor.

Mahayana also brought a new way of thinking about philosophy, for its aim was to destroy completely any faith in the validity of conceptual thought. Siddartha Gautama taught that man was devoid of any meaningful form of ongoing personal existence. The appearance of individual existence, he said, was part of the illusion from which man must free himself. The Mahayanists agreed that a self or soul did not exist, but they took this argument further, claiming that *nothing*, not even the Buddhist teachings, can be proven to exist separately, concretely, and inherently.[139] Their favorite example was that of a cart, which could be taken apart into wheels, an axle, and floorboards, thus proving (at least to their satisfaction) that there was ultimately no such thing as a cart. But their analysis went deeper than this, for they thought about the nature of human reasoning and concluded that *any* proposition that could be put into words could be refuted. Generalizing from this observation, they said that ultimate truth *can never* be expressed in words, thoughts, or propositions that are themselves logically true and irrefutable.[140]

This put them in a difficult position, for having destroyed the very concept of logical truth, they could say nothing true about their own beliefs. To get around this problem, they propounded a dogma of relative and absolute truth. *Relative* truth prevailed at the lowest level of Buddhist practice, where logical reasoning was used to undermine faith in conceptual thought, and to help seekers to understand that ultimate truth cannot be expressed in words. Conventional ideas of right and wrong, or good and evil, were also confined to the relative truth level.[141] Once a certain level of meditational (and in Tibetan Buddhism, magical) practice had been achieved, however, the would-be Buddha could discard relative truth, much as a traveler leaves behind a boat he has used to cross a river. Once on the other side, the traveler passes beyond all distinctions and enters the realm of *absolute* truth. Absolute truth discards all moral distinctions and claims no ultimate difference between right and wrong, good and evil, truth and falsehood, or any other seemingly opposite pairs.[142]

Early Mahayana divided itself into several schools, the most important of which for our story was the so-called *Madhyamika* school, associated with the Indian sage Nagarjuna (ca. 150-250 A.D.). Nagarjuna commented on and systematized the teachings of the Mahayanist *Perfection of Wisdom* literature, refuting the teachings of Hindus and other Buddhist schools. He emphasized that anything that can be put into words cannot be absolutely true, for the truth always lies beyond all words and conceptions and can only be realized.[143] Once one realizes this intellectually, one is ready to grasp the ultimate (or absolute) truth intuitively or directly, through meditation or through various occult practices. The Madhyamika school gave rise to two subtraditions that would later be influential in Tibet: the Prasangika School (whose major thinkers were Chandrakirti, Shantideva, and later Atisha) and the Suatantrika School.[144]

The Hinayana and Mahayana schools were not denominations, nor were they a doctrinal division like that between Catholicism and Protestantism. Instead, Hinayana and Mahayana were fluctuating tendencies within an intact Buddhist tradition. The Mahayana school became progressively more dominant in India, while the Theravadin school of the Hinayana vehicle developed on its own, largely in Sri Lanka. During much of the history of Indian Buddhism, monks living in the same monastery might follow either tradition.

Buddhism Crosses the Silk Road

Buddhism's advance across Central Asia owed a great deal to one remarkable man, Ashoka Maurya (270-230 B.C.). Ashoka was the ruler of an empire[145] that spanned the Buddhist heartland of north India. In the eighth year of his reign, he led his forces in a bloody campaign against a neighboring kingdom. Appalled by the suffering he had caused, Ashoka renounced the use of force and turned to Buddhism for consolation. He certainly took his new faith seriously. From historical records it seems that he devoted virtually all the resources of his empire to improving the lives of his subjects. He created a special class of ministers to go out among the people and care for their needs, founded hospitals and stocked them with medicines, dug wells, planted shade trees, built roadside shelters for travelers, and asked to be kept informed of his subjects' welfare at all times. Though an ardent Buddhist, Ashoka granted religious freedom to his people.

According to tradition, Ashoka equipped some of his most able monks to go to other countries as missionaries. Ashoka himself is said to have brought Buddhism to Nepal, and monuments attributed to him are still to be seen in the Kathmandu Valley. To the west, Buddhism spread to the Indus Valley (in modern Pakistan) where Ashoka's missionaries proclaimed his Buddhist piety on stone pillars inscribed with his edicts in Greek and Aramaic.[146] Buddhism spread beyond the Indus to the kingdom of Bactria (of two-humped camel fame) in what is now northern Afghanistan, and to Sogdiana, behind the Pamirs in the southern part of modern Uzbekistan. As we saw in the last chapter, this was the general area where a flourishing Buddhist civilization arose within the Kushan Empire at around the time of Christ.[147] The Empire maintained active trading contacts with Rome, India, and China, and in its later years attracted adherents of Zoroastrianism, Manichaeism, Brahmanism, Buddhism, and Christianity. In this melting pot of religious ideas, Buddhism was exposed to religious currents from all over Asia, and this influx of new myths, legends, savior gods, magic, occultism, and other raw materials almost certainly influenced the Buddhism that entered Tibet. The oasis cities of the Silk Road became centers of eclectic Buddhist learning and culture, supporting great monasteries, temples, and libraries. Silk Road cities such as Kashgar, Khotan, Turfan, and Dunhuang[148] attracted traders and missionaries from all over Asia.[149] From the Silk Road, Buddhism entered China, there to become the only foreign system of thought to make a profound impact on Chinese civilization until modern times.[150] Buddhist teachers in China took their doctrines to Korea and Japan.

It was probably during this time that the Tibetans made their first tentative contacts with Mahayana Buddhism. The spirit-haunted Kingdom of Shangshung, which we met in the previous chapter, maintained trading contacts with a land called *Tasig*,[151] which at that time referred to the area immediately west of the Pamirs, specifically to the Sogdian and Bactrian regions of the Kushan Empire and its successor states. It is likely that Buddhist teachings spread from Tasig to Shangshung,[152] where Buddhism's propensity to absorb local religions met shamanism's pragmatic search for occult powers; the result was a synthesis of both beliefs later known as *Bon*.[153] Hence Bon is probably best though of as a blend of early Buddhist and shamanist beliefs, rather than as the pre-Buddhist religion of Tibet, as is often claimed.[154] For their part, the Bon practitioners maintain that their teachings were handed down from an ancient sorcerer-king known as *Tonpa Shenrab*.[155]

One of the remarkable things about the spread of Buddhism across Asia was its ability to enter cultures very different from that of its Indian homeland. The historian Raymond Dawson points out that at the time Buddhism entered China, the cultures of India and China were poles apart. Ancient Sanskrit and Chinese had virtually nothing in common as languages; the Chinese thought concretely while the Indians were wildly speculative; the Chinese were interested in ethics while the Indians loved metaphysics; the Chinese focused on the present, the Indians on unimaginably vast eons.[156] So the Mahayanists faced a serious problem of what modern scholars call *contextualization*: that is, how was Indian Buddhism to be made relevant to the highly civilized, but very different, Chinese? Indeed, how did such a philosophically oriented religion spread among the people of Shangshung, or any of the other shamanist peoples who were interested only in the practical control of nature and the manipulation of spirits?

Tantra

The Mahayana movement opened Buddhism to influences from other Indian religions, particularly if their practices offered a shorter path to enlightenment. Prominent among the other schools was *yoga*, which appeared as a distinct movement on the Indian scene between 300 and 500 A.D.[157] In its original form, yoga was a set of mental and physical disciplines aimed at aiding meditation by stopping the action of the mind.[158] Yogic masters, or *gurus*, exercised complete control over every aspect of their students' lives, a tradition that would later become entrenched in Tibetan Buddhism. Yoga claimed followers both inside and outside the Buddhist monastic community. The latter formed bands of free-living ascetics called *yogins* (or *yoginis*, if women) who might or might not be attached to any particular philosophical school. By late in the first millennium, sexual yogic practices had become common to both groups.[159] These practices prepared the way for another cult called *tantra*.

The word tantra refers to any of a set of religious texts which appeared in north India and the Kushan area between the seventh and tenth centuries A.D. By extension, tantra came to mean both the texts and the rituals they describe. Buddhist tantras are based on philosophical monism: they assume that the world is illusory, and that breaking free of illusion unites man with the ultimate. But their appeal was that they claimed to offer a "short path" to enlightenment that could replace the lifetimes of moral effort required by classical Buddhism. An accurate description of tantra as it was practiced in the first millennium in India is not for the fainthearted, for the "short path" to liberation involved a set of sexual yogic practices, some licentious in the extreme, which dominated Mahayana Buddhism during the last centuries of its existence in India.

Indian tantra tried to break through illusion by exploiting the so-called "union of opposites." Tantric rituals normally took place at night in isolated places or cemeteries.[160] Since the fiercest and most bloodthirsty deities were thought to have the most spiritual power, ancient tantric yogins invoked them with magic spells, supplicated them with cannibalistic rites, and coerced them to descend into images or symbols of themselves.[161] Thus controlled, they became subject to the will of the yogin, who could identify himself with them and use their powers to gain supernatural and material benefits,[162] including the power to become a Buddha, the power to gain prosperity, women,[163] control of the weather,[164] good harvests, exorcistic powers, immunity from poison, the ability to become invisible, to pass through solid objects, to fly, to assume different appearances, to send out emanations of himself, to coerce others to do his will, to cure disease, and to grant wishes to others.[165] In fact, as with shamanist practice, much tantric teaching was concerned with simple magic for obtaining worldly benefits.[166] The overtly sexual yogic rituals were taken to symbolize the union of opposites around which tantra revolved. Tantra's sexual imagery (its gods are often depicted as locked in sexual embrace) and use of intoxicants and human flesh as ritual substances eventually scandalized even a culture long used to Hindu eroticism, and it was persecuted and driven underground in some areas. It was not destroyed, however, and sexual practices continue in tantric Buddhism today.[167]

The Buddhist tantras themselves are texts that describe these rituals and list the magic spells used to coerce the deities. Tantric texts teach strict living to the new initiate, and but allow sexual practices and alcohol[168] to the advanced practitioner who has passed into the realm of absolute truth and so is free from the claims of morality.[169] Tantra kept its occult spells and rituals secret by handing them down only from teacher to disciple[170] and through a secret language known only to initiates.[171] From yoga, it borrowed certain occult gestures called *mudras* which are believed to help the believer along the short path to liberation. It supplemented these with *mantras*, magical spells or phrases whose meaning is known only to a few initiates.[172] The mantra's essential character as a magic spell is revealed by the fact that they were not *translated* into the Tibetan scriptures, but merely *transliterated* as a chain of meaningless syllables, lest they lose the power felt to reside in their original Sanskrit

The Rise of Tibetan Buddhism

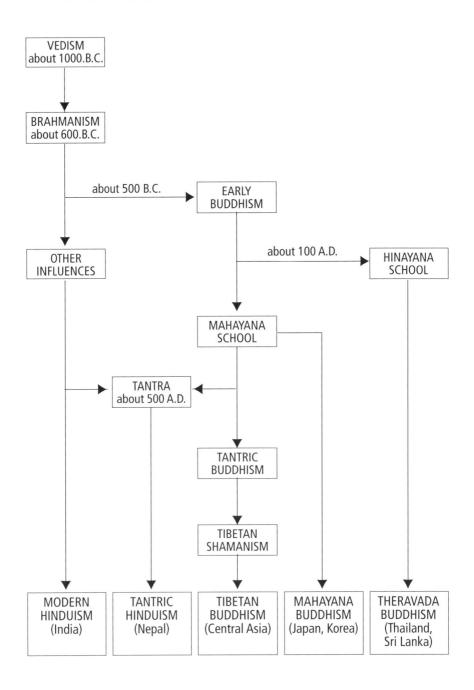

form. Even mantras which are repeated tens or hundreds of thousands of times by Tibetan monks are often no more than gibberish to them.[173] Also prominent in tantric practice are mystical diagrams whose most common form is the *mandala*. Mandalas are ritual patterns or designs into which deities are coerced, and in this sense they differ little from the spirit traps of the shamanists. They are commonly used for Tibetan Buddhist rites such as the Kalachakra initiation, which has been given to so many people around the world by the fourteenth Dalai Lama.

The Kalachakra tantra dates from the tenth century[174] and is one of the most complex of all the tantras.[175] The abridged version includes encyclopedic, apocalyptic, and ceremonial elements. The encyclopedic element contains instructions about astrology, calendrical calculations, imaginary cosmologies, and fantastic realms of time, as well as descriptions of alchemy, mystical anatomy, invisible energy channels, and Buddhist theories of ideal atoms.[176] The apocalyptic element focuses on a cosmic war predicted for the year 2424 of the present era, in which barbarian hordes whose prophets include Adam, Moses, Jesus, and Mohammed will invade the earth.[177] (Though there are symbolic elements to the description of this war, it is believed to refer to coming real historical events.[178]) But the invaders will be defeated with help from the mythical land of Shambhala, and a Buddhist golden age will dawn.[179] The ceremonial element offers instructions for a three- day empowerment in which participants imagine an enormous five-level palace occupied by 722 spiritual beings, whose power they invoke and into whose likeness they try to transform themselves. An associated system of vows aims at creating unquestioning obedience to spiritual teachers, maintaining the secrecy of tantric practice, and giving rules for tantra's sexual rituals.[180]

It is a testament to Indian Buddhism's elastic view of truth that a religion renowned for its teaching on non-violence was able to accept as canonical even tantric texts which referred to the use of ritual sex, human flesh, alcohol, corpses, women, and skulls. This is even more remarkable for the fact that the references in the original texts were to literal acts and substances, and there is no doubt that these things were actually procured and used in Indian tantrism.[181] In later centuries, the Tibetan government felt it necessary to control the translation of tantric texts into Tibetan, for some were seen as acceptable, and some were so wildly licentious that their translation was officially banned.[182] With time, however, imagined objects replaced the original items, at least in most Tibetan Buddhist practice. The horrific deities remain the same.

Tantra enjoyed wide influence. In the mid-17th century the Mongols built a monastic college especially dedicated to the study of the Kalachakra tantra, and similar institutions were founded in China, Mongolia, and Buryatia.[183] In these colleges students tried to visualizes their familiar deities, and to become what they saw; some Tibetan Buddhists even claimed to be able to physically materialize tantric deities in front of them. In tantric thinking, by visualizing a "liberated being," you can become one yourself.[184]

Though rejected by most non-Tibetan Buddhists, the tantric path eventually took its place alongside the Hinayana and Mahayana schools as so-called "Vajrayana" or "Diamond Vehicle" Buddhism. As Tibetan monks later explained it, the Buddha gave Hinayana teachings to disciples of low intelligence, Mahayana teachings to students of average ability, but reserved his supposed tantric teachings for a only a handful of his most promising followers.[185] Be that as it may, the magic and occultism of tantric Buddhism was powerfully attractive to the shamanist cultures of Central Asia, who were always alert for more powerful ways to force the spirits to do their bidding. It was this link between shamanism and tantra that caused the tantric form of Mahayana Buddhism to spread across Central Asia. Even in sophisticated China, simple magic was the contextual bridge by which Buddhism gained a popular foothold.[186]

Under the stimulus of tantra, Mahayana Buddhism further multiplied its Buddhas, boddhisattvas, and spirit beings by assigning female consorts to them all, as well as bringing myriads of tantric demons and deities into its already crowded pantheon.

Maintaining such a complex religion required education on a grand scale, and the larger north Indian monasteries began to offer courses in various aspects of Buddhism and its many paths to salvation. Some of these teaching monasteries grew into Buddhist universities, the most famous of which was Nalanda, a scholastic center whose libraries, observatories, and prayer-halls awed even the highly educated Chinese pilgrim Hsüan Tsang, who visited it in the seventh century. Nalanda and other monasteries were the source from which the Tibetans would bring tantric Buddhism into Central Tibet.

By the time that Mahayana Buddhism entered Tibet, it had become so transformed by tantric rituals, magic, and sorcery that it would have been unrecognizable to Siddhartha Gautama had he been alive to see it. His moderately ascetic philosophical religion for the dedicated few had been replaced by an all-too-worldly religion of magic and sorcery, encumbered with thousands of gods, godlings, demons, spirits, metaphysical Buddhas and consorts. An exuberant sexual practice and imagery had taken the place of the simple morality espoused by Siddhartha Gautama. His path of self-reliance had become the path of dependence on priests, wizards, and sorcerers. The decline of Buddhism into gross superstition, the resurgence of Hinduism, and the Muslim invasions of the Middle Ages all played a role in the final collapse of Buddhism in India. The land where Siddartha walked is today the home of the Hindu farmer and the Muslim shopkeeper. All that remains of Indian Buddhist culture are a few shrines and ruins, and the pilgrims from all over East Asia who come to visit them.

Summary

If the major actors in this story were characters in a grand historical drama, the shaman would certainly be the most pleased with himself at the intermission. He emerged into recorded history with a fully formed set of beliefs, and by the end of the nineteen centuries covered in this chapter, he was still a prominent figure in Central Asian religious life.[187] In most places between Siberia and the Himalayas, his beliefs and practices were unchanged, because only he offered a way to control the frightening and malignant spirit world. To take advantage of the exciting new techniques offered by tantra, the shaman had only to accept some philosophical speculations that were of little consequence to him or his people, for shamanism always revolved around power, not truth. Every people needed a man or a woman who could see the future, control the weather, heal diseases, ensure a good harvest, and answer vital questions. And even if the people would one day call themselves Buddhists, when trouble arose in their daily lives would they in fact be any less devoted to the shaman? Would that be changed if in Tibet the shaman had to wear a red robe instead of a special shaman's coat? Why, even the Dreamer would recognize him!

The tantrists could also gloat about their success. They had emerged in the middle third of the first millennium as a small sect of lascivious practices. Within a few centuries, their teachings dominated Mahayana Buddhism through the ancient appeal of sexual religious ritual.[188] Perhaps unwittingly, the yogins had borrowed the shaman's technique of manipulating the spirits for spiritual ends: "visualize a liberated being and become one yourself!" Within a few centuries, tantric doctrines had found a permanent place in both Hinduism and Buddhism, and their future was secure.

If the shamans and the tantrists had reason to be happy, the Vedic fathers of monistic pantheism would perhaps be happiest of all. Their ideas about reality laid the foundations for both Hinduism and Buddhism. Their views became the dominant understanding of reality held by millions of people across East Asia.

The Mahayana philosophers of ancient India would have reason for mixed feelings at this point in our story. On the positive side, their fanciful reconstruction of the historical Buddha and his teachings would spread to the most populous countries of Asia and become the most widely known form of Buddhism in the world. Yet they had used dialectical logic in the same way that a suicidal terrorist uses explosives. Employing logic to destroy logic, they undermined the very foundations of rational truth, putting themselves in the self-contradictory position of the philosopher who said, "No statements are true." Once they did away with rational thinking as a bridge to spiritual truth, there was no way for them to be sure that the experiences offered in the domain of so-called "absolute truth" were in fact true. The Mahayanists were forced to flee into an imaginary realm where the only "truth" lay in the arbitrary wanderings of human minds which had been systematically emptied of rational contents. When such an approach was blended with the sexual rituals of tantra, subjective "truth" very quickly led to subjective morality, and the Tibetan people would eventually become accustomed to seeing in their religious leaders outrageous behavior which few other religions would tolerate.[189]

Of all the actors in our story, the Buddha himself fared the worst of all. A speculative sage who offered his followers a philosophy of metaphysical mysticism, in the end he fell victim to his own view of reality. His Mahayanist and tantric successors repudiated his very existence, modified his teachings beyond recognition, taught the doctrines of other religions in his name, made his simple philosophy complex beyond recognition, and buried it under layer upon layer of fantastic mythologies, imaginary universes, and prolix commentary until it became arguably the most complex religion in the world. Multiplied, deified, and victimized by his own view of reality, in the end the Buddha had indeed passed beyond worldly existence, but not in the way he had imagined.

CHAPTER 4

Children of the
Water Mouse Year

The Qaidam Desert is an expanse of salty wasteland lying at the northern edge of the Tibetan plateau. In the spring of 1898, a small caravan could be seen making its way across this desolate wilderness, bound for Lhasa. At the head of the little party were Petrus Rijnhart, a Dutch missionary, and his wife Susie, a Canadian physician. Their infant son, three local servants, and 17 ponies filled out the expedition, whose intent was to reach the very heartland of Tibetan Buddhism in order to do evangelistic and medical work. But a month into the journey, two of the servants deserted and thieves stole five of the pack animals. Barely four weeks later, Petrus and Susie were stunned by the sudden death of their baby, whose first birthday they had just celebrated. Still determined to reach Lhasa, they pressed onward until confronted by an official of the Tibetan government, who told them that as a matter of policy, foreigners were not allowed to visit Tibet. He demanded that they return the way they had come. But the Rijnharts were not to be dissuaded from their goal, and they negotiated with the official until they obtained his consent to leave Tibet towards the east, following the headwaters of the Mekong River. While traversing this remote and difficult region[190] they were set upon by bandits, who robbed them of their animals, caused their remaining servants to flee, and killed Petrus Rijnhart, leaving the newly widowed Dr. Susie as the only survivor of this tragic expedition.[191] The Rijnhart party was one of many nineteenth century attempts to enter Tibet for purposes of evangelism, trade, diplomacy, or simple adventure. Yet most such attempts failed dismally due to the Tibetan government's determination to exclude outside influences from their country. As we shall see, this policy was rooted in religious beliefs that had entered the country many centuries before. Ironically, Tibet's isolationism would lead to the destruction of its lamaist theocracy.

Tibet's Age of Kings and the First Diffusion of Buddhism

Tibet enters recorded history in the middle of the seventh century A.D.[192] as a unified kingdom with its capital in the Yarlung Valley, southeast of Lhasa. The early Tibetan kings were believed to be a line of semi-divine beings who descended to the earth and returned to the heavens by means of a sacred cord,[193] a version of the world-axis that any shaman would recognize.[194] But a palace coup is said to have caused the loss of these magical powers,[195] and the kings of Tibet seem to have been mortal from that time onward. This new line of kings ruled the fertile Yarlung Valley, whose abundant crops fuelled a regional military machine which engaged neighboring China on a vast scale. In the eighth century, the Tibetans launched raids against the Silk Road cities of the Tarim Basin, the Gansu Corridor, and even the heartland of China, occupying the Tang Dynasty capital of Changan (near modern Xian) in 763.[196] By the early ninth century, the Tibetans controlled an Inner Asian empire stretching from Baltistan and Gilgit in the west to China in the east, including both the northern and southern arms of the Silk Road.[197] Buddhist civilizations flourished in all the countries surrounding the newly powerful Tibetans,[198] and it was not long before their faith began to influence the young monarchy.

The most famous of the early Tibetan kings was a man named Song Tsen Gampo (ca. 609-650 A.D.).[199] By threatening Tang Dynasty China's western frontiers, he demanded and received as wife a certain Chinese princess named Wen Cheng. Legend credits her with making the first tentative contacts between Tibet and its Buddhist neighbor to the east. She encouraged cultural exchanges with the Tang court, and brought young and educated Tibetans under the influence of Chinese Buddhism. The Tibetan nobles realized that Buddhism could not flourish without a standardized written language, so in the middle of the seventh century, Song Tsen Gampo sent a minister named Thön Mi Sambhota for language studies at the Buddhist universities of India. It is said that Thön Mi returned with a 30-consonant, four vowel Tibetan alphabet, which the king put into general use.[200] This alphabet, and its associated literary form of Tibetan, was used in the Tibetan Buddhist scriptures, and later taught wherever Tibetan Buddhism spread in Central Asia.[201]

After Song Tsen Gampo's death, Tibet's military fortunes waxed and waned until the reign of his successor Ti Song De Tsen (ca. 755-797 A.D.).[202] Ti Song De Tsen invited Chinese and Indian Buddhist missionaries to Tibet. Apparently persuaded by their preaching, he declared Buddhism the state religion and founded the country's first Buddhist monastery near a place called Samye, southeast of Lhasa. Samye is said to have been the scene of a famous debate between the representatives of Chinese and Indian Buddhism. The Chinese missionaries advocated a simple, direct approach to enlightenment known as *Chan* (the ancestor of modern Zen). The Indian Buddhists advocated the tantric path, with its promise of occult magical powers. Given the appeal of such powers to people who had lived under the shamans for centuries, it is not surprising that the tantrists won the debate and gained official support.

Though the Tibetan historical record focuses on the progress of tantric Buddhism, shamanism was by no means dead during the latter part of the first millennium. The bulk of the population were still shamanist by outlook and practice. In the west of Tibet, in the former kingdom of Shangshung, shamanism had already absorbed certain teachings of Central Asian[203] Buddhism and was incorporating these into what would later be known as the *Bon* religion. It is likely that the ancestors of the Tibetan Buddhist *Nyingma* school also accepted Buddhist teachings from a Central Asian source at about this time.[204] Yet it seems clear from Buddhist historical sources that shamanists stoutly resisted the advance of tantric Buddhism for several centuries.[205] The details of this contest are now buried in myth, but in the end, tantric Buddhism won at the political level because it had royal patronage, and brought with it literature, art, and intellectual contact with the more advanced civilizations of China and India. But shamanism continued to thrive at the popular level, and it introduced to tantric Buddhism many shamanic practices that give folk Tibetan Buddhism its distinctive character to this day.[206]

One of the most colorful figures of this early period was the tantric sorcerer Padma Sambhava, the legendary founder of the Nyingma sect of Tibetan Buddhism. An archetypal Central Asian shaman, this semi-historical sorcerer was said to have forced Tibet's local gods and demons to become protectors of Buddhism. An excerpt from his adventures will give some idea of their fantastic nature: "When the Guru reached *Nam tan kar nag,* the white fiendess of that place showered thunderbolts upon him, without, however, harming him. The Guru retaliated by melting her snow-dwelling into a lake; and the discomfited fury fled into the lake *Tan pa mo pa,* which the Guru then caused to boil. But though her flesh boiled off her bones, still she did not emerge; so the Guru threw in his thunderbolt, piercing her right eye. Then came she forth and offered up to him her life-essence, and was thereon named "The Snow White, Fleshless, One-Eyed Ogress of the Vajra."[207] After many such exploits in Tibet, Padma Sambhava is said to have gone on to the Himalayan kingdom of Sikkim, where he is venerated as the founder of Sikkimese Buddhism, and to Bhutan, where he holds a similar position. Whether or not he actually lived is an open question, but he is universally credited with founding the oldest sect of Lamaism, the Nyingmas. By them he is worshipped as an equal of Siddartha Gautama, and well he might be, for his activities allowed Tibet's native shamanists to preserve the cult of their deities by claiming their conversion to Buddhism, and so preserve their traditional Tibetan faith against pressure from its Buddhist competitor.[208] The Nyingmas claim authority for their beliefs and practices by appealing to *terma,* or teachings that Padma Sambhava supposedly hid in caves for discovery at a later time. The Nyingma monks say they are still discovering these teachings today, no longer in written form, but in visions and revelations.[209] Even Nyingma monks outside Asia hail Padma Sambhava as "the Buddha of our time" and as the power that lets their disciples cut through their illusions and realize liberation.[210]

After the death of Ti Song De Tsen and the legendary exploits of Padma Sambhava, the Tibetan empire entered a long period of decline. Military reverses pushed the Tibetans out of their commanding position on the Silk Road, and dynastic squabbles at home weakened the monarchy.[211] Tibet's shamanists, still politically powerful, are said to have staged a persecution of the Buddhists under King Lang Darma, who was murdered by a Buddhist monk shortly thereafter (around the mid-ninth century A.D.). The Tibetan empire fell apart into petty states[212] and Buddhism seems to have been eclipsed until the eleventh century.

It is likely that these political upheavals enhanced the Tibetans' interest in the magic and sorcery of tantra. From a very early period in Central Asian history, occultism was not regarded as mere superstition, but as a kind of supernatural technology which had very practical political, military, and diplomatic uses. In a prescientific age, magic seemed the best way to deal with problems for which there was no other solution. Since the only criterion of success was efficacy, and since tantric Buddhism was free of doctrinal restraints, kings of the first millennium sought improved "magical technology" as eagerly as the leaders of modern states seek improved military technology. And tantric Buddhism had magical technology in abundance. The Tibetans realized this and began to import it from India wholesale.

Tibet's Age of Fragmentation and the Second Diffusion of Buddhism

During the next phase of Tibetan history a series of scholar monks called the Great Translators played a prominent role in the so-called Second Diffusion of Buddhism.[213] By translating almost the entire body of Indian tantric literature into Tibetan, they laid the foundations of the major schools of Tibetan Buddhism. Near the end of the tenth century, the Tibetan king Yeshe Od sent the monk Rinchen Sangpo (ca. 958-1055) to Kashmir[214] to study tantric doctrines and collect Buddhist manuscripts. He finally returned to Tibet after a total of 17 years abroad, having translated over 150 separate medical and tantric texts into Tibetan. Yeshe Od also invited to Tibet a renowned tantric teacher known as Atisha[215] (982-1052 A.D.) who had taught at several of India's Buddhist universities. Offered a large sum in gold for his teachings,[216] he came to Tibet in 1042 to reform some of the more extreme expressions of tantric practice — by this time some tantrists engaged in orgies of murder, cannibalism, and ritual sex.[217] Atisha directed his disciples in the more philosophical aspects of tantra, reformed monastic rules and discipline, and enforced the tantric principle of absolute submission of the disciple to his teacher. Atisha's disciples became the nucleus of the second great school of Tibetan Buddhism: the Kadampas,[218] who three and a half centuries later would be reorganized into the Gelugpa sect.[219] [220]

Shamanism and tantric Buddhism continued to influence each other deeply during this period. The practitioners of Bon were forced to adopt much Buddhist teaching and to systematize their doctrines so as to defend them against those of Indian Buddhism.[221] The result was a mixture of shamanism and Buddhist tantrism called Transformed Bon (or *Gyur Bon* in Tibetan). Tantric Buddhism in turn absorbed much shamanist belief and practice; e.g. the shaman survived as the oracle or monk-sorcerer, compelling the local spirits to do his will and converting them to protectors of Buddhism. The exploits of Buddhist missionaries such as Padma Sambhava or Atisha were cast in shamanist terms, and the Buddhists appealed to the occult power of shamanism for the authority of their teachings. In the end, Bon survived as a numerically small but geographically widespread sect.[222] At the folk level, shamanism continued to have a very strong influence upon the beliefs and practices of the average Tibetan (a subject to which we will turn in the next chapter).

As Padma Sambhava's Nyingma order, Atisha's Kadampa order, and the Bon sect struggled for dominance, yet another school of Tibetan Buddhism was forming, centered around one of Tibet's most colorful figures, Marpa the Translator (ca. 1012-1096).[223] Born to wealthy landowners in southern Tibet, Marpa was an aggressive child who began Buddhist studies at the age of 12. Like his contemporary Rinchen Sangpo, he left Tibet for a broader education in the universities of India. There he met the famous sorcerer Naropa and the hermit Kukkuripa. Kukkuripa (the name means "dog-man") was an strange figure even in the bizarre world of tantric myths. It is said that he spent years meditating in a cave with only a dog for company. One day, the dog transformed itself into a spirit-being[224] who gave Kukkuripa the highest form of enlightenment. Thus delivered by his pet, he moved to an island in the center of a poison lake, where surrounded by a pack of dogs, he taught the secrets of tantrism to his famous disciples Naropa and Marpa.[225]

When Marpa returned to Tibet, he settled down to work as a farmer and trader. His biography depicts him as a violent man, fighting with his kindly wife Dakmema and beating his disciples in fits of drunken rage. Secretly, however, Marpa taught his cowed group of students some of the strangest of occult practices and translated yet more tantric texts into Tibetan. One of Marpa's disciples was the poet Milarepa (c.1052-1135) who became one of the most famous figures in Tibetan literature. When his father died, Milarepa and his mother fell victim to greedy relatives who robbed them of their home. Seeking revenge, the young Milarepa became a powerful tantric sorcerer who used black magic to destroy his wicked relatives, only to be consumed by remorse for taking revenge. His repentance at the hands of Marpa is the basis for one of the most famous scenes in Tibetan literature. To make him work out his bad karma, Marpa commanded Milarepa to build a tower. When the tower was completed, Marpa told him to tear it down again, only to insist that it be built once more. In this way Milarepa had to build his tower five times over while Marpa kicked, beat, and cursed him for his efforts. In the end Marpa agreed to teach Milarepa his occult secrets. Putting his tower ordeal behind him, Milarepa went on to become a famous saint, hermit, and literary figure. His supposed autobiography (known as *The Hundred Thousand Songs of Milarepa*) is written in an entertaining, personal style. It is widely known in Tibet, and has appeared in English translation.[226] Milarepa's disciples started the third order of Tibetan Buddhism, the Kargyupa sect.[227] The Kargyupas were hermits and never became very successful on the religious scene. They split into a variety of sub-sects of which one, the Drukpa, established itself in Ladakh and in the Himalayan kingdom of Bhutan, where it remained prominent into the twenty-first century.

A contemporary and one-time teacher of Marpa the Translator, the Tibetan scholar named 'Brog Mi, was deeply interested in tantric texts such as the famous *Hevajra Tantra*. After taking an initiation into the practices of the Hevajra, 'Brog Mi translated it into Tibetan, from which it became one of the basic texts of the Sakya[228] order. This order took its name from a monastery founded in 1073 by a lama known as Konchog Gyalpo. The head lama of the Sakyapas later played an important role in bringing Tibetan Buddhism to Mongolia.[229]

During this formative period of Tibetan history, tantric Buddhists sorted themselves into a spectrum of orders with varying degrees of emphasis on shamanism, tantrism, and monastic discipline. Those who preserved the most from Tibet's native shamanism were the Bon and Nyingma sects. The Sakyas and Kargyupas (and their descendants the Drukpas) saw themselves as direct heirs of certain Indian tantric masters. The Kadampas (and their descendants the Gelugpas, described below) emphasized monastic discipline.[230]

The labors of the Great Translators left Tibetan Buddhism with one of the largest collections of sacred literature of any major religion. The person responsible for arranging it was the scholar Pu Tön[231] (1290-1364), who edited all the Buddhist and tantric texts translated over the previous three hundred years. This great mass of material, most of which was commentary on other texts,

Major Schools of Tibetan Buddhism

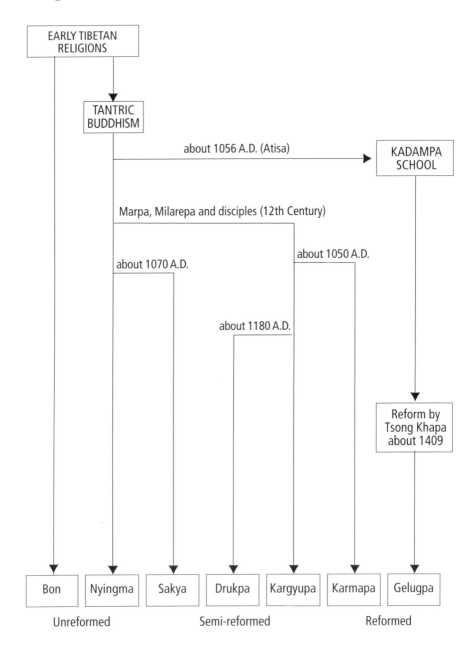

ran to 225 volumes. The collection was called the Tengyur,[232] and it became one part of the voluminous Tibetan Buddhist scriptures. The other part, known as the Kangyur,[233] was a veritable encyclopedia of Buddhism. Its 1,083 separate works were divided into a 108 bulky volumes that required a dozen yaks to move, and a small village to house the wooden blocks from which it was printed. The Kangyur and the Tengyur together form a massive collection of over 4,500 separate works, a modern edition of which runs to 65,000 pages in 120 volumes.

Pu Tön's work brought the era of the Great Translators to a close. Together, these men had shaped Tibetan Buddhism's major schools of thought and codified its beliefs into the Kangyur, Tengyur, and other works. As these texts were being finished, a Kadampa monk from northeast Tibet named Tsong Khapa (c. 1357-1419) troubled by the loose discipline of his fellow monks, began a series of reforms in monastic organization and discipline which earned him wide respect and transformed his Kadampa order into the *Gelugpa* ("virtuous way") sect. Tsong Khapa's reforms extended only to the discipline of the monks, not to their doctrines, however. The "reformed" Gelugpas put the same emphasis on magic spells, rituals and sorcery that the other "unreformed" schools did.[234] Tsong Khapa himself was a devoted tantrist, and his extensive commentaries on the early tantric scriptures became a standard for the Gelugpa order.[235] Magic and tantric occultism remain integral parts of Gelugpa teaching to this day.[236]

The Gelugpa order constructed several of Tibet's most famous monasteries. In 1409 Tsong Khapa founded Ganden monastery (east of Lhasa), while his successors built the great monasteries of Drepung (1416) and Sera (1419). The Gelugpas were also active in Tibet's second city, Shigatse, where they built Tashilhunpo monastery in 1445. Such monasteries became centers of religious, economic, and political life not only in Tibet, but across Inner Asia. The British diplomat Sir Charles Bell estimated in the 1920s that there were almost half a million monks in Tibet, an incredible number considering the harsh climate and lack of natural resources.[237, 238] Yet there were similar numbers in other countries. In 1921, just before the Communist revolution, nearly half of the male population of Mongolia was resident in Buddhist monasteries.[239] Even well into the twentieth century almost 15% of the male population of the Indian state of Ladakh, and 20% of the male population of Buryatia[240] was to be found in monasteries. The reasons for these remarkable figures are found in Tibet's history. From the time of King Ti Song De Tsen (ca. 791) monasteries had been free of taxes, and were given landholdings, serfs, and legal immunities.[241] Such advantages made the larger monasteries prominent in trade, and many of them became islands of wealth in desperately poor societies.

The power of the monasteries was based on a custom by which families gave a five or six year old son (not always voluntarily) to a local monastery for life.[242] The child was put under the guidance of a senior monk, who taught him reading, writing, and basic Buddhist doctrines. After he mastered these, the boy was eligible to pass through several higher grades of study. At each level, he had to memorize and obey an increasing number of rules. If the young monk showed exceptional promise, his study might be rewarded by a prestigious theological degree, which could open a career in government or administration. The majority who were not so gifted were sent to learn trades or to do menial work for their fellow monks. There were monk cooks, monk bakers, monk farmers, and even a kind of monk soldier. These latter might band together in small armies in order to attack other monasteries in times of civil unrest. (A great deal of such inter-monastic warfare took place during the Mongol rule of Tibet in the thirteenth century.) The larger monasteries held thousands of inmates; their wealth and private armies allowed them to become power bases for politically prominent monks.[243]

The Dalai Lamas

In the year 1174, a twelve-year-old boy named Temuchin was abandoned to die on the steppes of Mongolia. Temuchin and his family had lost a struggle for control of their Kiut Mongol tribe, and in the harsh world of twelfth-century Mongolia there was no place for losers. The Kiuts forced the boy and his widowed mother out into the desert, where both were expected to die.[244] But this did not happen. After eight years of hardships, Temuchin returned to his tribe and seized for himself the leadership he had been denied as a child. In a series of lightning conquests of neighboring tribes he extended Kiut rule across all Mongolia. In 1206 the newly united Mongols made Temuchin their ruler and gave him a new title: Genghis Khan. In the next twenty years, Genghis conquered most of north China, sacked Peking, and forced his way across the Silk Road. In campaigns of great violence and brutality, he destroyed kingdom after kingdom, from northeastern China all the way to southern Russia. Tibet was spared from invasion in 1207 only by its early and peaceful submission to his rule.

Just before his death, Genghis Khan divided his great empire among his descendants. One of these, a grandson named Kublai, was the governor of a border province between China and Tibet. In 1253, Kublai met a Tibetan Sakya monk by the name of Phagpa, who impressed the superstitious Mongol with his mastery of occult powers. While not personally converted to Tibetan Buddhism, Kublai eventually made Phagpa his personal chaplain and secular ruler of all Tibet.[245] When Kublai assumed complete control of the Mongol Empire in 1260, Tibetan Buddhism gained a powerful patron. Phagpa was set in charge of all the religious communities in the Mongol empire. Tibetan monks and lamas were invited to the Mongol Court at Peking, where they held great influence with the government. Marco Polo, who visited Kublai's court about 1280, records that the Tibetans used their magical powers to maintain favor with the credulous Mongols. Tibetan sorcerers supposedly controlled the weather around the Khan's capital city, and caused the Khan's drinking cup to rise to his lips untouched by any human hand.[246] When Polo asked him why he did not become a Christian, Kublai cited his miraculous drinking cups and replied that his sorcerers had the power of controlling bad weather,

Flowchart of the Major Schools of Tibetan Buddhism

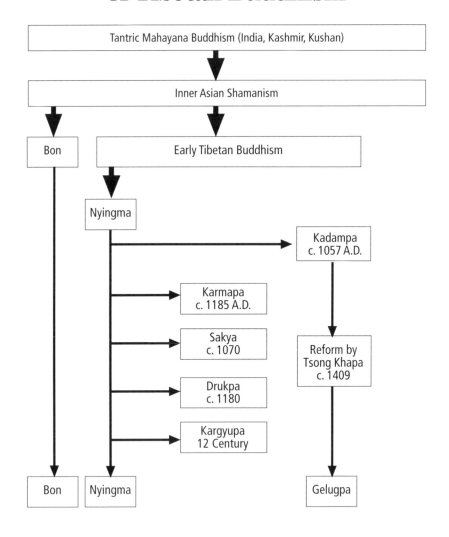

making idols speak, and predicting the future. He pointed out that Christianity offered no such practical benefits, and that Christians even denounced occult practices as black magic.[247] Evidently impressed by these powers, Kublai decided to employ Tibetan monks in laying the foundations of higher culture among the Mongols. He actively promoted lamaism by building monasteries in Mongolia and at his court in Peking. He appointed Tibetan monks to important positions, where they introduced tantric Buddhism to the shamanist Mongols. While most of them still clung to their ancient shamanist ways, Tibetan Buddhism began to make its first penetration into Mongolia.

After the Mongol empire broke up in the fourteenth century, the surviving Mongol tribes continued to be led by the descendants of the great khans. Tibetan dealings with these latter-day khans gave Tibetan Buddhism its most famous institution and spread lamaism across most of Inner Asia. In the mid-1500s the head of the Tumed branch of the Mongols, Altan Khan, became the ruler of a new Mongol confederacy.[248] Like his predecessor Kublai, Altan Khan had an interest in Tibet's affairs, and in 1578 he invited Sonam Gyatso, the head lama of Tsong Khapa's Gelugpa sect, to meet him at Lake Kokonor (modern Qinghai Lake). Like Phagpa and Kublai Khan 200 years before, the Tibetan monk and the Mongol Khan formed a relationship of priest and king with an exchange of honorific titles. Sonam Gyatso received the Mongol name *Ta-le* (rendered in English as *Dalai*) Lama, and in turn bestowed the name "King of Religion, Majestic Purity" on Altan Khan. But there was more to their meeting than mere politeness. Altan Khan, who had made tantric Buddhism the state religion of Mongolia the year before, received the blessing of Tibetan Buddhism's most respected leader. In return, he supported Sonam Gyatso's Gelugpa order over its Karmapa rivals for power in Tibet. For his part, Sonam Gyatso gained the right to travel and preach in Mongolia, where he enjoyed remarkable success in extending the power and influence of lamaism. Together, Altan Khan and Sonam Gyatso began a Tibetan Buddhist revival that became the greatest single influence on Mongol life and culture.[249]

Sonam Gyatso died in Mongolia in 1588, and his death forced the Gelugpas to find a new Dalai Lama. The first time they had faced this problem was in 1472, when their leader, the abbot of Ganden monastery, had died. At that time they borrowed from the Karmapas the idea of a line of reincarnating monks: as one such monk died, his successor would be "discovered" in a child born about the time of the previous lama's death.[250] If the child passed various mystical tests, he was taken to a monastery and raised as a monk. Not only did this idea appeal to the mystically minded Tibetans, but it gave the Gelugpa monks a chance to shape the views of their future leader from early childhood. When Ganden's abbot had died, its monks "discovered" a successor in a child they named Gedun Gyatso. This second Gelugpa leader traveled widely in Tibet, increasing support for his order and building up the monastery of Drepung, which by the time of his death held over 1,500 monks. He in turn "reincarnated into" Sonam Gyatso, who received the title of Dalai Lama from Altan Khan. Sonam Gyatso's two predecessors were given the title posthumously; they are now known as the first and second Dalai Lamas.

The young Gelugpa school still held no secular power in Tibet; it was purely a religious order. After Sonam Gyatso's death, however, the Gelugpas called in their Mongol patrons to support their choice of the next (fourth) Dalai Lama. Fearful of the increasing Mongol influence in the country's affairs, the king of Tibet tried to eliminate it by attacking the large Gelugpa monasteries near Lhasa. The fourth Dalai Lama (himself a Mongol) escaped, but died shortly afterwards. The embattled Gelugpas picked a fifth Dalai Lama, a young man named Ngawang Gyatso, this time (in 1618) calling in a Mongol army to back their choice. The arrival of the Mongols touched off a bloody civil war in which the Gelugpas crushed their rivals and made themselves masters of Tibet.[251]

The new Gelugpa leader, Ngawang Gyatso, was one of Tibetan Buddhism's greatest figures. An able administrator and politician, he was the first Dalai Lama to assume complete control of Tibet. He used his power skillfully, loosening his ties with the Mongols whose armies kept him in power, yet retaining their religious devotion to him as Dalai Lama. In this way he consolidated and extended Gelugpa control over large areas of Inner Asia. His achievements at home were equally impressive. He united the country after a bitter civil war, proclaimed himself and his four predecessors to be incarnations of Chenrezi,[252] the Buddha of compassion, and built the great Potala palace in Lhasa. By the end of his reign he had made himself master of the Gelugpas, head of the Tibetan government, and living god: offices which were claimed by all succeeding Dalai Lamas. Through his bold seizure of power and adroit administration, Ngawang Gyatso gave Tibetan Buddhism the form it retained until the mid-twentieth century.

Tibetan Buddhism Spreads Across Inner Asia

The reign of the fifth Dalai Lama (1617-1682) began a time of rapid expansion for Tibetan Buddhism. In the three hundred years since the fall of Genghis Khan's empire, the shamanist Mongols had become devout Tibetan Buddhists. Mongol monks studied in the great Gelugpa monasteries of Lhasa and brought their faith back with them to Mongolia. The political alliance between the Mongols and the Gelugpas flowered into a deep and enduring religious relationship which was actively encouraged by the Chinese. China had suffered centuries of attacks at the hands of Inner Asian nomads, and as a matter of state policy its government was quick to support the spread of a pacifist religion like Buddhism, even to the point of providing the Mongols with their own line of reincarnating Buddhist lamas called *hutugtus.*[253] The Qing Dynasty brought Mongolia under the direct control of China in the mid-1700s and actively promoted lamaism as the state religion. By the beginning of the twentieth century, 14% of the adult male population of Mongolia were to be found living in the country's 800 monasteries.[254] The Mongol historian Baabar points out that the spread of Buddhism severed his country from the developed world of the time, educated the elite few at the expense of the masses, and impoverished the Mongols by sending expensive gifts to Tibet.[255, 256] China, which for so many centuries feared the barbarian hordes from the Tibetan west and the Mongol north, was never to be troubled by them again.

From Mongolia, Tibetan Buddhism spread to the Buryat Mongols living around Siberia's Lake Baikal. By the beginning of the twentieth century, Buryatia had 37 monasteries and 15,000 monks, or one in five of the adult male population.[257] Their Siberian neighbors, the Turkic-speaking Tuvans, also embraced Tibetan Buddhism, with 4,000 monks living in 25 monasteries during the 1920s.[258] Tibetan Buddhism also entered the shamanist Yugur, Tu, Daur, and Ewenki (Tungus) cultures. Tantric Buddhism did not displace the native shamanist beliefs of these groups, but entered a more or less easy coexistence with them. The Torgut Mongols accepted Tibetan Buddhism and migrated all the way across Central Asia to European Russia (about 1620). They settled on the banks of the lower Volga River, where they became known as the Kalmyks. Three hundred years later, this small group of Mongols played a crucial role in bringing Tibetan Buddhism to North America.

Tibetan Buddhism also spread to the east. The Naxi, Pumi, and Nu peoples (now in northern Yunnan Province, China) and the Jiarong and Qiang peoples (of modern Sichuan Province) gradually accepted Tibetan Buddhism, which also penetrated south into the Himalayas. Here lay the kingdoms of Jumla and Mustang, which controlled all of what is now western Nepal. Both these kingdoms adopted Tibetan Buddhism, and today they remain one of the few places where Tibet's ancient culture can still be seen in its original form. Nepal, where Ashoka had planted Buddhism in the third century B.C., was a predominantly Hindu kingdom whose borders enclosed minority peoples closely related to the Tibetans. Most of these tribes (e.g. the Gurungs, Tamangs, Lhomi, and Sherpas) lived in parts of the country where there were frequent opportunities to exchange goods and ideas with the Tibetans, thanks to the yak caravans threading their way across the Himalayas trading in salt.[259] Tibetan Buddhism diffused through these ethnic groups with varying degrees of success. Some groups, like the Bhotias and Sherpas, maintained strongly Tibetan Buddhist cultures, while others continued to practice varying mixtures of shamanism, tantric Buddhism, and Hinduism.[260] Nepal's Hindu rulers invaded Tibet in 1788 and again in 1855, barring the expansion of Tibetan Buddhism further to the south.

As early as the tenth century Buddhism had spread to Ladakh, a mountain kingdom at the far west end of the Himalayas. Gelugpa monks began to arrive in Ladakh in the early 1400s, followed by representatives of the Drukpas, a subsect of Milarepa's Kadampa order. Despite Ladakh's nominal submission to the Muslim rulers of Mogul India, the cultural and religious ties between Ladakh and Tibet remained strong.[261] Tibetan Buddhism also took hold in at the other end of the Himalayas, in the border state of Sikkim. According to tradition, the sorcerer Padma Sambhava laid the foundations of Sikkimese Buddhism in the eighth century. The historical founder of Buddhism in Sikkim, however, was a Tibetan monk called Lha Tsun Chenpo. Born about 1595, Lha Tsun was a famous scholar whose great learning impressed even the fifth Dalai Lama. Convinced by a prophecy that he was to convert Sikkim, Lha Tsun used his shamanic powers to "fly" over the Himalayas and find a man named Phuntso Namgyal, whom he made king of Sikkim in 1642. The new king cultivated close relations with the fifth Dalai Lama, and under his patronage Phuntso Namgyal encouraged the spread of Nyingma Buddhism. Missionary monks came to Sikkim from Tibet and translated the Buddhist scriptures into the language of Sikkim's original inhabitants, the Lepchas. By skillfully combining the animist beliefs of the Lepchas with their own doctrines, the monks made rapid progress in converting Sikkim's aboriginal people to Buddhism.[262] The Tibetan-related Bhotias of Nepal and Sikkim also had little difficulty accepting the faith that had taken such a firm hold in their ancestral homeland.

East of Sikkim is the kingdom of Bhutan. The advent of lamaism in the country is said to go back to the time of the Tibetan King Song Tsen Gampo, who established two monasteries in Bhutan. Padma Sambhava supposedly visited the country a century and a half later, and he is popularly credited with bringing tantric Buddhism into Bhutan. A cult grew up around his legend, and he is widely worshipped by the Bhutanese to this day. The historical beginnings of Buddhism in Bhutan go back to 1616, when a Drukpa lama named Ngawang Namgyal made himself both secular and religious head of the country. A shrewd politician, he was able to retain his power despite repeated efforts by the Gelugpas to dislodge him. Though remote from the center of Drukpa Buddhism in faraway Ladakh, Bhutan remained staunchly Drukpa. It remained a tributary state of Gelugpa-ruled Tibet until 1951, after which became a monarchy protected by India.[263]

Spiritual and Cultural Effects of Tibetan Buddhism

By the 1600s, the monks of the Gelugpa order were powerful enough to impose their religious and political will upon Tibet. They filled government positions with monks and set up a theocracy[264] in which religious rather than pragmatic principles guided the actions of the state. The lamaist government showed little interest in the events of the outside world and did what it could to keep outside influence at bay. In the year 1792 (the Water Mouse Year according to the Tibetan calendar) the Lhasa government announced a formal ban on all Westerners entering Tibet.[265] To the ruling monks this must have seemed a natural policy, for isolation was a central theme in tantric Buddhist doctrine. Tibetan monks performed individual retreats lasting months or even years. A few even immured themselves for life in caves.[266] Other monks went alone to the hills to meditate. Monasteries were built at remote sites, often on a hilltop or rocky ridge away from settled areas.[267] Tibetans were also isolated from each other by large distances, low population density, and difficult terrain that promoted dialect differences and regional alliances. Isolating Tibet from the outside world must have seemed like a reasonable policy to the Tibetan government of the day, but it was to have long-lasting consequences which were ultimately fatal to the lamaist theocracy.

During much of the second millennium, the world of the average Tibetan was as wide as the lonely valley in which he or she was born (or if a pilgrim, nomad or trader, the territory which in which he roamed). Most monks and village Tibetans remained unaware of any social or intellectual alternatives to their station in life, for government policy as well as formidable physical barriers insulated them from the neighboring civilizations of Islam in the west, India in the south, and the Chinese world in the north and east. Tibet became an "island in the sky"; physically, intellectually, and politically isolated from the great cultures surrounding it. Creativity withered and intellectual life shrank to conserving, classifying, memorizing, and commenting on the vast amount of scriptural material imported from India and China during the seventh and eighth centuries. The catalog and the memorized list became the paradigmatic tools of Tibetan intellectual life.[268] Artists followed strict standards of subject matter, line, proportion, and color.[269] Artistic achievement was measured by conformity to norms established centuries before. Writers used established metaphors found in metaphor dictionaries.[270] There was no popular literary culture, for only the monks and government officials could read, and they lived in intellectual, and to some degree, social isolation from the communities on which their monasteries depended.[271] Since tantric Buddhism is a gnostic religion whose secrets are revealed only to dedicated initiates, it never developed as a truly popular movement in Tibet or elsewhere.[272] This allowed shamanist practices and beliefs to continue to flourish at the popular level.

This separation of the tantric elite from the shamanist masses persisted for centuries and had many important effects on Tibetan culture. The monks defined and controlled the high culture of reading, writing, and arts, and kept this knowledge to

themselves, so the common people came to feel that education, literacy, and religion were matters best left to the monk
"experts." Since the simple observance of ritual was enough to
satisfy the religious impulses of most people, shamanist beliefs
continued to thrive at the folk level, where they had already
propagated themselves by oral tradition for millennia. From
this layer of folk shamanist belief emerged many characteristi-
cally Tibetan religious phenomena: symbols such as the
windhorse, artifacts such as the stone piles found on high places
across Tibet, traditions such as tying bits of cloth to tree branches
or burning juniper branches to increase one's good luck or
lungta, setting aside animals for mystic purposes, changing
someone's name to deceive spirits in case of bad luck, doing
divination with various objects, belief in *lu* water spirits, helper
spirits, demons, oracles, prayer wheels, circumambulation of
holy places, burning incense, and many other customs. These
shamanist folk traditions helped to give tantric Buddhism its
distinctly Tibetan flavor and defined popular religious culture
for centuries to come.[273]

Tibetan Buddhism in Modern Asia

From the death of the Fifth Dalai Lama in 1682 to the
death of Twelfth Dalai Lama in 1875, the isolationist policies
of the Tibetan government kept the outside world at bay. By
the end of the nineteenth century, however, this situation began to change. Rising British power in India led to a series of
border skirmishes in Sikkim in 1888. In 1901 the Thirteenth
Dalai Lama authorized a diplomatic mission to Russia, which
heightened British Indian fears of a Russian threat to its northern border. This and other events caused the dispatch of a British military expedition to Central Tibet in 1904, which withdrew after securing treaty privileges.[274] An armed Chinese mission to Lhasa appeared in 1910, but withdrew in 1912 after
the Chinese Republican revolution. These events should have
persuaded the lamas that they could not remain aloof from the
world for very much longer. Indeed, developments in faraway
Europe were about to bring profound changes to the Tibetan

Buddhist world. In 1917 the Russian Bolshevik Party overthrew the country's newly elected Provisional Government, leading to a bitter three year civil war between the Communists and their adversaries (known as the Whites). By 1920 the retreating White Russian armies had invaded Mongolia and begun a reign of terror. The Moscow government sent its forces into the country to destroy the Whites and set up a Soviet-style regime. In 1924, what was then known as Outer Mongolia declared itself the world's second Communist country. The border region known as Inner Mongolia remained in Chinese hands.

Soviet Mongolia's bitterly antireligious government lost no time in launching a campaign of terror against the lamas and their monasteries. Leading Buddhists were jailed or shot, and their monasteries destroyed. By the outbreak of World War II, institutional Tibetan Buddhism had virtually ceased to exist in Mongolia, Buryatia and Tuva.[275] The Mongols were forced to swallow the bitter dregs of Stalinism until a democracy movement reformed the government in 1990. With the beginning of religious freedom, Tibetan Buddhism enjoyed a revival of sorts, and long-closed monasteries were reopened and refurbished. Mongolian monks expressed a desire to spread basic Buddhist teachings among the people, and to strengthen their links with Tibetan Buddhists in other countries. The fourteenth Dalai Lama encouraged local monks to pursue these aims during his repeated visits to Mongolia.

Just as the Communists set out to destroy Tibetan Buddhism in Mongolia, a similar effort began inside the Soviet Union itself. In 1928, the government started a campaign to suppress institutional Buddhism. The number of monks and lamas in the country shrank from some 16,000 in 1915 to about 300 in 1960. Religious toleration returned with the breakup of the Soviet Union in 1991, and three traditionally Tibetan Buddhist groups remained in Russia by the beginning of the twenty-first century: the Tuvans, the Buryats, and the Kalmyks. The Kalmyks were the descendants of the Torgot Mongols who migrated to European Russia in 1620. Though cut off from Lhasa, they remained active Buddhists right through the end of the twentieth century. During

World War II, Stalin suspected that the Kalmyks were collaborating with the invading Germans, and in 1943 he deported the entire Kalmyk population to Siberia. In the turmoil following the German retreat, about a thousand Kalmyks managed to escape from the Soviet Union and were eventually resettled in the United States, in 1952. The rest of the Kalmyks were allowed to return from Siberia after the war, and today they live in the Republic of Kalmykia, on the broad plain where the Volga River empties into the Caspian Sea.

Russia's other Tibetan Buddhist groups are the Tuvans and the Buryats. The Tuvans are a Turkic-speaking people who live in their own republic on the borderland between the Gobi and the forests of Siberia. The neighboring Buryats are Russia's largest Tibetan Buddhist group. Though many Buryats remain shamanists and a few have converted to Orthodox Christianity, Tibetan Buddhism remains a strong cultural and religious influence in Buryat life. Buryat scholars are known in the Russian Republic for their expertise in Tibetan and Mongolian studies. As in Mongolia, the demise of Communist rule brought a rebirth of Tibetan Buddhism in Russia. In July of 1990, Tibetan Buddhism was declared the state religion of the Tuva Republic. Monasteries in the Buryat, Kalmyk, and Tuva Republics were repaired, and training programs for monks re-established. In European Russia, a Tibetan Buddhist center reopened in St. Petersburg, and Tibetan Buddhism began to spread among some ethnically Russian young people.

The Communist revolution that began in Russia and spread to Mongolia continued in China. After the victory of the Maoist forces in 1949, the Chinese government asserted its control over Tibet in the 1950s. Tibet's religion and culture were vigorously suppressed, and during the Cultural Revolution (1966-1976) Maoist gangs destroyed what was left of Tibet's culture. At the beginning of the twenty-first century, institutional Buddhism in Tibet persisted only in a few state-controlled monasteries, but the folk religion remained a powerful force among the Tibetan people.

Tibetan Buddhism in its original form can still be found in India and the Himalayan states of Nepal and Bhutan. Nepal, which during the twentieth century was the world's only officially Hindu kingdom, was home to many Tibetan Buddhist tribal groups. Perhaps the best known of these were the Sherpas, famous for their mountaineering exploits on Mt. Everest and other high peaks of the Himalayas. Lesser known Himalayan peoples like the Tamangs, Bhotias, Magars, and Gurungs also practiced Tibetan Buddhism, though in some areas these groups were strongly influenced by their Hindu neighbors. For much of its history, Sikkim had a Tibetan Buddhist ruling class over its Hindu majority. Though only a third of Sikkim's population was lamaist, it was served by no fewer than 35 monasteries, some of which were important centers of Tibetan studies, such as the Karmapa monastery at Rumtek. The last king of Sikkim, Palden Thondup Namgyal, was a devout Tibetan Buddhist who founded the Namgyal Institute of Tibetology at Gangtok, and was actively interested in propagating his faith. In April 1975, Sikkim was annexed by India.

Bhutan remained the world's only officially Tibetan Buddhist nation-state. In the twentieth century approximately 70 percent of Bhutan's population was lamaist, and Tibetan Buddhist cultural influences remained very strong among the dominant people group, the Ngalops. Tibetan Buddhism had an unchallenged place as a culturally and politically unifying force in this small but ethnically diverse country. Tibetan Buddhism was also a vital force in parts of India. In Ladakh, India's northernmost province, there were 40 major and 60 minor monasteries. Even in the latter half of the twentieth century there were by some estimates 15,000 monks and nuns. Ladakh's most famous monastery, Hemis, is the seat of the Drukpa school, while the picturesque Lamayuru monastery is a Di Gung Pa (Kagyupa) institution. There are also a number of Gelugpa centers. Tibetan Buddhism remained the religion of most Ladakhis, though many are Muslims and a small number are Christians.

Elsewhere in India, Tibetan Buddhism thrived among the Bhotias, Tamangs, and other tribal groups of the Himalayan

frontiers. But perhaps the country's greatest Buddhist influence comes from the 100,000 Tibetans who fled Tibet with
the Dalai Lama in the 1950s. Most of these people were devout Buddhists who left Tibet in order to practice their religion.[276] Within a few years of their arrival in India, monasteries
or branches of the four main sects appeared in every Tibetan
settlement in the country.[277] In a bid to preserve their culture,
the exiled monks collected what Buddhist literature they could,
and published it in Tibetan and in English translation, setting
the stage for the spread of Tibetan Buddhism outside Asia.

International Tibetan Buddhism

The West has held a long fascination with Asia, going back
to the days of the fanciful kingdom of Prester John[278] in the
Middle Ages. During the late nineteenth and early twentieth
centuries, the advance of science, technology, and economic
development in the West left many people disenchanted by the
loss of simplicity, spirituality, and mystery in their lives. Just as
their ancestors sought hope in finding the spiritual kingdom of
Prester John, so modern Europeans longed for a fairytale kingdom where the values that had been lost in their own societies
could perhaps be regained. In this subliminal fantasyland, rulers of sublime spirituality governed a peaceful realm of beauty,
harmony, natural balance, and spiritual liberation.[279] As the Asian
land most isolated and different from the West, Tibet was a
tempting metaphor for these romantic dreams, which were just
waiting to be exploited by writers of sufficient talent.

The first such author was Rudyard Kipling, whose 1901
novel *Kim* featured a Tibetan monk who becomes attached to
the novel's namesake hero. As depicted in the novel, the monk's
highly romanticized religious beliefs seem much more at home
in London than Lhasa.[280] A line of much less talented theoso-
phists, escape artists and con men (such as the Englishman who
passed himself off as the so called "Lama Lobsang Rampa"[281])
continued to romanticize Tibet in the popular press during the
early years of the century. But no one did more to embed

Tibetan Buddhism in the West's romantic imagination than the British screenwriter James Hilton, whose 1933 novel *Lost Horizon* told the story of four unlikely adventurers (including one dreadfully stereotyped Christian missionary) who are swept away to a mythical Tibetan valley called Shangri-La. The story's escapist theme made it an instant success during the economic depression of the 1930s. Heinrich Harrer, an Austrian mountaineer taken prisoner by the British during the war, escaped to Tibet from an Indian prisoner of war camp, and remained in the country for seven years. His naively sympathetic picture of Tibetan Buddhism was published in 1953 as the book *Seven Years in Tibet* (which, like *Lost Horizon,* was made into a popular movie).

When the Chinese asserted control over Tibet in the 1950s, the Dalai Lama's government and thousands of monks fled to refugee camps in India. There they preserved their traditional culture as best they could, and tried to gain international support for restoring the Tibetan theocracy. Desperately short of resources, the Tibetan exiles in India appealed to the West for funding and political help. All the conditions for Tibetan Buddhism to spread internationally were in place by the middle of the twentieth century: a class of people who were disenchanted with modern life and who held a highly romanticized view of Tibet, a Tibetan exile administration in need of funding and political support, and the ability of both groups to travel internationally. As small groups of Tibetan refugees settled in Europe and America, the Tibetans saw a chance to raise support for their cause. In the early 1960s the first monks and lamas began to arrive in Europe. By 1963 the first European Tibetan Buddhist meditation center had been started by Lama Chogyam Trungpa in Dumfriesshire, Scotland. In the 1970s Tibetan Buddhist meditation centers opened in France and Sweden, and by the end of the decade a Tibetan Buddhist movement was spreading widely in Europe.

Tibetan Buddhism entered North America somewhat earlier. In 1952, a group of Kalmyk Mongols who had escaped from the Soviet Union settled in the eastern United States. One of their spiritual leaders, the Mongol Lama Wangyal, started the first Lamaist study center open to Americans. Tibetan lamas soon followed, many of them setting up Tibetan studies centers at major American universities. By the 1970s they had established Tibetan departments at state universities in Washington, California, Colorado, Wisconsin, and Indiana. All four sects established meditation centers in major cities across North America, and by the end of the twentieth century there were monasteries or Tibetan Buddhist study centers in major cities around the world.

How had an obscure, complicated, and deeply superstitious religion made such a successful transition to Western culture? First, it found a ready audience among those who felt alienated from a society which they perceived as fragmented, hurried, unspiritual, materialistic, and disconnected from the natural environment. Not a few became Buddhists because they felt the Church had failed them.[282] Such people were ready for a spiritual remedy from the mysterious East; a (literally) magical cure that offered solitary meditation and control of their own spiritual destiny. Second, Tibetan Buddhists skillfully used the entertainment industry and the international human rights movement (as well as certain aspects of the environmental, peace, and popular psychology movements) as bridges to mainstream Western culture. Third, the form of Tibetan Buddhism taught in the West was a highly philosophical form of tantric Buddhism, from which the superstitious elements of folk Buddhism had been discarded as not appealing to Western taste. This "refined" form of Tibetan Buddhism spread internationally during the late twentieth and early twenty-first centuries.

Summary

Like people, cultures make choices that bring them nearer to or farther from God. Since the dawn of history, the Tibetans valued the power of their shamans, who healed their sick, drove out their demons, controlled their weather, and foresaw their future. With no higher doctrines or revealed truths to guide them, the Tibetans found in tantric Buddhism a magic greater and more powerful than any their shamans possessed. It became their "pearl of great price,"[283] and they gave much treasure and centuries of scholarly effort to importing from India all of it they possibly could. The lamas taught their religion to other peoples whose shamanist worldview had prepared them to receive it, expanding the limits of Tibetan Buddhism to its natural borders with Hinduism, Islam, Chinese traditional religions, and Russian Orthodoxy. In Tibet, Mongolia, and elsewhere, the monks set up theocracies which stifled social change and suppressed the innovations[284] that were changing the face of Outer Asia.

By the end of the nineteenth century, it was apparent to outside observers (not all of whom were friendly) that the lamas' isolationism was a fatal weakness. Change-rejecting societies quickly find themselves at a serious political and military disadvantage to change-accepting ones[285] and the lamas' rejection of change was yet another chapter in this ongoing human tragedy. It is perhaps surprising that the lamaist theocracy in Tibet maintained itself as long as it did. But the arrival at the capital city, Lhasa, of a British Indian army in 1904, and a Chinese army in 1910, were signs that the monks could not keep the world at bay forever. Nor did they change even after watching the destruction of institutional Buddhism during the 1930s in Mongolia. When Tibet's turn came, it was too late. By the middle of the twentieth century, lamaist theocracies had been destroyed almost everywhere they had once existed (Bhutan being the only major exception). Paradoxically, the resulting diaspora of lamas gave new life to Tibetan Buddhism and gave this previously obscure mystery religion a worldwide presence.

CHAPTER 5

Folk Tibetan Buddhism

Culture can kill.

Pemba was a 20-year-old man who left his home in southern Tibet in search of a better life. Making his way over the snowy Himalayan passes into neighboring Nepal, Pemba settled among other Tibetans in Kathmandu, Nepal's capital city, and found a job in a small restaurant. It didn't pay much, but his employers were fellow Tibetans and treated him well. One day Pemba got sick. At first it was just a fever, but within days he began to cough up blood. His employers recognized the symptoms immediately: *tuberculosis.* Fearing for their health, they fired Pemba from his job and turned him out of his quarters, leaving him homeless and unemployed. Friends brought him to a local hospital, where the diagnosis of tuberculosis (TB) was confirmed; a serious case, but definitely curable. There was just one problem — Pemba could not speak Nepali (the national language of Nepal) and his doctors and nurses could not speak his dialect of Tibetan. The food was strange, too: rice and lentils instead of the tea and roasted barley that he was used to. Alone in a strange place, unable to talk with others, given strange food to eat, he lost his will to live and left the hospital. He died two weeks later. Cultural differences, as much as a medical illness, were responsible for Pemba's death. While he lived in the Tibetan community he could stay with Tibetans, speak Tibetan, and eat Tibetan food. When his illness forced him into the surrounding Hindu culture of Nepal, however, he could do none of these things. Pemba developed what is now called culture shock, and in his case it proved fatal.

Culture has to do with the different ways that human groups respond to the world around them. Some of these ways are obvious. For example, Europeans eat their food with knives, forks, and spoons. The use of silverware is taught from childhood, and failure to use it would be a subject for comment, if not shock, at most tables in Europe. In many Tibetan Buddhist cultures, though, people eat with chopsticks. Food is cut up into small pieces so that it can be eaten this way, and even small children can use their chopsticks well enough to get that last grain of sticky rice out of a bowl. Other cultural differences are not so easy to see. In North America, two people who have a difference of opinion will generally try to talk things out openly and honestly. They may even have a public argument and still remain friends. In Tibetan Buddhist cultures, open disagreement with another person is considered very rude, especially if a younger person disagrees with an older one. Everyone expects both parties to preserve the appearance of agreement in public, even though they might disagree violently in private. This is not considered dishonest or hypocritical, but simply a basic rule of courtesy. Anyone coming into a Tibetan Buddhist culture would be expected to behave accordingly.

Culture is more than how people eat their food or behave in public, however. Culture is meanings organized in patterns. It is a tool that people use to cope with the world around them. As we saw in Chapter Two, most of Inner Asia is a cold, high-altitude desert unsuitable for growing crops. In order to survive in these areas, the ancestors of today's Tibetans and Mongols developed a nomadic lifestyle based on the herding of yaks, sheep, horses, and other animals. As we have seen, the magical technology of shamanism helped these peoples cope with the everyday problems of life, death, and the spirit world. Because they shared similar environments, lifeways, and cultures, the peoples of ancient Inner Asia possessed a common cultural foundation even before the arrival of Buddhism. Lamaism simply absorbed the rituals, gods, and spirits of shamanism into its own belief system.[286] In this way, shamanism and tantric Buddhism became the common source for beliefs and values, not just for the Mongols and Tibetans, but for all the peoples whose lives and cultures were influenced by the Tibetan form of Buddhism.

This process was roughly similar to the one that gave Western Europe a common cultural foundation. Though the British,

French, and Germans are distinct peoples who speak different languages and have different customs, all of them share the "foundation culture" of Western civilization. All three peoples look back on a common heritage from ancient Greece and Rome. Historically, all three derived their values from Christianity. And all three continue to share with each other: the French read Shakespeare, the English listen to Beethoven, and the Germans appreciate French impressionist paintings. In the same way, the peoples of the Tibetan Buddhist world have a foundation culture. All of them share an intellectual and spiritual heritage from ancient India, all of them derive their values from shamanism and Tibetan Buddhism, and all continue to share their cultures with one another. The Bhutanese read Milarepa, the Mongols build their temples in Tibetan style, and the Tibetans imported much of their art from Nepal. For someone from outside the Tibetan Buddhist world, understanding this foundation culture is like having a master key that fits all the locks in a given building. With this key, one can begin to understand peoples as diverse as the Buryats, the Tibetans, and the Sherpas.

The foundation culture of Buddhist Inner Asia has a number of features that are present, at least to some degree, in almost every culture in the Tibetan Buddhist world. These ten features include: 1) shamanism, 2) a lively folk religion, 3) an occult-magical view of life, 4) belief in luck, merit, and offerings, 5) ideals of detachment and nonviolence, 6) Tibetan Buddhism as a part of ethnic identity, 7) Tibetan language, 8) religious specialists, 9) Tibetan religious art and architecture, and 10) pastoral nomadism. In the remainder of this chapter we'll explore these features and see what effects they have on everyday life.

1) Shamanism

As we saw in Chapter Two, shamanism appeared sometime during the prehistory of Inner Asia. Shamanist peoples also believe in spirits associated with animals and with objects in the natural world, a worldview known as *animism*.[287] For purposes of this book, the term shamanism embraces three core meanings: 1) the shaman, 2) the techniques he or she uses to coerce the spirits, and 3) the animistic beliefs associated with the shamanic worldview. Shamanism is a local religion in the sense that it focuses on the immediate environment of a given people. It assumes that humans and animals are interchangeable, that animals are spiritually powerful beings who can serve as tribal totems or symbolic ancestors, that personal power, good fortune, and luck can be maintained through proper rituals, and that symbolic death and resurrection mark the activity of the shaman. It assumes that there is a world of malignant spirits and personified natural forces intent upon harming human beings (fear of spiritual beings is a dominant theme in shamanism). Shamans address this fear by trying to ward off evil and helping people to live "in harmony" with the spirit world. The central concern of shamanism is success (whether or not its techniques ward off evil, find game, cure sickness, etc.) and it does not concern itself with ultimate questions such as morality or man's purpose in life. Because shamanism has no codified doctrines or philosophical systems, it coexists easily with Tibetan Buddhism (in Asia) or Christianity (in Russia or North America).

The encounter between the native shamanism of Inner Asia and tantric Buddhism began at least as early as the seventh century, and it has continued to the present. In Tibet the two belief systems accommodated each other by means of synthesis. The Tibetans preserved the cult of their shamanist deities by claiming their "conversion" to Buddhism, and by incorporating into folk Tibetan Buddhism shamanist *symbols* (e.g. the windhorse[288] and the swastika[289]); *artifacts* such as the stone piles[290] found on high places across the Tibetan Buddhist world; *practices* such as walking around sacred objects, tying bits of cloth to tree branches or burning juniper branches to increase one's personal energy, setting aside animals for mystic purposes, changing one's name to deceive spirits, doing divination with various objects; and *beliefs* such as belief in the *lu* water spirits and various helper spirits. The spirit journeys of the shaman are still made today by Tibetan Buddhist oracles and by certain special persons called *delogs* who are believed to die, visit the spirit world, and "resurrect" themselves after a period of a few days.[291]

In other parts of the Himalayas and in Siberia, Tibetan Buddhism is just beginning (in historical terms) to enter various shamanist cultures. It is not yet strong enough to establish monasteries or to train monks within these cultures, though an itinerant monk may serve as a priest in the same village where there is also a native shaman. In such settings, tantric Buddhism and shamanism coexist with one another. This situation is not uncommon among the Tamangs and other minority peoples of Nepal. A similar situation exists in Mongolia and certain parts of Siberia, where Tibetan Buddhism has established an institutional presence in the form of monasteries, but it has not yet displaced shamanism entirely. In these cultures, shamanism and Tibetan Buddhism coexist as parallel belief systems, often with some shamanist resistance to the advance of Tibetan Buddhism. Regardless of its relationship to tantric Buddhism, shamanism in some form is present in all Tibetan Buddhist cultures, either as a parallel religious phenomenon or as an integral part of Tibetan Buddhism. In many cases the two are so closely intertwined that it is no longer possible to tell them apart, especially at the folk level.

2) A Lively Folk Religion

Most people in the Tibetan Buddhist world are unconcerned with gaining enlightenment, meditating, or practicing tantric rituals. Like their shamanists ancestors, they see religion as a means to solve the problems of everyday life. A sick child, a lost yak, guidance for the future, or the most auspicious day to get married are the sorts of issues for which people turn to folk religion (which in this case is the set of beliefs held by the majority of people who are not monks or nuns). It is a set of beliefs and practices that is outside of, and may even be contrary to, what might be thought of as "orthodox" or "doctrinal"

Buddhism. The world of folk Tibetan Buddhists is filled with aggressive spirits, capricious gods, malignant demons, and personified natural forces who share the world with humans. These spirits are hostile to humans, and their existence is only important because of their effects on human life, not for any religious or philosophical reason.[292] These evil spirits lurk in all of life's shadows, waiting for the chance to strike. The ordinary Tibetan, or Ladakhi, or Bhutanese lives in constant fear of them and of the evil they may bring. No trouble is too great, no journey too long, and no cost too high to avoid the spirits, or to placate them once they have been offended. When a folk Tibetan Buddhist is troubled by sickness in the family or by business reversals, often their first thought is to locate the spiritual source of the trouble.

There are a number of ways to do this, including sorcery, mediumship, astrology, consulting an oracle, or doing divination. In cultures where shamanism and tantric Buddhism are integrated, the monks or lamas will perform the required rituals, while in areas where shamanism thrives independently of Buddhism, lay shamans are recognized as the experts. *Oracles* are people who specialize in fortune telling, and virtually every Tibetan Buddhist society has these amateur and professional seers. The Tibetan government maintained a state oracle who played a crucial role in enthroning the fourteenth Dalai Lama just as the Chinese People's Liberation Army was about to enter Tibet.[293] In the Tibetan Buddhist countries of the Himalayas, everything from common household decisions to major affairs of state are submitted to oracles for guidance. Trips are delayed, rituals cancelled, and important decisions postponed until the oracles make their decisions.[294] The oracles have a wide variety of fortune-telling tools at their disposal. Some interpret rosaries, others use dice, cards, arrows, animal bones and entrails, books, stones, pebbles, or butter lamps. Still others interpret animal behavior or go into trances. Unfavorable answers from these procedures mean that expensive rituals must be performed to ward off whatever evil is foreseen. In at least one case, an oracle has been known to load his dice to give unfavorable results,[295] so that his customers will have to pay for expensive rituals to ward off evil.

Every Tibetan Buddhist culture has shamans who compel the spirits to do man's bidding. Shamans specialize in trances, exorcisms, curses, and weather control. In a typical encounter, the shaman will enter a trancelike state during which he moans, sweats, writhes, and cries out in an abnormal voice. Some shamans demonstrate superhuman strength during their trances by twisting metal objects with their bare hands, or jumping up and down with heavy weights on their backs.[296] After demonstrating possession by the spirits, a shaman's words are taken as the utterance of whatever spirit possesses him. There are also *witches* who are believed to harm others with magical powers, and *mediums:* people who are possessed by one or more spirits. Known as *lha pa* in Tibetan, mediums serve as channels through which spirits can communicate with people.

Some of these encounters can be quite dramatic. The anthropologist Christoph von Furer-Haimendorf observed one seance in a Sherpa household where a young girl had been ill for some time. The family called in a medium, who went into a trance and was soon possessed by a spirit. The spirit complained that the family had been mistreating it by placing their boots in the spirit's corner of the house. As the medium related the spirit's complaint, the sick young girl pleaded with the spirit: "Please do not kill me, but let me live!"[297] Less dramatic but more common is the use of astrology, which is applied to almost every important decision in every corner of the Tibetan Buddhist world.[298] Horoscopes are cast for births, weddings, funerals, and many other occasions. They are available on an annual basis, or for an entire lifetime. Astrology also plays a prominent role in traditional Tibetan medicine. Astrologers, diviners, oracles, and sorcerers are all a part of the attempt to deal with the uncertainties of everyday life. For the sick child there is the spirit medium, for the anxious farmer there is the diviner, and for the prospective bride there is the astrologer. All these occult technologists make their living from fear: fear of the spirits, fear of the gods, fear of the future.[299] This fear puts a great emotional and economic burden on most folk Tibetan Buddhists.

Why don't people realize this and just get rid of these oppressive beliefs? One reason is that the most widespread alternative (a "modern" or "scientific" worldview) does not provide answers to the questions that shamanists and folk Tibetan Buddhists ask. Shamanism has endured from the dawn of history because it excels at manipulating the spiritual world for the sake of human beings - at least so far as people in shamanist societies are concerned. Shamanism and tantra are both what might be called "humanistic technologies." They are *humanistic* in the sense that their magical techniques put man at the center of existence and manipulate everything else for human benefit.[300] They are *technologies* in the sense that they are like tools which put humans in control of spiritual forces in the same way that scientific technology puts humans in control of physical forces. Shamanism gives people the sense that they can control what is actually beyond their control. This false sense of security is comforting in the face of an uncertain and dangerous world.

3) An Occult-Magical View of Life

Shamanism and tantric Buddhism are founded on what might be called occult-magical thinking. The term *occult* literally means "hidden", and in this case it refers to belief in spirits or in powers which cannot be seen. The term *magical* refers to the belief that these powers can be manipulated through spiritual technology. In shamanism, that technology is the shaman's trance and spirit-coercing formulas, while in tantric Buddhism, mantras (magical spells) and mudras (magical gestures) are believed to have the power to manipulate occult forces.[301] Occult-magical thinking assumes that reality is unitary and that there is no barrier between the physical, the psychological, and the spiritual. Anything that is possible in the mind is also possible in the physical world. For this reason, events that defy physical laws are believed to happen every day, as a part of the normal course of life. Expressed in terms of a Western worldview, in the Tibetan Buddhist world, the line between fantasy and reality is very thin, and sometimes nonexistent.

In philosophical terms, this kind of worldview fits very well with tantric Buddhism's insistence that there is no such thing as propositional truth (i.e. truth that can be expressed in words) because it is the nature of truth to *include* all opposites.[302] For Mahayana Buddhists, "truth" as opposed to "falsehood" is an alien category of thought derived from non-monistic religions.[303] Because ultimate truth always lies at a deeper level than humans can put into words, tantric Buddhists can quite sincerely see all religions as good and their teachings as similar to those of Buddhism. Any apparent contradiction between religious systems melts away in the ultimate unity of all opposites. To insist otherwise is to show that one has not understood the foundations of the world around us.

Sociologists call this view of the world *intuitional thinking*.[304] Intuitional thinking accepts the world at face value, and takes things as true if they appear to be so. And from a Buddhist point of view, this makes perfect sense, for there is no reliable test by which we can tell if a thing is "real" or not. Intuitional thinking and an occult-magical view of life complement each other in such a way that the magical is never very far away. The sociologist Robert Ekvall told the story of a group of hunters who were camped on the grasslands of northern Tibet when a thunderstorm passed over a distant lake. Impressed by the sight, the hunters commented on their belief that a dragon in the thunderstorm was drinking the lake water. Ekvall offered them 500 ounces of silver for the dragon's body, and the hunters proceeded with a serious discussion of just how one could shoot this thunder-dragon.[305] Even for Tibetan Buddhists who have received a Western education, and for people from Europe or the Americas who have converted to Tibetan Buddhism, the thin line between fantasy and reality sometimes disappears. In December 1981, an American camera crew went to India to film the cremation of a famous lama. After the cremation had begun, the crew reported seeing the top of the lama's skull fly up into the air without coming down to earth. Later during the cremation, the lama's eye, tongue, and heart supposedly flew out of the fire and fell at the feet of another monk. The local Tibetans and Sikkimese took all these "miracles" in a matter-of-fact way. They explained them in great detail to the American film crew, who reported the story at face value.[306] In one Himalayan nation, the government still makes some decisions based on the predictions of astrologers.[307] This is not to say that there aren't any skeptics in Tibetan Buddhist countries, but in traditional cultures they must be rare. The Austrian traveler Heinrich Harrer said that he never met anyone in seven years in Tibet who had the slightest doubts about Buddhist teachings.[308]

A magical view of life is not limited to simple country folk. A similar belief was shown by a young Tibetan friend who holds a degree in economics. He told of a magic charm which could be worn around one's neck. This charm, he insisted with all seriousness, would make a man invulnerable to bullets.[309] He knew this because the charm-seller had demonstrated its power by firing a pistol at an charm-protected goat, and the goat had emerged from this experience unharmed. The possibility that the gun had been loaded with blanks evidently had not occurred to this well educated friend. Tibetan literature is filled with similar tales of the fantastic and the bizarre. Flying demons, monks who change their appearance at will, powerful lamas who force disembodied minds into dead bodies,[310] and a host of other strange tales are a part of the heritage of Tibetan Buddhism.

Intuitional thinking and an occult-magical view of life are not superstitions that can be eradicated by education, but enduring cultural characteristics which have persisted through the centuries. In Mongolia, where the former Stalinist government sponsored intensive antireligious education for over sixty years, there was a re-emergence of Tibetan Buddhism virtually as soon as religious liberty was restored.[311] The same thing happened in Russia when the Soviet period came to an end. Occultism is still a vital force even in twenty-first century Tibet, despite some of the most violent antireligious campaigns of the Cultural Revolution having occurred there within the previous 50 years.[312] Though modern technology and economic development are having a great impact on many parts of the Tibetan Buddhist world, the old ways linger on. For many years to come, the Tibetan Buddhist world will be a land of faith, where anything can happen.

4) Luck, Merit, and Offerings

Among the central concerns of Inner Asian shamanism are personal energy, good fortune, and luck. In folk religious thinking, having these things lessens the likelihood of disease or misfortune. The Buddhist concept of merit (discussed below) operates similarly, in the sense that good things are likely to happen to people who have a store of merit, and bad things are likely to happen to people who don't. Both merit and personal energy can be increased or stored up by the proper rituals (sometimes the same ones). They can also be lost or depleted, in which case a monk or shaman can help to restore them, or at least mitigate the consequences of losing them. In order to understand how merit and personal energy interact with each other in the Tibetan Buddhist world, a short review may be helpful.

Siddartha Gautama told his followers that good deeds earn *merit* that can be stored up like treasure in a vault.[313] But bad deeds earn *demerit*, which accumulates in a similar fashion. At death, the balance of merit and demerit determines automatically, without the intervention of any supernatural judge, whether an individual gets a good rebirth (e.g. as a human) or an evil rebirth (e.g. as an animal or a hell-being).[314] Unfortunately, people earn demerit all the time without realizing it, but they can only gain merit by conscious effort to do so. Because demerit accumulates faster than merit, there is great pressure to find ways of earning merit faster than it can be canceled by demerit. The Tibetans seem to have had a special talent for inventing new ways to make merit; many of which are unique to the Tibetan Buddhist world. Just reciting the magic formula *om mani padme hum* is enough to guarantee that one will never be reborn[315] and gains the merit of thousands of lifetimes of effort in a single moment. Thoughts and sensations can make merit. Seeing a temple or a prayer flag is meritorious. Merely wishing others to be free from suffering creates merit.[316] Paying a monk to read the Tibetan Buddhist scriptures creates merit, even if one cannot understand what is being read. Ten times the merit can be made by hiring ten monks to read ten different scriptures aloud and at the same time.[317] Acts of personal service to monks and monasteries create great merit. Giving a child to a monastery creates merit for his family, as does contributing to the cost of his support.[318] Carrying a monk's baggage, guiding him on a journey, or repairing the monastery in which he lives creates merit. Counting off rosaries and walking around shrines are daily merit-making activities for many Tibetan Buddhists.[319] Going on a pilgrimage to sacred places makes merit, and the amount of merit increases with the length and difficulty of the journey. The Mongols considered it meritorious to die on such a journey, especially in Tibet. Even animals can make merit for themselves by being ridden or led on a pilgrimage.

So great is the need for merit and so time-consuming is the process of making it that the Tibetans invented an entirely new class of religious appliances to ease the load. The most famous of these artifacts is the prayer wheel, a round metal container in which magic formulas are placed. Rotating the wheel has the same effect as saying the magic formulas. Larger prayer wheels may contain a single magic formula repeated up to a hundred million times.[320] Wheels may contain many different mantras. A prayer wheel at the Nyingma Institute in Berkeley, California, USA, is wrapped with 198 different prayers imprinted on over 200,000 sheets of paper.[321] While most prayer wheels are turned by hand, some are wind, water, or candle powered, and the author has seen several run by electric motors.[322] Some modern Buddhists have placed mantras on rapidly-spinning computer hard disks. Of course, none of these merit making activities are of the slightest practical benefit to anyone but the person actually making the merit, though the lamas would claim that others do benefit in a mystical way from the compassionate mind of those who make merit as part of the boddhisattva path.

As we have seen, humans desire to control their circumstances by manipulating their gods with offerings and sacrifices. The shamanist cultures of Inner Asia had a rich variety of animal (and sometimes human) sacrifices. The early Buddhists tried to suppress these rituals, or at least replace actual victims with symbolic substitutes.[323] Such *substitute offerings* were probably the first to be made a part of Tibetan Buddhist life. In place of an actual animal or human victim, an image of wood, dough, or butter was placed before the god or demon to be worshiped. Such substitutes (called *torma* in Tibetan) were often made to look like animals, gods, or people. Demons or gods could be invited to enter the torma to receive food offerings or listen to requests for favors. In certain rituals the gods or demons could be forced to enter torma figures, and either bribed with gifts or physically destroyed.[324] Blood sacrifice (in symbolic form in the monasteries, in actual, if occasional, practice at the folk level) survives today in many Tibetan Buddhist cultures.[325]

Display offerings are found in almost every Tibetan Buddhist home. Generally there is a small altar shelf supporting pictures of gods, boddhisattvas or lamas, in front of which are placed bowls of milk, grain, water, flower, or incense offerings. Money may also be presented, and in certain tantric rituals beer, meat, and even human flesh may be used.[326] An electric light or yak butter lamp is kept burning before the offerings twenty four hours a day. Another kind of display offering (with roots in shamanism) is the pile of stones to be found at the top of mountain passes and in other locations from the Himalayas to Mongolia. Travelers carry clean white stones to the top of the pass, then decorate the heap with prayer flags. *Redemptive offerings* are less commonly performed but important because they illustrate Tibetan Buddhists ideas of redemptive sacrifice. There are two types of redemptive offerings in folk Tibetan Buddhism. In the first, the redeemer buys a laboring animal such as a horse or a yak, and then sets it free in a pasture. The redeemed animal may be marked with special threads passed through a hole in its ear, and need never suffer the hardships of field work again. A more common variant of this kind of redemptive offering is the purchase of an animal (perhaps a fish or bird) about to be killed for food.[327] In either case, the redeemer gains merit for having saved the animal from further suffering or death.

At least up to the mid-twentieth century, another type of redemptive offering called the scapegoat ritual was practiced in some places.[328] In one form of the ritual, the sins and misfortunes of an individual or a community were placed upon an image of dough, which was then thrown away in some wild and uninhabited area. Occasionally a domestic animal (often a goat) would be selected, symbolically loaded with guilt, and sent out to be killed by whoever finds it. The scapegoat ritual used to be enacted at Lhasa each year by a member of a special class of "professional scapegoats." These men (often beggars) would go from house to house, taking the guilt of the household upon themselves in return for gifts of money. At a special ceremony which followed, the "scapegoat" would be driven out of town into some remote place from which he would not return for several months. In Tibetan thinking, being a scapegoat involved contact with so much sin and evil that scapegoats were never drawn from among the monks or higher social classes.[329]

Methods of gaining luck and methods of gaining merit may overlap. The display of prayer flags is a shamanist practice for gaining good fortune that found its way into Tibetan Buddhism. Burning incense and walking around holy sites are other shamanist customs which have found their way into Tibetan Buddhism. Both merit-making and luck-seeking rituals have in common the hope of manipulating the supernatural to conform to human wishes.

5) Ideals of Detachment and Nonviolence

The second of Siddartha's four truths states that suffering arises from attachment, i.e. an emotional connection to people, things, or one's personal identity. To encourage his followers to sever their attachments, Siddartha embraced the ideal of the holy man who leaves home and family to seek enlightenment in the forest or monastery. In so doing he began a long monastic tradition of physical, social, and emotional isolation from the world. Tantric Buddhism, with its secret practices and occultism, gave a further impetus to this ideal of detachment.

Because Buddhism discourages close relationships with others, Tibetan Buddhist cultures tend to offer greater degrees of freedom to the individual, especially in the case of women. Compared to the family-centered cultures of India and China, there is less sense of obligation to the family. Children are free to leave home, especially for religious purposes, and fathers have somewhat less control over other family members than their counterparts in surrounding countries. For many Tibetans a father is an emotionally distant person who may be gone on prolonged pilgrimages or business trips. Respect, but not love, attaches to his person.[330] Many Tibetans do not know who their fathers are. The very relaxed view of sexual morality common in Tibetan Buddhist societies has greatly weakened the institution of marriage. Marital breakup is fairly common, with divorce rates of up to 30 per cent among some peoples.[331]

Among many Tibetan Buddhist peoples, it is considered an act of great merit to give a child as young as five or six to a monastery, where he will be raised as a monk[332] regardless of his inclinations or wishes.[333] The popularity of this practice is shown by the fact that in Mongolia before the Communist takeover, half the male population was found in monasteries. In Tibet in the 1940s the figure was 20 to 25 per cent, and in modern Sikkim and Ladakh the figure is 10 to 15 per cent of the Tibetan Buddhist population.[334] Even many older Tibetans tend to withdraw gradually from family responsibilities in favor of prayers, rituals, and other merit making activities.[335] Among the Sherpa people of Nepal, parents of married children will sometimes leave everything they own to their children and become hermits, supporting themselves by begging.[336]

Tibetan Buddhist monasteries are the living expression of the religion's ideal of withdrawal from the world. They are often built in remote or inaccessible places such as mountain ridges or cliffs. In many orders, solitary retreats up to several months long are a routine part of initiation. While on such a retreat, a prospective monk may have to repeat mantras or memorized scripture portions up to 100,000 times, or even more.[337] Initiates take vows of lifelong commitment to heterosexual celibacy,[338] and pledge themselves to keep over 200 monastic rules, many of which are designed to enforce withdrawal from everyday life.[339] For monks and lay Tibetan Buddhists, there is even a series of meditations aimed at cutting links with others. In one such meditation, the monk focuses on the thought that every living thing, even his own mother, has been an enemy in thousands of past lives.[340] The Buddhist emphasis on withdrawal into self for the purpose of liberation has loosened the normal ties that hold individuals together. Husbands and wives, parents and children feel its insistent tugging on their closest relationships. It is no wonder that one sociologist called Tibetan Buddhism "a religion of antisocial individualism."[341]

The ideal of *nonviolence* has a long history in Buddhism, and Tibetan Buddhists have interpreted it chiefly for the benefit of animals. In the spring of 1948, the Austrian traveler Heinrich Harrer, then a refugee in Tibet, was placed in charge of 1,500 men who were constructing a dike in front of the Dalai Lama's Summer Palace in Lhasa. The work frequently came to a halt when workmen discovered an earthworm or other small creature at the tip of a shovel. The dirt was carefully moved and the creature set aside in a safe place before digging resumed. No one wanted to be guilty of killing an animal.[342] This ideal once even played a role in Tibetan statecraft. After the third Dalai Lama and the Mongol chief Altan Khan met at Lake Kokonor in 1578, the new Dalai Lama insisted on an end to animal sacrifices in the Khan's Mongolian empire.[343] Three centuries later, the thirteenth Dalai Lama insisted that a British military expedition withdraw from Tibet, in part because warfare was bad for animals.[344]

Because of possible harm to animals, the production of food is associated with demerit. Farming accumulated demerit because breaking up the soil inevitably kills some of the worms and insects that live in it. Deliberately killing animals for food accumulates a lot of demerit, and if at all possible Tibetans will have it done by someone of another religion (usually a Muslim) or by someone so poor they have no other possibility of employment.[345] Thus the simple act of eating imposes a burden of demerit on Tibetan Buddhists that can scarcely be imagined by those of other faiths.[346] Even unconsciously taking life is sinful. Killing small insects by stepping on them is one way in which demerit can be accumulated without being aware of it. So serious is it that the monks say a magic formula to guarantee that every little creature that dies under their feet will be reborn in paradise.[347] Pest control is often out of the question. Mice and rats are major beneficiaries of this policy of nonviolence, and rare is the home or temple that does not have its share of them. Lice in clothing, or flies in tea, are picked out and thrown away alive.

6) Tibetan Buddhism as Ethnic Identity

For most people in the Tibetan Buddhist world, tantric Buddhism is an inseparable part of one's ethnic identity. To be a Tibetan, or a Mongol, is to be a Buddhist. To be anything else is to deny one's group identity and to commit a form of treason. Like so many other aspects of the Tibetan form of Buddhism, this reflects the ancient particularism of shamanism, where land and space and gods are local, and there are unbreakable bonds among people, the land they inhabit, and the gods they serve.[348] The political expression of this is theocracy. The ideal of government by the monks (*chos srid* in Tibetan) spread throughout the Tibetan Buddhist world, and shaped the political institutions of every country where Tibetan Buddhism gained a foothold.

The links between the state and religion were strong from the very beginning. Mahayana Buddhism had entered Tibet under royal sponsorship, and flourished there in part because of its political links to the Chinese court. From the time of Song Tsen Gampo, Tibet's kings took the title *chö gey* (meaning "religious king"[349]). Though most of Tibet's kings supported Buddhism, many sat lightly on their thrones because of the frequent attempts of the larger monasteries to overthrow them. This struggle ended in 1640 when the fifth Dalai Lama, backed by a Mongol army, seized control of the country for his Gelugpa order. The Gelugpa monks and their successors remained in power until the mid 1950s.

The pattern established in Tibet was reproduced elsewhere. The rulers of neighboring Sikkim were also known as the *chö gey*. Bhutan was ruled by a line of lama kings drawn from the Drukpa order.[350] In Mongolia, the government lay in the hands of reincarnating monks known as *hutukhtus*. Only the Himalayan hill tribes (who were subject to Hindu and Muslim conquerors) and the Mongol tribes in Russia had secular or non-Buddhist governments. The theocracies of Mongolia and Tibet were overthrown in the twentieth century, and the last king of Sikkim lost power when his country was annexed by India in 1975. Even so, Tibetan Buddhism still provides a strong unifying force for the people of Bhutan (now ruled by a line of constitutional monarchs) and for the Tibetan exiles in India. In these cultures and others, to be a Tibetan, or a Drukpa, or a Sherpa, is to be a Tibetan Buddhist.

7) Tibetan Language

In ancient India, Sanskrit was the accepted medium for religious communication (much as Latin had been in medieval Europe). Over the centuries, Buddhist scholars coined thousands of terms for philosophical and metaphysical ideas, deities, and states of meditational consciousness which together formed an incredibly rich and complex religious vocabulary. As the Tibetan monks translated the voluminous tantric scriptures, they compiled lists of Sanskrit words and made up standardized Tibetan equivalents.[351] When their work was finished, written Tibetan had become a sophisticated medium for expressing even the most abstract and specialized Buddhist ideas.

The classical religious form of Tibetan became the country's standard written language,[352] used for scriptures, sacred texts, commentaries, poems, and other literature. A formal and highly stylized language, classical Tibetan changed very little over the centuries. Spoken Tibetan changed at a much faster pace, so that within a few centuries native Tibetan speakers had to make a special study of the written language just to understand it. English speakers can get the gist of this situation by imagining that modern books were published in the language of Chaucer or Shakespeare. For many Tibetans, the written language came to be valued more as a religious symbol and focus of cultural identity than as a practical way to communicate.

Classical Tibetan literature is almost all religious in content. The bulk of it is occult or tantric in nature and dry in style, but there are some texts in a lighter and more personal vein which make colorful reading for the non-Buddhist. Notable among these are the biographies produced by Marpa, Milarepa, and their successors. The biography of Milarepa is widely known for its humor and sage sayings, even outside Tibet.[353] As Tibetan Buddhism spread across Inner Asia, non-Tibetan peoples adopted the Tibetan sacred texts as their own. Monks in China, Mongolia, and Russia learned written Tibetan in order to read the scriptures, so that eventually Tibetan became the sacred language of the entire Tibetan Buddhist world, a trend which continues in modern times as Tibetan Buddhism spreads outside Asia. Written Tibetan has become the universal means of religious communication for Tibetan Buddhists, be they Himalayan tribal peoples, Siberian Buryats, or students in European or North American universities.

Beyond its status as a lingua franca (and *lingua sacra*) for Tibetan Buddhists, the written Tibetan language is the subject of very strongly held attitudes and beliefs among Tibetans themselves. A religious book written in Tibetan may be the focus of great outward respect simply because it is written in Tibetan. Even the sacred texts of other religions may be treated in this way, though their meaning may be rejected. Many Tibetans consider the written form of their language to be the only acceptable way to communicate about religious ideas. With the assertion of Chinese control over Tibet in the mid-twentieth century, the entire canon of Marxist-Leninist and Maoist political theory was translated into written Tibetan, much as the Buddhist canon had been translated during the seventh century. As a result, new forms of written Tibetan emerged (collectively called modern literary Tibetan) and are in daily use by the government and media.[354]

8) Religious Specialists: Monks and Shamans

The peoples of the Tibetan Buddhist world are dependent on religious specialists to conduct their business with the transcendent world. Only the shaman has the call of the spirits and the ability to manipulate them. Only the monk knows the tantric rituals and magical formulas. Lay Tibetan Buddhists are excluded from the religious learning of the lamas because most do not have the time or money to learn meditation or to study the sacred texts.[355] Monks and shamans possess knowledge not accessible to lay people, and this puts them in a position of power over them. As the Tibetan proverb declares: "Without the lama in front, there is no approach to the ultimate."[356] The same can be said of the shaman.

Monks have great authority in most Tibetan Buddhist cultures. The laity are taught to venerate their spiritual teachers even above the historical Buddha. The Third Dalai Lama wrote in his 16th century text *Essence of Refined Gold* that since every aspect of spiritual development depends on pleasing one's spiritual teacher, one must not allow oneself to think that he may have faults.[357] Historically, this practice of encouraging the lay believers to venerate the monks and lamas as spiritually infallible has strengthened the bond between monks and the people and inculcated an attitude of unquestioning faith.[358] This cultural attitude explains the strong devotion that the Tibetans and other Tibetan Buddhist peoples have to their monks and lamas, and probably also explains the origin of the English term "lamaism."

The reliance of folk Tibetan Buddhists on rituals performed

by religious specialists increases the power and prestige of the monks while placing the focus of the laity on mere performance of the proper rituals. Monks or lamas perform most of the rites connected with births, deaths, exorcisms, offerings, and rituals on which daily life depends. For example, a recently deceased relative can be guided to rebirth in a paradise only through the ceremonies of the lamas, especially if the deceased did not make sufficient merit on his own.[359] Even though the monks maintain that pure motives are vital for gaining merit, their emphasis on rituals, and the outward performance of religious duties by lay people, works against any kind of inward moral or spiritual transformation. As a result, most lay Tibetan Buddhists devote themselves to one of the boddhisattva cults, or confine themselves to making merit and avoiding trouble from evil spirits.[360]

9) Art and Architecture

The arts are an important part of the common culture of the Tibetan Buddhist world. Perhaps the most ancient of these is painting, for there are rock paintings and tomb decorations dating from the Stone Age period of Inner Asian history. From at least the eighth century onwards, the Tibetans decorated their monasteries with colorful paintings and wall hangings whose subjects were always religious. Perhaps most impressive were the great temple banners called *thangkas*, displayed on religious holidays. These cloth paintings, done according to strict rules of composition, depicted scenes from the lives of tantric saints and divinities. Highly stylized murals and frescoes are another important form of temple art. Among the most common of these is the so-called "wheel of life," which illustrates the causes of suffering and rebirth.[361]

The spoken arts also have a long history in Inner Asia. Epic poetry is popular throughout the Tibetan Buddhist world; the most popular being the fifteenth century *Gesar* epic. Gesar, the hero, was the son of a sky god who led his tribe in wars against Tibet's neighbors. The most famous of his adventures are recited in a cycle of stories called the *Eighteen Great Fortresses*, though there are more than 30 parts to the entire Gesar cycle. The Gesar Epic was sung by wandering bards called Gesar singers, who spread the epic widely across the Tibetan and Mongolian speaking areas of Inner Asia. *The Secret History of the Mongols* is a similar cycle of stories about the Mongols and their khans. Both are available in English translation.

Chant is a kind of rhythmic speech that is common in Tibetan culture. It is used by schoolchildren as an aid to memorization, and by monks for recitation of religious texts. Perhaps the most famous are the so-called "thick-voiced" chants of the tantric monks, groups of whom have given performances while touring outside Asia. Within Tibet, each dialect area has its own style of folk song and dance. Nomad songs may feature a soloist who begins singing with a shout or a loud call. Other styles may employ solo voice or choruses, with or without instruments, or antiphonal singing. There are songs for different occasions, such as drinking or harvest, and songs for expressing feelings like love or homesickness. Mongols specialize in so-called throat- or overtone (*hoomi*) singing as a folk art. Overtone singing has its roots in shamanism.

Popular musical instruments in the Tibetan Buddhist world include the dulcimer, flute, various types of fiddles, lutes, drums, and bells. Cymbals and horns are also used in the liturgical music heard in monasteries.[362] Instruments may combine with singers in ensemble music (*nang ma*), which was especially popular in Lhasa in the early 20th century. Both Tibet and Mongolia have operatic forms (called *lha mo* in Tibetan and *durh* in Mongolian). In Tibet the operatic repertoire consists of eight or nine works which in content are similar to Tibetan folk tales. The stories are filled with supernatural beings, and the human heroes live happily ever after by following the principles of Buddhism.

The written word is represented by religious texts written in classical Tibetan. Each monastery in the Tibetan Buddhist world has its store of sacred texts. While few would have a complete copy of the Kangyur and Tengyur, virtually all would have a set of texts of some type. Texts were produced using laboriously carved wooden blocks about 7 x 28 cm. (or four inches wide by twelve inches long). Tens of thousands of these blocks might be used to print the Kangyur or the Tengyur, but fewer are needed for shorter texts or for other uses like prayer flags or charms.[363]

Tibetan architecture also spread across Inner Asia. The early Tibetan Buddhist monks had to house hundreds or even thousands of men in a cold, dry, and almost treeless country where there was danger of attack by thieves or monks from rival monasteries. They built flat-roofed, fortress-like buildings of stone or dried brick, often with inward-sloping walls covered with whitewash and decorated (in Central Tibet and Mongolia) with a band of brown or ocher at the top. Sometimes monasteries were built on cliffs or ridge tops, making them look as though they were rising out of a mountain. The Potala palace in Lhasa is perhaps the best known example of this style, though the famous hilltop fort at Gyantse is more dramatic. The Potala and other Tibetan buildings inspired imitators throughout the Tibetan Buddhist world. Monks from Ladakh and Bhutan copied the architectural styles of Tibet, as did the monasteries of faraway Mongolia. Even the Chinese Emperor Qian Long built a replica of the Potala Palace at Chengde, northeast of Beijing. In Siberia, where wood was more plentiful, the monks built in a native style but still preserved many of the decorative features of Tibetan architecture.

10) Nomads of Inner Asia

Since most of Inner Asia is high, dry, and agriculturally unproductive, herding animals often represents the best (or the only) human use of its lands. Much of Inner Asia produces limited pasturage, and that only at certain seasons, so that herders must move their animals from place to place in order to sustain them throughout the year. People who follow this lifestyle are called nomadic pastoralists, and they are an important part of most, but not all, Tibetan Buddhist peoples. Pastoral nomadism is a very important feature of life among the Mongols and the Tibetans, the two largest Tibetan Buddhist groups by far. It is also practiced among other Tibetan Buddhist groups such as the Kalmyks, Tuvans, Buryats, Yugur, and various Tibetan-related groups in northern India and the Himalayas.[364]

Nomads get almost everything they need from their animals, which makes them largely independent of their sedentary neighbors.[365] Since nomads depend on lands which are too remote or unproductive for others to use, they tend to be sturdy, independent people who are quite resistant to change by outsiders. Like their colleagues elsewhere, Inner Asian nomads tend to associate with one key species of domesticated animal, even though they keep other species as well.[366] For example, the key domesticated species in Inner Asia are the yak (in Tibet), the horse (in Mongolia), and the reindeer (in Siberia). Sheep, goats, and camels are also raised, and provide different products at different times of the year.[367] Caring for mixed groups of animals insures the nomads against catastrophic losses due to diseases or extreme weather, but also makes grazing requirements and migration patterns much more complex.[368] Nomads may not rely on their animals completely, but may also engage in trade in non-animal products. For example, the nomads of Tibet have for centuries participated in the cis- and trans- Himalayan salt trade, which was not only economically important, but also allowed exchange of religious ideas between Hinduism and Tibetan Buddhism.[369]

Tibetan nomads occupy the coldest and least productive areas in all of China, and they form one of the highest societies on the entire planet. Their sheep and goats graze in areas up to 5,400 meters above sea level, while their yaks may graze at 5,500 meters and cross passes over 6,000 meters high. The average annual temperature on the grasslands of their northern plains is below freezing for over 200 days a year, and temperatures can drop to minus 40 degrees Celcius in winter.[370] Tibetan nomads live in tents and rely on animal dung for fuel, so living conditions can be quite harsh. Grass grows only in the summer season, so from September to May the animals must forage on dead plants.[371] For this reason the nomads try to conserve the strength of the animals by minimizing travel and generally do not range far from their home base, yet they still must make a series of sub-migrations to maximize the grazing available to the different kinds of animals they herd.

Among the Mongols, nomadism is founded upon horse culture. The horse has a prominent place in the language and culture of Mongolia;[372] it is said that Mongols are born and die on horseback.[373] Mongol nomads live in *gers*, (also known in the West as *yurts*) which are circular tents supported by a collapsible wooden lattice. Nomads live on the steppes in family groups, which may become larger or smaller as grazing conditions dictate. As in Tibet, climatic conditions may be extreme and nomads may face large losses in animals after a single bad winter; it is possible for a wealthy nomad to become a poor one after a single snowstorm.[374] Living with such capricious natural conditions tends to encourage and reinforce the shamanic worldview that has been handed down in such cultures from time immemorial.

Summary

The difficult environmental conditions in Inner Asia, together with humankind's innate desire to control the spiritual world, created ideal conditions for the growth of shamanism and pastoral nomadism in cultures from Siberia to the Himalayas. The cultures of Inner Asia shared many similarities long before tantric Buddhism came on the scene. The appearance of tantric Buddhism not only reinforced the foundational worldviews and attitudes that were already present in Inner Asia, it added new elements of language, ethnic identity, and art that were not present before. Yet the core values of Tibetan Buddhist peoples remain deeply rooted in their shamanist past. For the folk Tibetan Buddhist, it is these values which lie at the cultural heart of the Tibetan Buddhist world.

CHAPTER 6

Christ on the Silk Road

J ust to the west of Kabul, Afghanistan lies the city of Bamiyan, once famous as a center of Buddhist learning. The monks of Bamian were cave-dwelling artists who carved colossal Buddha images[375] in stone and decorated their temples with colorful frescoes. At the beginning of the first millennium, Bamian was a part of the kingdom of Bactria, a center of religious innovation from which Mahayana Buddhism expanded eastward along the Silk Road to China. Had he wished to do so, a monk from the area of Bamian could have joined a camel caravan north to the city of Samarkand (now in Uzbekistan) which lay on the main east-west portion of the Silk Road. Turning west, away from China, he could have joined another caravan to Bukhara (later famous for its carpets) and Merv, and crossed the desert of what is now Turkmenistan into Persia. Exchanging his two-humped Bactrian camel for a one-humped dromedary, he could have followed the Silk Road westward to Baghdad and Damascus, where local trade routes would have taken him south to a small Roman province on the western shore of the Mediterranean. Had he actually made this journey at the beginning of the first century, he might have had three wise companions.[376]

The early Christian Church came into existence when the entire Mediterranean world had been united under the government of the Roman Empire.[377] The Romans built an extensive network of roads to link major cities; these highways made travel safer and easier than it had ever been before.[378] The early Church took advantage of such roads to establish itself in urban areas all around the eastern Mediterranean.[379] It appears that people in these cities were attracted to the early Church not because it had any set program of preaching or evangelism, but because of what it *was* — the faith, hope, and love of the Christians being expressed in a way that they could understand and appreciate.[380] The fact that the Church grew first in cities, and by virtue of the quality of the Christians' lives, will be important later on in this story.

The Christian Church had links to the East from a very early date. Jews from Parthia (now northern Iran), Media (now northwestern Iran and Azerbaijan), and Elam (now southern Iraq) were present at Pentecost;[381] and their homelands lay directly on or near main branches of the Silk Road. Syrian Antioch, where the followers of Jesus were first called Christians,[382] was the third largest city in the Roman Empire[383] and a major Mediterranean terminus of the Silk Road.[384] The city where Saul of Tarsus was converted, Damascus, also lay on a branch of the Silk Road. The Christian Church spread along these physical links to the East from a very early date. The Silk Road city of Edessa, in Mesopotamia, was an early Christian center,[385] as was Armenia.[386] By the third century, Christianity had reached the Kushan Empire, where it made its first contact with Buddhism and continued its long journey eastward into China.[387]

Early Nestorian and Catholic Missions to the Mongols

Christianity was well established in the East by the time it was challenged by the teachings of Nestorius, a fifth century bishop who was condemned in a dispute over the divinity of Christ.[388] Though Nestorius was judged without a hearing and it is by no means clear what his views actually were, he was exiled to Egypt, where he died embittered and obscure. His followers fled to the east, where they began one of the greatest missionary movements in the history of Christianity. The Nestorians believed in telling everyone about their Savior, as one of their surviving documents attests: "The disciples of the Messiah understood clearly and decided distinctly what to do; they went forth into all parts of the world, saying, "Preach ye my words to all the races of mankind . ."[389] In obedience to their missionary vision, Nestorian merchants and missionaries made their way eastward along the Silk Road, settling in strategic oasis cities like Merv, Samarkand, Kashgar, and Dunhuang. They built churches and translated the Bible into local languages. By the seventh century, the Nestorians had reached Chang An (modern Xian), capital of Tang Dynasty China, and spread their faith widely through China, Mongolia, and at least the very northernmost parts of Tibet.[390] So successful was this great missionary effort that by the year 800 most of the world's Christians lived east of Damascus.[391]

One of the peoples converted by the Nestorians was the Mongol Kerait tribe. The Keraits had been early allies of Genghis Khan, and many of them had married into the Khan's family. As Genghis and his successors conquered the known world, Kerait Christians found themselves holding positions of power and influence at the heart of the world's greatest empire. Perhaps because of this, Christians enjoyed religious toleration almost everywhere in the Mongols' vast domains. Since all the old borders had been erased by the Khans' conquests, the Keraits and other Christians could travel safely and easily almost anywhere they wished to go. Even travelers from distant Europe could now reach Central Asia, as two famous Italians did in the mid-thirteenth century. In the year 1266, Kublai Khan sent these two uncles of Marco Polo back to Europe with a request to the Pope for: "an hundred persons of our Christian faith . . . able clearly to prove by force of argument to idolaters and other kinds of folk that the Law of Christ was best, and that all other religions were false and naught; and that if they would prove this, [the Khan] and all under him would become Christians and the Church's liegemen."[392] When he sent this message to the Pope, Kublai Khan was the most powerful ruler on earth, and his invitation seemed to offer a grand opportunity, unparalleled in history. What thoughts must Niccolo and Maffeo Polo have had during their three year journey back to Italy! The conversion of all of Asia must have seemed at hand.

When the brothers reached the shores of the Mediterranean again in April of 1269, they learned that the Pope, Clement IV, had died the previous year and that no successor had yet been chosen. When a new Pope was selected three years later, he could find only two men who were willing to go as missionaries to the Mongol Court. These two men set out with the Polo family (this was the trip that Niccolo's son Marco made famous) but they were frightened by the perils of the journey and turned back. Kublai Khan never received his hundred missionaries.[393] One of the greatest opportunities ever presented to the Christian church had been irretrievably lost. In the event, Kublai decided to use Tibetan monks to lay the foundations of higher culture among the Mongols. Kublai actively promoted lamaism by building monasteries in Mongolia and at his court in Peking. He appointed Tibetan monks to important positions, which they used to introduce tantric Buddhism to Mongolia. While most Mongols remained shamanists, Tibetan Buddhism had made its first penetration into Mongol life.

Why didn't the Nestorians seize the opportunity the Pope had missed? Nestorians had been at home among the Mongols for several hundred years. They had stood at the threshold of power in the world's largest empire. They eagerly translated the Scriptures into local languages. Yet when the Mongol Empire collapsed in the mid 1300s, Mongolian Christianity collapsed with it. Why did the Nestorians' vital, vigorous missionary movement become almost extinct in Central Asia? Several answers to this question have been suggested. One is that Nestorian Christianity itself had lost much of its purity and orthodoxy in the six hundred years since it was introduced to China. At least some of the priests said regular masses for the dead. William of Rubruck, who visited the Khan's court in 1254, noted that many of the Nestorian priests were addicted to wine.[394] A second reason for the ultimate failure of Christianity at the Mongol Court was occultism. As a shamanist people, the Mongols valued religion because it gave them power over demons and spirits. They encouraged contests among the religions in their empire to see which one offered the greatest control over these forces. The occult mysticism of Tibetan Buddhism, so close to the Mongols' own shamanism, held a natural appeal that the Nestorians (and later Catholics) found hard to match.

A third reason for the Nestorians' decline may have been the influence of Buddhism, which had arrived in Central Asia over a thousand years before the time of the Khans. The Nestorians found it difficult to translate their ideas into Chinese or Mongolian without using words already laden with Buddhist meanings. For example, in one Nestorian document, the "Discourse on Rest and Joy" we find Jesus telling Peter: "Know you Simon Peter that if any of you wants to prepare himself for 'the Victorious Way,' as a rule he must get rid of both 'motion' and 'desire' before everything else …If he is of 'non-desire' and is of 'non-action,' then he may be pure and serene…understand and demonstrate (the truth)…be all illumining and all pervading. And to be all illumining and all pervading is nothing but the concatenation of cause and effect which will lead (people) to the state of rest and joy."[395] Non-desire and non-action are Taoist terms, and the remainder are Buddhist concepts. While some later Nestorians apparently tried to blend Christianity and Buddhism, others had a difficult time making the Gospel clear in a language so strongly influenced by Buddhism. Finally, most Nestorians were members of the upper classes of Mongol society. Their missionary vision, like that of the Catholic fathers after them, seems to have been to convert the highest levels of society first. In doing so, the Nestorians' Gospel message was forced to compete with other religions, like Tibetan Buddhism and Taoism, which were also trying to reach the upper classes. Weakened by competition and compromise, and fatally identified with the ruling class, Nestorian Christians could not stand firm as the Mongol empire began to topple. When it finally fell, they fell with it.

The Early Catholic Missions to Tibet

By the end of the seventeenth century, Tibet had extended its religious dominance across a vast area of Central Asia. From Siberia to the Himalayas, and from Manchuria to the Volga, people in Inner Asia looked to Lhasa as the center of the Tibetan Buddhist world. It was not long before such a large block of non-Christian peoples attracted the attention of the Church. Though the Nestorians were undoubtedly aware of the warlike Tibetans,[396] they made no sustained effort to evangelize them as they had the Mongols. After the Nestorian Church declined in the 1300s, the Catholic church sent increasing numbers of missionaries to China and other parts of Asia, but it was not until the seventeenth century that it sent envoys to Tibet proper.

The first of these intrepid missionaries was the Jesuit Father Antonio de Andrade, who set out from India in March of 1624.[397] After disguising himself as a Hindu pilgrim, Andrade outwitted hostile local officials, made his way north to the Himalayas, endured altitude sickness and snow blindness, fought his way over a 5,500 meter pass into Tibet, and finally reached Tsaparang, capital of the western Tibetan kingdom of Gu-ge. (Gu-ge was a successor state to the Shangshung kingdom where Central Asian Buddhism had first entered Tibet.) There he impressed the king and queen with his piety, and they gave him permission to return, establish a mission, and preach the Gospel. In August of the following year, Andrade came back with four companions. So interested was the king in their work that he requested instruction in the Catholic faith, and himself laid the cornerstone of the Church of Our Lady of Hope — the first Christian church in Tibet.[398] But this promising beginning soon fell afoul of Tibet's worsening political situation. This was the time when the Gelugpas were fighting for control of Tibet, and the troubles which led to Tibet's civil war were already beginning. The lamas of Tsaparang, alarmed at their king's interest in the new religion, incited a revolution.

Andrade was transferred from Tsaparang to India in 1630, and reports of the revolution did not reach him until the following year. He sent Fathers Francisco de Azevedo and John de Oliveira to see what could be done to save the mission, but they realized that without outside help their journey would be fruitless. The two fathers decided to visit Ladakh to enlist the help of its king, Sengge Namgyal, in quieting the political situation in Tsaparang. Sengge Namgyal received the two fathers kindly, even giving them permission to preach in Ladakh, but he could do nothing about the revolution in Tsaparang. The mission that Antonio de Andrade started amid such optimism in 1624 collapsed just 11 years later.[399] He was perhaps unfortunate in arriving in Tsaparang just as the kingdom of Gu-ge was about to fall. It was this timing, as well as the jealousy of the lamas, that doomed his mission to failure.

The Jesuits did not abandon their hopes for a church in Tibet, however. As Andrade's mission was faltering, the Jesuit fathers Cacella and Cabral were entering the little kingdom of Bhutan. The Bhutanese monarch received the two missionaries warmly and invited them to stay in Bhutan to preach and start a church. Though the two were touched by the king's liberal offer, their goal was Tibet, and they still had a difficult journey ahead.[400] Cacella and Cabral struggled on over the wastes of southern Tibet to reach Shigatse, seat of the great Tashilhunpo monastery that Tsong Khapa's followers had set up in 1445. They were warmly received, but Cacella's untimely death in Shigatse in 1630 prevented the founding of a mission and the long journey came to nothing.

Inspired by Andrade's work at Tsaparang, the Italian Jesuit Ippolito Desideri went to Ladakh in 1714, looking for a way to get to Tsaparang and Lhasa. The news in Ladakh was discouraging. Lhasa could be reached only by a brutal five month journey across the robber-infested deserts of western Tibet. Desideri's only hope of survival was to join a well-armed caravan, and he began to pray that one would form soon. On October 9, 1715, his prayers were answered as Desideri and his small party joined a Mongol princess on her way to Lhasa to become a nun. Her kindness to Desideri on the bitterly cold winter journey saved his life and the lives of his companions more than once.[401] On March 18th, 1716, Desideri and his party reached the capital of Tibet, where he had a sad parting from his Mongol princess. Their friendship was deep, and in their parting one senses Desideri's heart for sharing his faith: "I pray to God constantly and fervently to recompense her for all the benefits bestowed on us, to illuminate her, convert her, and grant her eternal salvation."[402] Like Andrade before him, Desideri arrived in Tibet during a time of political unrest. Ten years before, a Mongol Khan named Lha Sang had invaded Tibet, stormed Lhasa, deposed the sixth Dalai Lama, and set himself up as governor. Despite his bloodthirsty past, this unsavory character received Desideri kindly, giving him permission to stay in Tibet and preach freely. In response, the scholarly Jesuit devoted himself to the study of the difficult Tibetan language. He recorded that each day he " . . made it a rule to study from early morning to sundown, and for nearly six years took nothing during the day save tea to drink." His study was rewarded by a fluency in written and spoken Tibetan rarely achieved by foreigners.

Desideri had been trained in medieval Scholastic theology, which tried to justify the Christian faith using philosophical methods, some of which were similar to those used by Tibetan monks in their debates.[403] As a result, he was able to write five major works on Christian theology in Tibetan, in a style that monks and lamas were used to reading. In these books, he critically examined Tibetan Buddhist ideas and set forth Christian alternatives. His command of Tibetan scholastic idiom was so great that monks crowded his rooms day and night, eager to read his works and debate with him. Desideri used his natural gifts to win friends in high places, notably in the court of Lha Sang Khan, and spoke about his faith with many well-placed government officials. So great was the confidence they placed in him that Desideri was given rooms in Sera monastery and allowed to say mass. In 1719 Desideri's superiors in Rome decided that further work in Tibet should be carried on by the Capuchin fathers,[404] and at their insistence Desideri left Lhasa in April, 1721. He had accomplished a great deal in five years, and was probably one of the ablest representatives of the Christian faith ever to set foot in Tibet. His brilliant approach to explaining the Christian faith to Tibetan monks using the tools of medieval Scholasticism was a stroke of genius, one that deserves further development in modern times. His withdrawal from the field for merely administrative reasons seems one of the less fortunate episodes in Church history.

Desideri's Capuchin successors opened a small dispensary and translated catechisms and other Catholic literature into Tibetan. In a step they probably regretted later, the fathers distributed this literature in some quantity among the monasteries of Lhasa. Though a few monks showed interest, much of the literature was trampled on the ground in contempt, and two monks who had been so bold as to read it were flogged for their curiosity. An air of suppressed hostility entered the volatile relationship between the lamas and the missionaries, and it needed only a spark to cause an explosion. The fathers continued their medical and evangelistic work with quiet persistence. In October 1726 they opened a chapel and friary, and by the spring of 1742 their services were attended by 27 baptized converts and some 60 enquirers. Plans were made for baptizing 12 more new believers, but in May of 1742 the mission came to a catastrophic end.

In an incident at the end of April, one of the new converts, a man named Pu Tsering, publicly refused to bow down before the Dalai Lama. The general consternation over this had barely subsided when only days later another convert openly refused to recite a mantra. That same evening an angry crowd of 400 monks threatened the Regent with a revolt if the Christians were not expelled from the city. A trial followed during which twelve of the Christians were sentenced to be flogged on the back of the legs just above the knees with 20 lashes each — 50 lashes was considered a death sentence. This punishment permanently crippled its victims. Among the converts was a nursing mother who was exempted from punishment by the court, but who voluntarily submitted to the flogging for the sake of her Christian testimony. Though the believers endured this trial with great fortitude, the fathers were forced to close their mission and withdraw to Nepal. They were hardly out of the city when a mob attacked and destroyed their chapel, of which nothing now remains but the bell.[405]

What had been accomplished in the 120 years since Antonio de Andrade's mission began at Tsaparang? Both Andrade and Desideri had been well received by the local authorities, and both received permission to preach their doctrines openly, yet both Catholic missions were ended by the monastic authorities when people either professed faith in Christ or appeared about to do so. Two small mission churches had been founded, but both were closed and later physically destroyed by the very people the fathers had hoped to serve. In 1769, as a sad postscript to the Lhasa mission, the Capuchins' small group of converts requested that a priest be sent to them. So far as is known no priest went, and nothing more was ever heard of the tiny group of believers.

Why had Catholicism failed to find a home in Tibet? One reason may lie with the missionaries. Of all the Capuchin and Jesuit fathers who served there, apparently only Desideri and Andrade learned the Tibetan language well enough to make their teachings clear to the rulers of Tibet. Both men served in Tibet for only five years, Andrade from 1625 to 1630, and Desideri from 1716 to 1721. This brief residence by the most able of the fathers was not enough to get their missions off to a good start. Another factor was politics. Andrade arrived in Tsaparang just as the lamas were about to seize power from the King of Gu-ge, and Andrade's arrival merely provided the excuse they needed for a revolution that was coming anyway. Desideri's mission also arrived in turbulent times (after Lha Sang's overthrow of the sixth Dalai Lama) but Desideri's intelligence and personal charm seem to have carried the day. Had he been in Tibet during the final crisis faced by the Capuchin fathers, the tiny Catholic community might have survived.

The First Protestant Missions to Inner Asia

Fifty years after the Catholic mission at Lhasa collapsed, another Christian missionary movement began. Like its Nestorian and Catholic predecessors, the Protestant mission to Tibetan Buddhists would be geographically widespread, yet in most cases it would fail to establish a vital indigenous church. Like much else in Protestant missions, the effort began with the English missionary William Carey (1761-1834). Born into a poor family, Carey was converted at the age of eighteen, and grew rapidly both in his faith and his vision for a world lost without Christ. In 1793 he set sail for India, where he supported himself as an indigo planter while preaching the Gospel and translating the Bible into local languages. In March of 1797, Carey and a friend visited Bhutan, probably with a view towards beginning mission work there. Though favorably received by the local officials, Carey's hopes to begin a mission in Bhutan were not realized, and he was forced to remain at his already established work in Bengal.[406] He maintained his interest in things Tibetan, however, and in 1826 he published a Tibetan-English dictionary, possibly based on a manuscript compiled by the Capuchins.[407]

Other Protestants, inspired by Carey's example, gained a vision for sharing Christ among Tibetan Buddhist peoples. In 1817 the London Missionary Society sent three missionaries, Rev. Edward Stallybrass, William Swann, Robert Yuille and their families to work among the Buryat Mongols in southern Siberia. The Russian government gave them 7,000 rubles to erect church buildings in the town of Selenginsk, near the southern shore of Lake Baikal. From their newly established base, the missionaries went on preaching tours among the Buryats, and translated the Old Testament into Mongolian. In 1840 the Tsar's government ordered them to leave Russia, but they continued their translation work outside the country and completed a Mongolian New Testament in 1846. Like other attempts to offer the good news of Christ to Tibetan Buddhist peoples, this one carried a heavy cost: Mr. Yuille, his wife and two children, and the first wife, second wife, and child of Mr. Stallybrass died on the field.[408]

A second effort to reach the Mongols was similarly difficult. In 1870 the London Missionary Society sent a Scotsman named James Gilmour to Mongolia. Gilmour was a keen student of both Mongolian and Chinese, and when he had mastered them he traveled thousands of miles across Mongolia teaching, preaching, and doing medical work. In a single nine month period this tireless and devout man treated 5,700 patients, preached to over 23,000 people, sold over 7,000 pieces of Christian literature, and traveled 1,800 miles. One trip took him into Siberia, where he tried without success to find any trace of the London Missionary Society's earlier work near Lake Baikal. Gilmour suffered great loneliness after the death of his wife in 1885, the more so because his two sons had to be sent home to be educated. His feelings of loss must have been compounded by the meager results of his preaching. After 12 years of work among the Mongols, only one person had professed faith in Christ. In the remaining eight years of his life, only a handful of Mongols became Christians. James Gilmour never saw the Mongol church for which he had labored so diligently.[409]

Gilmour's story inspired others to work among the Mongols. In 1893 a young Swede named Frans August Larson went to Mongolia with the Christian and Missionary Alliance. He joined a small group of missionaries working among the Mongols of the Ordos Desert. During his language studies, Larson and his American wife realized the need for formal language study materials, so they began work on a Mongolian-Swedish-English dictionary. They were well into completing this project in 1900, when the Boxer rebellion spilled out of China into Inner Mongolia. As the border country burst into violence, all except one of the Scandinavian Alliance Mission workers were killed, and the Larsons' Mongolian dictionary and all the mission's property were destroyed. Larson himself led a daring escape across the Gobi Desert which saved 17 adults and six children from almost certain death. His camel caravan took 36 days to reach Urga (modern Ulaan Baataar) where the other missionaries left for home by way of Siberia. Larson's family was left penniless in the heart of Mongolia, and he was forced to get a job with the Mongol Ore Company to support them. After earning enough to get his family back to America, Larson returned to Mongolia to work as a railroad surveyor and an agent of the British and Foreign Bible Society. He traveled widely throughout the country, distributing Scriptures and sharing his faith in fluent Mongolian everywhere he went. He retired in

1913. Other missions worked among the Mongols, too, though most of them concentrated their efforts in the more heavily populated areas of Inner Mongolia. The American Board Mission began border work in 1865, the Swedish Mongolian Mission in 1898, and the Irish Presbyterians in 1901. So far as is known, none of these efforts bore any lasting fruit, and again, a great cost was paid in human life and suffering.

The story was similar elsewhere in Asia. The Moravians, inspired by the London Missionary Society's work in Siberia, sent Edward Pagell and William Heyde to set up a mission in Mongolia. Pagell and Heyde intended to reach their field by way of India and Tibet, but could not get the permission they needed to enter Tibet. In 1853 they settled in north India. After *32 years of prayer*, the Moravians finally received permission to enter Ladakh (then known as "Little Tibet"). This remote land had long been closed to missions, and the Moravians made the most of their opportunity, establishing mission stations in several strategic centers including Leh, the Ladakhi capital. The Moravian missionaries were marked by their great devotion, faithfulness in prayer, and high standards of scholarship. In 1857 they were joined by the brilliant German linguist Heinrich August Jaeschke. Like Desideri before him, Jaeschke made a detailed study of the voluminous Tibetan scriptures. He discovered that these classical texts were not like European books, written for any educated reader to understand, but more like notebooks, written in an arcane and very stylized format for students who already knew the secrets of tantric Buddhism. In this very conservative classical language, Jaeschke found a rich technical and religious vocabulary refined by a thousand years of native Tibetan scholarship. Though this classical form of the Tibetan language was learned by every educated member of the society, it was inaccessible to the uneducated, who could not understand it even if it were read to them, for the spoken dialects of Tibetan are quite different from the written form.[410]

Near the end of his preparatory studies, Jaeschke faced the crucial question of which language he should use for his New

Testament translation. Though his own Moravian denomination stressed the importance of having the Scriptures in the vernacular, Jaeschke realized that he faced an impossibly large number of vernaculars, each of which would be understood only in a limited area. The vernaculars also lacked the depth of religious vocabulary he needed for a Bible translation. Beyond that, the Tibetan people themselves felt quite strongly that vernacular forms of their language were wholly inappropriate for religious use. So Jaeschke chose to make a single, widely readable, theologically precise translation written in a form culturally acceptable to the Tibetans, rather than attempting a large number of vernacular translations which, while perhaps more understandable, would probably be rejected. He published several books of the New Testament between 1861 and 1875, all printed in Tibetan-style books called *pechas*. The first complete Tibetan New Testament was finally published in 1885, two years after the death of this great pioneer scholar of the Tibetan language. Other linguists published a Darjeeling-dialect based translation of the New Testament in 1903, which remained in print through most of the twentieth century. A whole Bible based on Moravian scholarship was published in 1948, and a revised version of the New Testament, also based on Moravian scholarship, was published in 1970. All these versions have had both critics and defenders, with controversy centering on the tensions between literary and colloquial expressions, intelligibility, and dialect favoritism.

While Bible translation efforts were going on, the Moravians did not neglect their other work. They held two Sunday services in Leh: one for Christians, one for inquirers, as well as three midweek meetings for prayer, hymn singing, and the telling of Bible stories. Drama, music, singing, and the use of painted scrolls called *thangkas* were a part of these meetings. From the 1870s onward, native evangelists ranged as far afield as Zangskar and Baltistan.[411] Among the Moravians were some first-rank linguists and scholars, who produced a Bible story book for children, a catechism, a book of theology, tracts, Christian poetry, hymns, Scripture portions, and many other Christian books, as well as Ladakh's first newspaper. Nor were the practical needs of the Ladakhi people forgotten. There was a medical clinic, leprosy work, a guesthouse,[412] a school, a mission farm, and a handicraft production and marketing scheme. By the time the expatriate missionaries had to leave in the 1950s, the Moravian church in Ladakh had about 140 communicant members.

The Moravians were not the only group to work among Tibetan Buddhists on the Indian subcontinent. The venerable London Missionary Society and several smaller groups sent missionaries to Tibetan Buddhist tribal peoples in northwest India, between Ladakh and Nepal. To the east, individual missionaries began work among the Lepchas of Sikkim as early as 1841. The Bible was translated into the Lepcha language and large numbers of Lepchas turned to Christ. The Scandinavian Alliance Mission began work near Darjeeling in 1892, and set up mission stations in several places in Sikkim and along the Bhutanese border. The Himalayan states of Nepal and Bhutan, home to many Tibetan Buddhist peoples, remained firmly closed to Christian missions through the end of the nineteenth century.

Protestant Missions Among Tibetan Buddhist Peoples in China

For China-based missions, the outskirts of Tibet were a natural frontier that soon attracted a missionary presence. The China Inland Mission surveyed Tibet's northeastern limits (the Tibet-Gansu border) in 1888 and established mission stations shortly thereafter. In 1895 it was joined by the Christian and Missionary Alliance, and both societies continued to work in this strategic area for many years.[413] The China Inland Mission also surveyed Tibet's eastern frontier (the Sichuan-Tibet border) in 1877, and twenty years later opened a permanent station at Kangding. Several smaller missions followed; one set up a printing press for Christian literature in Tibetan. The Roman Catholics were active at 12 small mission stations in this region, from which they recorded over 1,600 converts by the

1920s.[414] Both frontiers were lawless areas, and opposition to the presence of foreigners was occasionally violent. In the city of Pao-an, Tibetan sorcerers pronounced a curse on the Alliance missionaries, who barely escaped with their lives before a group of angry Tibetans completely destroyed their mission station. In 1873 the Catholic mission at Batang was demolished, in 1881 a priest was murdered, and in 1887 the Chinese government ordered the temporary closure of mission stations on the Tibetan border. In 1905 and 1906, a revolt broke out at Batang during which two priests were killed, and converts who would not deny their faith were shot. While efforts continued on the periphery of Tibet, some missionaries were eager to press on to Lhasa itself.[415] Several individuals made heroic efforts to reach it, but almost all of them failed, some at the cost of their lives. Tibet proper remained as firmly closed to missionaries as ever.

But the work continued along Tibet's eastern borders. In the late 1940s, on the eve of the proclamation of the People's Republic of China, approximately 50 missionaries (20 of them Chinese) were laboring on Tibet's borders. Within a few years most if not all the foreigners had been compelled to leave, though some of the Chinese were able to remain. In 1959 when the Chinese government asserted its control over Tibet, the fourteenth Dalai Lama and thousands of other Tibetans fled to India. Christian missions played a prominent role in the relief efforts that followed, but the Tibetan exiles showed little interest in what was to them an alien faith.

The Church Begins to Grow

Tibetan Buddhist peoples were subjected to dramatic and violent changes during the course of the twentieth century. In Russia, traditional life under the Tsars came to an end in 1917, followed by a bitter civil war and 70 years of militantly atheist rule. The Soviet government made intense and systematic efforts to suppress any form of religious expression. Buddhist monasteries in Buryatia, Kalmykia, and Tuva were closed or destroyed. Monks were shot, sent to prison, or returned to secular life. In

1943 the Kalmyk people suffered a mass deportation at the hands of Joseph Stalin. With the end of Soviet rule in the early 1990s, the more egregious abuses came to an end, and the peoples of Russia enjoyed limited religious freedom. Protestant churches appeared or reappeared in Kalmykia and Siberia, but they remained under pressure from the strongly nationalistic Russian Orthodox Church.

Mongolia also endured all the horrors of Stalinist rule from the mid 1920s until the democratic reforms of the 1990s. Under Stalin's direction, institutional Tibetan Buddhism was virtually eradicated, and monks suffered the same fate as their colleagues in the Soviet Union. The collapse of Communism seven decades later left Mongolia a free, but deeply impoverished country. When it reopened to the outside world, Christians from many countries sought to work in partnership with the Mongolian people through programs providing education, medical assistance, and social services. Within a decade, the Church had grown to include thousands of baptized indigenous believers, with Mongols in leadership roles. This remarkable story is told in more detail in the next chapter.

The early years of the Peoples' Republic of China were a dark and frustrating time for Chinese Christians, and for the expatriate believers who had made so many sacrifices to help them during the first part of the twentieth century. Officially, the Maoist government rejected Christian missionaries as agents of foreign imperialism, but in fact the Maoists probably feared the Church more deeply as a source of political values opposed to their own atheist materialism than as foreign spies. Under the Maoists and their successors, Christians were persecuted, tortured, shot, sent to labor camps, and mistreated in many other ways. Despite this, the Chinese Church survived and even grew in numbers.[416] In the last two decades of the century, the government extended a limited official tolerance to Christianity. Under this policy, expatriate Christians returned to the country and began to make significant contributions to China's development, even in the more remote areas of the country where many Tibetan Buddhist peoples live.

The twentieth century saw dramatic change in the Himalayas as well. Nepal abandoned an isolationist policy in the 1950s and opened to the outside world. Though officially a Hindu theocracy, within two decades a small but rapidly growing church appeared among the majority Nepali population. Three decades later, churches appeared among minority ethnic groups such as the Tamangs and Lhomis, who had traditionally been Tibetan Buddhist. Even long-closed Bhutan made a tentative and limited opening to the outside world, and a small indigenous Church came into being. The growth of the Church in Tibetan Buddhist areas of the Himalayas in the last half of the twentieth century was largely due to the work of indigenous Christians who worked with quiet persistence in the face of great hardships.

Summary

From its very earliest days, the Christian Church had links with Asia. Moving eastward along the Silk Road, Christians had established churches in Mesopotamia, Persia, India, and the Kushan Empire within 500 years of Jesus' death and resurrection. During the next 500 years, much of the Church's Inner Asian presence was confined to the Silk Road, north of which lived marauding steppe tribes, and south of which lived the warlike Tibetans. Only at the distant Chinese end of the Silk Road did Christianity begin to establish itself and expand. The second millennium saw a great Protestant and Catholic missionary movement which established itself on the Russian, Indian, and Chinese frontiers of Inner Asia. But only during the last third of the millennium did this movement become strong enough to send its first tentative feelers across the borders of Inner Asia. For most of the 2,000 years covered in this chapter,[417] Inner Asia remained what it had always been: remote, inaccessible, and resistant to change from outside the region.

With few exceptions, the lamas who ruled Inner Asia were lulled into a fatal slumber by their Tibetan Buddhist worldview.

They disregarded or minimized the significance of the scientific, political, and military changes happening all around them in Russia, Europe, India, Japan, and China.[418] With the rise of Communist governments in Russia, Mongolia, and China, Inner Asia was dominated by an alien and militantly anti-religious ideology which swept away the old ruling elites and forcibly integrated traditional societies into the fabric of modern nation states within a generation or two. When change finally came to Inner Asia in the twentieth century, it was catastrophic for institutional Tibetan Buddhism. But the shock of these changes seemed to "wipe the slate clean" for many people, and led them to ask fundamental questions about their lives. As soon as some degree of religious freedom was restored, the Church grew rapidly in some areas. At the beginning of the twenty-first century, there were new and confident national churches in places where just a hundred years previously few people had ever even heard of Christianity. We shall see an example of such a Church in the next chapter.

CHAPTER 7

Miracle in Mongolia

By Hugh P. Kemp[419]

Mongolia is a country that looks to both the past and the future. Since the glory days of empire in the thir-teenth century, Mongolia has borne the weight of Ming overlords, Manchurian exploitation, feudal poverty, and Buddhist theocracy. During the twentieth century, she has emerged from seventy-odd years of Soviet style communism until in 1990, democratic elections created a new environment that facilitated social and political change. With these changes, the Christian church in Mongolia grew from nothing to a body of thousands of national believers. Why, after such a long pe-riod of spiritual drought, did the Mongolian Church burst into flower with such powerful exuberance? Why did it grow so rap-idly when the Church was either unknown or barely struggling to exist in other parts of the Tibetan Buddhist world? And what lessons does it offer for those who testify to Christ in the Ti-betan Buddhist world today? The answers to these questions, as with so much else in Mongolia, lies in the history and char-acter of this remarkable people.

Who are the Mongols?

The Mongol homeland is a well defined area, incorporat-ing the grasslands of north-western China in the east and the Gobi desert in the south, and bordered by Lake Baikal in the north and the Altai mountains in the west. The state of Mongolia (formerly the Mongolian People's Republic or MPR) is the only Mongolian political entity, conforming roughly to this geo-graphical area. Mongol tribes also live in Buryatia (in southern Siberia) and the Inner Mongolian Autonomous Region of

China. A small pocket of Mongol cousins lives in Kalmykia, an area in European Russia near the head of the Caspian Sea.

The Mongols are a Turkic people who are descended from the remnant of the Mongol Empire founded by Chinggis Khan in the early thirteenth century. The predominant tribe in Mongolia is the Khalka, who occupy the centre and east of the country, and who comprise about 80 per cent of Mongolia's population. There are three other main groupings which are easily recognised: the Oirod, the Buryat, and the tribes of Inner Mongolia. The Oirod Mongols are located in the western regions of Mongolia, as well as in China's Xinjiang and Qinghai provinces. The Kalmyk (sometimes called the Torgut) Mongols of Russia are also Oirod. They are regarded by Khalkas as distant cousins. There are exile populations of Oirod Mongols in France, New Jersey (USA), Taiwan, Hong Kong and Germany. Most of these groups left Chinese Inner Mongolia during the rise of Communism in the 1950s.

The Buryat Mongols live north of Mongolia in Russia's Buryat Republic. There are also Buryats in Mongolia proper, and as far south as China. The Mongols of the Inner Mongolian Autonomous Region of China comprise numerous sub-tribal groupings (called "banners"), and are referred to corporately as simply "the Inner Ones" by the Khalka of Mongolia. In summary, any Mongol tribal group related in an historical and geographic way to the Khalka tribe of modern Mongolia may be generally regarded as ethnically Mongol. The Manchurians of China and the Moghuls of India, although very distantly related to the Mongols, fall outside this definition. Other distant relatives, like the Uighurs, played a role in the transmission of the Gospel to the Mongols in the first millennium, but are now a distinctly non-Mongol group. Christian witness has occurred amongst all of these tribal groups at different times.[420]

A Brief History of Mongolian Christianity

The Mongols have had considerable contact with Christianity since the seventh century A.D., when Eastern Syrian

Christians were active throughout Central Asia. Five distinct periods of Christian contact are recognizable: pre-Empire (635-1245), Empire (1245-1368), post-Empire (1368-1765), pre-Modern (1765-1990), and Modern (from 1990). Each period featured a dominant mission group: first the Eastern Syrians (also referred to as Nestorian), then the Franciscans, the London Missionary Society (LMS), the Swedish mission, the Catholic order *Congregatio Immaculati Cordis Mariae* (CICM), and then the Evangelical Alliance Mission (TEAM) and other Protestant groups.

At first these efforts focused on the heart of the Mongol Empire (the Khan's capital was at or near Karakorum, until Kublai shifted it to Da-tu, now modern Beijing), then Kalmykia, Buryatia, Inner Mongolia, then Outer Mongolia. This geographical sequence meant that there was also an ethnic sequence: the first Christians were among the Turkic tribe of Keraits (then holding future Mongol territory and consequently quickly conquered by Chinggis), then the Mongols descended from Chinggis and his family, then the Kalmyk, the Buryat, the Oirod of Inner Mongolia, then lastly the Khalka of Mongolia proper.

The pre-Empire era could be called the "Period of Contact" (635-1245). It began with the arrival of the "Luminous Religion" in Central Asia as documented on the Nestorian Monument, an eighth-century three metre high granite stele now in the Xian County Historical Museum in Xian, China. The "Luminous Religion" is the Tang Dynasty name for the Eastern Syrian Church, which in later Catholic literature is referred to as "Nestorian," and in modern Mongolian as "niestor." Nearly two centuries prior to the ascendancy of Chinggis Khan, the Kerait tribe converted en masse to this Syrian-Nestorian Christianity, and other pre-Mongol tribes in the Central Asian hinterland were also influenced by Nestorianism. When Temujin was ordained Chinggis Khan at the grand parliament, or *huraltai* of 1206, he was well on the way to conquering these neighbouring tribes and absorbing them into his growing sphere of influence. It was with these conquered Nestorianised tribes that the Mongols first encountered Christianity. In 1245, the

Franciscan Jean de Plano Carpini arrived at the Khan's encampment or *ordo*, and introduced the Mongols to Catholic Christianity.

During the ensuing "Empire Period" (1245-1368) the Mongols were at the height of their world power. Diplomatic missions were exchanged between Catholic Europe and the Mongol Empire during the so-called "Pax Mongolica" when Chinggis' sons and grandsons ruled. These embassies were mainly between the Popes and the Il-Khans of Persia, and Kublai Khan's China. The papal ambassadors were mainly Franciscans; it is quite legitimate to speak of a Franciscan mission to the Mongols.

The following "Post-Empire Period" saw no recorded Christian witness to the Mongols during a four hundred year period of Chinese domination (1368-1765). Ming dynasty emperors tolerated a limited Jesuit presence in China, but the Jesuits had no special interest in the Mongols. Ming xenophobia ensured that the Chinese coast and the Mongol/Russian border were closely monitored. Periodic Mongol uprisings failed to produce another Mongol state or to throw off first the Ming, then the Manchurian yoke. The Mongols remained a forgotten people, a mere shadow of their former selves, destined to insignificance in the shadow of emerging China and Russia.

After centuries of neglect, the Christian church remembered the Mongols again in 1765. In that year the Moravian Brethren established a mission among the Kalmyk Mongols at a site called Sarepta (now part of the city of Volgograd). This "pre-Modern" or "Period of Rediscovery" lasted from 1765 until 1990. The London Missionary Society (LMS) sent workers to Buryatia, building on the momentum generated by the Moravian mission in Kalmykia. By the first decades of the 19th century, the LMS and a number of other Protestant mission agencies had established work in Inner Mongolia. None of these missions met with great success in numbers of converts, though a small congregation of Kalmyk Christians emerged, as well as two Mongol congregations in Inner Mongolia. The Catholics returned in 1865, this time represented by the CICM

(*Congregatio Immaculati Cordis Mariae*).

In 1846 a complete Mongolian Bible translation was published by two LMS missionaries, Stallybrass and Swan, in a high form of the Buryat-Mongol dialect. This Bible and related tracts were the main tool of evangelism in subsequent years, where much itineration across the steppe was done by missionaries based in Kalgan (modern Zhangjiakou) and other Chinese border towns. Swedish missionaries penetrated as far inland as Urga (at the site of modern day Ulaanbaatar), where they ran a medical clinic and small farm from 1919 to 1924. During the Communist years of the Mongolian People's Republic (1924-1990), no evangelism was attempted. If there had been any fruit from the Swedish endeavours, it was swept away with Marshal Choibalsan's religious purges of the 1930s and 1940s. Meanwhile, in Inner Mongolia, both Catholic and Protestant Christian witness continued through the Republican years of China (1912-1949) into the 1950s when the rise of Communism led to an exodus of Inner Mongols to Hong Kong, Taiwan, and elsewhere, and the closure of much Christian missionary effort in China generally. Efforts continued by means of radio and secretly imported Bibles (specifically a 1952 revision of the LMS' 1846 New Testament), and then by TEAM missionaries among diasporan Mongols.

The "Period of Establishment" (the Modern Era) commenced in July 1990 when democratic elections were held in the Mongolian People's Republic, and subsequently a new Constitution was drawn up. Also in 1990 two Mongolian men returned from study in the Soviet Eastern bloc, where they had become Christians. Towards the end of the year, the first 12 Protestant missionaries arrived in the country and the United Bible Societies was distributing its translation of the New Testament, named *Shin Geree*. By August 1991, there were about 140 believers in three public congregations, and by the end of 1992, there were around 1,000 believers in four congregations in Ulaanbaatar and one in Darhan, Mongolia's second city. In early 1993 a church was planted in Mongolia's third largest city, Erdenet. By 1994, there were 3,000 Christians in ten churches in Ulaanbaatar and spread throughout five provinces, and by 1997 there were more than 6,000 Christians in more than 20 churches in Ulaanbaatar and a Christian presence in all 18 provinces. Estimates by 2004 have put the number of active Christians between 12,000 and 30,000 meeting in up to 150 groups and/or churches, nationwide.[421]

The CICM established a Catholic congregation in July 1992 in Ulaanbaatar and opened its own multi-purpose building in the summer of 1996. The Russian Orthodox church returned to Ulaanbaatar as well, celebrating its first communion service on March 16, 1997 after being absent since 1931.

Religion and the Mongol State

By the end of the twentieth century, the Mongolian world view had been shaped by four major influences: the veneration of Chinggis Khan, the religions of both shamanism and Tibetan Buddhism, and the secular philosophy of Communism.

In the early 1990s public pictures and statues of Lenin were replaced by memorials to Chinggis Khan. Slogans commending the glories of the Communist regime were replaced with the quotes and deeds of Chinggis. Young men and women wore lapel badges with the great khan's picture. School textbooks were re-written; the Soviet image of Chinggis as the "marauding barbarian" was replaced with a vision of Chinggis as "noble statesman."

It cannot be understated how much the modern Mongol sees himself in the light of Chinggis Khan. Chinggis is esteemed as a great political figure: the founder of the Mongol nation and the father of its people - the conqueror who established the greatest land empire the world has ever seen. Chinggis' military prowess is the object of great pride. When democratic changes opened the door to new paths in 1990, there was much rhetoric about following in the footsteps of Chinggis: "We were great once, and so we can be great again."

The glorification of Chinggis Khan during the early 1990s produced a Chinggis cult. He was venerated at shrines and held up as a model statesman. Sons, vodka, furs, and travel agencies were named after him. His spirit, still militant, inspires Mongol youth to assert their Mongolian identity in the face of new forces jostling for priority on the nation's agenda. During the last decade of the twentieth century Chinggis was re-invented, re-interpreted and re-venerated.

His legacy is still found in the *yasa*. This is a word meaning "tradition" or "customs" in modern Mongolian, but which also means "law" or "legal tradition." It is probable that Chinggis established a *yasa*, or legal code, for his troops and administrators. The existence of the *yasa* is described in full by Juvaini, an eye witness in the Mongol court: "...[Chinggis] established a rule for every occasion and a regulation for every circumstance; while for every crime he fixed a penalty. ... He gave orders that ... these *yasas* and ordinances should be written down on rolls. These rolls are called the Great Book of *Yasas* and are kept in the treasury of the chief princes. Whenever a khan ascends the throne, or a great army is mobilized, or the princes assemble and begin [to consult together] concerning affairs of state and the administration thereof, they produce these rolls and model their actions thereon."[422]

The *yasa* dictated tolerance towards all religions as a fundamental political policy binding on subsequent khans. Juvaini summarises: "Being the adherent of no religion and the follower of no creed, he (Chinggis Khan) eschewed bigotry, and the preference of one faith to another, and the placing of some above others; rather he honoured and respected the learned and pious of every sect, recognising such conduct as the way to the court of God. And as he viewed the Moslems with the eye of respect, so also did he hold the Christians and idol worshippers (that is Buddhists) in high esteem. As for his children and grandchildren, several of them have chosen a religion according to their inclination, some adopting Islam, others embracing Christianity, others selecting idolatry (Buddhism) and others again cleaving to the ancient canon of their fathers (that is, shamanism).... But though they have adopted some religion they still for the most part avoid all show of fanaticism and do not swerve from the *yasa* of Chinggis Khan namely, to consider all sects as one and not to distinguish them from one another."[423]

This tolerance towards all religions was the expression of a pragmatic political policy. The khans did not embrace or neglect any one particular religion out of conviction. They were more interested in the conquering of nations to acquire booty. Religious tolerance simply made it easier to govern the conquered. Such tolerance was conditional, however, on absolute obedience to the khan, to whom politics and religion were distinctly separate. A subject's personal religious convictions should not compromise political allegiance. Priests of all religions were expected to say prayers on behalf of the khan for the benefit of the empire. Tax concessions and other privileges were conditional on all priests of all creeds praying for the welfare of the khan.

This political obedience did have religious overtones, however. To obey the khan was to obey God/Heaven (*munkh tenger*). The Mongol khan understood his conquering mission as commissioned by *munkh tenger*. *Munkh tenger* had chosen the khan to exercise divine authority in the whole world, and therefore the Mongol khan was conquering in *munkh tenger's* name. This messianism left the Mongols indifferent to religious conflict and sceptical about doctrinal arguments. They showed little concern for the doctrines and truth claims of the religions they encountered in their conquests. Political pragmatism, driven by messianic conviction, was the motive behind a tolerant religious policy. The actual religious beliefs of the conquered peoples were of little consequence.

This initial conquering messianism softened somewhat during the reign of the khans subsequent to Chinggis as there was a shift to peaceful rule. Once a people had been conquered, they had to be governed, and this administrative role did not sit well with the natural instincts of the Mongol aristocracy. The khans had to curry the favor of the conquered peoples' wealthy classes to ensure effective rule. This led to the so called "Pax Mongolica" (or "Peace of the Mongols") during which the religious tolerance implied in the *yasa* was given full expression. When Kublai took the throne in the east as fifth and last of the Great Khans (1260), he shifted his capital from Karakorum to Da-tu (Beijing) and had to win the favour of the ruling Confucian bureaucracy to run his empire. In the west, the Il-Khans, descending from Hulegu, Kublai's brother, embraced local religion (sometimes Islam, sometimes Nestorian Christianity) to varying degrees in order to appease the local emirs, bishops, and petty nobility. As long as subjects were obedient to the *yasa*, individual belief was one's own choice.

By the reign of the eighth Il-Khan of Persia, Oljeitu Il-Khan, Hulegu's house had become so influenced by the sedentary Muslims that they had lost their conquering vitality as a nation. Oljeitu gave a wake-up call: "Let us return to our ancient religion."⁴²⁴ Oljeitu was appealing to return to ancient Mongol shamanism. But this call came too late. And here is the inherent weakness of the religious pragmatism of the *yasa*. The *yasa* was not a viable religio-legal framework for a sedentary population. Mongol shamanism was a religion of a people on the move; a people in close contact with nature. When the initial nomadic militarism had conquered all that it could, the subsequent Khanates had then to govern sedentary populations. These populations, for example the Muslims in Persia, took advantage of the religious freedom that the *yasa* afforded them, and so the House of Hulegu conceded much to the Muslims to offset the continual threat of internal revolution. As a result, the House of Hulegu eventually lost its Mongol character by adopting Islam and consequently merging into cultural and religious milieu of the Persians.

The legacy of the *yasa* influenced Mongolian religious policy and worldview into the twentieth century. The post-Communist constitution of 1992, as interpreted in the Law of the Relationship of Church and State (November, 1993) endorsed three official state religions: shamanism, Tibetan Buddhism and Islam, and ensured freedom of religious expression for Mongolia's citizens. The apparent tolerance implied by this law is perhaps better thought of as "indifference." As in the *yasa* of Chinggis, one's religion is seen to be inconsequential to the welfare of the state, so long as the state's citizens are obedient to the law. The law endorses three religions practiced by the majority of Mongols; the law's intent was descriptive rather than prescriptive.

The Mongol Worldview in Modern Mongolia

If shamanism was the core belief system in the Mongol worldview by the end of the twentieth century, it was overlaid in important ways by the religion that the Mongols imported from Tibet. Outwardly, Tibetan Buddhism might have seemed to be the dominant partner in this relationship. Tourists of the 1990s, walking the streets of Ulaanbaatar, would notice Gandan monastery and its temple dominating the hill in the western sector of the city. In the provinces they might notice monasteries reopening and novices being recruited, encouraged by periodic visits from the fourteenth Dalai Lama. On the surface, it seemed that Tibetan Buddhism was the main filter through which the Mongol interpreted his world.

Inwardly, however, twentieth-century Mongols still viewed Tibetan Buddhism as a foreign religion. Many were adamant that Buddhism was an import and were quick to point out Tibetan words in the language as foreign words. For formal rites of passage many would go to a Tibetan Buddhist temple, but the normal daily rhythms of life might well be dominated by shamanistic influences. The local Buddhist lama would be consulted for the most auspicious day for a wedding, but the first ladle full of tea would be flicked with the fourth finger to the four points of the compass as an offering to *tenger*, the ancient sky-god whom Chinggis worshipped.

To add to this religious mixture, Soviet Communism also influenced the Mongolian worldview, although not pervasively. Atheistic Communism heavily suppressed all religion with purges in the 1930s, and the 700 odd Tibetan Buddhist monasteries in Mongolia were either leveled or turned into museums. Monks were killed or secularised while the nomads were organised into production units. The State took over everything and owned everything.

Communism as a worldview led to a practical atheism amongst the Mongols. It bred a class of civil servants who in post-Communist Mongolia were neither shamanist nor Tibetan Buddhist. They were disillusioned that the high ideals of the Communist state to which they had given their lives collapsed overnight in 1990. It also bred a generation of young people who knew nothing of either ancient shamanism or Tibetan Buddhism. The result was a religious void in society. Certainly the older Mongols still interpreted their world through the "blue glasses" of the ancient sky-god-based shamanism, while a remnant of priests did so through the "yellow glasses" of Tibetan Buddhism (the Buddhist sect in Mongolia is the Yellow sect). The dominant worldview however became atheism: it was the party officials, bureaucrats and emerging youth who viewed the world through the "red glasses" of Communism.

Changing economic fortunes from 1990 brought new challenges to the Mongols: new television programs, easier access to the Internet, new religions arriving at the borders, and the ever tempting lure of consumerism. With an emerging worldview dominated by market reform, economics soon became a key frame of reference for the new entrepreneurial Mongols who began importing all sorts of goods from China, Russia, and more lately Japan and Korea. The early 1990s witnessed huge social upheaval, accentuated by the collapse of the state welfare system. Domestic violence, unemployment and underemployment, medical and nutritional mismanagement, and a poor work ethic all contributed to a social agenda that seemed overwhelming. Inflation, privatisation, and market reforms left thousands poorer, indebted, abused, and marginalised.

Mongolian Cultural Characteristics

Shamanism, Buddhism, and Communism each left their marks upon the broad social canvas of Mongolia, but what of the individual Mongol? What can be said of the way that he or she interacts with the world? What were the Mongols like as a people at the turn of the twenty-first century?

137

One of the first characteristics that struck the author in the early days of his time in Mongolia was the Mongols' innate forthrightness and lack of guile. There was little desire to take unfair advantage of a foreigner: exchange rates and taxi fares were fairly quoted. Whether this was a remnant Communist ethic, or a winsomeness born of the isolation of the Central Asian steppe was open to question. Mongols still preferred the traditional values of a full bowl of fermented mare's milk (*airag*), a noble mother, and a good horse.

This is not to suggest, however, that the Mongols of this period were naive rustics. For much of the late twentieth century, a whole world of education in the best universities behind the iron curtain was at the disposal of the Mongolian population. By the end of the Communist era, almost all Mongols, even remote nomads, were literate in the Cyrillic script, and were able to read a Bible when the chance to do so arose.

An unchanging aspect of life in Mongolia is a Mongol's love for the steppe. It is in his very being. In the summer, people return to their families on the steppe: urban life is seen as a necessary evil, but real life happens in the countryside. "To go to the countryside" is a universally accepted excuse for absence at the office or a late return at the beginning of the semester. Anything to do with the steppe is glorified: the quality of the mares' milk, the freedom to hunt, and the leisure to socialize. Legends of the steppe abound: songs are sung of horses, battles, hunts and lovers. Any Biblical themes to do with Creation, nomads (the patriarchs of Genesis), and the deeds of heroes and heroines (David and Goliath) are embraced enthusiastically.[425]

Kinship structure is fairly loose. Mother is especially honored (or rather it is often grandmother). The family is an extended family, with aunts looking after nephews and nieces, and parents being absent for long times for study or work. During the Communist regime, there was a genuine gender balance in the work place, including the academy, but even so, women were still expected to run the household. Mother usually controls the money. A nomad's tent, or *ger* with its door open, implies open hospitality; there is much visiting, socializing, drinking, toasting, and singing. Distant cousins will carry the title of brother or sister: the nuclear family is often hard to discern.

As in other parts of the Tibetan Buddhist world, shamanist beliefs persist in Mongolian life. Because of fear of evil spirits, children are not named until they are well past the risk of infant mortality. Children may be named "Not this," or "No name" to fool the evil spirits so as not to risk the child's life. Gifts of milk, food and prayers are offered to the spirits who live in the mountain passes: *obo* (cairns of rocks with prayer flags) dominate all the high places; travelers are expected to stop and circumambulate the *obo* and offer some gift to the spirit resident there. Talismans are common: luck and fate are forces to be reckoned with every day. The author once commented on the fine quality of a friend's new lambskin coat. That evening on the way home on the bus it was slashed and ruined by a pickpocket. The friend interpreted the incident (much to the author's embarrassment) as being caused by the author, because he had drawn an evil spirit's attention to the coat's beauty. The fear of evil spirits casts a long shadow.

The summer festival of *Naadam* includes three days of passionate support for wrestling, archery and horse racing (the "Three Manly Sports"). Nomads will travel weeks into provincial centres for the events: bets are placed and legends are made. Soldiers in the imperial leather uniforms of Chinggis' day parade on horseback through the cities; the nine-yak-tail banner is honored. The winter festival of *Tsagaan Sar* (or "White Moon/Month") marks the beginning of the lunar new year in February. Older relatives are honoured, toasts for the new year are made, and there is much eating and drinking.

Birth of the Modern Mongolian Church

Between 1990 and 1993, Mongolia experienced immense changes. Democratic elections overthrew the communist Mongolian People's Revolutionary Party (MPRP), and the country experienced two heady years of democratic reform. The

Constitution was re-written, there was talk of Mongolia becoming an Asian economic tiger, the Soviets began leaving, and Mongolia threw its doors open to the outside world. A check came with the re-election of a restructured MPRP in 1992, but nevertheless, democratic and open market reforms had come to stay.

These changes were not as sudden as they seemed. During the mid to late 1980s reform had been in the air. Some Christians had visited the Mongolian People's Republic on tourist visas, praying for the day when it would open. Internal restlessness grew and news of the changes in Soviet Europe trickled back. A youthful ground swell, inspired by the rock band *Honk* ("The Bell") picked up momentum, and it is only the grace of God and the constraint and wisdom of the nation's leaders that Ulaanbaatar did not have a Tienanmen Square incident in 1990.[426, 427]

In these first three years, two tools were immediately available for evangelisation: the United Bible Societies' (UBS) New Testament (*Shin Geree*), and Campus Crusade's film *Jesus*.

Work on the Khalka *Shin Geree* started in 1972, and was completed 17 years later, in 1989. The project involved over 30 Mongols and six Bible translation consultants. In July 1990, the first 5,000 copies were being printed in Hong Kong by UBS, ready for an opportune moment for shipment to the Mongolian People's Republic. When she threw off the Communist system, a modern colloquial translation of the New Testament was ready. The warehouse in Hong Kong was soon cleared and 3,000 more copies were ordered. This was surely an example of God's perfect timing for a nation.

Hand in hand with UBS' *Shin Geree* was the *Jesus* film. This was used extensively throughout Mongolia. Groups of Mongolian Christians would go to a provincial center, show the *Jesus* film either outdoors or in the local cinema, preach, sell *Shin Geree* (or Gospels of Luke) and give an appeal for commitment to Christ. Such endeavours would often bring a house group together and so a church would be planted. Video editions of *Jesus* soon became available and continued to be used in homes and smaller venues. The effect of the dual use of the *Jesus* film and the New Testament *Shin Geree* cannot be underestimated: they both received exceedingly wide distribution and have been instrumental in hundreds of Mongolians coming to know Christ personally.

Shin Geree and the *Jesus* film spoke directly to a new generation of Mongolian youth who witnessed the collapse of Communism and for whom the Tibetan Buddhism of their parents and the shamanism of the grandparents were unattractive, powerless and irrelevant. There was in effect a huge spiritual void waiting to be filled. Consequently, the first three to five years of Mongolian church growth was among the 14 to 25-year-old age group, and often among girls. Nevertheless, by the mid 1990s this disparity had started to even out, with more young men and older people in the churches, often facilitated by specialist home groups.

From a missions strategy perspective, in 1990, Mongolia was a clean slate. The country had had no recent history of missions, no western colonial history, no established church, no recognisable Christians, and no Bible. It was a grand opportunity to get evangelistic strategies right. It was also a tempting venue to experiment. It is significant that the two key evangelistic tools in the early days were non-sectarian and interdenominational. The early missionaries of the 1990s and the Mongolian Christians were all keen to evangelize Mongolia as quickly and effectively as possible. It was no surprise that the period from 1990 to 1993 was characterised by a heady flurry of activity.

The 1993 Law on the Relationship of Church and State

In December 1993, there appeared in the newspaper the text of a new "Law on the Relationship of Church and State." Foreign Christians reacted immediately, claiming that it discriminated against Christianity on the grounds that the law named Tibetan Buddhism, shamanism and Islam (the latter a concession to the Khazak minority) as Mongolia's official state religions. Tibetan Buddhism was declared to be the predominant religion which would receive state patronage. The implication was that to be a genuine Mongol, one was naturally a Buddhist.

The formulation of the law was inevitable. Naming Tibetan Buddhism as the state religion was merely describing what already was, and conceding that there would be two other official religions alluded perhaps to the toleration embedded in the ancient *yasa*. The fact that Christian numbers had been growing so quickly between 1991 and 1993 was certainly a factor in the formulation of the law. The timing of the publication of the law implied it, although nowhere was this stated explicitly.

Wariness continued amongst the Christian community in light of Mongolia's southern neighbor's track record of meddling in religion. The new law dictated that the State would control the location of all *sum*. *Sum* was translated as "church," but it is a generic term meaning any religious building or entity, like a temple or even a mosque. No religious teaching could occur outside of registered *sums*. The Law demanded that all *sums* register with the government. This of course meant each Christian church or congregation, but it also meant every Buddhist temple and monastery, as well as any mosques.

The foreign media and the embassies showed immediate and intense concern over the new law. United Nations resolutions on freedom of religion were discussed, and eventually a small consortium of Democrats and Christians took the Government to the Constitutional Court, on the grounds that parts of the law were unconstitutional. The Constitutional Court sent the law back to Parliament, ordering three clauses to be rescinded. In this revised version, the law allowed public preaching and witness, but still all *sums* had to be registered. No *sum* was allowed to meet in State-owned halls, and the State would control the number of clergy in any religion. The most immediate problem for Christian churches was that there were no alternative meeting places, as private ownership laws had not yet been introduced, and consequently there were no alternative venues other than State or City owned halls.

Article 4.2 of the law put a high place on the unity of the Mongol people, their historical and cultural traditions and civilization. Legislators saw post-1990 Christianity as a threat to this, and that is partly why Tibetan Buddhism was reaffirmed as the official Mongolian religion. The challenge to the Christian church was to present Christ to the Mongolian people in Mongolian ways. Eventually, Christians settled down to await the outcome. Singapore and Hong Kong had similar laws regulating church-state relationships, and Christian churches there seemed to do fine.

The First Decade: 1990-1999

Among all the Tibetan Buddhist people groups in Central Asia, the response of the Mongols to the Gospel has been a pleasant reprieve in a hard-fought spiritual battle. In some ways, the people of Mongolia are different from other Tibetan Buddhist peoples (an underlying shamanism, recent Communism, the legacy of Chinggis, political independence), but in other ways, they are very similar. How can we account for the seemingly sudden success of the Gospel? Are there lessons from Mongolia that can be applied to other parts of the Tibetan Buddhist world?

As we think about these questions, first place must be given to the providence of God in the birth of the Church in Mongolia. In many ways it was God's time for Mongolia and Christians could only stand back, watch God at work, and rejoice. It was in fact a re-birth, considering that Christianity had a significant influence during the Imperial era. Nevertheless, there were at least four factors vital to the Church's rapid growth. These were: 1) an accessible, easily-readable translation of the New Testament; 2) cooperation among Christians, and between Christians and the government; 3) a focus on church planting; and 4) an emphasis on leadership training.

The New Testament

Underlying the rapid growth of the church in Mongolia was UBS' *Shin Geree* New Testament. Yet from its first publication it was the subject of heated controversy.

Shin Geree was translated and published in a time when there were no Biblically-trained Mongols to review it critically. Its intended readers would not have access to commentaries or Bible dictionaries for many years to come, so "the aim was to give as much information as possible, and in a way which the totally uninformed would find comprehensible and easy to read."[428] Such translations are technically known as dynamic-equivalent translations, and are often made when the intended readership needs extra help in understanding the Biblical text.

Critics charged that *Shin Geree* was "a paraphrase" and had "too much explanation within the text" and so "was not close to the original." They believed that generic words within the Mongol language should have been used to preserve the literal meaning of the original text. Much of their criticism focused on the word for "God." *Shin Geree* used a phrase meaning "Lord of the Universe," but its critics argued that the word *burhan* (which they championed as a generic term for "deity") should have been used instead. As a result, the Mongolian Bible Translation Committee (MBTC) was set up in 1994 to work independently on a more literal version, translating anew, and using *burhan* as the key word for "God." Thus two main New Testament translations emerged between 1990 and 1997: the United Bible Societies' *Shin Geree* and the MBTC's *Shin Geree: Bibel.*

By the end of the twentieth century the Mongolian Church itself had not yet resolved this issue, but in the providence of God, disputes over terminology did not slow the growth of the Church. The key point was that there was a colloquial Khalka-Mongol version of the New Testament available as soon as Mongolia opened to the Gospel. Moreover, almost everyone in Mongolia was literate and could read it. And lastly, curiosity played a big part: here was something new to Mongolia, well presented and well distributed. The New Testament had a context; it was usually coupled with the *Jesus* film and good preaching. Any terminology questions were explained or discussed in the context of a worshipping Christian community.

Cooperation

With a clean missiological slate confronting them, it was tempting for expatriate Christians to act independently in Mongolia. Some did so, but most realized the benefits of working together. There was an encouraging amount of grass-roots cooperation, vision sharing, and praying together. Formal and informal partnerships gave rise to various aid and development projects, an international church and an international school, the Union Bible Training Centre (UBTC), and the Mongolian Centre for Theological Education by Extension (MCTEE). Joint planning also resulted in an annual ministry consultation, city-wide evangelistic campaigns, a combined "March for Jesus" through the streets of Ulaanbaatar, music-writing workshops, combined worship services, joint Easter and Christmas celebrations, and united legal efforts in response to the 1993 Law on the Relationship of Church and State. A single project in the countryside might feature an evangelistic team from one of the Ulaanbaatar churches, donated woolen clothing from a foreign aid agency, and a resident foreign teacher from yet another international Christian agency.

There was cooperation with the government, too. Christian agencies provided English teachers, veterinarians, teacher trainers, agriculturalists, doctors, aid-workers, financial consultants, and environmental specialists either under direct contract to government departments or in partnership with inter-agency government projects. Christians promoted the spiritual welfare of the nation, but also witnessed to the love of Christ by providing vital services for the physical welfare of Mongolia. In this way Christians gained credibility with the government.

Joint work by Protestant, Catholic and Orthodox Christians was a frontier of partnership that was still being explored in the 1990s. Exactly what form it would eventually take was not clear, but a united front would have surely spoken volumes to the nation. Mongols have had exposure to Orthodox Christianity due to the large numbers of Russians who lived in the country during the Communist era. The Catholic order of the

CICM gained a presence in Mongolia due to an invitation by past-president Ochirbat for Rome to establish a Papal embassy in the country. In the late 1990s the CICM had its own building, a viable congregation and was involved in much charity work in Ulaanbaatar.

Church Planting

Church planting was the major emphasis of the expatriate Christians who entered Mongolia in the 1990s. With a population of only 2.5 million, some saw the possibility of winning the whole nation for Christ, and many Mongol Christians, too, believed this was attainable. Even though foreign Christians made a genuine effort to learn the Mongol language, it was the Mongols themselves who kept the momentum for the evangelization of their own people. And who better to do it? Some churches systematically prayed through, evangelized, and established house groups in stairwells, then buildings, housing estates, suburbs and so to whole towns.

In the summers, teams of Mongol Christians went out from Ulaanbaatar and traveled to the provinces to preach, distribute literature and show the *Jesus* film. A house group was often established and the team would then stay on to teach the new believers for a number of weeks. One member might stay on further, or the whole group might return to Ulaanbaatar. After a few months, emerging leaders would be brought to the capital for further training, or Mongolian Bible teachers would be sent to care for the new house group. The new daughter church was encouraged to attend a winter and/or summer camp of the mother church in or near Ulaanbaatar for a week. Leaders were identified and given further training. One Ulaanbaatar church planted 19 daughter churches before its own sixth anniversary.

Expatriate Christians wisely preached the Great Commission right from day one of preaching the Gospel. The Mongolian church grew up familiar with its responsibility to reach out to its own country, and to the nations of the world. Mongolian evangelistic teams had gone to Buryatia (in Russia) and Hohhot (in Chinese Inner Mongolia) by 1996. Within Mongolia itself, Mongols began to evangelise the Khazaks, the Chinese and the residual Russian population.

Leadership Training

With the Mongols quite capable of evangelizing their own country, expatriate Christians found themselves quickly (and rightly) working behind the scenes in a supporting role. Granted, 1990-1993 saw expatriates doing the evangelizing, the organizing, and the church planting. But certainly by 1995, the Church was taking on a Mongolian face and fewer foreigners were seen "up front." The Law of the Relationship of Church and State ensured a lower profile for expatriate Christians. With trainable leadership identified, expatriate Christians found a place in teaching and training the emerging Mongolian pastors, evangelists, and church planters.

By the turn of the century, leadership training had become a high priority for mission in Mongolia. Individual churches experimented with training their own people; Sunday school teachers, home group leaders, and the like. The Union Bible Training Centre, an inter-church and inter-agency Bible College, was set up to provide high quality, in-country leadership training. The Mongolian Centre for Theological Education by Extension was started in 1995, providing distance learning courses to pastors who couldn't come into Ulaanbaatar for training. A number of Mongol leaders won scholarships to seminaries and Bible Colleges in America, Singapore, Australia, and Europe.

Others were called to produce resources for the church. A number of translation and research projects were started to equip pastors with books in Mongolian so that there would be no need for them to learn other Asian or even European languages in order to use Bible references or to read Christian literature.

The Mongolian Church
at the Close of the Century

At the end of the twentieth century, Mongolian Christians faced three long-term challenges. The first of these was to understand the Mongol Christian Church's place in history, right back to the planting of the Nestorian Church. Christianity in effect pre-dates Tibetan Buddhism amongst the Mongols, and it can be rightly argued historically that Christianity, especially Asian (as opposed to Western) Christianity has a legitimate place in Mongolia today. Christian Mongols also needed to think clearly about their own culture and experiment with ways of expressing Christian truth and worship in Mongolian ways. The challenge of "mongolizing" Christianity into culturally appropriate forms will be ongoing.

The second challenge was to play a significant role in nation building. In the late 1990s Mongolia began "opening the books" on 70 years of Communism. Atrocities, missing persons, purges and mismanagement were beginning to be addressed. There was a great opportunity for Mongolian Christians to preach, demonstrate, and lead the nation in acts of genuine reconciliation, which would bring honour to Christ and His Church. With the legal precedent for toleration set down by Chinggis in the *yasa*, the Mongolian church had every right to be in the forefront of political and social change. However, this in and of itself is a major challenge: how long does the spoon have to be to dine with Caesar? At best, the state has historically been tolerant of diverse religious expression in as much as religion should support the political status quo. The Christian church should always pray for wisdom in its relationship with the State, and genuinely seek to incarnate itself into the Mongolian psyche, worldview and culture.

The third challenge was that of Tibetan Buddhism. The immense social changes of the 1990s led to a natural renaissance of Tibetan Buddhism in Mongolia as in other parts of the Tibetan Buddhist world, due to the renewed freedom to express the religion of pre-Communist Mongolia. Idols were rebuilt, novices recruited, lamas began writing in the newspapers, and once again began to dictate the rhythms of family and national life. Many of the young Christians know little of Tibetan Buddhism, observing it only from afar, but nevertheless pressed upon to embrace it to some degree. With a growing diasporan Mongolian population around the world, Tibetan Buddhism may well act as a cultural glue during times of transition. Nevertheless, Christian churches are being established today amongst diasporan Mongolians resident in Korea, the United States, and throughout Asia.

By the end of the twentieth century the Mongolian Church was aware of and seeking to address the great spiritual struggle ahead of it. It was a church reborn on solid historical precedents in a time when the nation was at its most crucial turning point. In a land that has witnessed warfare for centuries – both in the grand clash of great civilizations as well as inter-tribal disputes and bickerings – the Christian church simply cannot afford to be sectarian and dysfunctional. There is a growing consensus among both Mongolian and expatriate Christian leaders that the way forward for the church in Mongolia must be one of unity. The Mongolians display character that would be a credit to any missionary: a simple life style, agility, the ability to survive in a harsh climate, innovation, and daring to go anywhere and do anything. In God's timing, and in his grace, Mongolia's modern Christian church will continue to bear a solid witness to Christ in the nation and graciously continue to live out the power and truth of the Gospel.

CHAPTER 8

Susan's Journey

I t was a long, hot climb up to the Tibetan monastery for Vivian and her friend John. By the time they reached the monastery's tea shop they were ready for a rest. As they entered, they were greeted by an Australian girl named Susan. Susan had recently become a Tibetan Buddhist, and she was living at the monastery while she studied for her initiation. She told John and Vivian about her lama's *dharma* teachings, and the difference these teachings had made in her life. After listening closely to Susan's examples, Vivian and John talked with Susan about their faith in Christ. Susan replied: "You've found a way that helps you, but I've found that the Buddha dharma helps me. And if Christ is the only way to salvation, then one of us is right and the other is wrong, and that simply can't be. All religions are just different ways of getting to the same place."

Susan's reply is familiar to many Christians who have Tibetan Buddhist friends. From a Tibetan Buddhist viewpoint, all religions are equally true because ultimate truth lies beyond any apparent contradictions in doctrine. Tibetan Buddhists often compare the world's religions to different paths up the same mountain. One path may be steep, another more gradual, but all of them reach the top.[429] But is this an accurate view? Are Christianity and Tibetan Buddhism really just different paths up the same mountain? One way of finding out is to follow each path step by step, to see where it leads. In this chapter we will follow the path of Tibetan Buddhism in Asia, while in the following chapter we will follow the path of the philosophical form of Tibetan Buddhism that has become popular internationally.

To begin, it may help to consider whether the "different paths" are in fact "paths." The Buddhist way of life truly *is* a path in the sense that the traveler makes progress by his or her own effort. If that effort ceases, progress stops. The first step on this path is to recognize that one is in control of one's ultimate spiritual destiny, and that the proper set of practices (applied in the right order) will result in spiritual liberation. The Christian way is not a path in the sense that the traveler makes no progress by his or her own effort. Indeed, the first step is to recognize that one's own moral efforts are completely useless in attaining the ultimate goal. The traveler's progress depends entirely upon God's undeserved favor; it is made only in complete dependence on Christ who is himself the way to salvation.[430] In terms of spiritual effort, the Buddhist way is a path to be walked, the Christian way is a vehicle to be ridden.

Each path has a guide. Susan's teachers told her that to follow the Buddhist path, she must find and rely on a qualified spiritual teacher or guru. While reading a famous text by the third Dalai Lama, she learned that she would be expected to give this teacher offerings of material things, devotion, practice, personal service, and always to consider him as faultless and infallible.[431] Total surrender to her teacher would be essential in the tantric phase of her spiritual practice.[432] By contrast, God Himself is the faultless and infallible Guide on the Christian path. Jesus taught that material things, devotion, service, faultlessness, and infallibility belong to Him alone.[433] Jesus never encouraged cult-like devotion to merely human teachers, and no doubt many Christians have been saved from abuses by this teaching.

Step One: The World Around Us

As she began her spiritual journey, Susan took the world for granted, believing implicitly that what she saw, heard, and touched was actually there. But her spiritual teacher's first lesson had been that no one can trust the evidence of their senses, because our human perception of the world is mistaken.[434] Tibetan Buddhism takes its view of the world from the monistic pantheism of the Vedic and Brahmanic sages (see Chapter Three). In this Indian view of the world, nothing exists independently because everything is part of an ultimate, impersonal ground of existence which is neither good nor evil. It is devoid of personality, intention, or emotion. It simply *is*. The Mahayana Buddhists undermined even this idea of an absolute by claiming that nothing is ultimately real, and that a "void" or "emptiness" is the foundation of the universe. Jesus' view is much different. He said that He was one with the good, self-existent, and personal God who made everything there is.[435] This God made a real world, distinct from Himself, for man to live in. God's world is a good place for man to be, because God made it. Best of all, man is created to have a relationship with God who is wise, holy, good, free, loving, gracious, merciful, forgiving, and just; in other words, with a God who is personal and who cares about man in a real sense. Jesus' God is not an "it," but a Person.

Susan's lama told her that the things that are "truly real" lie beyond what we can see or know.[436] He said that on this deeper plane, everything is the same as everything else. Apparently opposite things like good and evil, or truth and error, are part of the world of mistaken perceptions and have no ultimate meaning.[437] Once men and women reach an intuitive realization of the emptiness of the universe, and rid themselves of the illusion that they are unique personalities, they have no further need for ideas like good and evil.[438] Again, Jesus' view is much different. He taught his disciples that truth and goodness are rooted in the character of God.[439] Good and evil are more than just rules for proper behavior, they are absolute categories with eternal significance, and man can never rise to some metaphysical plane where they do not make a difference. Good and evil will matter for all eternity.

Susan's lama also taught her that nothing has a permanent existence of its own.[440] Men and women and the world around them are like phantoms in a twilight zone between reality and fantasy. Far from having souls, or even stable personalities, people are just ever-changing manifestations of the law of cause and effect.[441] Much to her surprise, Susan found that this was not just an abstract philosophical idea, but a part of the everyday thinking of her Asian Tibetan Buddhist friends. Jesus always treated his listeners as real people with real fears and real hopes for the future. He based his teachings on the fact that God made each person with a unique and lasting personality. As unique men and women, people can have a unique relationship with a personal God. As Jesus said: "For my Father's will is that everyone who looks to the Son and believes in him shall have eternal life, and I will raise him up at the last day."[442]

Jesus told his followers that not only are people real, but what they see and hear and feel is real, too. Jesus' attitude towards reality can be seen in the way he treated one of his disciples named Thomas, who had doubts about whether Jesus had really risen from the tomb. Jesus appeared to Thomas and commanded him to look at his risen body, to see the prints of the nails and feel the wound in his side. Convinced by the evidence of his senses, the disciple cried, "My Lord and my God!" Because of events like this, the early Christians insisted that God had appeared in history in a real and tangible way. As one of them wrote of Jesus: "That which was from the beginning, which we have *heard,* which we have *seen* with our eyes, which we have *looked at* and our hands have *touched,* this we proclaim concerning the Word of Life."[443] Men and women need not grope for the truth in a metaphysical fog, because God has revealed the truth in a form available to everyone.

Step Two: Unseen Things

Susan's lama told her that when she died, an impersonal life force would leave her body and be reborn in another body shortly afterwards.[444] Like other Tibetan Buddhist teachers, Susan's lama offered five proofs that rebirth is a fact:

1. Different people have different temperaments and abilities. Some people always seem to be happy while others are gloomy. Some children are good at mathematics while others excel at music. The reason for such differences is that all of these people have had previous lives in which they were happy or sad, or gifted with ability in mathematics or music.

2. If people have minds and personal characteristics now, then they must have had them in the past. Since nothing can

arise without a cause, people's present personalities arose from personalities in former lives.

3. Things that happen in dreams are actually occurrences of a previous life. One respected monk wrote that if one often dreams of flying, then in a past life one was able to fly.[445]

4. Supposed incidents have occurred in which people could recall past lives.

5. Buddhist scriptures teach the doctrine of rebirth.[446]

None of these "proofs" demonstrate the reality of rebirth, of course. To say that individual character arises from events in a previous life is an assumption, not a proof. The same argument applies to dreams as a "proof" of former lives. While there have been instances of people claiming to remember past lives, most of these people lived in places where there were social, cultural, or even monetary rewards for making such claims.[447] Finally, if the doctrine of rebirth is true, it is strange that even the most accomplished lamas cannot remember their own past lives, though a few have claimed to be able to do so.[448] When examined closely, the doctrine of rebirth remains an unproven assumption.[449] In place of rebirth, Jesus proclaimed a resurrection. As he told one of his friends: "I am the resurrection and the life. He who believes in me will live, even though he dies; and whoever lives and believes in me will never die."[450] Jesus' promise of resurrection excludes the possibility of rebirth and re-death. Resurrection to a joyous and eternal personal relationship with God offers a better hope than a dreary succession of rebirths followed by the metaphysical extinction of nirvana.

Susan's lama taught her that those who do evil in this life will pay for it in the next, and those who do what is right will be rewarded.[451] This arrangement seems fair on the surface, and all Tibetan Buddhists seem to believe it, but it is marked by a number of serious flaws. To see them in action, consider the following case: Dawa is a Tibetan friend who is serious about her religious life. She tries to gain merit for her next rebirth by practicing meditation, giving generously to the local monks, and being kind to animals. But like all people, Dawa occasionally does things she knows aren't right. How will the law of karma work in her life? First of all, Dawa's good works will earn a certain amount of merit, and her faults will earn a certain amount of demerit. But even Dawa's slightest fault will earn far more demerit than her good works will earn merit, because the system is set up to work this way.[452] When Dawa takes stock of her merits and demerits, she finds that even though her good actions outnumber her bad ones, the demerit built up by her faults outweighs the merit built up by her good works.

Anxious about this, she tries to make more merit. Because Dawa can "sin" without knowing it, but can only make merit when she consciously tries to, her demerits accumulate at a faster rate than her merits. In this way Dawa accumulates a colossal load of karmic debt that she can never repay. Now suppose that Dawa dies. Because of her demerits, she is reborn as a beggar girl named Mingma who is abandoned in the street. But Mingma cannot remember her former life as Dawa. She has no idea why she is suffering from hunger, cold, and abuse. Even worse, in her unhappy new life as Mingma she accumulates new sins. The balance of her merits and demerits grows steadily worse. Mingma's poverty prevents her from making merit through religious ceremonies and expensive gifts to the monasteries. Awash in a sea of karmic debt, Mingma becomes a living illustration of Milarepa's proverb: "Religion is forbidden to the poor."[453] The story of Dawa and Mingma shows why rebirth and karma can never reward good actions or punish bad ones. Since people's personalities perish at death and only an impersonal life force is reborn, no one *ever* suffers for their own sins. Mingma suffered because of the sins of Dawa, whom she had never even met. This is not justice, but pointless misery.[454]

Sociologists have studied the effects of this belief upon Tibetan Buddhist peoples. Most Tibetan Buddhists who do not become monks or nuns assume that they will be reborn as human beings. Those who do good in this life will be reborn rich and powerful in the next life, while those with little merit will be reborn poor and despised. The rich often do not care about the poor, for the poor are only suffering the bad results of their bad deeds in a previous life. The poor suffer in silence, for the system teaches them that the rich have earned their privileges by good deeds in past lives.[455] But Jesus breaks any such link between wealth and virtue, or poverty and punishment. On one occasion he met a man who had been born blind. Jesus' disciples asked him whose sin had caused the blind man's suffering, and he replied that it was no one's fault, and restored the man's sight. At another time Jesus was told of a building collapse that had killed 18 people. He asked his listeners: "Do you think that they were more guilty than all the others living in Jerusalem? I tell you, no!"[456]

For people like Dawa and Mingma who are burdened with a crushing load of karmic debt and who can't afford expensive rituals, Tibetan Buddhism offers little hope of escape.[457] But Jesus said: "Come to me all you who are weary and burdened, and I will give you rest." Jesus offers forgiveness of sins and freedom from the burdens that so many Tibetan Buddhists carry. He brings men and women into a new relationship with Himself that no karma can ever destroy, for nothing can separate us from God's love.[458] Not only does Jesus offer a better hope for mercy, he also offers a better hope for justice. Take the case of Lha Sang Khan, who by treachery and murder deposed the sixth Dalai Lama in 1706. Lha Sang was himself murdered in 1717, but even his own death would not have erased the karmic debt he had built up during his bloodthirsty career. Suppose that Lha Sang becomes a worm for his next thousand rebirths in order to work off his karma. How can a mere worm possibly suffer the justice that is due to Lha Sang Khan? This is where Jesus offers a better hope. He once told the story of a rich man who completely ignored a beggar outside his gate. The rich man had no concern for others and thought only of himself. In the end he died and went to hell, while the poor man he had ignored went to heaven. The rich man in hell is still himself, not a dumb animal or another person. He knows that he is suffering for his own sins. He recognizes the poor man in heaven and begs for mercy, but finds that it is too late. Justice must be served.

The theme of justice and eternal judgment was often on Jesus' lips. He constantly warned of God's final judgment upon all men. In many parables and stories he taught that those who did not believe in Him and those who would not demonstrate their belief by the quality of their lives would be eternally condemned.[459] Yet He invited all men everywhere to leave their sins and come to Him for forgiveness and mercy. This ideal balance of justice and mercy is unlike anything in the dreadful round of suffering facing Tibetan Buddhists like Mingma and Dawa.

As she made her way to the monastery each morning, Susan noticed the temple pictures of the gods. Gods (*lha* in Tibetan) are another part of the unseen world of Tibetan Buddhism. Susan's lama told her that the gods are only projections of peoples' minds, and have no reality of their own. But her Tibetan friends know many gods, most of which have two forms: a fierce, threatening form with multiple heads and arms, and a benign form that is absorbed in its own happiness. The benign gods are just as weak, disinterested, and uncaring about the human world as they have been since the shaman first sought their favor at the dawn of history. These gods must constantly be bribed with food and invoked with costly rituals. The Sherpa people of Nepal feel that these rituals must be performed often, or else the gods may just go away.[460] The fierce forms are either the earth and locality spirits known so well to the people of ancient Shangshung, or the bloodthirsty tantric deities imported from Kashmir and India for their supposed magical powers.[461] The primary emotion evoked by these petty godlings is *fear:* fear of sickness or misfortune if they are not placated, fear of disaster if their power is mishandled in some way. By contrast, Jesus had much to say about God. He told his listeners that God was not remote at all, but intimately concerned with their everyday affairs. They could even trust him for their daily needs, as Jesus explained: "So do not worry, saying `What shall we eat?' or `What shall we drink?' or `What shall we wear?' For the pagans run after all these things, and your heavenly Father knows that you need them. But seek first His kingdom and His righteousness, and all these things will be given to you as well. Therefore do not worry about tomorrow, for tomorrow will worry about itself."[462] No rituals are needed to keep the interest of Jesus' God, for He loves the creatures He has made.

Step Three: The Doctrines of the Middle Way

Susan's first steps on the Tibetan Buddhist path brought her to accept that everything in the universe is empty of ultimate existence, and that she must realize this emptiness for herself through a direct mystical experience.[463] This first step made her what philosophers call a monistic (everything is one) pantheist (everything is god). Her second step along the path was to accept the doctrines of rebirth and karma. In the third step, she accepted Siddartha Gautama's basic teachings, and became a Buddhist. Siddartha Gautama's followers summarized his teachings in a set of principles known as the "The Four Truths" (see Chapter Three).

1. The first of Siddartha's truths was that all life involved suffering, and he made this point in a graphic way. One day a mother came to him carrying a dead child in her arms. She begged the famous teacher to restore her child to life. Siddartha listened, then sent her out to get a mustard seed from a house where no one had suffered the same grief and loss that she had. After a long search, she returned empty handed.[464] Jesus was faced with the same situation. He was entering a town one day when a funeral procession emerged from the city gates. A widow had lost her only son, and the mourners were carrying him out to be buried. When Jesus saw the widow, he told her not to cry, and restored her son to life.[465] Jesus' and Siddartha's views of suffering and death could not have been more different. Siddartha saw suffering as a disease to be cured by withdrawing from the world and denying its existence. Jesus saw suffering as an evil with the seeds of redemption in it, and held up his own suffering as a model for all who would follow Him. He told his disciples: "If anyone would come after me, he must deny himself and take up his cross and follow me. For whoever wants to save his life will lose it, but whoever loses his life for me will find it."[465]

2. In his famous "Sermon on Burning," Siddartha taught that all of humanity is aflame with covetousness, desire, and greed.[467] He believed that these experiences are wrong not because they are offenses against a righteous God, but because they contribute to man's illusion that he is a unique individual. It is this illusion that causes rebirth and suffering. Jesus always encouraged people's natural sense that they were individual, personal beings. He held out the promise of eternal life with a personal God: "For my Father's will is that everyone who looks to the Son and believes in Him shall have eternal life, and I will raise him up at the last day."[468] And again: "I am the resurrection and the life. He who believes in me will live, even though he dies; and whoever lives and believes in me will never die."[469]

3. Siddartha taught that the only way to be free from suffering was to eliminate desire; at first by leaving acts of selfishness, later by withdrawing from the world, and finally by losing one's personality in the Buddhist void. From the beginning Buddhism was a monastic religion whose highest virtues could only be realized by cutting attachments to home, family, neighbors, and even oneself. But Jesus encouraged, and even commanded, his followers to be involved in the world. Love for God and others was at the center of his teachings: "Love the Lord your God with all your heart and with all your soul . . and your neighbor as yourself," he said.[470] The love that Jesus preached was not just a benevolent attitude towards others, but a practical love that applied itself in everyday life. To show what it was like, He told the story of a man who was beaten, robbed, and left for dead. A foreigner found him and bandaged his wounds, helped him to an inn, nursed him back to health, and paid his bill.[471] This is the kind of love that Jesus commanded: it is involved in the world.

4. Finally, Siddartha taught that a path of simple morality and good works could set men and women free from suffering. At first one practiced such virtues as nonviolence (not killing animals), chastity, telling the truth, and abstaining from theft,

drugs, and alcohol. In later stages of the path one gained the magical powers which were so sought-after by the shamanist peoples of Central Asia. All four steps of the path were taken by one's own self-effort over many lifetimes. Jesus taught his disciples that their own efforts to lead a good life were not good enough to meet the standards of a holy and righteous God. The only one good enough to meet God's standards was Jesus himself. Through faith in Jesus, God would accept Jesus' righteousness as the believer's own. This promise of forgiveness of sins and an eternal personal existence with God was what Jesus called the good news.

These, then, were Siddartha Gautama's Four Noble Truths, and he encouraged his followers not to take them on faith, but to see if they were true in their own mystical experience. Mysticism was at the heart of Siddartha's way of deliverance. Because it is a completely personal experience (I cannot see your vision, and you cannot understand my dream) mysticism cannot be judged by any outside standard. The inherent subjectivism of the Buddhist path led to so many new interpretations of Siddartha's teachings that tantric Buddhism accepted all the gods, priests, sacrifices, and rituals that Siddartha himself had rejected. As we saw in Chapter Three, his simple religion of self reliance was swept away by a cataract of mysticism, magic, and occultism. Jesus always pointed to an objective standard, encouraging his listeners to judge his message by the rule of the Hebrew Scriptures.[472] Based on this standard, all were welcome to see for themselves that Jesus' teachings were not his own, but God's. As He said: "My teaching is not my own. It comes from him who sent me. If anyone chooses to do God's will, he will find out whether my teaching comes from God or whether I speak on my own. He who speaks on his own does so to gain honor for himself, but he who works for the honor of the one who sent him is a man of truth; there is nothing false about him."[473]

Step Four: The Great Vehicle

After taking her first three steps, Susan was a Buddhist. But her lama spent very little time talking about Siddartha Gautama and his teachings. Instead, he encouraged her to dedicate herself to saving all the beings in the universe by becoming a *chang chub sempa*, or boddhisattva.[474] The ancient Indian Mahayana Buddhists taught that every person could become a Buddha by postponing their own entrance into nirvana while working for the enlightenment of others. They called the mere wish to do this *compassion*, and praised it as Mahayana's greatest virtue. In Tibetan Buddhist thinking, compassion is a mental attitude that comes from meditation. The person who is meditating considers the sufferings of others and thinks how nice it would be if they were free from suffering.[475] They then resolve to devote their own meditative practice to ending the suffering of every being in the universe. In other words, a person becomes compassionate merely by thinking about compassion,[476] one of the many ways in which Tibetan Buddhism substitutes pleasant thoughts for good deeds. But Jesus had a very different kind of compassion. When He felt compassion, he urged others to pray,[477] healed the sick,[478] raised the dead,[479] and fed the hungry.[480] His compassion did not withdraw into itself, or merely wish for the benefit of others. It expressed itself in action. Jesus taught his listeners that those who believe in Him would show the same kind of compassion that He had.[481] As one of his disciples later said: "Dear children, let us not love with words or tongue but with actions and in truth."[482] Jesus' compassion is involved in the needs of real people in the real world.

The Mahayanists taught that truth has a dual nature, relative and absolute. Relative truth is for religious novices, who need the guidance of ideas like good and evil to avoid accumulating demerit. But in Tibetan Buddhism, good and evil have no ultimate meaning, because ultimate truth is *inclusive:* that is, all seeming opposites are really the same.[483] Ideas of good, evil, and conventional morality are like a boat that a traveler uses to cross a stream. Once across, the boat is no longer useful and is left behind. In the same way, tantric Buddhists no longer need to worry about good and evil because they have crossed the stream into the realm of so-called absolute truth. In this way, they believe themselves to have transcended conventional morality.[484] Jesus had much to say about truth. His truth is the same for the humblest sinner and the greatest saint, for in His view, good and evil are not shadows that fade away in a metaphysical fog, but eternal truths rooted in the nature and character of God, whose essence is goodness and whose Spirit is truth. As he told his listeners: "If you hold to my teaching, you are really my disciples. Then you will know the truth, and the truth will set you free."[485] In Jesus' world, truth is naturally *exclusive*. When the truth comes, error and falsehood are exposed. Jesus taught that He was himself the truth, and His word is the standard of truth by which all others are to be judged. Since He is himself the single, simple truth, other approaches to God and other attempts to find ultimate meaning for man are doomed to failure. As Jesus put it: "I am the way, and the truth, and the life. No one comes to the Father except through me."[486]

Step Five: The Dark Side

As an Australian Buddhist, Susan was only vaguely aware that her Tibetan friends believe in a lively (and often terrifying) spirit world. Her lama moved through this world with the aid of tantra, which he said she could learn once she had made more spiritual progress. Though the tantric scriptures claim his authority, tantra was unknown to the historical Buddha. It is a gnostic religion whose secret rituals are shared only with carefully initiated disciples, who study under the complete control of a tantric master. Central to tantric practice are magic rituals, sometimes using human body parts,[487] which exploit the occult power of wrathful deities in order to become enlightened in a single lifetime. Jesus knew nothing of secret doctrines for the select few. As he said to his disciples: "What I tell you in the dark, speak in the daylight." He proclaimed the truth openly to all, and his way of salvation was the same for all. His disciples recognized this transparent and open quality in Jesus' life. One of them wrote of the coming of Jesus: "In him was life, and that life was the light of men. The light shines in the darkness, but the darkness has not understood it."[488]

The Goal: Nirvana or Heaven?

Siddartha Gautama's *Sermon on Burning* taught his disciples that the entire world is aflame with the desire for personal existence. When a Buddhist destroys the illusion that he or she is a unique and independently existing personal being, these flames are extinguished. Rebirth and suffering end, and the Buddhist's impersonal life-force merges with the void (i.e. enters nirvana). Later Buddhists taught that one could delay entry into nirvana for the benefit of others; or perhaps seek rebirth in one of the many paradises (Buddha fields). Jesus taught that man's ultimate goal was an eternal and joyful fellowship with God. Christians do not enter some vague metaphysical state of extinction, but continue to be unique people, even having personal names.[489] They would enjoy the company of other believers and of the God who made them. Nor would there ever be any suffering. As one of Jesus' disciples wrote after a vision of heaven: "There will be no more death or mourning or crying or pain, for the old order of things has passed away."[490]

Susan's spiritual journey began with a search for meaning. In Tibetan Buddhism she found something excitingly exotic and quite different from the other religions she had tried. Her lama taught her that her world was not a real place, and that her personality was just an illusion. She believed that her unhappiness was a residue of unremembered sins in lives forgotten long ago. Convinced that the only way of escape lay in mystical experiences, she turned away from her friends, her family, and even her own personality to seek peace in tantric Buddhism. As time passed, Susan's natural gift for compassion and caring dwindled away in a self-centered search for liberation. When her lama told her she was ready for tantric practices, she meditated for weeks and repeated magic formulas literally hundreds of thousands of times.[491] After years of mystic rituals, secret teachings, and merit making, she spent her time sitting in the dark, trying to visualize a multiheaded half-human deity[492] whose appearance frightened her more each day. Her lama told her that when she could become what she saw, she would be well on her way to liberation.

Susan's Christian friends followed a different teacher, Jesus Christ. Jesus' teachings begin with real people who live in a real world. All of these people, the best and the worst alike, are imperfect in God's sight (and, if they are honest, in their own sight as well). Their only hope is in God's certain mercy. Those who trust in God's mercy have no need of magical formulas, mystical experiences, or withdrawal from society. Instead, they are in the world and doing good. They feed the hungry, they give the thirsty something to drink, they invite the stranger in, they clothe the naked, they care for the sick, and they visit those who are in prisons (the kinds without bars as well as the places for criminals).[493] Susan's insistence that the Buddhist way and the Christian way are two paths to the same goal could not be more mistaken. Tibetan Buddhism is the path of mystic occultism, superstition, and ultimate despair. Jesus Christ's is the path to life.

Tibetan Buddhism and the Life of Nations

Tibetan Buddhism has had profound effects on the lives of individuals like Susan's. What about its effect on entire peoples? How has Tibetan Buddhism changed the lives of the Central Asian peoples who accepted it?

1) **Monism:** The philosophical heart of Buddhism and Hinduism is belief in the unity of all existence, or what philosophers call *monism*. In Chapters Three and Four we saw that this view of reality leads to a fatally compromised view of truth. The denial that things truly exist on their own had tragic consequences in the lives of millions of Hindus and Buddhists. If the world around us isn't "really there," then any sort of objective record of

history is pointless, as is any meaningful investigation by the natural sciences. In such an environment, the roots of modern science, education, technology, and health could not develop, and for many years these foundations of a better material life were deliberately excluded from Tibetan Buddhist countries.[494] While other Asian nations were developing in the nineteenth and early twentieth centuries, the Tibetan Buddhist world languished in poverty. Japan leaped from feudalism into modern times in the 40 years between the Meiji Restoration in 1868 and the Russo-Japanese War in 1904. China built shipyards, foundries, and textile mills during the same period. And India developed its own system of railroads, irrigation schemes, and manufacturing concerns.[495] None of these things happened in any predominantly Tibetan Buddhist country. All remained tightly closed to outside influences, at tremendous cost to their national well being. To the present day the Tibetan Buddhist world is among the least developed parts of Asia. In the end, even the Tibetans saw that the single minded pursuit of their religion had cost them dearly. In the refugee camps of India, increasing numbers of Tibetans realized the link between their religion and their lack of economic and political development.[496] The sad irony is that one of the world's most religious peoples was kept in ignorance, poverty, and fear for generations.

2) **The World as Illusion:** If the world around us isn't "really there," then critical thinking is pointless, and what sociologists call *intuitional thinking* comes to dominate intellectual life. Reality and fantasy became impossible to separate from each other. It is not an accident that modern science arose in Christian Europe and not in Hindu India or Buddhist Tibet. This is not because European Christians are smarter or in some way superior to Inner Asian Buddhists. It is because they believed that a divinely created world is significant because God made it, and therefore it was worth investigating.

3) **Rebirth and Karma:** Belief in an endless cycle of rebirth governed by the iron law of karma gives rise to a circular view of history in which progress is impossible and human destiny unchangeable. Fatalism rooted itself deeply in both Hin-

duism and Buddhism, causing profound effects at all levels of society, from the apartheid-like caste system to the root causes of ancient India's grinding poverty. If poverty, suffering, and other social ills are simply the results of evil deeds in forgotten lives, then there is no point in trying to alleviate suffering or better the lot of the poor and oppressed.

4) Merit and Offering: The resources demanded by merit-making and offerings diverted time, effort, and money into unproductive channels. Though the choice to do this was free and politically unconstrained, the diverted resources undoubtedly accounted for a significant fraction of the gross domestic product of even larger states like Tibet and Mongolia,[497] to say nothing of smaller and poorer areas like Ladakh, Bhutan, or Tuva.

5) Detachment: The ideal of detachment has shattered family life in many Tibetan Buddhist countries. The withdrawal of the old, the retreat of the young in monasteries, and the fragile status of marriage has taken a heavy toll on the integrity of the family.

6) Tantra: The gnostic ethos of tantra permeated the monasteries and caused the monks to keep even their written language to themselves, resulting in illiteracy and poverty for the common people. From tantra came the belief that monks had supernatural powers, and on this basis were best qualified to govern. The identification of Tibetan Buddhism with the state retarded political progress, since questioning the state was the same as questioning religion. A single-minded preoccupation with religion blinded the leaders of most Tibetan Buddhist countries to the political developments that took place around them during the pivotal nineteenth and early twentieth centuries. The Chinese encouraged the rule of the lamas in Mongolia in order to keep the country weak and divided, a policy which succeeded brilliantly from 1689 to 1911. While some of the Dalai Lamas were able men who served their people well, others were weak or in their childhood at critical times in Tibetan history. The weakness of the sixth Dalai Lama provided the occasion for a Mongol invasion. Later, the government of Tibet deliberately closed the country to trade and economic development from 1792 to 1959. The fourteenth Dalai Lama was made ruler of Tibet when he was only 16, just when China's Maoist government asserted its control and the Tibetans were in need of experienced leadership. Overall, the lamaist theocracies of Tibet and Mongolia failed catastrophically in leading their respective peoples through the challenges facing them at the end of the second millennium.

7) **Shamanism**: The animistic beliefs of the shamans, taken over and modified by the lamas, kept the people in a state of fear and dependency. As we have seen, the shamanic world swarms with evil spirits who must be placated, worshipped, and manipulated. The commonest decisions of everyday life are made in a haze of fear and ignorance exploited by oracles, astrologers, and spirit mediums. There could be no clearer illustration of the fact that man's ideas about God do, in fact, matter.[498]

Tibetan Buddhists Look At Christianity

Having looked at Tibetan Buddhism through Christian eyes, it would seem only fair to look at Christianity in the light of Tibetan Buddhism. But just as with adding fractions, religions really need to be expressed in common denominators in order to compare them meaningfully. Stripped of its philosophical trappings, tantric Buddhism is a *technique*, a status it shares with its shamanist sibling. Tantra puts man at the center of existence and seeks to manipulate both nature and supernature for human benefit. At its very core, tantra is magical in the sense that it is what one *does* to manipulate the supernatural in one's favor. Christianity is in essence a *religion*, a status it shares with its Judaic parent. Both Christianity and Judaism put God at the center of existence, and humanity in a decidedly secondary position. For the Christian, truth has a very hard-edged exclusivity about it; for it draws very sharp lines between orthodoxy and heresy. To compare an occult-magical technique with a major world religion claiming ultimate truth is a hazardous undertaking indeed.

From a Buddhist point of view, it seems impossibly narrow-minded to assert that one religion is absolutely true while other religions are not. The unity of opposites and the inclusive nature of truth are so deeply ingrained in Tibetan Buddhist thinking that even when two religions make logically incompatible assertions, they can both be accepted as ultimately true, for (from a Christian perspective at least) the categories "true" and "false" have lost all ultimate meaning.[499] Thus the Tibetan Buddhist is entirely sincere, as well as doctrinally orthodox, in asserting that all religions are different paths to the same goal. For these reasons, a truth-based comparison of Tibetan Buddhism and Christianity is impossible *in principle,* for there is no commonly agreed standard on which both religions could agree that a statement is true.[500] This of course does *not* mean that Christians should avoid friendly dialogue with Buddhists! It only means that there is not a commonly agreed standard of truth between the two faiths by which they could determine in principle, on philosophical grounds, which one of them is true.

Since both shamanism and tantric Buddhism are technique-focused rather than truth-focused, from their own side they can (and do) live at philosophical peace with Christianity, Islam, or any other religion. Most Tibetan Buddhists can appreciate Jesus Christ as yet another of the religious teachers of whom their own tradition is so full. Some even regard Jesus as a past incarnation of Buddha. The problem comes with the fact that Christianity and Islam are *missionary* religions. Because most people in the Tibetan Buddhist world sense a deep unity of language, culture, ethnic identity, and religion, the idea of conversion to any other religion causes deep offense. It carries overtones of treason, betrayal of ethnicity, and group shame which most Christians from outside Asia find difficult to understand. For these reasons, people in many parts of the Tibetan Buddhist world say that it is impossible to be both a Christian and a Tibetan, Bhutanese, etc. The sense of outrage at conversion is compounded when well-intended Christian social, medical, or development ministries are perceived as a form of payment for conversion to Christianity, a charge which Tibetan Buddhists (including the fourteenth Dalai Lama) have made again and again.[501]

Another perceptual problem for Christianity has been its missionary methods. Tibetan Buddhist missionaries to countries outside Asia are usually monks who have completed advanced Buddhist studies. They are well-educated within their own tradition and exemplify values that are treasured by Tibetan Buddhist culture. The representatives of Christ to Buddhist Central Asia in former times were often scholarly diplomats like Andrade, Cacella, and Cabral; or first-rank scholars like Desideri, Francke, or Jaeschke. These men had personal qualities which earned them a respectful welcome even in monastic circles. In later years, Tibetan Buddhists were to meet less educated representatives of the Christian faith, whose modern values were more likely to clash with traditional Buddhist culture. At the end of the twentieth century, a North American missions movement appeared which stressed the sociological, as opposed to the spiritual, roots of church growth. It tended to speak about missions in technological terms, and to refer to people groups as "targets." Naturally, this raised barriers of prejudice which had little to do with the message of the Christians, but much to do with their lack of adequate preparation for their task.

Some Tibetan Buddhists have perceived Christian missions as an attempt to change or destroy indigenous cultures.[502] (Western converts to Tibetan Buddhism have been among the most vocal in making these charges.) The reality of the twenty-first century is that there is no such thing as a static culture; *all* cultures are changing. Good mission methods take careful account of those changes and equip local people to deal with them on their own terms. They leave people with a socially positive view of themselves and their potential to act for good in their society. By contrast, Christian mission methods that are culturally insensitive, or that empower youth at the expense of age, or that rely on methods and values borrowed from the Western entertainment industry, do not represent a positive contribution to Tibetan Buddhist societies. Christian missions need to consider their methods very carefully, always seeking to live out the life of Christ in ways that local people can understand and appreciate. We will explore this subject further in Chapters 11 and 12.

CHAPTER 9

Christil and the Western Buddhist

A ndres is a comparative religion professor at a major European university. Each term of the academic year, he teaches his students about the world's major religions, contrasting their histories, philosophies, and development. Though raised in a nominally Catholic home, Andres is a Tibetan Buddhist who reads the Tibetan scriptures and practices daily meditation. On weekends, he and a small group of friends meet for dharma practice. From time to time they go on longer retreats to receive teachings or special empowerments from visiting lamas. Andres finds his life as a Buddhist both fulfilling and exciting. He has visited Tibet and India, learned other languages, and met many like-minded friends. As a person who is comfortable in the world of ideas, he appreciates the philosophy of Tibetan Buddhism, with its rigorous formal logic, elaborate psychology, and exacting analysis of metaphysical issues. He finds an intellectual depth in it that he feels is lacking in Christianity. As he once commented to a friend, "Christianity is a good path for some, but it is a philosophically inferior religion."

In the last half of the twentieth century, Tibetan Buddhism became a truly international religion. As small groups of Tibetan refugees settled in Europe and North America in the early 1960s, they established teaching centers and attracted small groups of disciples. By 1963 the first European Tibetan Buddhist meditation center had been started by Lama Chogyam Trungpa in Dumfriesshire, Scotland. In the 1970s Tibetan Buddhist meditation centers opened in France and Sweden, and by the end of the decade, the Tibetan Buddhist movement was spreading widely in Europe. Tibetan Buddhism entered North America somewhat earlier. In 1952 the Mongol lama Wangyal, spiritual leader of a group of Kalmyk Mongols who fled from the Soviet Union to the United States, started the first Lamaist study center open to Americans. In the following decade, other monks set up Tibetan studies centers at major American universities. By the 1970s they had established Tibetan departments at state universities in Washington, California, Colorado, Wisconsin, and Indiana; eventually all four sects of Tibetan Buddhism established meditation centers in major cities across the United States and Canada. By the turn of the millennium, Tibetan Buddhism had become an international religion, with teaching centers on all six continents.[503] As it continued to spread outside Asia, many people like Andres were attracted to it. Those from European or American cultural backgrounds were often called "Western Tibetan Buddhists" (or "Western Buddhists" for short).

There are a number of reasons why Tibetan Buddhism appeals to people of non-Asian backgrounds. Some try Tibetan Buddhism for its novelty, exotic appeal, or no-guilt, "do-it-yourself" approach to religion. Others are "spiritual tourists" who may have tried other Eastern religions, rock music, drugs, or Zen before Tibetan Buddhism, and might try anything from herbalism to Zoroastrianism afterwards. But beyond these superficial motives lie deeper needs. The author has met many Western Buddhists who have come from broken or abusive homes, or whose past is so painful they find it hard to discuss. Often these people are sincerely looking for answers that will quench their pain and give meaning to their lives. Such people (and there are many) are really searching for the love of Christ without knowing it. They may have chosen Tibetan Buddhism simply because no one has yet demonstrated God's love for them. Other people find Buddhism intellectually attractive. Outside Asia, Tibetan monks present tantric Buddhism as a philosophical religion with valuable contributions to make to society at large. They have been quick to identify Buddhist doctrines with the concerns of the human rights, environmental, and peace movements. Such contacts serve as "bridges" across which important segments of a given non-Asian population can be introduced to tantric Buddhist teachings. Similar links have been formed through the language, sociology, and comparative religion departments of major colleges and universities. Tibetan Buddhists have used these contact points to introduce their religion to a wide audience.[504] More traditional means of spreading lamaist teachings include local study groups, retreats, and Tibetan cultural programs. Some of these centers offer courses in Tibetan art, culture, language, philosophy, or Buddhist perspectives on the environment or world peace as a way of attracting converts, interest, and funds.

The form and emphasis of the Tibetan Buddhism taught in these centers differs from that described in Chapter Five. The religion's shamanist and folk Buddhist beliefs and practices have been discarded and Tibetan Buddhism is presented as a philosophical system, sometimes through a prescribed Western-style curriculum leading to a degree. A typical curriculum might include classes in Tibetan language, meditation, philosophy, and logic. Students engage in formal debates with each other in order to sharpen their knowledge of Buddhist logic and to learn how to defend key doctrines.[505] This focus on logic and philosophy is important to many Western Buddhists, especially those following the Dalai Lama's Gelugpa school. Perhaps more than any other school of Tibetan Buddhism, the Gelugpas have tried to set their faith upon a firm logical and philosophical foundation, much as the Scholastic philosophers of the European Middle Ages tried to do with Christianity. Because of its parallels with the medieval Scholastic movement, the Buddhist philosophical system is sometimes called *Buddhist scholasticism*, and its method of inquiry *Buddhist scholastic logic*.[506] Gelugpa Buddhists have applied these philosophic tools to basic doctrines like emptiness, rebirth, karma, and the two truths in order to justify their beliefs and persuade their followers that such teachings are reasonable. Because these philosophical doctrines are such an important part of Tibetan Buddhism as it is taught outside Asia, it's useful to look critically at some of them and examine the reasoning that is used to support them. The Christian who can tactfully and considerately raise questions about these teachings can help a Western Buddhist friend see them from a fresh perspective.[507]

Looking Into Emptiness

As we saw in Chapter Three, Tibetan Buddhism claims that all the objects we see around us are in fact just momentary products of the law of cause and effect, mistakenly perceived by our minds as though they are independent, self-existing objects. Gelugpa Buddhists would say that all phenomena around us, and we ourselves, are "empty" of an independent, inherent existence. The classical Buddhist example of this situation is walking into a darkened room and mistaking a coiled rope for a snake. Our mistaken perception of the rope causes our cry of fright at the "snake." Buddhist logicians elaborate on this example by teaching that all things are composed of certain ideal parts (e.g. color, form, shape, etc.). By a special kind of analysis using Buddhist scholastic logic, they try to show that all objects and people are just collections of these ideal parts, and so they have no existence of their own.[508] The classical example is that of a cart. According to Buddhist logic, a cart is not the same thing as its parts, different from its parts, in its parts, having its parts, or the shape of its parts. Since, under this type of analysis, no such thing as a cart can be found, there is really no such thing as a self-existent cart. In the same way, since all objects are not the same as the sum of their ideal parts, they have no inherent, permanent existence of their own. Or, as the Dalai Lama would say, things have only a "certain level of conventional, relative existence."[509] We will comment on this argument shortly.

It is important for non-Buddhists to see that this is not the same as saying that *nothing* exists. Gelugpa Tibetan Buddhists would say that theirs is a "middle way" between the position that *nothing* exists and that things *inherently* exist (that is, exist really, substantially, and on their own). To assert that nothing exists would be to fall into *nihilism* (the belief that there is no being in the universe) with its attendant self-contradictions and absurdity. After all, if nothing exists, what is the point in Buddhism or any other religion? However, to admit that things actually do exist on their own would contradict the teaching of the historical Buddha. To give things some form of "conditional" or "conventional" existence is the obvious compromise, and different schools of Buddhism have attempted this in different ways over the years.

What are non-Buddhists to make of such claims about the world around us? Many Western philosophers have wrestled with these questions, including Descartes, Berkeley, Kant, and Hegel. From a Christian perspective, we may argue along with Descartes that God in His integrity would not place us in a universe that only seemed to exist, but such an argument is unlikely to convince a Buddhist. Reasoning along other lines may be more helpful. To propose, as the Buddhists do, that our senses can be fooled is one thing. But to claim that *all of our senses* deceive us *all of the time* is another matter entirely. Why should we assume that our senses are totally untrustworthy? We may indeed mistake a rope for a snake, but we have other senses to tell us that the rope is in fact not a snake. We can turn on the lights to get a better view of it, we can feel its braided strands, and smell the greasy hemp from which it was made. We can see that it doesn't slither away when we cautiously poke it with a stick. It doesn't eat, sleep, or produce baby snakes. If we are brave, we can pick up our "snake" and tie it in knots, or use it to lead our yak to greener pastures.

Likewise the cart. According to Buddhist scholastic logic, the wheels, axle, floor, and reins are not the cart; neither is its color, form, shape, or size; therefore there is no such inherently existing thing as a cart. In fact, multiple lines of evidence lead us to believe that our cart is real. We can take a pragmatic approach and drive it, or an empirical approach and describe the parts from which it was made, or an historical approach and talk to the cart maker. If we trust none of these methods, we can watch the plodding gait of our horse when hitched to the cart, and compare it to his eager trot when freed of it. We would be in little doubt that the horse believed in the cart even if we did not!

If others do not see our cart and we are hallucinating, then our doctor may demonstrate the tumor or the chemical imbalance of the brain which disorders our perception. We may need surgery or medication to set our senses right again, but even in this case the problem lies objectively and demonstrably within us. When we leave the hospital, our phantom cart will be gone. Of course, even ardent Tibetan Buddhists are born with the sense that the world around them actually exists. The strength of this perception is proven by the lengths to which they will go to try to remove it. Tibetan texts prescribe an extensive and complex series of mental exercises, prayers, tantric rituals, and multistage meditations (just one such stage taking six months of practice) to remove the sense of seeing things as humans normally do.[510] Even when one completes this procedure, the ability to "see" the emptiness of things lasts only as long as one remains in deep meditation. If Buddhist emptiness really is a basic property of all things, why should such an arduous process of auto-suggestion be required to see it? And what of the vast majority of mankind who have neither the time, the leisure, or the money to spend years in meditation?

As taught in Tibetan Buddhism, realizing the emptiness of *things* is only the first step in realizing the emptiness of *people*. The same arguments and meditations used to show that *things* do not exist are applied to humans to show that *people* do not exist, i.e. that they lack a durable identity or "self." The technical term for this teaching is "selflessness."[511] When a Tibetan Buddhist says that a person is selfless, he is not talking about someone who jumps into a lake to save a drowning child, but about this idea that people lack a permanent, inherent, personal identity (or "soul"). As the Dalai Lama says, the "person" is only a label put on the bundle of ideal qualities that, in Buddhist psychology, make up a human being. In reality, he claims, there is no such enduringly existing person.[512] This does not mean that people lack personalities. It does mean that, according to Buddhism, those personalities lack any ultimate basis in reality.[513]

The contention that people exist on the same level as dreams or hallucinations, or are anything less than fully real, raises interesting questions for Tibetan Buddhism. As the Diamond

Sutra says: "although innumerable beings have been led to nirvana, no being at all has been led to nirvana."[514] That is, since there are no fully existent beings, none have entered nirvana, and none ever can be led there. If none can be led there, what is the point in becoming a boddhisattva "able to benefit all sentient beings"? Why should anyone devote themselves to the welfare of others if they only exist on the same level as dreams and phantoms? Why bother with the fate of mere karmic streams? Tibetan Buddhists treat these questions as a paradox, skirting the issue that there can be little justification for morality or responsible behavior if people do not really and inherently exist. Moral issues aside, the Buddhist model of the self as just a bundle of ever-changing ideal qualities held together by karma seems flawed in other ways. If the self were such a bundle of constant changes, then there would be no way for such a "self" to know that change had occurred. Take the example of a student in a two year university course. She begins her first year, spends nine months studying, ends the first year, begins a second year, studies for a further nine months, completes her second year, and receives a degree. In order for her to have the experience called "getting a degree," there must be at least a relatively unchanging "self" to recognize: "I studied for one year, then another, then received my diploma." If there were no such self, there would be no "experience" of going to school, merely a succession of memories of classes. There would be no constant yardstick with which to measure change, no way to organize experiences. Life would be just a succession of perceptions without possibility of reasoning or communication.[515] If our student were a Tibetan Buddhist, she might say that she was in fact "not the same person now" as she was in her first or second year of school. But if this really were the case, how could she know? Who is recognizing that the "I" of two years ago is not the same as the "I" of today, if there is not some stable entity which had both experiences and can compare them to each other? To say, as some Tibetan Buddhists might, that her memory could fill this role is to divorce memory from personality in a way that is neither philosophically or scientifically convincing.

Science also leads us to believe that an enduring self is an important characteristic of living things. Every person has his or her own unique pattern of genes, encoded within each of the body's cells by a substance called DNA.[516] Because each person's DNA is as unique as their fingerprints, the police in Western countries commonly use a criminal's DNA to tie him to the scene of a crime with almost total certainty. The human immune system has a similar ability to distinguish self from non-self.[517] This unique, one-of-a-kind property does not stop with our genes or our immune systems, however. The cells of the brain share this uniqueness and extend it in a curious way. Most of the body's cells replace themselves by dividing to produce more cells. This is the reason we can heal a cut finger or recover from a surgical procedure. The cells of the outermost layer of our skin, for example, are not the same cells we had last month, and in this sense we have a new skin every month or so. But most of the cells of the adult brain lose this ability to reproduce. Once the brain is completely formed, most of its nerve cells divide no more for the remainder of the life of the individual. Each person is left with a set of unique brain cells throughout normal adult life. So if the functioning of our brains is at least in some way related to our personalities, then at the physiological or brain level, we have a ground for personality that lasts through an entire lifetime.[518]

Buddhists argue that memory and the unconscious account for the sense of self.[519] This argument is refuted, however, by the fact that drugs or diseases which decrease or abolish memory leave at least a core sense of self intact. In fact, from a medical perspective, memory and the sense of self are two different functions. One can be lost without the other. Such facts tell us that a unique identity, or "self," is a basic biological property of both humans and animals. It is literally "built into" each cell in our bodies as a real and lasting characteristic. Yet, our sense of self is not just a biological fact, like the color of our hair. It is a fact with great spiritual significance, as pointed out in many places in the Bible. Christians can encourage their Tibetan Buddhist friends that their natural sense of self is in fact good and right, and can find its fullest expression in Christ.[520]

Born Again

Another basic Tibetan Buddhist doctrine is the teaching that each "individual" (understood as a stream of causes and effects flowing across aeons of lifetimes) has been born, died, and reborn countless times. According to Tibetan Buddhist teaching, humans are generally reborn in subhuman states, where they remain in suffering for ages before eventually being reborn as a human again. This state of affairs has no beginning - it regresses infinitely into the past, so that a being having a human body now has been through every other possible state of existence and every possible relationship to other beings countless times. This teaching is known as the doctrine of rebirth, and as we saw in Chapter Three, it is basic to Tibetan Buddhism. Without rebirth, the law of karma could not operate for more than a single lifetime, and only a very few people would ever have any hope of reaching enlightenment. The personal circumstances of individual Buddhists, once thought to be the result of actions in previous lives, would become meaningless. There would be no point in devotional practice, merit making, or offerings; no benefit to oneself in the practice of kindness to others. In fact, all Buddhist doctrine would become meaningless for the disbeliever in rebirth.[521]

The doctrine of rebirth as taught by Tibetan Buddhists raises a number of interesting logical problems. If in fact our earth had a beginning, as the Bible teaches and most scientists seem to believe, the cycle of rebirth could not extend infinitely into the past. Rebirth could have begun no earlier than the appearance of life on earth. In fact, because rebirth is said to be caused by ignorance, rebirth could have begun no earlier than the first appearance of morally responsible beings on the earth. When this was pointed out to the Dalai Lama, he suggested that rebirth had begun on other worlds.[522] However, if scientists are correct in thinking that the universe had a definite beginning, this only moves the difficulty one step back. Rebirth (caused by ignorance or by a mistaken view of reality) could only begin when life that was capable of *having* a view of reality appeared

181

on the scene. If the universe had a beginning, it is hard to see how the Tibetan Buddhist doctrine of rebirth could be true.[523]

Attempts to prove rebirth by Buddhist scholastic logic are based on assumptions unlikely to persuade the non-Buddhist. Such efforts involve assumptions about the mind being made up of various ideal factors whose validity is unrecognized by non-Buddhists. Within such writings are abundant examples of pre-scientific attempts to account for the facts of heredity and genetics (the scientific study of inheritance). For example, the Dalai Lama asserts that infants know how to eat as soon as they are born because they learned to eat in a previous life. (If humans were in fact reborn as animals as often as the Buddhists claim, this would make for some interesting infant feeding patterns!) In the same text the Dalai Lama claims that no factor of the parents' mind is a cause of the mind of their children.[524] If this is true, it would be impossible to explain the well-described tendency to inherit mental illnesses (e.g. schizophrenia or manic-depressive disorder), personality traits, or specific talents and abilities. Of course, these are only a few of the many conflicts between the observed facts of genetics and the Tibetan Buddhist idea of rebirth. Modern Buddhists appreciate this and have suggested that the "personal continuum" enters the body at conception, and that genes are physical means by which karma is transmitted.[525] If this were so, identical twins (who have the same genes) would also have the same karma. How then could we explain the death of one twin in an accident, or an illness that strikes one but not the other? We might say that different karmic streams had entered each twin, but then their genes would no longer be the transmitters of their karma.

Another traditional Tibetan Buddhist "proof" of rebirth is based on the supposed cases of past-life recall. Some Tibetan Buddhists claim to be able to train themselves to remember previous lives, but the training takes years of practice and is supposedly accompanied by the ability to fly, become invisible, multiply the body, and dematerialize. Even in the Tibetan Buddhist community, such gifts seem to be rare at best.[526] Purported cases of past life recall are often prejudiced by financial or social benefits to the person recalling the past lives. Rebirth also lacks the capacity for justice that Buddhists ascribe to it. Let us suppose that Joseph Stalin or Adolf Hitler is continuously reborn as a worm for the next thousand years. Certainly a human consciousness imprisoned in the body of a worm would suffer agonies. But worms do not have a human consciousness. Though they may be able to react to stimuli that humans would describe as painful, they are completely unaware of this since they lack consciousness, and are unable to suffer in any meaningful sense. The worm that writhes in the beak of a hungry bird is displaying reflex actions only, not suffering. (The distinction between suffering and pain may be new to the reader, but the two are quite different processes.[527]) So to return to our example, if Hitler or Stalin were reborn as a worm, it would affect the life of the worm not at all, and neither Hitler nor Stalin would suffer for their crimes. Where then is the justice in karma and rebirth? The Dalai Lama says that when we face difficult times in life, we must think about the law of karma and realize that our troubles are the result of our own actions in the past.[528] Yet if rebirth as a human is as rare as the Tibetan scriptures say it is, it becomes very difficult to believe that in the time since morally responsible life appeared on earth anyone has had enough lifetimes to accumulate bad karma. And to assert that the system began in some other world is nothing but fantasy thinking. Without a retreat into mysticism, there is no way to square the apparent origin of our species or our planet with the doctrines of rebirth and karma.

Double Trouble

From ancient times, Tibetan Buddhist thinkers realized the conflict inherent in their views of self and suffering. If there really is no ultimate personality or "self," then there is no one left to suffer or be delivered from suffering. Likewise, there is no reason to do good to others when neither we nor the person we benefit has any real existence. Tibetan Buddhism resolves this dilemma by talking about the "ultimate truths" (*don dam bden pa*) and "relative truths" (*kun rdzob bden pa*) that we met in Chapter Three. Ultimate or absolute truths are seen only by highly accomplished Tibetan Buddhists, and then only during deep meditation, while relative or conventional truths are seen by a less involved process called "conventional valid cognition."[529] It is said that only Buddha can see the world from the perspective of both truths at the same time.[530] The ethical problem with this system is that two truths lead to two moralities — one for the spiritually elite, and one for everyone else. For example, the Buddhist scriptures explicitly state that monks should not drink any alcohol or have sexual relations with women. But an authoritative text for those taking the Tibetan Buddhist Kalachakra initiation states that these rules are only for those who are still subject to taking rebirth as lower beings. It goes on to say that the Buddha allows the higher monks and lamas to have sexual intercourse with women and drink alcohol.[531] Even the Dalai Lama acknowledges that ritual sex is used as a technique in Tibetan Buddhism.[532] Nominally this is allowed for advanced tantric practitioners only, but it still represents a double standard. Such double standards may be what led one group of Western Buddhists to publish a statement that spiritual teachers should not meet their own needs at the expense of their students by demanding money, time, labor, or sex.[533] Western Buddhists who have recently joined a dharma group may not be aware of these practices, but should be aware of some of the tantric rituals that may compromise their health or well-being.

Saying No to God

Explicit arguments against the existence of God are not a prominent feature of Tibetan Buddhism. However, direct arguments against the existence of God are found in the Buddhist Pali Canon (composed in the first century B.C.) and Tibetan Buddhists would, in general, agree with these arguments. Of course, since the writers of the Pali Canon lived in ancient India, most of their writings are directed against Vedic and Hindu concepts of deity rather than against Biblical ideas. Some modern Buddhist writers however, especially those reacting to the impact of Christian missions, have adapted the early Buddhist scriptural arguments against the existence of gods and applied them in attacks against the Judeo-Christian concept of God. A response to these arguments lies far outside the scope of this book, and the reader is referred elsewhere for discussion of them.[534] A brief review may indicate their general categories, some of which will be familiar to any Christian who has lived or worked on a university campus.

1. God and the Soul: Buddhists take note of the New Testament link between God and the human soul. Since the Buddha taught that there is no such thing as a soul, he held that belief in it was spiritually harmful.[535] Buddha's reasoning was directed against the Brahmanistic idea of an eternal soul that was essentially one with God, an idea which does not appear in the New Testament. Most Buddhists would still object to the Christian concept of the soul as an enduring personal entity, however, on the basis of Buddha's "no self" doctrine. As we saw above, this doctrine relies on Buddhist philosophical arguments based on ancient assumptions (e.g. the five *skandhas*) that are questionable in the light of modern science.

2. God as Creator: Since Buddhist and Christian views of the world around us are so widely divergent, it is not surprising that the Judeo-Christian concept of God as the Creator of the universe is difficult for Buddhists to understand or accept. The Biblical idea of Creation differs radically from the Buddhist view that the universe is nothing more than a chain of causes and effects reaching into the beginingless past. Such a view makes a creator unnecessary and eliminates the need to explain the origin of rebirth. If scientists eventually prove the Biblical contention that the universe had a definite beginning in time, then Buddhists may have to reconsider their views of rebirth or retreat to a fundamentalist position that the Buddhist scriptures take precedence over scientific observations.

3. God and the Problem of Evil: The Buddha observed evil and suffering, and reasoned that if a god created this world, he was responsible for the evil in it.[536] Modern readers will recognize this as a form of the argument put forward by Pierre Bayle in the seventeenth century: "Evil exists; if God were omnipotent He could destroy evil; if God were good He would destroy it; but evil continues, so therefore God is either impotent, malevolent, or nonexistent." A discussion of the Christian responses to this argument is beyond the scope of this book, but the argument itself is certainly not conclusive.[537]

4. God and Morality: Since Buddhists object in principle to the idea of God, and maintain that all moral accounts are settled through the law of karma, it is not surprising that they object to the Judeo-Christian concept of God as a Judge and moral Lawgiver.[538] Thus the Christian idea of people having intrinsic moral value because they are created in God's image is not acceptable to Buddhists, who base their morality on empathy or sympathetic feelings: "If something is unpleasant to me, it is unpleasant to others and I should not do it," which Christians will recognize as a non-theistic version of Luke 6:31. Buddhists object to the idea of God issuing moral commands, on the theory that if God commands what is good because it is good, there is a standard of goodness outside God, and therefore He is not ultimately good. If it is admitted that the good is simply what God commands, then they feel God is arbitrary. Further, they argue that it is difficult to know what God's commands are, since differing traditions interpret the commands of God in different ways. The force of such arguments is based on the assumption that "God" is a philosophical concept subject to human analysis.

5. God as Experience: Evangelical Christians stress the importance of a personal relationship with Christ and the intimate personal reality of God in their lives. At least one Buddhist writer attacks these experiences as basically emotional and irrational, seeing them as conditioned by previous irrationally accepted beliefs. The same (Theravada Buddhist) writer dismisses Christian mysticism out of hand, relating it to drug experiences.[539] Interestingly, his arguments undercut all mysticism, including the central Buddhist experience of intuitive realization of emptiness. If experiences are invalid simply because they are subjective, then it is difficult to see how Buddhist enlightenment (a uniquely personal experience) is meaningful.

6. The Bible as God's Revelation: Buddhists in general place a strong emphasis on reasoning one's way to truth, and disparage accepting truths on scriptural authority. Though no Tibetan Buddhist would say that their scriptures are revealed by a god, the writings of at least major figures like Nagarjuna, Chandrakirti, and Tsong Khapa are regarded as being without error.[540] Still, Buddhists may ask how Christians can accept the Bible as divinely-revealed truth without logical proof from other sources that this is in fact the case. To do otherwise seems to them to be circular reasoning: "The Bible is God's Word because it says so in the Bible." In other words, as a minimum case, if God's existence can be irrefutably established by reasoning alone, then the possibility of His self-revelation can be independently checked. Or more simply: "Show us God by reasoning alone, and then we will see if your Bible is an accurate picture of Him." Here we meet a question that Western philosophy has wrestled with for a long time: Can the existence of God be proven by reason alone? It is significant that the medieval Scholastic philosophers, using methods quite similar to those practiced daily in Gelugpa monasteries, were unable to give a resounding *yes* to this question. While there are non-Scriptural arguments for the existence of God which many thinking people find convincing, it still is true that the nature and character of God cannot be discovered from unaided reason. But if God is really God, this is not surprising. He is quite likely to be beyond anything that humans can sort into logical propositions or even understand.[541] The Biblical writers knew this and filled their pages with figures, symbols and stories to tell us what He is like.

Christ and the Western Buddhist

The Tibetan Buddhist philosophical system that many Western Buddhists find so attractive is in fact a living fossil, formed in the thought world of ancient India and preserved in the bedrock of Tibetan scriptural tradition. Even in modern Tibetan

Buddhism, important philosophic arguments are based on ancient superstitions and dogmatic assumptions thousands of years old.[542] Profound assertions about the nature of man rest upon occult concepts of ideal body fluids, mystic channels, energy winds, and other ideas scientifically discredited and abandoned long ago. It could be argued that with its spread outside Asia, Tibetan Buddhists will have to reconcile their beliefs with the facts discovered by Western science and other philosophical systems, but there seems to be little evidence of this. At least in its native literature, Tibetan Buddhism has yet to take other, non-Asian and non-Buddhist worldviews seriously. It remains just as inward-looking and self-absorbed as it was a thousand years ago. It remains firmly rooted in an ancient system of dogma and intellectually ingrown commentary. What does this mean for those who are concerned to bring Christ to Western Tibetan Buddhists? Many Western Buddhists bring to this philosophy a set of assumptions and a non-Asian way of looking at things, that is fundamentally at variance with basic Tibetan Buddhist teachings on karma, rebirth, emptiness and two-level truth. The Christian can gently and tactfully encourage a Tibetan Buddhist friend to think critically about these doctrines in the light of the way they live and work in the secular world.

This is not to say that Western Buddhists can be argued out of Buddhism, by themselves or anyone else. People do not choose one of the world's religions by deciding whether it is logically plausible, but by seeing if there is some degree of "fit" between their needs and what a religion offers. But pointing out logical inconsistencies may be a first step in helping a Western Buddhist to think through some key issues, which itself may begin a process of spiritual growth. Meeting arguments and hostility against God with love, tact, and patience will help this process. A good starting point is to focus on the person and not their beliefs. Who are they? What personal needs have led them to seek fulfillment in Tibetan Buddhism? Why Tibetan Buddhism and not another spiritual path? Is Buddhism a passing interest or are they deeply committed to it? In what ways can Christ's love be made real (demonstrated) to them? A *person-centered* (how can I demonstrate to them who Christ is?) rather than a *doctrine-centered* (how can I prove to them that the Gospel is true?) approach is usually most helpful at the beginning of such a relationship. Confrontational approaches are of little use in sharing Christ with Western Buddhists or anyone else. Cornering people with Bible verses, denouncing Buddhism as Satanic, or pushing for on-the-spot prayers to receive Christ will not only make Western Buddhists feel manipulated and resentful, they will raise barriers of prejudice which will be hard to overcome later. There is certainly a place for Bible verses and prayers to receive Christ, but probably not in most initial encounters with most Tibetan Buddhists. Coming to Christ takes time, and that time is more often measured in months or years than in minutes.

CHAPTER 10

The Seven Pillars of Wisdom

B eth is a Christian student at a large university in Canada. One of her classmates is a man named Paul, a psychology student who has become very interested in Tibetan Buddhism. In the past few weeks he's been learning how to meditate, and he has gone on several retreats organized by a Tibetan monk who runs the campus dharma center. Paul told Beth that he intends to take Tibetan Buddhist initiation soon, and Beth wonders how she can talk about her faith with someone who says there is no God, just an "emptiness" that we can "realize by meditation." The issue concerns Beth deeply, for when she finishes college she hopes to work in a Christian health and development project in a Tibetan Buddhist area of Inner Asia. In that setting, she will be surrounded by Tibetan Buddhists on a daily basis. She hopes that they will see something of the life of Christ in her, and she wants to be able to share with them something of what she believes. When she told her friend Paul of her plans, he angrily accused her of trying to change their culture: "These people's culture and language are endangered already, and you're trying to destroy them by making them Christians. Do you hate them?" he asked her. Stung by his comments, Beth decided to take a day or two to think about what Paul had said.

In a day when world religions are becoming next-door neighbors, it seems fair to question the motives of people like Beth. Is it right for them to share their faith with those of other religions? Isn't religious proselytism an act of cultural imperialism that destroys native cultures and centuries-old beliefs? Isn't it racist to assume that people from one culture know what's best for those of another? Aren't missionaries (of whatever religion) just fundamentalist zealots out to make converts by whatever means they can? The answers to these questions depend on how one looks at religions generally. To those who feel that all religions are just superstition (or worse), little can be said. But others may be able to see that *some* kind of missionary activity is a logical consequence of any religion that professes to care about others. If a religion has what it feels is the key to human happiness and fulfillment, how can it refuse to share that with the rest of humanity?

Since ancient times Christianity, Hinduism, Islam, and Buddhism have sent their adherents into other cultures as missionaries. During the twentieth century, the Tibetans were among the most active of all Buddhists in sending emissaries to non-Asian cultures, making Tibetan Buddhism a world religion in distribution if not in actual numbers of believers. If it is legitimate for Tibetan Buddhists to send missionaries to non-Asian cultures, there would seem to be few grounds for objecting to an exchange of ideas in the other direction. As Article 18 of the United Nations' Universal Declaration of Human Rights says, "Everyone has the right to freedom of thought, conscience and religion; this right includes freedom to change his religion or belief, and freedom, either alone or in community with others and in public or private, to manifest his religion or belief in teaching, practice, worship and observance."[543]

Ever since Jesus sent the apostles to "go and make disciples of all nations," Christians have been sharing the good news of their risen Savior in virtually every nation on earth. Christian missions recognizes the equality of all people in God's sight, teaching that all need God's undeserved favor. Christian missions seeks to manifest the unconditional love of God for humanity in true compassion through such activities as medical, social, educational, and economic development projects among disadvantaged peoples. Christian missions as an enterprise seeks to affirm the positive aspects of the cultures it serves, in many cases giving them the tools they need (e.g. through literacy and education) to adapt to inevitable social change on their own terms.[544] The missionary outreach of the Church seeks to share the good news of Jesus Christ by example as well as by preaching. Missions done according to Biblical standards *never* seeks to manipulate, force, or bribe anyone to change their faith.

Instead, Christian missionaries serve as ambassadors of the King-dom of God to the peoples they serve.

Ambassadors for Christ

It was the Apostle Paul, one of the earliest and greatest of Christian missionaries, who first described himself as an "am-bassador for Christ."[545] An ambassador is a representative sent by one nation to another. A skilful ambassador understands the people, problems, and worldview of his or her host country. He uses this knowledge to represent the policies of his home government in terms that local people can understand and ap-preciate, even if they do not always agree with them. Just as the world's governments employ qualified diplomats to represent them, so God calls upon certain people as cross-cultural am-bassadors to represent his Kingdom. These people represent Jesus to the world. Like their diplomatic cousins, Christ's am-bassadors need to understand their host country's people, prob-lems, and worldview. They too can use this knowledge to rep-resent Him in terms that local people can understand and ap-preciate. This puts a great responsibility upon them to do the best job that they can.

No unskilled person would approach his government and say, "Send me out as your ambassador." Whoever wants to be an ambassador needs tact, a good education, plenty of experi-ence, and a deep understanding of international relations. Only if a budding diplomat proves to be well-trained and competent can he or she hope to be appointed an ambassador. In the same way, Christians like Beth, who feel called of God to represent Christ in another culture, need training and experience in their home countries before going overseas. Even the great mission-aries Paul and Barnabas gained experience as teachers (during the year they spent instructing the Christians at Antioch) and as representatives of the church (when they completed an im-portant mission to the Christians in Jerusalem) before God called them to go out as ambassadors.[546] Both men showed by expe-rience that they were prepared for whatever God told them to do. Only then did the Holy Spirit and the local church send them off to their missionary task.[547]

Not everyone needs the intensive preparation of a cross-cultural ambassador. For example, God calls many people in so-called "home countries" to support those he sends out as cross-cultural workers. Beth's friends and supporters need only a broad, general understanding of the Tibetan Buddhist world in order to pray for her in an informed way. Other Christians have friends, neighbors, or family members who have converted to Tibetan Buddhism, or they may meet Tibetan Buddhist immigrants and become friends with them. In either case, it can be very helpful to learn a bit more about Tibetan Buddhist beliefs and culture. This will help them to share their faith in ways that they are more likely to be understood and appreciated.[548] Still others may make short term visits to Inner Asia for study or tourism. In general, the more preparation that is put into such visits, the more rewarding they are for all concerned. Finally, the Christian professional or missionary who goes to live in Inner Asia needs the most preparation of all. Learning the language, customs, and culture of their host country will take several years. This is not to say that they can accomplish nothing for Christ if they aren't cultural experts or can't speak another language. Even if they know little about Asian culture, God's love in their hearts can be an effective tool of the Holy Spirit. A friend tells the story of a woman who came to a mission hospital in Kathmandu, Nepal. She had only a few months' leave from work in her home country, but she wanted to do all she could for the local people during that time. She volunteered to change sheets, run errands for the nurses, and bring food to the patients. Her manner was so cheerful, loving, and helpful that both the patients and the staff were deeply impressed, yet she was completely unable to speak the local language. Her love said it all.

Ambassadors in Training

Beth's local church gives her a lot of help in preparing for her future role as a Christian professional in Inner Asia. The church is realistic about missions and they know they aren't looking for a "perfect saint." They don't expect Beth to have an encyclopedic knowledge of the Bible, superb communication skills, the wisdom of Solomon, and a scholar's understanding of other languages and religions. But they do look for the *beginnings* of certain qualities in her, and they want to see that those qualities are starting to grow towards maturity in her Christian life. Beth's church helps her in the areas where she needed it, and as they do so, they watch with joy as God equips this young woman to be his cross-cultural ambassador. What qualities are they looking for?

A Firm Foundation

Beth's church knows that she needs to be settled in the basics of her faith and have a clear personal commitment to Christ. As we have seen in previous chapters, Tibetan Buddhism is a religion of occult mysticism and gnostic[549] philosophy. This being the case, Beth's church remembers what the Apostle Paul wrote to the church at Colossae: "See to it that no one takes you captive through hollow and deceptive philosophy, which depends on human tradition and the basic principles of this world rather than on Christ."[550] They feel that it's best if new Christians, people who are unsettled in their faith, or who have some kind of pre-Christian background in occult practices seek a ministry other than with Tibetan Buddhists. They know Beth needs more than just a firm grounding in the basics of her faith. They encourage her to gain the systematic understanding of Christian doctrine and apologetics that will be very helpful to her in talking with philosophically-minded Buddhist friends like Paul. Beyond these basics, they want Beth to make sure she has entrusted to the Lord not only her personal life, but also her career, her plans for marriage, and her finances. Her church wants to see in her a definite calling to serve in Asia that will

195

not fade away when the going gets tough. (This is especially important for married couples, as the stresses of life in a new culture will magnify natural differences in personality, language learning ability, and cultural adaptability.) If there is any problem in these areas, the church encourages its candidate missionaries to wait to go overseas until God has further prepared them for service.

Practical Holiness

Beth's church wants to see how her faith works out in the practical details of her daily life. They help her assess her strengths and weaknesses, and encourage her to grow in the areas of her life that need to change. Here are a few aspects of her Christian life that Beth's church helps her to think about:

1. The Small Things: Preparing for effective ministry begins in our own homes and in our daily affairs. Taking every opportunity to help others cheerfully with household chores, errands, and such will help in preparing for life in another culture, where we may have to live in much closer quarters with others than in our home country. Being flexible when confronted with the likes and dislikes of other people is one of the most valuable assets any Christian can have. "Where he leads me I will follow; what they feed me I will swallow" is an old missionary adage that applies to more areas of life than food.

2. Self Discipline: Regular study of the Scriptures is vital. Discipline in speech, even in relaxed social conversation, is a virtue which prevents many frictions and misunderstandings. Discipline in personal habits makes it easier for us to live with others (and for them to live with us!). Discipline of our emotions makes it easier to remain patient when faced with delays and frustrations.

3. Simple Lifestyle: Learning to live with little money and few possessions can be a great help in preparing for life in certain parts of Inner Asia. It trains us in separating the necessary from the nice, and helps narrow the economic gap that separates many expatriate Christians from the people they have come to serve.

4. Balance: All Christians do well to keep the Kingdom of God first in life, without getting distracted by differences with others over worship styles, mission methods, or by those ancient foes of the Christian, the world, the flesh, and the devil.

5. Prayer: The Apostle Paul urged Christians to "pray in the Spirit on all occasions with all kinds of prayers and requests."[551] Prayer links us with God. Through prayer we have access to all of God's power to help in any given situation.[552] Prayer is particularly important for those who are living and working in a Tibetan Buddhist culture. Such people should have someone praying for them as they introduce their Tibetan Buddhist friends to Christ. Prayer-partners need to pray both for the Christian (for encouragement, holy living, and spiritual protection) and for the Tibetan Buddhist.

Good Communication Skills

Diplomats are in constant touch with their home countries — sending reports, appealing for help, and receiving instructions. In the same way, ambassadors for Christ are in constant touch with their "home country": receiving instructions from God's Word, and sending appeals for help and guidance through prayer. An ambassador who no longer communicates represents no one but himself. Ambassadors also need to communicate "horizontally" with the people of their host country. Practical experience in leading evangelistic Bible studies and discipling others is an essential part of preparing to share Christ with Tibetan Buddhists. Beth's church sees that she is a woman of prayer, and that she has practical experience in relating successfully to people like her friend Paul.

A Consistent Life

Cross-cultural ambassadors need to know how to live out the life of Christ in their own culture before trying to do so in another one. Jesus' command that the apostles should make disciples in Jerusalem, Judea, Samaria, and the ends of the earth meant more than just "start where you are and move outward." The people in Jerusalem and Judea were Jews. The apostles could tell them about Jesus in terms that all Jews could understand. But Samaria was different. The culture was not the same, and there were high walls of prejudice to be broken down.[553] The Gentile world was something else again: the Roman Empire was filled with peoples of different cultures and languages who knew nothing of Israel or its God. Jesus was instructing the disciples to begin with their own culture first. Obeying his instructions, they gained experience among their own people[554] before trying to do so in another culture. Beth's church saw that she was leading Bible studies and sharing her faith in her own community, and this encouraged them to think that she could do so successfully once she arrived in Inner Asia.

Biblical Wisdom

Every government expects that its ambassadors will behave wisely, make good decisions and follow instructions carefully. In the same way, Christ's cross-cultural ambassadors need a firm foundation of Biblical wisdom. As the writer of Proverbs said:

> Wisdom has built her house;
> She has hewn out its seven pillars.[555]

The "seven pillars" metaphor indicates that wisdom is solidly founded, and will be there to support us in difficult times. Christians need maturity and wisdom to live Christ-honoring lives[556] and to meet the needs of their Tibetan Buddhist friends in sensitive, caring ways. This mature wisdom knows when to speak to a friend and when to be silent. It knows what to say to meet a another's need. It is "pure, peace loving, considerate, submissive, full of mercy and good fruit, impartial, and sincere."[557] It has much more to do with what we *are* than what we *know*. The effect of this kind of wisdom in a Christian's life is to cause others to seek its source. As Proverbs 11:30 says, "The fruit of the righteous is a tree of life, and he who wins souls is wise."

The Hebrew expression translated "wins souls" has a New Testament parallel in the idea of Jesus' disciples being "fishers of men."[558] This proverb shows us an inseparable connection between the pure, peace loving, mature wisdom manifest in a Christian's life and its natural result: others drawn to Christ by actions as much as words.

Jesus, too, felt that wisdom was an important quality for the representatives of his Kingdom. As he sent his disciples to preach, he warned them to be "wise as serpents, and innocent as doves."[559] How were the disciples to be "wise as serpents"? The Greek word used here for wisdom (*phronimos*) can mean thoughtful, discreet, or cautious. The New International Version translates it as "shrewd." What was there to be cautious of? Jesus knew that the Gospel is never proclaimed without risk. In the following verse He instructs the disciples to beware of those who would oppose their message and subject them to the physical risks of arrest and flogging. There are also spiritual risks involved, as the Apostle Paul noted: "For our struggle is not against flesh and blood, but against the rulers, against the authorities, against the powers of this dark world and against the spiritual forces of evil in the heavenly realms."[560] The occult is a part of the everyday experience of most people in the Tibetan Buddhist world. The Christian who enters that world needs wisdom to know what these occult practices are and how to deal with the forces behind them.

A Biblical Approach to Other Religions

Beth's church knows that she needs a solidly Biblical approach to other religions in general, and to Tibetan Buddhism in particular. They help her to think about whether she should ignore other religions, condemn them, study them, or use them as bridges to span the gap between themselves and Christ. Many answers have been given to these questions. Some have held that there are elements of truth in all religions, placed there as part of God's common grace to the world (Romans 1:20). These truthful elements may serve as a kind of preparation for the Gospel, in that they can make it easier for people to understand who Jesus is when they hear about him. For example, many Muslims who have come to believe in Christ feel that their former faith did teach things that were true about God, but that Christ helped them to know God in a deeper, more meaningful way. This is not the same as saying that other religions are sufficient for salvation, but it does point out that truthful elements in other religions can serve as a kind of bridge across which a person can come to Christ. Others hold that the world's religions are either devoid of truth or even satanically inspired. This line of argument follows the Apostle John's statement that "whoever denies that Jesus is the Christ is the antichrist."[561] In this view, other religions should be ignored, shunned, or condemned. Studying them is spiritually dangerous and has little to offer Christians who want to share their faith with others. Still other views hold that world religions represent man's best attempts to deal with the mysteries of life, or to evolve a belief system that will hold society together. Ultimately these views reduce religion to merely sociological significance, or see all religions as but different paths to the same goal.[562]

Which of these views should Beth adopt? Probably none of them alone is an adequate basis for a Christian approach to Tibetan Buddhism. The philosophical Buddhism that is so attractive to youth in Europe and North America denies the most basic Christian teachings, right down to the very existence of creation. Assuming that these doctrines can serve as a preparation for the Gospel takes too much for granted and can result in serious misunderstanding. The purely doctrinal side of Tibetan Buddhism seems to offer few if any bridges across which a person can come to Christ. Tibetan Buddhist culture, however, seems to offer several points of contact with Christian belief. These contact points, even though they are not areas of agreement, may be a way for folk Tibetan Buddhists to approach Christ. For example, there is a real fear of demons and evil spirits among most Tibetan Buddhist peoples. Jesus' mastery over these forces banishes the fear that shamanism and folk

Tibetan Buddhism create in their adherents. As for the other view, assuming that Tibetan Buddhism is unworthy of study makes it almost impossible to present the Gospel in terms that Tibetan Buddhists can understand.

A Christian approach to Tibetan Buddhism takes into account the fact that the doctrinal teachings of Tibetan Buddhism stand opposed to Christianity at virtually every point and at the most fundamental levels. Yet it also allows for careful study of Tibetan Buddhist life and culture in order to make clear to Buddhists just who Jesus is. A Biblical view of Tibetan Buddhism also acknowledges that lamaism cannot deliver men and women from the power of sin. Only Christ can save.[563] Integrity in cross cultural missions means living out the life of Christ *in a way that our listeners can understand and appreciate.* This means taking seriously the language, culture, and history of Tibetan Buddhists, and using this information to share Christ with them in locally meaningful ways. But is such an approach Biblical?

With Paul at Athens

By the middle of the first century, the early Church faced a crucial situation. Christianity was spreading outside its first toeholds in the synagogues of the Eastern Mediterranean. It was beginning to attract all kinds of people from across the Roman Empire. Some of these people worshiped a pantheon of unruly gods; others offered food and flowers to the spirits of woods, fields, and mountains. The Romans themselves said their Emperor was a god and should be worshipped. Virtually all of these peoples practiced occult rituals, magic, and sorcery of one or another kind.[564] None of them had any regard for the Hebrew Scriptures. So how could the early Christians make their message clear to people who did not share their Judaic heritage and culture? This was the problem faced by the Apostle Paul as he arrived in Athens on his second missionary journey.

Shortly after Paul entered this great center of Greek civilization, he was invited to preach before the Areopagus, a forum of the most learned intellectuals in this very intellectual city. Steeped in the proud traditions of Greek culture and philosophy, these men were as culturally different from Paul as can possibly be imagined. What would he say to these great philosophers who sat at the center of the civilized world? Let's listen as Paul begins his great speech to them.

"Men of Athens! I see that in every way you are very religious. For as I walked around and observed your objects of worship, I even found an altar with this inscription: TO AN UNKNOWN GOD. Now what you worship as something unknown I am going to proclaim to you. The God who made the world and everything in it is the Lord of heaven and earth and does not live in temples built by hands. And he is not served by human hands, as if he needed anything, because he himself gives all men life and breath and everything else. From one man he made every nation of men, that they should inhabit the whole earth; and he determined the times set for them and the exact places where they should live. God did this so that men would seek him and perhaps reach out for him and find him, though he is not far from each one of us. 'For in him we live and move and have our being.' As some of your own poets have said, 'We are his offspring.' Therefore since we are God's offspring, we should not think that the divine being is like gold or silver or stone — an image made by man's design and skill. In the past God overlooked such ignorance, but now he commands all people everywhere to repent. For he has set a day when he will judge the world with justice by the man he has appointed. He has given proof of this to all men by raising him from the dead." 565

At this point, Paul was interrupted by jeering and evidently stopped speaking. Enough of his speech is recorded, however, to give us a clear idea of how he proclaimed the Gospel to an audience that did not share his own cultural background. It is this feature of Paul's speech in Athens that makes it such a good Biblical model for cross-cultural ambassadors who want to live out the life of Christ in other cultures.566 Paul's approach to his pagan listeners is marked by spiritual maturity, cultural preparation, and a clear discernment of the spiritual issues at stake. He makes every effort to share his message in terms the Athenians can understand and appreciate. This effort must have been successful, for even though his speech was interrupted, God used it to bring people to faith in Christ.[567] Let's look at what makes Paul's speech such a clear Scriptural model for presenting the Gospel message to people of other faiths.

1. Spiritual Maturity: By the time Paul reached Athens, he was no novice, but a veteran missionary. He had been a leader in the church at Antioch.[568] He had preached to Jews and Gentiles, Roman officials and common people. In Lystra he had been mistaken for a god, then stoned and left for dead;[569] he'd returned to Jerusalem for a major Church Council,[570] set off on another missionary journey (this one to bring the Gospel to Europe), been imprisoned, beaten with rods, and delivered by an earthquake.[571] With amazing courage he continued to proclaim his message faithfully, even to the point of provoking a riot in Thessalonica.[572] Despite this, he still fearlessly preached in Athens the very message that had brought him so much suffering. Paul was a mature Christian. Not all of us today can have the spiritual maturity of the Apostle Paul, of course, but spiritual maturity remains a vital qualification for sharing the Gospel with Tibetan Buddhists. As we saw before, the basics of commitment to Jesus Christ as Lord and Savior must be settled in our hearts. Regular, disciplined Bible study and prayer must be a part of our lives. These basics should lead us to live out the life of Christ among people in our own culture. Paul had been through all of these experiences, and he stands before us in this passage as a model of a spiritually mature Christian whom God can use to accomplish great things.

2. Cultural Preparation: The Apostle Paul did his homework before bringing his message to the Greeks. Paul grew up in the Greek merchant colony of Tarsus, where he lived in close contact with Greek language and customs.[573] He probably studied Greek literature at some point, for in the middle of his speech to the Athenians (verse 28), he quotes the poet Aratus, whose

203

principal work *Phaenomena* was widely known in Greece, and which would have been recognized immediately by his listeners. Nor was Paul's study confined to the dusty classics. In 1 Corinthians 15:33 he quotes the Athenian author Menander, who was known for his romantic comedies! But Paul did more than just throw in a few lines from the Athenians' favorite poets. He actually changed the way he presented his message so that it would be more understandable to the Greeks. Instead of presenting a series of Scripture proof texts, as he had with the Jews at Thessalonica,[574] Paul used the form of linear, logical argument that was more familiar to Greek listeners. In other words, he used Greek thought forms to present his Gospel to the Greeks. He also presented his message in a way that fit the Greek worldview. Athens was renowned for the sheer number of its temples, and the Greek view of reality was dominated by its many gods. As culturally repulsive as this must have been to Paul, he did not rebuke the Athenians for their beliefs, but explained the Gospel using the temple of the unknown god as a starting place (verse 23). In other words, he kept his Gospel the same, but changed its packaging to fit a Greek worldview. There is a lesson here for every Christian who shares his or her faith with people of another culture. Rather than merely translating our favorite Gospel presentation into someone else's language, we need to go the extra mile, as Paul did. We need to know how our listeners think, and present our message in ways that make sense *to them*. This means taking their culture, their language, and their worldview seriously, and using what we learn to make the Gospel message clear to our listeners both by our words and by our actions.

3. Spiritual Discernment: Despite Paul's wide education in Greek culture, there is no record in Acts 17 that he took the time to appreciate the famous cultural monuments of Athens or admire its great art and architecture. Paul saw through the glories of ancient Greek culture to the spiritual poverty that lay behind them. He knew the Greeks needed Christ, no matter how religious they were. Like ancient Greece, Tibet has a rich and varied culture which has spread far outside its original homeland. As Greek culture became one of the foundations of Western civilization, so Tibetan culture spread from the Himalayas to Siberia and became the foundation culture of the Tibetan Buddhist world. Many young people from Western countries have found the exotic trappings of Tibetan culture almost irresistibly appealing. By contrast, Christians need spiritual discernment to look behind the rich and fascinating culture of the Tibetan Buddhist world to see the spiritual realities that lie behind it.

4. Appropriate Action: Paul put all of his knowledge and experience to use as he preached to the Athenians. Modern Christians need to do the same, applying what they learn about Tibetan Buddhist life and culture as they live out the life of Christ among their Buddhist friends. When the time comes for them to speak about what they believe, they will be able to put the claims of Christ before their Tibetan Buddhist friends in terms *they* can understand and appreciate. Paul's action in going to the Areopagus and speaking to the intellectual leaders of Athens also showed good judgment. Any among his audience who turned to Christ would be able to share the Gospel at the most influential levels of Greek society. This would provide the infant church with able leadership and help Paul's message to spread more rapidly.

5. Results: Although he was rudely interrupted by his listeners, Paul did see some results from his preaching. In verse 34 we read that several people believed his message. The phrase suggests that they became believers after some time, perhaps after they had learned more about Christ. In any case, Paul's effort to present the Gospel in a way the Athenians could understand was honored by God, and a number of men and women came to know Christ as a result.

Incarnational Missions

As the time for her departure nears, Beth begins to wonder exactly how she will share her faith with the new friends she will meet in Asia. While she has experience in teaching the Bible to Canadian college students, she wonders if this approach will

Incarnational Missions

Great Commission Matthew 28:18-20	Great Commandment Matthew 22:37-39

The Two Foundations of Incarnational Missions

be helpful to people who know nothing of the Bible and perhaps can't even read. How will she share the Gospel message with them?

Traditionally, Christian missions has been framed in terms of Jesus' Great Commission to " … go and make disciples of all nations, baptizing them in the name of the Father and of the Son and of the Holy Spirit, and teaching them to obey everything I have commanded you."[575] As applied in the recent history of Protestant missions, however, this narrow definition risks reducing the good news of Jesus Christ to the sort of mass media message found in commercial advertising. Treating the Gospel only as a simple verbal message can have a number of negative effects: a) it is easily promoted in mass marketing campaigns that

206

show scant respect for local cultures; b) it requires missionaries to make little investment in the language or culture of the people to whom the message is directed; c) Tibetan Buddhists easily confuse it with peddling Western culture; and d) it oversimplifies the Gospel by treating it as a simple verbal message with no need for a living example. In short, such an approach is not *incarnational* in the sense that it offers Tibetan Buddhists no living example of Christ.

An incarnational approach to missions takes Jesus' Great Commandment (to love our neighbors as ourselves) just as seriously as the Great Commission (to make disciples of all nations). Resting on these twin foundations, Christians who follow an incarnational model of missions learn the language, culture, and worldview of the people they serve, and present the Good News of Christ to them in ways that make sense locally. Incarnational missions takes seriously the physical, social, and spiritual needs of human beings, and meets those needs in real and practical ways. But the local people aren't the only beneficiaries of this approach. Incarnational missions offers the missionary the difficult, spiritually maturing experience of living out the life of Christ in another culture — a process that is sure to deepen his or her own appreciation of Christ's incarnation. Incarnational missions puts the focus on obedience and faithfulness rather than on "success." And it recognizes that *only in dependence upon the work of the Holy Spirit* can people come to Christ and the Church grow.

Preparing to Enter the Tibetan Buddhist World

Beth's church makes sure she's done some systematic study of the Bible and Christian doctrine, and encourages her to get a good general academic preparation. Some experience in apologetics will come in handy, especially with people like her friend Paul. Beth knows that making friends with foreign students living in Canada is excellent preparation for her future life in another culture. Though not everyone like Beth has the inclination, opportunity, or funds for more advanced studies, even a brief exposure to linguistics, anthropology, or comparative religion will be a great help. Beth learns all she can about Tibetan Buddhism and how it affects the lives and outlook of the people of her host country. She reads widely about Inner Asia and the people she's going to serve. She prepares to study their language, religion, culture, government, and even their sports until she understands how her hosts think about life. She wants to know what things are important to them and how they see themselves and the world around them. Of course, this is more than she can learn before she leaves for Asia, so she wisely decides to become a lifelong student of her host culture. Later in her career, she will find that almost everything she has learned was of value in making Christ real to people in her host culture.

As the time grew nearer for Beth to leave for Asia, she realizes excitedly, "this is really going to happen!" Like most people about to make a major change in life, she has some concerns about her future. Perhaps most people who are preparing to leave their home country experience some degree of apprehension, or even fear. It may be fear of unfamiliar customs, of causing offense by something we say, of strange foods or of physical dangers. But such fears, while real, can't be allowed to deter God's cross-cultural ambassadors. The Bible is full of commands not to be afraid.[576] When we face danger, discomfort, cold, heat, hunger, or other perils, faith in God's calling and his promise to be with us always[577] will strengthen us for whatever lies ahead. But fear is only one kind of obstacle to incarnational missions. Attachment to a comfortable life in one's home country, personal relationships with family or friends, and concern with career over God's calling are just a few of the difficulties that can get in the way. Dealing with these hindrances is the first step on the long road of obedience.

The occult is another area of concern for some people like Beth. European and American Christians are sometimes uncertain what to make of New Testament references to demons and evil spirits. Christians from outside Asia or Africa tend to discount the stories of Jesus' mastery over evil spirits[578] and Satan[579] as either allegorical material or as accommodations to first-century Jewish culture, because they have no personal experience with such phenomena. But no Christian has reason to be embarrassed by the Bible's reference to demons and spirits. As the Apostle Paul makes clear in the sixth chapter of his letter to the church at Ephesus, the Christian life involves struggle against spiritual forces. Anthropologists have documented spirit possession as a worldwide cultural phenomenon. Social scientists have written books about it[580] and even made films of spirit-possessed people.[581] Among folk Tibetan Buddhists, spirit activity and demon possession are accepted as everyday phenomena. Fear of gods, demons, and evil spirits is widespread, because they are believed to cause all sorts of misfortune in people's lives.

Multiple Scripture references[582] make it clear that Christians are to have nothing to do with occult practices. The most explicit passage warns: "Let no one be found among you who sacrifices his son or daughter in the fire, who practices divination or sorcery, interprets omens, engages in witchcraft, or casts spells, or who is a medium or spiritist or who consults the dead. Anyone who does these things is detestable to the Lord, and because of these detestable practices the Lord your God will drive out these nations before you."[583] This and the other passages give a strong warning to Christians who are tempted to be involved in any kind of occultism. Yet meeting Tibetan Buddhists, especially in Asia, brings Christians into contact with people who are deeply involved in the occult and the forces behind it. This is *not* to say that Tibetan Buddhists are evil people, or that they are to be shunned as spiritual lepers. Christians should rightly seek their friendship and be examples of God's love to them. Some Christians who do so, however, report experiences of spiritual oppression, which may appear as depression, anxiety, or experiences that they describe as supernatural in origin.[584]

Another concern for many people like Beth is dealing with opposition, which comes in various forms. The least common form is direct opposition from local people, who are almost always friendly and welcoming. More commonly, opposition takes the form of difficulty in dealing with various government bureaucracies, complying with local rules and regulations, and gaining permits and different types of permissions. Official demands for bribes, special favors, and even attempts at extortion are not unknown in the countries of Inner Asia. In addition to these sources of opposition, daily living in less-developed countries takes a lot of time and energy. Much of Inner Asia is bitterly cold in winter, and there may not be any adequate source of heat. In desert or steppe areas, blowing dust makes one dirty and there may not be enough water for washing. All these factors, taken together, can be very wearing. Christians must rely on a faith that won't let go when the going gets tough. This kind of battle-hardened faith is won only by experience, and there is no substitute for it.

Summary

A missionary outreach has been part of Christianity from its very beginnings. Christian missions is not an act of cultural imperialism perpetrated by fundamentalist zealots, but a practical manifestation of God's love for the world and its peoples. Those who would serve as cross-cultural "ambassadors for Christ" need careful preparation. A firm faith, practical holiness, good communication skills, and mature wisdom are essential qualities. A Biblical approach to other religions is essential if we are to engage the beliefs of world religions without accommodating to them. The Apostle Paul's speech to the Athenians serves as a model of how to do this. But more than words are needed. People need to meet Christ as He lives out His life through those who believe in Him. In other words, the Gospel must have skin on it to become real.

People like Beth know this, and they seek a solid foundation for ministry as they prepare to live and work in Inner Asia. Taking the time to prepare well is worthy of the task. It eases entry into a new culture, and keeps the new cross-cultural ambassador from making many mistakes which might have serious consequences later on. In the next chapter we shall see these principles in action as we follow Beth into Inner Asia.

CHAPTER 11

Christians in the Tibetan Buddhist World

A Quick Tour

On the way to her host country, Beth wants to take a quick tour of Inner Asia to familiarize herself with the region she will soon call home. She begins her tour in India, where she sees a growing Indian evangelical church openly preaching Christ. After visiting Ladakh and some north Indian hill stations, she flies to Bhutan, a Tibetan Buddhist monarchy where monks and lamas hold great influence with the government and where the local church struggles under many difficulties. A week later she visits Kathmandu, Nepal, where a growing national church is increasingly active in sharing Christ with Tibetan Buddhist minority peoples. The next section of her trip takes her across the Himalayas into western China, home to 70 per cent of the population of the Tibetan Buddhist world. Making her way across the mountains and high deserts of Inner Asia, she reaches Beijing and takes a train to Mongolia, once rigidly Stalinist, but now establishing its new identity in the modern world. The final portion of her trip is a brief foray into Siberia, home to two of Russia's three Tibetan Buddhist peoples. In all, her journey crosses the largely impoverished homelands of at least 60 different ethnic groups,[585] speaking 40 or more different languages,[586] whose governments are either widely tolerant or harshly repressive of local Christian churches. As Beth's tour demonstrates, the Tibetan Buddhist world is a very complex place. Each of the six countries with substantial Tibetan Buddhist populations has different social, political, linguistic, and economic conditions to which Christians must adapt. While all this diversity may seem confusing at first, there are some basic principles that can help

Christians like Beth live out the life of Christ in whatever culture they enter.

Learning a New Language

At the end of the tour, Beth returns to her new host country eager to begin her assignment. Everything seems wonderfully exotic and Beth is fascinated by all the new sights and sounds and smells. All around her, people are speaking a new language. Shop signs are in an unfamiliar script. Beth finds that she can't even buy groceries without help; worse than that, she's illiterate! Beth realizes very quickly that if she wants to relate to people in her new culture, she's going to have to learn their language.

Of Asia's approximately 2,000 living languages, about 40 are spoken by Tibetan Buddhist peoples. Each of these 40 languages belongs to one of two big language families: the Sino-Tibetan family (365 languages including Tibetan and Chinese) or the Altaic family (65 languages including Mongolian and various languages related to Turkish). Since most Tibetan Buddhist peoples live as minorities among a dominant majority (e.g. Tibetans among Han Chinese, Buryats among Russians), many of them speak two languages: their own local language (e.g. a Tibetan dialect), and the majority's national language (e.g. Mandarin Chinese). Even though many people are bilingual, they almost always use their own local language when they want to say what is truly important to them. The value of studying this "heart language" cannot be overemphasized. With a clear command of the local tongue, people like Beth can develop good relationships with others, learn their culture well, and use a local version of the Bible. Without good language skills, they may be limited to friendships with people who can speak English. Such people may be interesting and helpful, but they are usually not typical of the population at large. Monolingual foreigners will also have to depend on local translators, or maybe even limit communication of their faith to handing out literature they cannot read, videos they can't understand, or Bibles

Languages of the Tibetan Buddhist World

Country	Official Language(s)	Documented Living Languages	Major Languages Spoken by T.B. Peoples	Examples of Tibetan Buddhist Languages
Russia	Russian	100	3	Buryat Kalmyk
Mongolia	Khalkha	12	4	Buryat Tuvan
China	Mandarin	201	11+	Tibetan (3 dialects) Qiang Yugur Tu Mongolian
India	Hindi English	387 +	8 +	Tibetan Ladakhi
Nepal	Nepali English	120	6 +	Tamang Sherpa
Bhutan	Dzongkha English	24	5	Tshangla Khengkha

they can't study. As a result, they may be mystified when Tibetan Buddhist friends make comments like, "Jesus and the Dalai Lama are the same," or "Tibetan Buddhism is the same as Christianity."

Learning a national language, and maybe a local one as well, might look like a hopelessly difficult task. The years of study are long, the frustrations many, and the sacrifices great. But Christians who are called of God to share Christ in the Tibetan Buddhist world dare not do less than to take the way of the cross in learning the right language well. Those who do will gain more than the ability to speak to others. As the missions scholar David Hesselgrave writes: "Languages constitute veritable gold mines of information about the people and cultures that employ them."[587] Language students will learn a great deal about the spiritual worldview of their Tibetan Buddhist friends simply by understanding their spiritual vocabulary. This will be an enormous help to the students later on, when they are ready to share the Gospel verbally.

Among all the languages of the Tibetan Buddhist world, one has a preeminent position. The classical form of the Tibetan language has the same exalted place in Buddhist Central Asia as Arabic does in the Islamic world, or Sanskrit in the Hindu world. It is the "mother language" of Tibetan Buddhism and the source of many of its spiritual terms. Christians who understand Tibetan spiritual vocabulary have a long head start in making the Gospel clear even to their non-Tibetan listeners. Tibetan language is also important because its literature is more widely available than that of many other Inner Asian peoples. Reading Tibetan literature in the original or in translation is helpful to learn how Tibetan Buddhists see the world around them. Just as the Apostle Paul used his knowledge of Greek literature to make his message clear to the Athenians, the Christian who has read Milarepa or Tsong Khapa will have a much better understanding of Tibetan Buddhist ways of thinking.

Learning a New Culture

The people in Beth's new community not only speak differently from Beth, they act differently as well - sometimes in ways that surprise or even shock her. Before long, she realizes that it is not enough for her to *speak* as her local friends do, she also has to learn how to *behave* as they do. Beth is smart enough to realize that the more she knows about the local culture and ways of doing things, the less "foreign" she will appear. "After all," she reasons, "if Jesus was willing to come down from Heaven and learn the language and culture of his "host country," then I should be willing to do the same."[588]

Learning about a new culture can be lot of fun, and there are many ways to do it well. One of the best methods employs helpers who can teach the cultural basics they teach to their own children. Perhaps you can be "adopted" by a family with whom you have a close enough relationship to let them correct you when you make mistakes. If you can't find such a family, try to find a local "mother" to teach you basic cultural values, and a "father" to give you guidance and direction in relationships. While it is helpful if these people are Christians, they need not be. A local family can give you a lot of general information about the culture, such as expected roles for men and women, how decisions are made, or how to show respect. David Hesselgrave points out that learning about another culture has a number of very important advantages.[589]

1. It Makes Christians Believable: The Christian who knows little or nothing of a local culture will have little credibility in it. The less one knows of a culture, the more likely one is to make mistakes, some of which may be serious. Local people are often too polite to point out such blunders, but they have long memories, and serious mistakes can undermine one's credibility for years to come. Imagine a Buddhist missionary from an Asian culture who comes to your home country with little knowledge of its customs, culture, or religion. This person cannot speak your language well, has no apparent work, and relies heavily on books, tracts, videos to get his message across. How likely would you be to change your religion after talking with him or her? On a positive note, credibility is enhanced when Christians know how to live out the life of Christ in ways that are meaningful in the local culture.

2. It Keeps Communication Clear: A knowledge of local culture and of Tibetan Buddhism is essential for Bible study and for other settings where the Gospel is communicated verbally. People in any culture tend to compare the teachings of the Bible to those of their own religion. The Christian who cannot help a local person bridge the gap between a folk Buddhist worldview and a Biblical worldview will not be a very effective communicator of the Gospel message. By contrast, those with a good knowledge of local culture tend to be good at putting the truths of the Bible in terms that local people can understand.[590] They can illustrate Biblical truth in a local style with locally appropriate examples.

3. It Helps Evaluate Methods: Should Beth use Tibetan-style religious paintings in sharing the Gospel message? Is it alright for her to say that Jesus took on our karma? Should she put a Tibetan- or Mongolian-style scarf around a picture of Jesus? Some Tibetan Buddhist peoples have had a new year ritual in which a scapegoat took on the demerit of certain people. Would this be a good way for her to explain Christ's death? [591] Only with a deep knowledge of local culture can techniques such as these be evaluated. Unless research is very carefully done, double, wrong, or unintended meanings may be communicated. Particularly dangerous are shallow analogies like the Christian Trinity and the Tibetan Buddhist idea of the triple refuge, or the Dalai Lama's incarnation and Jesus Christ's. These kinds of superficial similarities lead to confusion and syncretism unless Christians make very clear and careful distinctions between the Christian and Tibetan Buddhist ideas behind them.

Key Cultural Indicators

Beyond credibility, clear communication, and evaluating methods, learning about the local culture helps Beth to separate the Gospel from her own cultural background. As she begins to learn about life in her new host country, she focuses on certain key issues or "cultural indicators" which include:

1. Face and Shame: Face (and its opposite, shame) are very powerful forces in many Asian cultures, and they are usually little understood by non-Asians. It is vital for anyone living in a face-and-shame culture to know how these two forces interact with each other, for at least two reasons. First, many difficulties between national Christians and expatriate workers, and many barriers to the Gospel, are created by expatriate Christians who do not know how to "give face" or prevent its loss. Second, people in face-and-shame cultures tend to have difficulty understanding the concepts of guilt and sin, so special care needs to be taken in explaining them. A complete explanation of face and shame is beyond the scope of this book, but is available in other references.[592] An important part of living in face and shame cultures is learning how to show respect to others. In non-Asian cultures, showing respect is mainly a matter of politeness and simply not being rude. In Asian cultures, however, knowing how to show respect is very important,[593] and should be learned by every Christian worker who is not already familiar with it.

2. Cultural Pride: Some cultures see themselves as high, worthy, and superior to others, while others see themselves as low, unworthy, and inferior to others. In the Tibetan Buddhist world, as a broad generalization, majority cultures tend to fit into the first category, and minority cultures tend to fit into the second. If Christianity is seen as a foreign religion, it may have a much harder time entering a "high pride" culture than a "low pride" one. High pride cultures tend to be self-interested and place little value on foreign things unless they are of immediate material benefit. This is very important to remember when adapting Christian materials for use in such a culture. In this case one would want to exclude references to foreign things and "localize" the materials as much as possible.

3. Hierarchy or Levels in Society: Some cultures divide themselves by rank and social status, while other cultures are of the "all are equal" school. A clue about this can be gained from whether a language has special terms for people of different status. Some languages have a simple system of polite titles, while others use elaborate linguistic devices to show the relative status of two speakers. The Central or "Lhasa" dialect of Tibetan is an extreme example of social hierarchy expressed in language — it employs an intricate system of honorific verbs, nouns, and titles to indicate social status. In cultures where social status is vitally important, credibility is linked to status. It is very important for a foreign Christian to understand where he or she fits into such a society in terms of social role and rank; he or she may have credibility only with equals or inferiors.

4. The Usefulness of Religion: Many Christians from a non-Asian cultural background might say that they value their faith because it is true, because it offers hope of eternity with God, or because it gives them meaning in life. For shamanists and folk Tibetan Buddhists, however, the crucial question is, "Does religion *work?*" People in these cultures tend to value a religion for what it can *do*, rather than because it offers meaning in life, a relationship with a higher spiritual power, hope for the afterlife, or forgiveness of sin. It may be more important to make clear what Christianity means for a *group* (friends, family, tribe) than for an individual. Christians need to help people in these cultures to see how Christ relates to concerns that are important their lives, while not allowing Jesus to be seen as just another powerful shaman.

5. Relationship to the Majority Culture: As mentioned above, most shamanist and Tibetan Buddhist peoples live as minority peoples within a majority culture. It's very important to understand how a majority culture treats its minority cultures. Unfortunately, racism is not just a Western problem, and some majority cultures have a "big brother complex" towards their Tibetan Buddhist minority peoples even at the best of times.[594] Some Tibetan Buddhist or shamanist cultures have adapted well to their majority cultures, while others consciously reject the majority culture. This has important implications for church relationships, language study, and ministry approaches. In general, it is more difficult for anyone to come to Christ if they must first be accepted in the majority culture.

6. How Decisions Are Made: One of the more important things that an outsider can learn about a culture is how decisions are made. Many people from outside Asia are accustomed to a democratic decision making process in which each person has an equal say and the majority rules. This type of decision making is very rare in Inner Asia, where recognized traditional leaders (e.g. older men, village elders) or appointed political leaders make most of the important decisions. Outsiders who expect to impose democratic decision making in a local church, development project, or organizational setting may be setting the stage for confusion and misunderstanding.

7. Social Structures: Human beings have many ways of forming social groups. The existence of these groups may not be obvious to outsiders, but they can be very important within the culture. For example, a tourist visiting a medium-sized Tibetan city in Inner Asia will probably notice both Han Chinese and local Tibetans living there. On probing more deeply, however, one finds that the Chinese have come from many different parts of the country, each with its own dialect, cuisine, and way of relating to other Chinese. The Tibetans also separate themselves into distinct social groups, such as farmers and nomads, speakers of Kham, Amdo, or Central Tibetan dialects, etc. These social and language distinctions are socially and economically powerful because they determine the networks of friendship and trade within the city. For example, when Tashi the Tibetan needs a new piece of furniture, he will probably go first to a store that is owned by someone from his dialect area, because a shop owner from any other dialect area will probably charge a higher price or even cheat him. If Tashi is invited to a Bible study, he may use similar criteria to decide if he can trust those who are present.

It is helpful to get an idea of how strongly people feel about their membership in social groups. Is it a vital part of their identity, or just an interesting fact about their lives? Would they socialize, conduct business, or intermarry with people from another group? Who are the group leaders, and how and why are they selected? Is the group mobile? Is the group an agricultural community that is fixed to the land, a nomad community that grazes animals in certain areas, or a migrant community whose members go back and forth between the city and the countryside? Beyond this information, it can be very helpful to ask questions about families (e.g. family values, how marriage decisions are made, who leads the family, who makes decisions), about groups and associations of all kinds, and about government policies, education, economics, and history.[595] In many parts of Inner Asia it is wise to avoid discussions about national politics.

Avoiding Mistakes

Beth knows that even though she's done her best to study her host culture before coming to Asia, she still has much to learn now that she has finally arrived. She wants to avoid causing offense as she makes new friends and learns the language. She asks many questions about the kind of behavior that local people expect from "religious" figures. For example, Beth learns that when a local boy enters a monastery, his tutors give him a set of lessons. One of these is a set of rules for proper behavior called the "Eight Acts of Low Born Persons." These forbid coarse language, impoliteness, proud speech, lack of foresight, poor manners, staring, sexual offenses, and theft. Other moral maxims include the "Ten Faults": disbelief in doctrine, lack of respect for teachers, being obnoxious to others, desiring what belongs to someone else, talking too much, making fun of another's trouble, swearing, getting angry, borrowing and not paying back, and stealing.[596] While Beth didn't need to be reminded not to steal or use coarse language, she learned she could easily offend others by not following local standards of restraint in speech, or by not showing respect to teachers or elders in locally appropriate ways. Non-Asians in particular are likely to give offense by speaking too much or too loudly, failing to show respect to elders, and by being what locals consider direct or brusque in manner.[595]

The wise Christian will live in a way that Tibetan Buddhists regard as holy, so far as is consistent with Scripture. A British missionary tells the story of a mistake made early in his career in China. While attending a language lesson with a local Tibetan Buddhist monk, a bug entered the room and distracted his attention. Annoyed, he raised his hand to kill it when the monk forcibly restrained him, asking: "Would Jesus kill it?" In an instant the missionary realized that his teacher would regard this as a grave sin that would reflect poorly on the name of Christ. The humbled missionary left that room with a new awareness of cultural differences.[598] While most Tibetan Buddhist peoples are very forgiving of mistakes by newcomers, some mistakes are far more serious than others. Every Christian should be aware of actions which may be trivial in one's home country, but which can be "ministry killers" among a Tibetan Buddhist people. Depending on the particular culture and circumstances, showing anger at a local person, killing an animal, or using alcohol just once can ruin relationships and negate the value of any further ministry.[599]

Geoffrey Bull, a missionary on the eastern frontier of Tibet in the late 1940s, learned this lesson the hard way. One evening he was invited to a well-attended religious debate with a famous local lama. The debate went badly for the missionary, who felt that the entire discussion was becoming a farce. Finally, in response to a question he felt was designed to make him look silly, Bull responded sharply to the lama. Later a Tibetan friend counseled him: "You became angry, you know. The thing is, you do not yet understand the ideas of Buddhist debate. The question he asked you was quite valid from the standpoint of Buddhism. Even if his question had not been reasonable, yet in the circumstances it should have been taken up reasonably."[600] Bull had to learn that local ideas of holiness are important.

Local standards are also important in churches. Tibetan Buddhists venerate their gods with great outward piety, often prostrating themselves full length on the ground before a sacred image. They handle their scriptures as materially holy objects, wrapping them in cloth and storing them carefully. However non-Asian Christians may feel about such practices, showing great outward respect to sacred things and religious persons is part of the way that Tibetan Buddhists understand holiness. Foreign Christians can give a poor impression of their faith when they talk loudly in a church, pray in casual postures, or handle their Bibles carelessly.[601] Any printed religious materials should be handled with respect. Another application of this principle is to adopt a simple lifestyle. Except in the case of "incarnate" lamas, most people in Inner Asia expect religious figures to live simply. Christians who go overseas burdened with many of the material goods of modern life will certainly make an impression on the local people, but it will not necessarily be one of holiness. Of course, standards of wealth vary enormously across Asia, and local conditions should be taken into account.[602]

Beth finds that eating local food and wearing local clothing shows her friends that she takes their culture seriously and accepts their ways (within Scriptural limits) as her own. The ability to drink Tibetan salted butter tea, or to eat Mongolian *buudz*, and enjoy them, is an essential social skill. An expatriate Christian in Nepal found that when she wore Tibetan-style clothing, her opportunities to talk with Tibetan women multiplied. Simply changing her mode of dress was seen as a gesture of respect to the Tibetan community. But identifying with a local culture goes deeper than simply putting on its clothes. Christians can also "put on" a Tibetan Buddhist view of the world, and learn to see life as Tibetan Buddhists see it. Beth realizes that she needs to continue learning the local language and culture until she can see the world in the same way that her friends do.

Ministry Multipliers

Once Beth has learned the basics of living in her new culture, she begins to think carefully about the things that will help her share Christ in a way that will be appreciated by people from a shamanist or folk Tibetan Buddhist background. Her train of thought begins when one of her new Tibetan Buddhist friends asks her: "Why are you here?"

1. Plausibility: The person who has a plausible, long-term, non-religious reason for his or her presence in a country tends to be better accepted than the person who stays only for a few weeks, or who is seen merely as a salesperson for a foreign religion. Christians who have a locally acceptable reason for their presence can enjoy a wide range of contacts with local people. For example, the Tibetans are avid traders. Christians who are involved in business or handicraft development projects will enjoy meeting many people in circumstances that Tibetans see as non-threatening. One Christian in Nepal met many local people by starting a joint venture in exporting Tibetan wool carpets. Many professional people work in the Tibetan Buddhist world as teachers, medical personnel, or aid and development workers. In an incarnational approach to missions, these activities are *never* "covers" or "fronts" for evangelism, but Christlike activities that meet real human needs and have eternal value on their own account.[603] They are the compassionate context in which local people can see the life of Christ lived out.

Tourism is a major industry in a number of Tibetan Buddhist countries, and facilities for tourists are becoming more common throughout Inner Asia. Short term visits to the area for purposes of tourism or providing technical assistance are becoming more frequent. Prospective Christian workers may come to Asia on orientation visits, prayer tours, or to visit local churches. It is very important that short term visitors receive a good orientation before leaving their home country and coordinate their activities with national churches or resident Christians. There are many parts of the Tibetan Buddhist world where the well-intentioned activities of uninformed Christians can do more harm than good. Short-term groups should remember that while their trip can be used of God, their credibility with local people may be limited if they are not linked with long term benefits in some way.

2. Humility: Christians are not the only ones who love their neighbors. One rainy day in the Himalayas the author and his wife were threading their way along a narrow track across a rain-slickened landslide high above a river. The way seemed especially dangerous when seemingly out of nowhere came a local man who guided us safely across. When thanked for his kindness, he simply replied: "I am a Buddhist," and left. His practical love for two people he had never met made a lasting impression on two people who had come to teach others about love. Christians should always keep in mind that only God's undeserved favor separates them from the Buddhists and shamanists they have come to serve. Christians have nothing they did not receive, nothing to boast about, no way in which they are morally or racially superior to others. This being the case, Christians have no reason to say bad things about the Buddha or Buddhists. The Church does not grow by destruction or disparagement of Buddhism or shamanism.

3. Taking Time: Shamanist and Tibetan Buddhist peoples need to come to grips with many unfamiliar ideas (e.g. God, creation, sin) before they can completely understand the Gospel. It is very important not to rush this process. Jesus often met people at their point of need without explaining to them the entire plan of salvation, and Christians living in Central Asia need be in no rush to share truths for which people are not yet ready. Indirect approaches often work well in Inner Asian societies. For example, Allan was a teacher who lived in Central Asia. In his city there was a large Tibetan Buddhist religious shrine called a *chorten*. On holy days, hundreds of people would come to walk around the chorten, spinning prayer wheels and saying mantras. Open evangelism was against the law in Allan's country at that time, so instead of preaching to the crowd, he walked around the chorten with the rest of the pilgrims, reading from local language Christian literature he had brought with him. The local people were surprised to see him reading a book in their language, and they started reading over his shoulder. A conversation began; soon people requested copies of the book for themselves. Another indirect approach is to encourage a Tibetan Buddhist or shamanist friend to try to keep his or her own moral standard perfectly for one week, or even for one day. If such a person is honest, they will soon realize that they don't always have pure thoughts about others or consistently compassionate motives. This is a natural starting place for a lesson on the place of sin in human life, and on Jesus Christ as the answer to that problem.

Sharing Christ in the Tibetan Buddhist World

Historically, Christians have tried to share their faith with Tibetan Buddhists in a number of different ways.[604] Some of them are summarized below.

1. The Doctrinal Comparison Approach: This method lists the major doctrines of a world religion, compares them with Christian beliefs, and presents an argument as to why Christianity is better. Such an approach is followed in Chapters Eight and Nine of this book. It was also used by the Apostle Paul in his speech to the Athenians in the seventeenth chapter of the Book of Acts. He noted the Athenians' professed belief in an unknown god, compared that god to the one true God, and implicitly claimed that Christianity was better because it offered life from the dead.[605] To take the same approach with Buddhism, we could point out that according to the doctrine of rebirth, people are trapped in an endless cycle: birth, death, and rebirth. This cyclic view of human history leads to fatalism and acceptance of social injustice. But the Bible asserts that the universe has a beginning and that history is moving towards the glorious conclusion described in the Book of Revelation. This belief leads to the hope of ultimate justice. Therefore Christianity is better than Buddhism (at least as far as an ultimate hope is concerned).

This doctrinal comparison approach is commonly used in comparative religion courses outside Asia, and it is easy to see why. It is simple, it follows Western ways of thinking, it makes Tibetan Buddhism easier to understand and evaluate, and it produces apologetic arguments that are convincing to Christians. However, when used as an evangelistic method, this approach tends to be ineffective, because: a) there is a tendency for Christians to oversimplify doctrines which they do not completely understand, or to be baffled by doctrines (e.g. those of tantra) for which there is no Christian counterpart; b) comparing similar categories of thought leaves Christianity open to the response "its the same as Buddhism"; c) it doesn't work well for shamanist peoples or folk Tibetan Buddhists whose interest in religion is defined by the practical benefits it will bring to them; d) it is a Western method which seems quite strange and unconvincing to most people in Inner Asia. In general, doctrinal comparison is better used as a teaching method for Christians than as an apologetic or evangelistic tool.

2. The Cultural Forms Approach: This technique looks for items within Tibetan Buddhist culture which can be adapted to Christian use. Had the Apostle Paul actually taken up residence in the Athenian temple of the unknown god (Acts 17:23) and used it as a teaching center, he would have been using this approach. Within Asia, a number of Christian groups have published Bible portions in the Tibetan scriptural format known as *pecha*. Others have put the life of Jesus in pictorial form on *thangkas*, or Tibetan religious paintings on silk rolls. Such approaches can make Christianity seem less foreign, but they also run the risk of sending wrong or syncretistic messages. The cultural forms approach can be helpful if it is thoughtfully and prayerfully used, but it should be attempted only with a thorough understanding of both the form and the function of an object in its original setting, and then only after wide consultation with the national church. Tibetan Buddhists may have strongly negative feelings about Christians who use items of Buddhist material culture to explain Christian beliefs. The key is to be very careful, selective, and prayerful in adopting such cultural forms.

3. The Physical Needs Approach: This form simply looks for physical needs and attempts to meet them; it was constantly used by Jesus. Christians have set up programs in health, education, and community development in many countries of Inner Asia. It works well in settings where openly Christian activity is not allowed by the government. It is an excellent expression of an incarnational approach to missions, and offers a wonderful opportunity to work alongside local people. It also expresses Christ's concern for the poor and for man's social and physical needs. It builds good will and fulfills God's command to love our neighbor. However, these activities have to be very carefully planned if they are to be sustainable from local resources. The time and energy spent in meeting physical needs can overwhelm any kind of spiritual witness. Meeting the physical, social, and educational needs of people is commonly misunderstood by Tibetan Buddhists as a form of payment for conversion to Christianity. Even so, meeting physical needs is still the most common form of Christian ministry in Inner Asia.

4. The Folk Religion Approach: This technique recognizes that Christianity has had its greatest numerical successes in dealing with animism and folk religions, and has been least successful in dealing with established "high" religions like Islam, Hinduism, or Buddhism. Advocates of this method argue that since the great majority of people are (in effect) folk religionists, why not treat them all as animists and simply bypass any apologetic based on, for example, Tibetan Buddhism? In practice, this approach looks at everyday problems such as dealing with evil spirits, providing for one's family, or gaining spiritual power, and tries to provide Christian answers. It has the great merit of avoiding direct confrontation with Buddhism. It also concentrates on something Christianity does very well, that is, interacting with animism and folk religions. On the surface it would seem to work well in shamanist or folk Tibetan Buddhist cultures. As we have seen, however, these cultures tend to look at religion in terms of "does it work?" rather than "is it true?" An approach purely at the folk religious level may result in a "what can Jesus do for me?" mentality. Foreign Christians who try this approach may be less effective communicators if they focus only on the folk religion level and do not understand a Tibetan Buddhist worldview.

5. The Direct Approach: This method follows apostolic example in preaching the Word of God directly to Tibetan Buddhist people, without using doctrinal comparisons, cultural forms, ministry to physical needs, or dialogue with folk religionists. It has been tried many times both in the Tibetan and Mongol portions of the Tibetan Buddhist world. In general, this approach works best for local Asian believers whose cultural background is very close to that of the people they are trying to reach. Historically, it has worked very poorly for non-Asians, or even for people from Outer Asia whose culture isn't sufficiently close to that of the people they are trying to reach.

6. The Community Approach: This is a modification of the direct approach. It was used by Catholic missionaries in Inner Mongolia and Sichuan in China up to 1949. As people came to Christ they were *withdrawn* from their larger social setting and brought into a mutually supporting community of believers, which was sometimes physically separated from the rest of the culture. Despite the fact that this approach would seem to violate some of the tenets of modern missions, in 1997 there were reported to be 2,000 ethnically Mongol Catholics in Inner Mongolia, with 2 Mongol priests and over 4,000 Tibetan Catholics in Sichuan and Yunnan.[606] In the early history of the Tamang church in Nepal, the withdrawal of some of the first believers into a separate community played a crucial role in allowing the church to grow large enough to withstand opposition from the majority culture.[607]

7. The Guru-Disciple in Community Approach: In this relationship-centered technique, a Christian teacher (*guru*) lives in community with a group of disciples. This time-honored teaching method was used by Jesus and the Buddha. The living-in-community model is very Asian, intensely relational, offers a living model of faith in Christ, and allows for learning by "watching and doing likewise." Its weakness is that it requires a setting where an openly Christian community life is possible. To the author's knowledge, Christians have never tried this approach in a planned and intentional way in the Tibetan Buddhist world.

The Fallacy of the Magic Key

Though these approaches (and others) have been used in the long history of missions to Tibetan Buddhist peoples in Inner Asia, none has proven to be a "magic key" that unlocks peoples' hearts. Much has been written about various techniques and strategies that are supposedly effective in planting the Church, but their track record in the Tibetan Buddhist world is not encouraging. While it is easy to point out historical or sociological factors that may have contributed to Church growth among the Mongols, Tamangs, or Lepchas, in the last analysis the Church grows only though the work of the Holy Spirit. There is no technical or methodological "magic key" that puts His work under human control. Success in missions is not a matter of technique but of long-term obedience and the sovereignty of God. In human terms it depends upon living out the life of Christ in ways that local people can understand and appreciate.

The Three Steps

By the end of her first few years in Asia, Beth had learned the local language and culture. She had a circle of local friends, and the work in her development project was going well. Some of her friends had asked questions about her faith, and she felt it was time to say something to them. As she studied her Bible one day, she found herself thinking about the Apostle Paul's famous questions, "How can they believe in the one of whom they have not heard? And how can they hear without someone preaching to them?"[608] In this passage, Paul was talking about the fact that people need a way to *discover* Christ. This may happen through preaching, friends, church attendance, films, books, audio media, or tracts, but the important point is that someone hears about Christ for the first time. After the discovery phase, a *relationship* with an individual believer or a local church allows an inquirer to see a living example of Christian faith in a way that is personally meaningful to them. A period of *instruction* about the Christian faith (or discipleship training) normally occurs during or after the relationship phase.

To give some Biblical examples, Simon Peter *discovered* Jesus when told about him by his brother Andrew.[609] He had a three-year *relationship* with Jesus as a disciple, which convinced him that Jesus was Lord;[610] during this time Jesus *instructed* him in the faith. Perhaps more typical was the experience of the early Christians in Jerusalem, who discovered Christ through the Apostles' preaching[611] came to know Him in relationship with the early Church,[612] and were instructed by the Apostles[613] in the content of their faith. These three general stages of progress towards Christ (discovery, relationship, and instruction) are ultimately under the timing and control of the Holy Spirit. Beth doesn't expect her friends to progress through these stages at a time of her choosing, and she doesn't try to put pressure on anyone to move faster than the Holy Spirit is working in their hearts. While no one claims that every new believer always goes through these three phases in this order, the three steps do offer a convenient framework for thinking about ministry. It may be helpful to consider them in a bit more detail.

1. Discovery: Historically, the discovery phase usually began when Christians arrived in places such as Kathmandu, Lhasa, Leh, or Urga (Ulaanbaatar) and began to preach the Gospel. In modern times, people may first hear favorable mention of Christ through radio broadcasting (e.g. in India) or the *Jesus* film (e.g. in Mongolia). People may also hear of Christ for the first time from government propaganda or other sources opposed to the Christian faith. Mass media have allowed large numbers of people to hear about Christ without Christians being physically present, which has had both advantages (audience size) and disadvantages (no living example). Ideally, the discovery phase is an attractive process during which the Holy Spirit persuades the non-believer that in Jesus Christ there is something good, something powerful, something transcendent. Miracles were a part of the discovery process for many early Christians[614] and healings continue to be so today in parts of the Tibetan Buddhist world. Dreams have been important for members of some tribal groups in Nepal. There are many people

Effective and Ineffective Relationships

Effective Relationships	Ineffective Relationships
Genuine and Long Term	Short term or 'Hit and Run'
Acceptance Not Conditional on Conversion	Acceptance Conditional on Conversion
Gives Face to the Buddhist	Condemns Buddhism or Shamanism
Dialogue	Argument
Models Christ's Servanthood	Domination by Christian
Patient	Impatient
Spirit-led	Program driven

in the Tibetan Buddhist world who have been touched by God in some wonderful way, but have yet to hear of Jesus. These people are like Nicodemus[615] or Cornelius[616] — they already know something of God, but want to know Him still better. A number of successful missionaries to Buddhists spent their careers looking for such people and investing time in them. One experienced worker makes a practice of searching for people with a sympathy for Biblical values. He looks for an openness to people of other backgrounds; a concern for the truth (he deliberately overpays shopkeepers to see if they will give him the right change!); an understanding of the need for grace and forgiveness; or a sympathy for the needs of their poorer neighbors. When he finds people like this, he spends his time with them.

Beth knows how to help her local friends discover Christ, but what about all the shopkeepers, government officials, taxi drivers, and other people she meets in the course of her day? How can she help them discover Jesus? She realizes that most of them aren't ready to hear the Gospel. As she reflected on the fact that people often come to Christ in stages, she discovered a way to help them take at least one step toward Christ. When talking with a government official, she mentioned that a part of her faith is doing good works among the poor and the disadvantaged. This is not a one-time Gospel presentation, but it might help the official overcome his prejudice against Christianity. He might even develop a positive attitude towards it. The next time he meets a Christian, he may be more open to being led another step or two towards faith in Christ. Once Beth began to approach her friends in this way, she realized that *every encounter could be eternally significant* even if she could not share the entire Gospel message. Beth discovered the practical truth of Paul's statement, "I planted the seed, Apollos watered it, but God made it grow. So neither he who plants nor he who waters is anything, but only God, who makes things grow."[617]

2. Relationship: Like most other people, Tibetan Buddhists meet Jesus most easily in the context of a relationship with a believer or a local church. But this kind of relationship is more than just a friendship. This kind of relationship *incarnates or models Christ in ways that Tibetan Buddhists can understand and appreciate;.* a relationship exemplified in the story of the Good Samaritan. It answers in practical ways the inquirer's question, "Does the God of the Christians really care about me?" Relationship can be one of the most enjoyable and rewarding aspects of ministry; it can also be one of the most difficult and time consuming. Relationships must be undertaken freely, with no strings attached. An "I'll be your friend if you'll become a Christian" attitude has no place in Inner Asia or anywhere else. Good relationships are free from material benefits to either side, thus avoiding allegations that Christians "pay" Buddhists to convert to Christianity. Relationships must also be free of coercion. Tibetans who have been pressured into using Western evangelistic methods have some very sorry tales to tell, which do not reflect well on the Christians who trained them. Many troubles arise when relationships are not honest, open, equal, and respectful, or where they are tainted by hope of gain (of converts or money) on either side. Some characteristics of effective and ineffective relationships are shown in the following table.

3. Instruction: Instruction of new believers should occur in the context of a relationship with a more mature Christian or with a local church. It is normally during this phase that the new believer's faith is filled with content through Bible study and other methods of teaching. Bible study can be fun and rewarding if a few basic issues are kept in mind. First of all, studying the Bible directly, *without* using ancillary material translated from another language, may be the best choice. If published Bible study materials are used, they should be well-translated, and more importantly, well-adapted. A "rule of thumb" test for good adaptation is to ask a local person to read, listen to, or watch the materials in question, and then ask if they sound as though they were written by a foreigner. If the answer is yes, it may be best to study the Bible directly or to use other materials. Bible study materials which do not address local concerns or which are not adapted to local ways of thinking may not be very effective, and they make Christianity seem like a foreign religion.

Second, the worldview of people in Inner Asia may be limited because they may have had very little exposure to the world outside their own town or village. Foreigners can forget that local people may need help in understanding the details of Biblical customs, culture, festivals, daily life, geography, and history. They may be at a complete loss to know where Israel is or who the Jews are, or whether Jesus lived in the first century or the nineteenth century. One Tibetan who read a Gospel for the first time wanted to know if Israel was a place in America. Teachers need to be aware of these issues and take the time to explain them to their students.

In Asia, it's generally more effective to use the Bible as a storybook rather than a set of theological proof-texts. People everywhere love stories, and the Bible contains the best stories ever told. Many Bible characters lived in circumstances not too different from those of modern Inner Asian nomads, so folk Tibetan Buddhists can often appreciate Bible stories without knowing a lot of background. But other parts of the Bible can be much harder to understand. The Biblical style of storytelling may be quite different from what Tibetan Buddhists are used to, and some material is very difficult for them to grasp (e.g. why does Jesus have so many heated arguments with the Pharisees?). As a general rule, it is good to take Bible stories in short segments, with frequent stops to let your Tibetan Buddhist friend tell you his or her understanding of the story.

Tibetan Buddhists may understand Biblical terms in non-Biblical ways. As Geoffrey Bull noted: "We take up and use a word in Tibetan, unconsciously giving it a Christian content. For them, however, it has a Buddhist content. We speak of God. In our minds this word conveys to us the concept of the supreme and Eternal Spirit, Creator and Sustainer of all things, Whose essence is love, Whose presence is all holy, and Whose ways are all righteous. For them, the Tibetan word God means nothing of the kind. We speak of prayer, the spiritual communion between God our Father and His children. For them prayer is a repetition of abstruse formulae and mystic phrases handed down from time immemorial. We speak of sin. For them the main emphasis is in the condemnation of killing animals."[618] The importance of defining terms is shown by an example from Tibetan history. In the seventh century A.D., Buddhist missionaries brought their Sanskrit language religious texts across the Himalayas to shamanist Tibet. The Tibetans had no words in their own language for the difficult philosophical terms so common in tantric Buddhism, so they compiled extensive word lists in which Buddhist meanings were assigned to Tibetan terms. This made for clear communication and kept their work at a high scholarly standard. Modern Christians face similar issues, and must understand fully both the Buddhist and the Christian meaning of the terms they use, and make the difference clear to their hearers.

This is especially important when it comes to central Biblical concepts like God, love, and salvation. Here are a few examples from Tibetan (the basis for spiritual terms among many Tibetan Buddhist peoples). All of these words are used in the older editions of the Tibetan Bible, and all of them have Buddhist as well as Christian meanings: 1) Compassion: (Tibetan *snying rje*) In Tibetan Buddhism, compassion is the *wish* that all beings may be free from suffering.[619] Tibetan Buddhist compassion is a mental attitude, while Christian compassion is always linked with action.[620] 2) God: (Tibetan *dkon mchog*) The Tibetan term can be used at the folk Buddhist level to refer in a general way to a supreme deity, but most often is used to mean the Buddha, his teachings, and the body of monks (the so called *Kön Chog Sum* or triple refuge). While Christian Tibetans use the term Kön Chok to refer to God, who is eternal, personal, holy, just and loving, none of these qualities is implied in the Buddhist sense of the term. 3) Incarnation: (Tibetan *sprul sku*) is a person who is a mystical emanation from a famous teacher or deity. Thus the Dalai Lama is believed to be the *tulku* of the god Chenresi, in the sense that Chenresi is using the Dalai Lama's body.[621] The root word "tul" (*sprul*) is used of apparitions, phantoms, and ghosts, and the tulku himself is thought by many to be only partly real.[622] The word "tul" is used in the Tibetan Bible of Jesus' appearance on earth[623] and Jesus' title of Savior (*skyab mgon*) is often used to refer to the Dalai Lama and other tulkus. This can cause confusion when Christians do not define their terms. One learned Tibetan read an entire tract on the life of Christ, and then asked if the tract referred to the Dalai Lama. It is no surprise that Buddhists often assert that Jesus was a tulku.[624] The distinction between this idea and the Christian sense of the word incarnation is very important. 4) Salvation: (Tibetan *thar pa*) in its Buddhist sense means to be saved from rebirth and suffering. The person who has achieved *thar pa* has entered nirvana. 5) Sin (Tibetan *sdig pa*) The Tibetan sense of the word is closer to the English words "offense" or "crime." A sin in this sense is a bad act that brings demerit on the sinner, but it has no connection with the idea of offending a righteous God. This is just a sampling of the words frequently used by Christians and Tibetan Buddhists when they talk with each other. Many other examples could be given. The point is that *Christians must clearly define their terms when they use words with Tibetan Buddhist meanings.*

Christians need to select and adapt Biblical material in such a way that it will be most easily understood by Tibetan Buddhists and make them want to hear (or read) more. The stories from Genesis are helpful in this regard, because they do not require a great deal of background information in order to be understood. Stories from Genesis are also helpful because they teach foundational truths that "set the stage" for the Gospel. Jesus' parables also have a transcultural appeal that Tibetan Buddhists appreciate. The Gospel of John has mystical elements that are appreciated by more educated readers. By contrast, Scripture verses that discuss obvious suffering, animal sacrifices, war, and death are probably not the best ones to study first. These things are all part of God's revelation and must be discussed eventually, of course. But there is little point in causing so much confusion at the beginning that our local friends have no desire to learn anything more about Christ.

Christians who preach among Theravada Buddhists in Thailand have found that their listeners appreciate the Gospel as a means of avoiding hell.[625] Folk Tibetan Buddhists believe in a hell strikingly like the one described in Dante's famous *Inferno*, only the Buddhist version is divided into eight hot and eight cold hells. Each hell has several sub-hells in which sinners are made to suffer until they work off their demerits. Folk Tibetan Buddhists tell vivid stories of the excruciating tortures to be found in the underworld, and there is genuine fear of hell as a place of possible rebirth in future lives.[626]

After key spiritual terms are defined, the major ideas of the Gospel message introduced, and Scripture passages selected, the Gospel message must be applied to life. Non-Asian Christians must be very careful to do this in a style that Tibetan Buddhists will not see as foreign. Examples of such styles include informality, directness, lack of obvious reverence for God and the Scriptures, and overt displays of emotion. Like most other peoples, Tibetan Buddhists prefer a native style in religious communication. For example, many non-Asians tend to think in terms of logical progression; most of them would agree with the reasoning behind the statement: "Two religions that teach completely opposite things cannot both be true." Tibetan Buddhists, however, view truth inclusively and think intuitively (see Chapters Three and Five). Most Tibetan Buddhists would therefore disagree with the reasoning behind the statement above. Another style preference is for rote memorization rather than understanding the general principles of why something happens. Tibetan scholars never tired of sorting their doctrines into easily memorized lists, and their literature is full of mnemonic aids like the four relations of speech, the eight acts of low born persons, or the ten faults. Though this style of education may seem difficult to non-Asians, it is the way that the people of most Inner Asian cultures learn best. Christians in Tibetan Buddhist lands might do well to concentrate instead on skillfully using stories, parables,[627] and easily memorized lists such as the Ten Commandments, the Nine Beatitudes of Matthew 5:3-11, or the Nine Fruits of the Spirit mentioned in Ephesians 5:22.

Meeting Objections

Any honest dialogue with people of another faith will bring forth a number of objections to the Gospel. The Scriptural principle for dealing with objections is found in 2 Timothy 2:24-26: "And the Lord's servant must not quarrel; instead, he must be kind to everyone, able to teach, not resentful. Those who oppose him he must gently instruct, in the hope that God will grant them repentance leading them to a knowledge of the truth, and that they will come to their senses and escape from the trap of the devil, who has taken them captive to do his will." To meet objections with gentleness, it is very important to know how to think like a Tibetan Buddhist. Remember that for Tibetan Buddhists, ultimate religious truth is not a series of propositions that can be thought about logically, but an experience that everyone must have for him or herself.

1. Different Paths to the Same Goal: Perhaps the most common of objections is that Christianity and Tibetan Buddhism are just different paths to the same goal. North Americans or Europeans who have converted to Tibetan Buddhism will often express this view, and for them reasoning step by step through both religions may be effective in showing them that this is untrue (see chapters Eight and Nine). Asian and some European and American Tibetan Buddhists will often appeal to the monistic idea that the truth lies beyond all apparent opposites like true and false. In this way, they can honestly and sincerely maintain that despite the most obvious differences between the two religions, they are the same in the end. Such people may be helped by the illustration that all the world's religions are in fact man's best effort to reach heaven by different paths, but there is one religion that begins in Heaven and comes down to man. This is the religion of the One who came from Heaven, Jesus Christ.[628]

2. Christians Kill Animals: A second objection may seem trivial to Christians but it is very serious to Buddhists; namely, that Christians kill animals, which is a very sinful act in Buddhist thinking. (Yet it is still practiced at the folk level in a number of places in Inner Asia.) The animal sacrifices of the Old Testament are particularly repugnant to Tibetan Buddhists, and some groups find the catching[629] and eating[630] of fish morally offensive. Discussion on these points should be postponed until the Tibetan Buddhist has had a chance to understand the Biblical concepts of a Creator God, the nature of sin, and the relationship of sin to death. Christians agree with Tibetan Buddhists that death is indeed a serious matter, but sin is an even more serious matter. So serious is it that God had to use the death of animals to show how wicked sin really is. By contrast, there are Bible stories which tell of God's care for his creatures, and some of these may be useful in helping Tibetan Buddhists understand the Christian attitude towards killing animals. Examples include the preservation of the animals in Noah's ark, the provision of God for his creation depicted so beautifully in Psalm 104, or the fact that God made a day of rest for animals.[631] In Christ's new kingdom the animals will not harm one another (Isaiah 11:6-9); for Buddhists this may be a beautiful picture of God's ultimate plan for the world.

3. The Emotional God: A third objection is that God is frequently depicted in the Bible as having human emotions which Buddhists view as either sinful or as showing undue attachment. In the Bible God is described as liable to anger,[632] jealousy,[633] and wrath.[634] Christians need to make clear the difference between man's sinful anger and God's righteous condemnation of sin, or between man's petty jealousy and God's concern for the honor of his name. These teachings are often best reserved for a later stage in the instructional process.

4. Christianity is Too Easy: Another common objection is that just receiving salvation as a free gift is too easy; people must work for their salvation. Here the Christian must make sure that the whole Gospel is preached. Believing in Christ means recognizing that we have not led a morally perfect life (and in fact are sinners), giving up living life our own way and starting to live according to God's way (repentance) and trusting Christ for salvation (faith). If this faith is genuine, it will show itself in acts of love towards others. In other words, following Christ involves an inward change that is every bit as challenging as making enough merit to have a better rebirth the next time around. Jesus encouraged those who wanted to follow him to count the cost first.[635] Tibetan Buddhists who do this may find that following Christ is even more costly than making merit or paying for shamanist rituals.

5. Leaving My People: A fifth and very serious objection to Christianity is that while the religion itself may be good, a person cannot be a good citizen of his nation and a Christian, too. In the case of the Ngalop Bhutanese, for example, to be a Ngalop is to be a Tibetan Buddhist. A Ngalop who accepts another faith may no longer be considered Bhutanese, and runs the risk of complete rejection by friends and family. Where religion and state are one, change of religion takes on the overtones of treason. Non-Asian Christians who have grown up in secular democracies often forget that accepting Christ may cost an Asian all of his or her family and social relationships. Unfortunately, it is often the newest believers who pay the highest cost. In such situations close fellowship with other Christians takes on added importance.

A related objection is that Christianity is a foreign religion. In response, it can be said that God, who could have sent Jesus to earth in any circumstances whatsoever, sent Him to be an Asian. The Bible was written mainly by Asians, and many of the cultural practices of New Testament times are still current in Inner Asia today. For instance, most Tibetan Buddhists would understand immediately why Jesus' disciples were surprised that He talked with a woman (John 4:27) or had washed their feet (John 13). People from Inner Asia often feel much more at home in Biblical culture than people from Outer Asia, Europeans, or North Americans do. Non-Asian Christians should never forget that the Bible can speak very powerfully to Asians in terms that they find especially meaningful.

Summary

Mature Christians like Beth who have solid spiritual foundations, who live holy lives in the context of a Tibetan Buddhist culture, who speak the right language well, and who have learned to think like Tibetan Buddhists, can do far more than just translate the Gospel message into a local language. They can live out the life of Christ in a locally meaningful way that makes the Gospel attractive to local people. Their living example provides a powerful testimony to the peoples of the Tibetan Buddhist world.

CHAPTER 12

The Way of the Cross

B eth's friend Richard is a single, 25 year old teacher with a degree in linguistics and two years' experience in teaching English as a second language. He is impressed by Beth's now-thriving ministry to nomads in Inner Asia. He sees what God is doing through her work, and he thinks that there may be an opportunity for him to do something similar. However, he is not quite sure how his skills might be used in Asia. His church also wants to be involved in ministry to the Tibetan Buddhist peoples of Inner Asia, so after consulting with a number of Christian groups working in the area, they decide to send a small study group to see the area for themselves.

Short Term Trips to Inner Asia

Many churches and parachurch agencies send people on short-term prayer or service trips to the Tibetan Buddhist world.[636] Short-term missions trips can be great successes which help and encourage those who send, those who go, and those who are visited.[637] Good reasons for short term trips include learning about missions firsthand, helping Asian churches, giving orientation to prospective full-time workers, and using technical skills to serve Tibetan Buddhist peoples. Short-term groups may be involved in education, construction, teaching, orphanage work, helping the disabled, economic development, or many other activities. In order to avoid being well-intentioned but unprepared "tourists for Jesus," Richard's group wisely makes sure it will be doing something that local Christians agree is needed, and that the group can actually provide. They check with their hosts about the best time to visit,[638] and learn everything they can about their destination from travelers, newspapers, books, magazines, and the Internet. They learn appropriate phrases for please, thank you, numbers to ten, and common phrases. Their pre-trip orientations cover health issues,[639] cultural topics,[640] security,[641] and realistic expectations for sharing their faith with local people.[642]

Sometimes short term groups can do more harm than good. One such group distributed large amounts of Christian literature while trekking in the Himalayas. Unknown to the trekkers, local officials were annoyed by the literature and threatened to cancel the visas of long-term Christian workers in the area. Another group's illicit literature distribution caused the arrest and interrogation of an innocent tour guide.[643] Another Christian went to a Buddhist holy place and handed out copies of a local pastor's life story, resulting in the threat of serious legal action against the pastor. (Fortunately, this unwise use of literature was stopped, and the pastor went on to plant the first church for his ethnic group in that area). Richard's church wisely avoids such problems by seeking advice from local churches and long-term workers in the area.

The Modern Silk Road

As they prepare for their trip, Richard's group reads the story of the first-millennium traders and missionaries who made their way along the ancient Silk Road. Richard's group will travel on a modern version of the Silk Road - one that is much more likely to use trains or jet aircraft than camels. Christian travelers on this modern Silk Road might still be traders or missionaries like their Nestorian and Catholic predecessors, but they may also be tourists, teachers, doctors, aid and development workers, language students, academics, technical experts, or short term visitors. Some of them are coming at the invitation of local churches that actively cooperate with the wider international Church. Others come at the invitation of Inner Asian governments who ask Christian organizations to contribute their medical, educational, or development expertise. Still others come to offer business, professional, or technical skills.

Christian professionals can make important contributions to the people of Inner Asia, and their service can be very effective in living out the life of Christ in ways that local people can appreciate. However, professional work in the Tibetan Buddhist world is not without its problems. A professional's work may be with the majority people of a given country, but his or her personal interest may lie with a Tibetan Buddhist minority group. Medical or other professional ministries may leave little time for language learning or other activities. Peter was an American doctor working in a government hospital in an Inner Asian country. He was expected to take care of his hospitalized patients, conduct a very busy clinic, and cover emergency cases at night. Not surprisingly, he was usually worn out and had little time outside his professional duties for sharing Christ with others. Many Christians who work in the Tibetan Buddhist world are busy professionals with schedules like Peter's. Often there seems to be no time for sharing the deeper significance of their presence. Still other professionals face the loss of their skills. In the twenty-first century, most technical and scientific fields are changing very rapidly. The professional who serves for even a few years in Asia may miss vital working experience with these new developments, and may be much less employable when they return to their home country. Richard's group meets some expatriate Christians who have sacrificed their professional skills to the point that they are no longer employable in their home countries. Such people often gain more in ministry skills than they lose in currency in their chosen profession, however. The group from Richard's church takes note of these problems and tries to make sure that any professionals they send to Asia will have appropriate care.

As their visit progresses, the small group from Richard's church meets and prays with local Christians, long term workers, and various Christian relief and development agency personnel. The group stays in local homes and talks with a wide variety of people. Their new friends give them a broad sense of what God is doing in this particular Inner Asian country, and the local church convinces them that they could make a meaningful contribution. The careful preparation they have put into their trip has paid off.

Lessons from the Past

After they return to their home country, the leaders of Richard's church reflect on their visit and begin to think more deeply about the broader Church's role in Inner Asia. They realize that their contribution to missions in the region will be just a small part of a large effort that has been going on for a long time. Over the last 1,300 years, Nestorian, Catholic, Orthodox, and Protestant Christians made attempts to share Christ with the peoples of Inner Asia. The Nestorians made the first effort, working among the Mongols from the eighth to the fourteenth centuries. Roman Catholic missionaries were active from the fourteenth century onwards. The Russian Orthodox Church tried to evangelize Tibetan Buddhist and shamanist groups in Kalmykia and Siberia. Lastly, the Protestants entered the Tibetan Buddhist world in 1797, and continued with widespread (though often small scale) efforts since then.

Few of these attempts to plant the Church enjoyed large scale success. In Russia, only the Buryats and the Kalmyks had any Christian witness at all, and only a small minority came to Christ. The Protestant effort to reach the Buryats lasted only 22 years and ended in 1840, while the Orthodox Church's attempt to reach the Kalmyks became tangled up in politics and failed almost completely.[644] The Protestant missionary effort in pre-Communist Mongolia came too little and too late. Only in the very last decade of the twentieth century did the Mongolian Church enjoy significant growth. Though much missionary effort was expended on the Indian and Chinese frontiers of ethnic Tibet, the harvest was small in proportion to the effort made, and Central Tibet was never effectively touched by the Gospel. While the Church grew to significant size among the Mongols in Mongolia, and among certain Tibetan Buddhist ethnic groups in the Himalayas, the larger picture was one of scattered individuals coming to Christ in small numbers. This situation compares less favorably with the history of church growth in Russia, China, and India, where Christian missions produced strong, if relatively small, national churches. The peoples of Inner Asia seemed to offer a less hospitable climate for Church growth than the surrounding peoples of Outer Asia. Why was this the case? Were Tibetan Buddhist peoples somehow "resistant" to the Gospel? Or were they receptive, but did Christians somehow use wrong methods in trying to reach them?

A look at Inner Asia suggests a number of factors which made it difficult for the Church to grow in the region during most of the first two millennia of missions effort. Not all of these factors were operating at any given place and time, but in the broader context of missions over the past two millennia they seem to have been important overall. These factors are:

1. Physical and Social Conditions: Most of Inner Asia is a high, dry, cold plateau separated from the more productive lands of Outer Asia by high mountains and large deserts. Because Inner Asia produces little food, people lived in small groups scattered over a large area.[645] Many lived as nomads whose lifestyle and economic self-sufficiency made them very resistant to change. The settled population lived mainly as farmers in very small communities where everyone knew everyone else. When the occasional Christian appeared in either type of society, he or she was easily persecuted and excluded, so the church found it very difficult to reach the "critical mass" it needed for growth. Because of the low population density, for most of its history Inner Asia lacked cities in which people could find anonymity and space for religious change.[646] In these circumstances there was no enduring place for an indigenous Christian church,[647] though the Catholic mission practice of encouraging new believers to settle in physically distinct communities did result in some Christian islands in the Tibetan Buddhist sea.[648]

2. Mass Monasticism: Unlike other Buddhist societies, Tibetan Buddhists practiced mass monasticism. Under this system, boys between the ages of seven and ten were placed in monasteries for life,[649] placing a huge pool of capital and labor in the hands of powerful lamas. In pre-Communist Mongolia, up to 50 per cent of the male population were monks.[650] In Tibet during the eighteenth century about one quarter of the men were monks;[651] in late twentieth century Sikkim and Ladakh, the figure was 10 to 15 per cent of the total population, with similar figures in other societies.[652] Mass monasticism gave most families a personal or economic stake in the monasteries, where political and economic power became concentrated in the hands of the most conservative elements of society. The monasteries used their political power to reject innovation, refuse modernization, and hold outside influences (including Christianity) at bay. For more than a thousand years this policy was successful in excluding the Church and everyone else, but in the twentieth century it ended in the destruction of the lamaist theocracy.[653]

3. Worldview Disparity: Christian missions came to Inner Asia offering ultimate truth to people who valued religion for its practical benefits. Kublai Khan spoke for many shamanist and folk Tibetan Buddhist peoples when he said he would not become a Christian because Christianity had no effective magic or sorcery, and because Christians condemned such practices as evil.[654] Human-controlled manipulation of the supernatural world is a core value in both shamanism and Tibetan Buddhism. This core value is directly opposed to submission to an all-powerful and all-knowing God. The disparity between these two values lay at the root of much resistance to the Gospel.

Were these three reasons the only factor which hindered the growth of the Church, or could Christians have done more to help the people of Inner Asia see their Savior more clearly? The missions scholar David C. E. Liao has shown that some peoples who are thought to be resistant to the Gospel actually have not had a fair chance to accept it. He has identified additional reasons why the church fails to grow despite years of missionary effort.[655] A number of these factors may apply to the Tibetan Buddhist world.

4. Minority Status: Most Tibetan Buddhist peoples live as minorities within a dominant culture, and they face the threat of cultural loss. Christians can unintentionally identify themselves with the dominant culture by using its religious and cultural forms. For example, expatriate Christians trained in Chinese or Russian language and culture may carry these forms over into their work among Tibetan Buddhist minorities. While some of these people do use Chinese or Russian for business or official purposes, most use their own language to say the things that really matter to them. An expatriate Christian who uses Chinese or Russian language or cultural forms marks himself as an alien, and his religion as a foreign religion. This situation is compounded when a new Christian's only option is to join a dominant-culture local church. New Christians in dominant-culture churches must learn a new language and culture if they wish to worship God in fellowship with others. For example, there are Tibetan Christians in the subcontinent who attend churches where Hindi, Nepali, or even English is used in worship, where the pastor is non-Tibetan, and where the dominant culture is Nepali or Indian. This situation places many barriers in the way of people who might otherwise want to come to Christ.

5. Country Focus: When Jesus sent the disciples to preach in the towns of Israel, He carefully defined the people to whom they were to go. They were not allowed to visit any town of the Samaritans or Gentiles, only the cities of their fellow Jews.[656] Their ministry was to be focused on the particular ethnic group whose language and culture the disciples understood best. Christians have not always been this clear about their objectives. In an earlier era, mission strategy was set by geography (e.g. China, India) rather than by the ethnicity or culture of the people (e.g. Tibetan Buddhist peoples). In Nepal, for instance, there many different ethnic groups, and over 120 different languages.[657] A focused effort with workers trained in the language and culture of one of these peoples will generally be more successful than a broad effort to reach the entire country.

6. Preparation Issues: Many of the early representatives of the Christian faith were scholars or diplomats who had the benefit of the best training their countries could give them. Through much of the nineteenth century, missions sent out well-educated people who had time for deepening their knowledge of the languages, cultures, and social sciences of the day. For example, the Moravian missionaries in Ladakh were renowned for their language ability, and they counted at least one famous linguist (Heinrich A. Jaeschke) among them. Jaeschke and others made detailed notes on the Buddhist meanings of Tibetan religious terms, and carefully distinguished these meanings from their Biblical synonyms. This meticulous scholarship is reflected in Jaeschke's Tibetan-English Dictionary, which remained one of the best sources of information for Christian students of Tibetan for well over a century after it was first printed. With such a mastery of the language, it is little wonder that the Moravians planted a church in Ladakh that remains to the present day. In later centuries this scholarly tradition gave way to a more hurried mass evangelism movement in which linguistic and cultural preparation did not always get the attention it deserved. The demands of professional work, pressure from home countries for evangelistic "results," time limits on visas, a short term orientation, and the generally more rushed pace of modern life tended to squeeze out time for good preparation. As a result, Protestant Christians as a whole were probably less equipped for ministry than some of their predecessors.

7. **Bible and Language Issues:** Protestant missionary culture was (and is) centered on the Bible. This focus on the Scriptures led to a number of worldview conflicts over the use of written religious materials, translation issues, and an over-reliance on widespread literature distribution. In most Tibetan Buddhist cultures, the Buddhist scriptures were reserved for the exclusive use of the monks. Ordinary people were not expected to understand them because they were written in classical Tibetan, which could not be understood without special training. So ordinary "folk" Tibetan Buddhists used their scriptures as magical objects, for example, in making merit or driving out evil spirits.[658] This was, of course, in direct conflict with the culture of most Protestants, who emphasized meaningful personal study of the Bible in vernacular translations. When given a Bible, many folk Buddhists would simply put it in a place of honor in their home, with no idea of ever reading it.

Sometimes translation issues hindered use of the Bible. Until the twentieth century, the Bible might have been available only in a majority or trade language and not in a dialect that local people could understand. Or the Bible was translated in a literary style that was beyond the reach of the uneducated reader.[659] The Bible also speaks in categories that are alien to Tibetan Buddhists, for the Buddhist scriptures are filled with serene speculations on philosophy, instructions for quiet meditation, and methods for achieving passionless peace. Yet a Tibetan Buddhist opens the Bible to find wars, animal sacrifices, and Jesus' sharp controversy with the Pharisees, who resemble the lamas in so many ways. Bible stories are also told in ways that are alien to many of the cultures of Inner Asia. The same issues appeared in Christian literature. As a local believer once said about a Mongolian translation of a foreign Christian book, "The words are Mongolian, but we Mongols don't think this way." In other words, the text had been well *translated* but poorly *adapted* to the way that Mongols think and express themselves.

An over-reliance on literature distribution also caused problems. For example, in 1919 and 1920, the missionary press at Kangding (on the Tibet-Sichuan border) produced 115,000 pieces of Tibetan language Christian literature. Yet one missionary in the area reported that only a few people could read, and of those that could, only a handful could read more than several paragraphs at a time with any degree of understanding. Even in early twenty-first century central Tibet, functional literacy rates were well under 50 per cent among farmers, while nomad groups remained almost entirely illiterate.[660] Sometimes Christians distributed their literature to segments of the population most likely to reject it. The Catholic fathers in Lhasa prejudiced the powerful monastic authorities against themselves when they distributed Christian literature in the monasteries (see Chapter Six). This set in motion the chain of events that culminated in the destruction of the very church they had planted. Similar events were repeated in Mongolia and elsewhere when Christian groups focused on the most visible, but least receptive, portion of the population. In other places booklets were given away wholesale, creating the perception that the Gospel was of no value. Much prejudice against Christianity resulted from the indiscriminate distribution of Christian literature to those who didn't want it or who were most likely to reject it.[661]

Christians can profit from these lessons of history by writing literature specifically for Tibetan Buddhists, by making sure that any foreign materials are well translated *and* well adapted, and by helping local Christian authors to develop their skills. Literature should carefully define Christian terms and take local needs, worldviews, and ways of thinking into account.[662] Literature and other media-based materials are most effectively used in the context of a personal relationship. It is often better to aim for "quality" literature distribution (to those who request it) rather than "quantity" distribution (to as many as possible).[663]

8. Spiritual Factors: Spiritual factors have blighted the growth of the church in the Tibetan Buddhist world. As we have seen, tantric Buddhism offers a utilitarian approach to religion which attempts to manipulate the supernatural for human benefit. This makes it very difficult for Tibetan Buddhists to understand a truth-based Gospel in which God is at the center of things and human beings are at the periphery. The cult of demonic protector deities[664] and the seeking of spirit possession also worked against the Gospel. In terms of Jesus' Parable of the Sower,[665] the hard and rocky soil of Inner Asia took a long time to break up. In some areas the seed of the Word was sown but the workers had to wait patiently for the young plants to appear. In one or two places the land is yielding its first crops.

9. Lack of Cooperation: Could the missionaries on the Gansu-Tibet border have learned something from the early pioneers of the Scottish Mission in Sikkim, or vice versa? What would have happened if James Gilmour of Mongolia could have talked with H. A. Jaeschke of Ladakh? Would the Protestant missionary effort have enjoyed greater success if the Tibetan Buddhist world had been seen as a whole instead of as disconnected parts? Beyond such strategic-level questions, would the Church have grown more rapidly had there been better cooperation among the various Christian groups trying to work in

Inner Asia? The experience of the Church in Mongolia and elsewhere suggests that transdenominational cooperation was a key element in the growth of the Church.[666] What would have happened if the churches had begun to cooperate in 1800?

In summary, the centuries-long effort to evangelize the Tibetan Buddhist world was less successful than it was hoped. Nestorian, Catholic, and Protestant workers were hampered by involvement in politics, focusing on countries rather than people, founding dominant-culture churches in which minority peoples felt excluded, operating with poorly defined goals and inadequate preparation, and sometimes failing to do their linguistic and cultural homework. In turn, Christians have been opposed by political, cultural, and spiritual factors over which they have had no control. Some missionaries (like James Gilmour, whose story is told in Chapter Six) appear to have done all the right things but labored in unripe fields. The combination of all these internal and external factors has produced less-than-hoped-for church growth. Despite the difficulties of the last several centuries, the opportunities for sharing Christ in the Tibetan Buddhist world appear greater in the twenty-first century than at any time in the past. Careful planning can avoid past mistakes and offer hope for a more abundant harvest in the future.

How Buddhists Accept Christ

While the obstacles between the Tibetan Buddhist and Christ are many, God can and does overcome all of them. What are some of the tools that God uses in bringing Buddhists to himself? Certainly one important tool is the Bible. The Tibetan Buddhist monk Tsering (see Chapter One) is not the only Buddhist to have come to faith because of the witness of the Scriptures. The Bible played a key role in the entirely indigenous movement to Christ of the Tamang people of Nepal. One Burmese military officer came to Christ because he was impressed by the beauty of the love of God as expressed in the Psalms.[667] As we saw in the last chapter, normally God uses the Bible in the context of a personal relationship with a believer or with a local church. Such settings are more likely to provide teaching that is especially tailored to the needs of Tibetan Buddhists.

While no extensive studies have been done among people coming to Christ from a Tibetan Buddhist background, a survey done among Thai people identifies a number of factors which they felt were important in their own journey to faith. The Thai survey looked at the relative effectiveness of people, evangelistic tools, and circumstances in bringing Thai Buddhists to Christ. The most effective *people* were, in order, 1) Christian neighbors and friends, 2) family members, 3) Thai evangelists, and 4) local pastors or elders. The most effective *evangelistic tools* were, in order, 1) church services and conferences, 2) leprosy clinics, 3) evangelistic teams, and 4) Christian books. Least effective evangelistic tools were radio programs, Gospel tracts, Christian schools and English teaching. The most effective *circumstances* were, in order, 1) fear of going to hell, 2) a feeling of hopelessness and failure, and 3) dreams and visions.[668]

While it may not be valid to apply these results from Thailand to the Tibetan Buddhist world, several principles seem to stand out. Neighbors, friends, and family members make the most effective evangelists.[669] The church itself is an effective means of winning others to Christ (at least when the church has the same culture and uses the same language as those it is trying to win). Direct, personal methods of ministry (the lives of Christian friends and family) are generally more effective than indirect or impersonal methods (radio, distributing tracts). This is not to say that radio ministries and tract distribution are useless, but they are best used in the context of a relationship.

Sound Strategies

A strategy is simply a method for achieving a goal. The history of Christian missions in the Tibetan Buddhist world suggests several principles of strategy which have helped to establish the Church in Inner Asia. None of them are "magic keys"; all are general principles that need to be adapted to each local situation.

1. Sound Strategies Are Clearly Defined: When He sent the disciples on their first preaching mission, Jesus defined their goal in terms of a single people group in one geographical area: preaching to the Jews of Israel. His command was so simple that it can be translated in just 21 English words: "Do not go among the Gentiles or enter any town of the Samaritans. Go rather to the lost sheep of Israel."[670] Stating goals in one or two sentences can be an aid to clear thinking. For example, a reasonable goal might be to plant a church among the Humla people living in northwest Nepal. The goal is limited to one people group with one language and one culture in one geographical area. Stating the goal in this way not only makes the task stand out more clearly, it clarifies the training and methods that will be needed to reach that goal. In this case, there will be a need for (preferably local) Christians who can reside in the region, learn the language, live out the life of Christ in ways that Humla people can understand and appreciate, form a church, train the local leaders, and leave for service elsewhere.

2. Sound Strategies Work Through the Local Church: Because they are already part of the culture, it is national Christians who are best at living out the life of Christ in locally meaningful ways. Their natural network of relationships makes them very effective at sharing their faith with others. By contrast, expatriate Christians often have resources that the local church does not. Outer Asian and other expatriate Christians can give technical help and support to the agenda of the national church when requested to do so. Because of wealth disparities between the Church in Inner Asia and the international Church, any such cooperation must be taken up in a spirit of servanthood to the local church.[671]

Expatriate Christians can cooperate among themselves to instill in the national church a vision for both missions and ministry to the poor. *Cooperation* among expatriate believers and their respective missions, churches, and development agencies sets a good example that will bear fruit far into the future. It also prevents much waste and duplication. If a *missionary vision* is not instilled in the local church from its formation, it may remain an isolated and defensive group of believers whose presence is barely tolerated by non-Christians. Local believers with missionary vision can bring their friends and relatives into the church without having to overcome all the cross-cultural obstacles faced by foreign Christians. This was an important factor in the growth of the Church in many places in the Tibetan Buddhist world, but it has been especially important in Mongolia and Nepal. Instilling a *vision for ministry to the needs of the poor and disadvantaged* is equally important. Mission- or Christian- assisted hospitals, schools, and social and development programs play an important part in meeting physical needs in some Tibetan Buddhist countries.[672] Good works and thoughtfully-planned outreach should work together in a unified witness for Christ.[673] In countries where public evangelism is prohibited, it is all the more important that Christian doctors, teachers, and engineers have a holistic view of their professional and Christian lives.

Local churches play a vital role in protecting new believers. In Inner Asia, the pressures against individual commitment to Christ are strong and persistent. The believer who has no fellowship or Bible training will find it extremely difficult to stand alone in a culture that opposes his or her beliefs and values. Christians who openly confess their faith may lose their jobs, bring serious trouble to their families, or even face imprisonment. These efforts at intimidation may be successful unless the new Christian is given support and encouragement by the local church. It is very important to encourage new Christians to join a local church. As Donald McGavran has pointed out, persecution is very effective against one person, less effective against a dozen, and least effective against a group of two hundred.[674] It is in fellowship with other local believers that the individual Christian has the best opportunities for spiritual growth and reaching maturity in faith.

New Christians can ease the strain somewhat by sharing their interest in Christ with their families at an early stage, perhaps in the presence of other believers. This gives the family some time to get used to the idea of one of their number becoming a Christian, and may result in other family members coming to Christ as well. While family conversions are to be encouraged, they are not equally likely in all Tibetan Buddhist countries. Family conversions may also be more difficult in areas where the local government is extremely hostile to Christianity.[675]

3. Sound Strategies Are Indigenous: Sound strategies address local concerns, use local media and local people. For example, when people in the Tibetan Buddhist world come to Christ, they bring with them remnants of their previous folk Buddhist or shamanist worldview. As a result, they often have concerns about using divination, astrology, or occult means of guidance; interpretation of frightening or recurrent dreams; dealing with spirit possession; living with unsaved family members; Christian behavior during Buddhist holidays; what to do when family members become ill or die; treating sin as demerit and good works as merit; luck and personal energy; and the belief that only church leaders should read or study the Bible. Sound strategies address these concerns in the teaching ministry of the local church.

The Tibetan Buddhist world has an incredibly rich tradition of folktales, proverbs, songs, stories, art, epic poetry, music, and literature, many of which can serve as artistic models for Church use. Whether the Gospel is put into words or pictures, its message can be presented using local forms to meet local needs. Christian workers often forget that translating a book, a film, or a video into a local language is only the first step in making its message understandable. The second step is making sure that the message is expressed in terms familiar to Tibetan Buddhists. The third step is giving such materials a local flavor using artwork that follows local patterns and motifs. Tibetan Buddhism has a long tradition of using religious art (e.g. thangkas) for teaching purposes. Cultural objects may be adapted to Christian use if their form and function in their native setting is clearly understood and if the local church feels they are appropriate.

Good strategies recognize the *principle of non-transferability:* that is, they recognize that a method that works in one place doesn't always work in another. This is especially true of evangelistic methods which may be highly successful in the culture where they were first developed, but which may be inappropriate when transferred somewhere else. An evangelistic technique developed for Australian college students who value informality is not likely to work among Bhutanese government officials who value social distance. Evangelism based on entertainment events might work well among young people in Tokyo or Singapore, but they may cause people in Inner Asia to feel that Christianity is foreign and superficial. Different situations call for different solutions.

The people of many Tibetan Buddhist lands see Christianity as a foreign religion. A study from Thailand found that evangelistic campaigns and village meetings in which foreigners were involved were relatively ineffective in winning Thai Buddhists. Only when foreign participation was reduced, and indigenous elements added to the presentation, were village campaigns more effective.[676] In the late nineteenth century, European missionaries enjoyed great success among the Tibetan Buddhist Lepcha people of Sikkim. Many Lepchas turned to Christ, but along with this spiritual renewal came an acceptance of Western culture. The modern Lepcha writer A. R. Foning notes that "...among our Christian kinsmen there is a definite trend to display with pride, like the proverbial peacock, the plumes of Western culture in almost everything that is displayable. More often than not, suit, hat, and tie proclaim that a person is a Christian convert."[677] While most Christians working in Asia would deny consciously trying to import their own culture to the countries in which they work, the aspects of their culture that seem most foreign to local people tend to be the very aspects of which foreigners are least aware. Informal worship styles, non-indigenous music and art forms, absence of symbolism, and church structures that empower youth at the expense of age seem so natural to many expatriate Christians that they are unaware of how powerfully these things broadcast that Christianity is a foreign religion.

In some areas, association with foreigners may be politically unsafe. In such places foreign Christian workers may do well to refrain from attending a local church whose members might be endangered by their presence. If church attendance is permissible, it is well for foreigners to put themselves under the leadership of the local church, who must suffer the consequences if something goes wrong.[678] Christian workers must be exceedingly careful that their actions do not embarrass or harm local believers. Careless publicity in mission or secular publications can do a great deal of damage. Jesus often warned those he had cured that they should say nothing about their healing.[679] Modern Christians can learn from this that undue publicity can hinder God's work. Finally, in some areas there may be no local church, and it will be best for foreign Christians to concentrate on finding and discipling one or more local believers rather than attempting widespread evangelism. These local believers will remain long after the foreigner has left, and may they form the nucleus of a new church.

Christian workers who can affirm local culture (within Scriptural limits) will go far in planting a truly indigenous church. Such a church will not be seen as a "foreign body" by those yet to be won to Christ. Where foreign presence is necessary, its profile should be kept very low. Meetings should be conducted in the local language with as few foreigners present as possible, at least until a local church is firmly established. When a larger foreign presence is necessary, Christians from other parts of Inner Asia, or Christians from Outer Asia, may be more suitable than non-Asian Christians. In any case, the vital need is for well prepared, culturally sensitive believers who can share Jesus Christ in a locally appropriate way.

4. Sound Strategies Equip People for Service: Sound strategies equip both local and expatriate believers to live out the life of Christ in ways that nationals can understand and appreciate. Local Christians need different types of training than expatriates, and the nature of their training should be determined by the local churches themselves. Expatriate Christians should remember that issues that are important in their home

257

countries may not be so important in Inner Asia, and that the local church may have spiritual needs in areas where expatriate Christians have little relevant experience. Expatriate Christians should be trained for language and culture learning that extends over the entire course of their careers. Such training should focus on the enduring skills and qualities that will let others see Christ in them. Continuing education for Christian workers should encourage lifelong learning about the anthropology, art, festivals, folktales, geography, history, literature, music, religion, sociology, and even sports of Inner Asian peoples. Beyond these basics, virtually no area of study is irrelevant. Almost anything that Christian workers can learn about a people can help them to reveal Jesus Christ more clearly.

5. Sound Strategies Pay Attention to Social Structures: All societies have some kind of structure that defines the position of various groups within it. In most Inner Asian societies some are nomads, others farmers; some speak this dialect, others that; some are among the "in" group, while others are outcasts. The group that may be most responsive to the Gospel may be the least visible to outsiders. Even the rich and powerful may be more responsive to the Gospel than the poor and downtrodden, or just the reverse may happen: those with nothing may accept Christ more readily than those with everything.[680] While sociological information may suggest who may or may not be likely to respond to the Gospel, missions is ultimately an activity of the Holy Spirit, and it is well to remember that it is not under human control. When God does move among a particular segment of society, the new believers from that group have the advantage of working within their own subculture to reach their peers.[681]

Who are the subgroups most likely to respond to the Gospel? From a human perspective, that may depend on the particular culture and its attitude to change. Within the past 50 years, entire peoples have had to adjust to new ideas, tourism, economic development, and the other onrushing forces of modern life. Rising educational and economic standards are displacing animist beliefs and even raising some questions about the doctrines of the lamas. The segments of society which are bearing the brunt of these changes may also be the segments most responsive to the Gospel. Examples might include students, workers in the tourist industry, and younger professional people.

Historically, the least responsive group in any Tibetan Buddhist society has been the monks. In the past, a great deal of Christian effort was focused on the monks because they were virtually the only people who could read, and because they were the most visible segment of society. They were also the group in society that had (and has) the most to lose by converting to Christianity: a privileged position in the culture, a great deal of accumulated merit, and social and economic status. Much evangelistic effort has been focused on the group least likely to respond to the Gospel. This is not to say that monks should not be evangelized, but only that evangelistic resources can be concentrated on segments of Tibetan Buddhist society that are more likely to respond, without neglecting others.

6. Sound Strategies Have an Endpoint: Lastly, good strategies have an *endpoint* at which local Christians will become self-governing and foreign Christians will go on to serve in other areas. This is one of the striking things about the Apostle Paul's ministry. Even in major centers like Ephesus and Corinth, Paul stayed only about two years before moving on to other cities.[682] His apparent method was to gather a group of believers, instruct them, appoint local leaders, and then leave.[683] Good strategies will follow his example and aim for withdrawal of foreign workers at the earliest possible time. Failure to do this can cause needless friction with local believers and delay the spiritual maturity of the local church.

The Way of the Cross: Incarnational Missions

By the start of the twenty-first century, the Tibetan Buddhist world seemed more open to Christian presence than in many years past. This new openness calls for Christians to take the way of the Cross in serving the peoples of the Tibetan Buddhist world. Both Asian and non-Asian Christians must have the willingness to be discipled for personal spiritual growth, the courage to enter spiritual struggle, the persistence to spend years in the study of difficult languages, the discipline to study Tibetan Buddhist cultures thoroughly, and the diligence to apply appropriate methods to local situations. Christians who have these qualities will be able to share Christ with Tibetan Buddhists in terms they can understand and appreciate.

Studies and strategies are only helps along the way, not formulas for guaranteed success. Who will accept Christ and who will reject Him is not something that humans can engineer or control. We cannot tell in advance whose heart the Holy Spirit will open, for He is God's instrument, not ours. As Jesus said: "The wind blows wherever it pleases. You hear its sound, but you cannot tell where it comes from or where it is going. So it is with everyone born of the Spirit."[684] Yet we can expect that with diligent application of Scriptural principles, direct dependence upon the Holy Spirit, and believers willing to take the way of the Cross, *the Church can grow in the Tibetan Buddhist world.*

SPECIAL SUPPLEMENT:

Sharing Christ with Tibetan Buddhists in Diasporas

by David Housholder

Any movement of a people emigrating from their home land into other parts of the world can be identified as a *diaspora* ('A dispersion of a people from their original homeland'),[685] but of particular significance to us are the large-scale emigrations of people from the Tibetan Buddhist countries of Inner Asia. These dispersions take people from countries most of us will never have the opportunity to visit and bring them to places where we can pray for them, care for them, and share Christ with them. While there has so far not been a great amount of research on most of the Tibetan Buddhist peoples in diaspora, good information is available on two such groups: the Mongols and the Tibetans.

In this chapter we will look briefly at the Mongol diaspora in the United States, and then in greater detail at the worldwide Tibetan diaspora. The chapter will conclude with suggestions for ministry with diaspora Tibetans — suggestions that would apply to any Tibetan Buddhist people group we might encounter outside their Inner Asian homelands.

The Mongol Diaspora

The "Mongol diaspora" is a river fed by multiple streams that flowed through numerous countries until finally emptying largely into the United States (which now has the largest population of Mongols outside Asia).[686] The river is a coming to-gether of Kalmyks and Buryats from Russia, as well as Mongols from China's Inner Mongolia Autonomous Region, moving in some cases from Mongolia to Tibet and from Tibet to India and beyond. In other cases the flow was via Russia (after the communist revolution) into Europe. The flow might well have been stopped in Europe when the post World War II situation made survival difficult for the Kalmyks living there. But on August 31, 1951 the US Congress passed a law granting Kalmyks the right to immigrate as Europeans, not as Asians, easing their entry into the USA. In late 1951 and early 1952, 571 Kalmyks came to Lakewood, New Jersey, and Philadelphia, Pennsylvania. As we saw in Chapter Four, it was due to this migration flow that the first Tibetan Buddhist monastery in the United States was established by Mongols. After 20 years the Kalmyk community, by then doubled in numbers, began moving into New York, Washington DC, West Virginia, Florida, Arizona, Texas, New Mexico, and California. Their numbers did not grow dramatically, largely because the initial immigrants were mostly older people. But the community has remained close-knit and eager to work toward maintaining its cultural identity, thus avoiding an acculturation process that would lead to the loss of traditional values. To support that goal while also showing its links with the USA, the Kalmyk-American Cultural Association was founded in Howell, New Jersey, in 1997.

In an event similar to that which enabled the Kalmyk immigration, Inner Mongolians were granted an enlarged immigration quota by the United States in 1965. As a result of these special immigration quota exceptions, by the beginning of the twenty-first century there were about 5,000 Mongols in the United States, most living in major cities such as New York, Philadelphia, Chicago, or Los Angeles, as well as in the state of New Jersey. In 1988, Professor John Hangin Gombojab,[687] a Mongol credited with initiating Mongolian studies in the USA,[688] founded the Mongolian Society at Indiana University (Bloomington, Indiana), the precursor to The Mongol-American Cultural Association (MACA).[689] Another association, the West Coast Mongolian Cultural Foundation, is the 2002 creation of Dr. Shirchin Baatar, a senior software engineer in Silicon Valley in California (USA) who remembers, at age four, learning to ride a horse as a member of a nomadic family in Mongolia. The "West Coast Mongolian Cultural foundation's goal is to preserve Mongolian Heritage among Mongolians in the West, [and to] deliver Mongolian Culture to American people."[690] At heart the purpose of such associations is preservation of culture and heritage and the desire that others should see the culture through the eyes of those for whom it is precious. Related to these goals is the fear of loss of culture. How can we share Christ with these people without making them feel we are demanding they abandon what they treasure in memory and community? Before we try to answer that question, we need to look now at another diaspora, that of the Tibetans.

The Tibetan Diaspora

For most people, pre-1959 Tibet and its inhabitants seemed to be of another world, a land of Shangri-La and a people of romantic mystery (see Chapter Four). Even Tibetan Buddhism was widely unknown; it was only in 1948 the first site for instruction in the religion outside Asia was established when Johns Hopkins University (in the USA) hired Telopa Rinpoche to teach Tibetan Buddhism. But in 1959 the veil of mystery parted as thousands of Tibetans, including the Dalai Lama, trekked their way south out of Tibet into Nepal, Sikkim,[691] Bhutan, and India. Most were settled into refugee camps set up by gracious host governments and began creating new lives in settings radically different from their places of origin. Adjusting to life in the new settings was difficult. Replacements had to be found for traditional occupations that could not thrive outside of Tibet. People found their settlements to be islands set in a sea of confusing cultures, and found themselves susceptible to diseases they had not dealt with before. They attempted to preserve as much of their home culture as possible, the women persisting in wearing heavy woolen clothing even in the heat of South India being one visible testimony to that attempt. The exiles had entered the world outside Tibet. These Tibetans in diaspora were safe and their communities grew, but they did not prosper.

Though other people groups have spread around the world in their own diaspora, the world's attention is repeatedly drawn back to the Tibetans through media coverage, films, and the public role of the Dalai Lama. It is no accident that the Tibetan profile is high. It is the intention of the exiles that members of the Tibetan diaspora be part of an international public relations process to keep the world aware of the situation in the land of Tibet and to seek for an eventual return of the "exiles" to the high plateau. And even though they must adapt to some degree to the host cultures in which they live, they also want to create an environment in which traditional Tibetan culture (language, dance, festivals, and so on) is preserved. They take this as an obligation, fearing their cultural heritage is being diluted or deliberately drowned out among Tibetans in China. So while there are only some 140,000 Tibetans in this international diaspora, compared to millions of Tibetans living in various parts of China, it is the Tibetans of the diaspora that have captured the world's attention, interest, and in many cases, sympathy.

In a sense there are two Tibetan diasporas. There is that of Tibetan peoples and there is that of the Tibetan form of Buddhism. Since that first instructional site at Johns Hopkins in 1948, many Tibetan Buddhist dharma centers and monasteries have been founded around the world, their leaders modifying and re-packaging the religion to the tastes of the "open-to-experiment" West. But that really is a separate diaspora. Those dharma centers and monasteries may rarely be visited by the members of that other Tibetan diaspora, the peoples themselves. So while the dharma centers in the western world draw in scores of curious or devout westerners there is no essential relationship between them and the Tibetan communities.

So while there were Tibetan lamas and dharma centers in various countries around the world by the early 1960s, the Tibetan diaspora was still largely confined to South Asia, with only a few Tibetans able to move into other countries. The beginning of the international spread of Tibetans came in 1967, when the Dalai Lama appealed to the international community to accept Tibetan refugees as immigrants. Switzerland was the first nation to respond because, according to Swiss government, the "Tibetan tragedy aroused national sympathy of a free alpine people for another mountain people in great need." The original plan of the Swiss government was to resettle Tibetans in high mountain areas, where they could live the life of Old Tibet and find pastoral work. However, during that time Swiss manufacturers were short of labor, so some Tibetans were resettled in a more modern setting.[692] By 2004 there were 3,000 Tibetans in Switzerland, one-third of those having been born there. A major center for Tibetans in Switzerland was the village of Rikon, where Tibetans made up 20 per cent of the population of 1,500 people. Even though only 10 per cent of the Swiss Tibetans lived there, at the beginning of the twenty-first century it was the heart of the Tibetan presence in the country because it was there that the Dalai Lama had established a monastery to support the new Swiss Tibetan community. Eight monks lived at the monastery and taught language and meditation. There were also seven Tibetan schools in other parts of Switzerland. Such schools represented yet another attempt to preserve culture and tradition, something the Tibetans were eager to do even though many who came to Switzerland took Swiss citizenship.

The second country to respond to the Dalai Lama's plea was Canada. In 1970, Canada received 228 Tibetan exiles, just short of the 240 immigration slots they had offered. By 1997 that number had increased, but only to 600 persons. From 1998 to 2001, one thousand Tibetans seeking refugee status entered Canada from New York. Because many of those thousand were young singles with poor English skills, they were eligible to be on welfare support,[693] in contrast to the earlier invited immigrants. By 2002, the Tibetan population of Canada was stated to be 1,850, but unofficial estimates by members of the community suggest there could be 5,000 to 6,000 living mostly in Toronto with smaller groups in Bellville and Lindsay (Ontario), Calgary, Montreal and Vancouver.

The third country to respond to the appeal was the United States. Seventeen Tibetan lamas had come in 1960, invited to lead eight centers for Tibetan studies established by the Rockefeller Foundation. And the Office of Tibet was set up in New York in 1964, primarily to represent Tibetan issues before the United Nations. In the late 1960s, 27 Tibetans immigrated to the U.S. to work as lumberjacks for the Great Northern Paper Company in Portage, Maine. But by 1990 there were only about 500 Tibetans settled in northeastern, northwestern, and central cities of the United States. Additional Tibetan presence would take an act of Congress — and that's exactly what happened, the step that made the USA the third county to give an official invitation in response to the Dalai Lama's appeal.

During the 1980s and 90s, the Dalai Lama asked the United States to resettle some Tibetans in the USA where they could multiply their earning power to contribute more to the support of the refugees in South Asia as well as to better support the traditional government in Dharamsala, India through the *rangzen* dues, a tax paid by all Tibetans in exile from age six on. In 1991 the Tibetan US Resettlement Project was passed by the US Congress and the door was opened to a greater international dispersal of Tibetans. In 1992, a thousand Tibetans, chosen through a lottery system from those in the camps in India, arrived in the USA and were placed in cluster groups in 18 states. The locations chosen were cities where there was some already existing relationship with Tibet, or some representative presence related to Tibet (a university department, a monastery, or a dharma center, for example). When these initial thousand had obtained jobs and established themselves, they were permitted to bring in their family members, so the numbers grew dramatically over the next few years. By 2005 there were over 10,000 Tibetans in the USA, and community leaders estimated another 3,000 who were undocumented. There were Tibetan communities and Tibetan Associations (formed wherever there were more than 15 Tibetans in a city) in 30 cities in the USA, the largest concentrations being in the New York City area and in Minneapolis, Minnesota.[694] Some people did not remain in their original resettlement settings for long. Most of the St. Louis group, for example, moved to Minneapolis. By the early years of the twenty-first century the largest communities were in the Northeast (especially the New York City area — about 3,000), the Midwest (mostly Chicago and Minneapolis — about 2,500), and the Western states from Washington down through California (another 1500).

In 1998 the Planning Council in Dharamsala reported significant Tibetan populations had also been established in Taiwan (1,000), Europe (other than Switzerland) including Austria, France, Liechtenstein, and Russia (640), Australia and New Zealand (220), Scandinavia (110), and Japan (60).[695]

This international spread of the peoples of Tibet is a gift from God to those who would seek an opportunity to share his love with Tibetans. We are constrained by biblical mandate to emulate the Father in the way he cares for the many-faceted needs of the foreigner in our midst [696] and by Jesus' commendation of those who take the initiative to welcome the stranger into their community.[697] While some of the readers of this book will have opportunity to travel into areas historically connected with the Tibetan Buddhist peoples, many more of us will now be able to have opportunities to share God's loving care with Tibetans because they are living in our own cities or in cities to which we can travel easily and where access can be more open and free than in some of the traditional Tibetan Buddhist lands.

In sharing Christ with Tibetan Buddhists in the lands of their diaspora, the principles already presented in this book are applicable. But there are some other issues important to note.

1. In contrast with the diaspora of other peoples like the Kurds or the Gujaratis or the Somalis, the Tibetan diaspora takes on a different character because it was initiated and encouraged by the exile authorities in India. Initially people moved from Tibet partly to escape persecution but also to protect and preserve their language, religion, and culture, fearing the potential eradication of their heritage by the Chinese. Representatives migrated beyond the South Asian host lands that initially welcomed them into (particularly) Europe and North America in order that they might prosper economically in a way that would enable them to support the people in the South

Asian camps and to support the traditional government, with a long-range goal of restoring Tibet as an independent nation. They do not want their Tibetan identity to be diluted through a process of assimilation with the host culture. They may settle in fully, even take citizenship, but still have hope for a renewed Tibet. And since there is widespread understanding in the community and in the leadership that to be Tibetan is have a commitment to the traditional government and to the preservation of their cultural heritage (which includes being a Buddhist[698]), Tibetans in diaspora may be more resistant than other people groups to anything that would seem to have the potential of weakening any part of that identity. Changing one's religion, therefore, could be seen as repudiating one's identity and loyalty, a break from community commitment.

2. Tibetans in diaspora settings are reported to work more than the average "native" person in the same area. In most cases husband and wife both work and are likely to do a lot of overtime work or to have more than one job. They seek this over-employment so they can support their own families as well as family members still in the camps in Nepal and India.[699] A study of the community in one city found many Tibetans working in hospitals as dietary aides, in housekeeping, in transport, and a few as nursing assistants. Others work in hotels doing housekeeping or in restaurants as cooks or bus boys. A smaller number work in the Tibetan handicraft stores and restaurants. One consequence of the long work hours is that, "With both parents working, children and youth are usually left by themselves after school to run around on their own without supervision, and the youngest ones have to stay in day care."[700] So we may have a harder time scheduling personal visits into Tibetan homes or, even more so, gatherings which involve Tibetans. It does, however, give a clue to ways we can minister to Tibetans. We'll discuss that more below.

3. Since many of the Tibetan immigrants come to other countries from the camps in India, the culture and language background for daily life for many of our immigrants is Indian, not Tibetan. They may have a stated need to preserve the Ti-

betan language and culture, but for many of them, especially the younger generation, the language they are called upon to preserve is ceasing to be a living language. So while they may use Tibetan for rituals, they are just as likely to sing Bollywood[701] film songs in Hindi, and negotiate daily life in English (in North America) or German (in Switzerland). Dr. M. S. Thirumalai, who has studied populations of immigrants in the USA, says the Tibetans "have a close affinity with the Indian ethos....We need to understand that the immigrant Tibetan population is not from Lhasa but from...metropolitan cities of India. Most of these people have never even been to Tibet. Their original home is indeed Shangri La for them. The real world is the world of Hindi cinema, Indian curry, biriyani, chappati and purees!"[702] It could be, therefore, that as we plan a meal to share with our Tibetan friends that a South Indian *masala dosa* might say "home" to them as much as would a *momo* (a traditional Tibetan meat pastry). And, even more important, while they might welcome a chance to see the *Jesus* film in their own dialect of Tibetan, they might enjoy even more the Hindi version! A Tibetan believer may be more comfortable worshiping in Hindi than in either Tibetan or the national language of the country in which he or she is living. But such believers may also be comfortable with English, especially those who were educated in Christian boarding schools in India. People who have worked with exiled Tibetans report there is considerable "code switching and code mixing," with conversation involving elements of several languages.

4. The Tibetans in diaspora are not a single homogeneous group. There are affinities created by language dialect or by sect of Tibetan Buddhism, even though Tibetans report they can understand and communicate with each other even if they came from areas where different dialects were spoken. An Amdo Tibetan may more quickly assist a newly arrived Amdo, seeing the Kham immigrant as a more distant cousin. New immigrants, especially those coming directly from Tibet, say they are laughed at and treated with disdain and resentment by the Tibetans who have lived in an area longer, due to differences in accent,

mannerisms, social etiquette and in their vision for a future Tibet.[703] While we do not have to fully understand these distinctions nor be able to discern specific backgrounds of the people we befriend, we need to be aware of this dynamic.

5. Viewing films about Tibet and Tibetans is useful for expanding our understanding of their history and traditions, but we must remember that neither the Tibetans in Tibet nor the Tibetan peoples in diaspora are fully like the Hollywood version of Tibetans. To think we have seen a true glimpse of Tibetan life through watching these films is a bit like seeing a film about the daily life of Cistercian monks living in a monastery in France and then thinking we know all about the daily life of all Roman Catholics in Argentina. The complex realities of life are far greater than the cinematic distillations.

6. Reports from various diaspora settings agree that the Tibetans are highly concerned about preservation of the Tibetan culture, but when asked what that must include it is language and dance that are almost universally named. There is no strong appeal for teaching *thangka* painting or Tibetan cooking or even for religious instruction.[704] There are good things in any culture, things worth preserving, and nothing is more precious to a people than the heritage of language. We need to look for and affirm those things they bring from their culture that are good. Dr. Thirumalai notes that the competitive spirit in the job setting, the insecurity they may feel in this immigrant setting, and the fact that many lack professional skills or certification may influence them to abandon the morals and ethics that would have prevailed in their culture and advises Christians to help them maintain the best elements of their culture.[705]

How can we become effective in sharing Christ with Tibetan Buddhists in diaspora settings?[706] First we need to examine our motives for wanting to reach out to Mongols, Tibetans, or other peoples from Inner Asia. If we go among them because we fantasize they are a unique people who are somehow more exotic or exciting than others to whom we might go, or if we somehow think that a Tibetan or Mongol coming to the knowledge of the Lord Jesus Christ is of more value in

God's eternal plan than for one of our neighbors who is like ourselves to make the same commitment to the Lord, or if we think our own status in the Christian community will be enhanced if we share Christ with a person from an exotic country, then we should stop and review the fact that God loves all people and counts none as more important than another. We are to reach out because we love God and we love people, not because we love labels. We focus, in a book like this, on a certain set of people groups because historically those groups have had less opportunity to hear God's good news, and we want to be certain they have that opportunity.

With our motivation tested, the beginning point of this ministry (as it should be with any other) is prayer. As one worker wrote, "First of all, we must listen to the Lord and the Holy Spirit and what he is directing us to do or say *before* following any dos or don'ts. It's especially effective to have a small group of people who commit to join us in regular prayer for this work. Having the right motives and holding the need of the Tibetans in prayer before the throne of God we then look to see whether there are any Tibetan Buddhists in our own area. How is that done?

A first step is to check the telephone book for Tibetan or Mongol businesses (restaurants, craft shops). A visit to such shops, expressing our interest to the proprietors to learn more about their people who are living in our area, and looking for posters or newsletter announcing events in the local ethnic community can give us a start in knowing about the Tibetan Buddhist peoples near us. We can even visit dharma centers or monasteries, if there are any in our area — they may have information about the local Tibetan Buddhist community. Taking the Tibetans as an example, one might check in the phone book for common names such as Dolma, Tsering, Tenzin, [707] and look up the addresses on a map. Are there any areas where there seem to be clusters of Tibetans? That would be a good neighborhood to visit. You can also inquire from the school system whether there are Tibetan speaking students in the schools. In North America the public schools are free to tell you the mother tongues of their students even if they can't give you specific names of students or families.

Once you have located some people what do you do next? One worker writes: "When you have located some Tibetans in your area it's easy to get involved. The first step? Just 'hang out' in a Tibetan store, restaurant, etc. Go there, talk to people. If there's a Tibetan-American Foundation or something like that, volunteer, get to know the community, and attend community events if there are some." In making these contacts don't be the overeager or over-helpful western problem solver. Listen much *before* you offer any help or solutions. Learn about their concerns and the local community's needs.

If you are serving a local Tibetan exile community, keep in mind that the political issues related to China and Tibet are important to the Tibetans (especially to the older generation), but that these issues are theirs, not yours. They don't expect you to become a political activist on behalf of Tibet in order to be their friend. There is no need to paste a "Free Tibet" bumper sticker on your car or to display the Tibetan flag in your home or at programs to which you invite Tibetans to show your interest in their community. Our Lord loves people, not political entities. It's true that God is concerned for justice for the oppressed, but the issues related to China and the land of Tibet are multi-sided. We certainly don't want our Tibetan ministry activities to be handled in such a way that it would alienate ministry we might have among Chinese people in our area.

Even though we are not caught up in the political issues of the traditional Tibetan government, we must respect the Dalai Lama and others for the intensity with which they have worked to hold the Tibetan community worldwide together and to present an attractive picture of a people honoring their ancestral homeland. Even though we disagree with the religious understandings of the Dalai Lama and the other Tibetan Buddhist religious teachers there is no need to treat them with disrespect. These leaders are following the highest path they know. Many suffered greatly to maintain their commitment to a way they believe is the best way of life. The idea (sort of a conspiracy theory position) that there is a back room somewhere with secret meetings in which the Tibetan leadership is planning the spiritual overthrow of the world is probably more Hollywood than reality. They do want to spread Buddhist concepts, but they do so because they believe they provide a better way to live for the world. It's more likely the Western Tibetan Buddhists who take a more aggressive or proselytizing approach. Dr. Thirumalai suggests that the preservation, translation, and dissemination of Tibetan Buddhist thought is more a goal of American converts to Tibetan Buddhism than of the Tibetans themselves.[708]

The one essential key to being effective in ministry with any Tibetan Buddhist ethnic group is, in one worker's words, to "*be a friend*, whatever that looks like. Just help. Also, let them help you.[709] Just be there for each other. Being willing is more important than having the right skills. Love them, invite them over for dinner." Another wrote, "Reaching Tibetans with the love of Christ is about being friendly, building a relationship, being a friend. It is letting God's love flow through you to your Tibetan friends. It's difficult for people in the task-oriented, time-pressured Western cultures to understand what it means to 'be a friend.' We may call someone a friend when we mean we know their name and wave a greeting to them when we by pass each other. In the Tibetan culture a 'friend' is one you can depend upon, someone who will be there for you when needed. Special invitations are not needed to drop over to visit a friend, and the value of time together is not measured by how much of some task was accomplished."

And a commitment to friendship cannot be dependent on some anticipated response from the other person. It is not right for us to focus mainly on our Tibetan Buddhist friend's acceptance of Jesus as Lord and Savior. God enables us to sow the seed, but we might not reap the harvest. Our friendship will certainly result in opening a window through which to see God, whether our friend embraces Jesus immediately or not because the Word does not return void.[710]

Spending time with people as a friend will open opportunities for sharing the good news of the gospel, but many of our prescribed approaches to evangelism in the western countries are meaningless to our Tibetan Buddhist friends. As we have seen earlier in this book, the Christian worldview presuppositions (e.g., that there is a God who acts and interacts and loves) underlying those approaches are alien to them. In many cases our Tibetan Buddhist friends may never have given serious thought to God because belief in God is not central in the thought of Tibetan Buddhism. Yet as they hear your testimony it can bring them to a place of realizing God is real and is important. "In general, the gospel will be much better received when it comes up naturally, and you can talk about your own experience" always trying to avoid Christian clichés and specialized vocabulary.

Here are some ideas for developing ministry. Some of these things can be done by an individual, but it is even better to have a small group working together in these projects.

1. Invite your Mongol, Tibetan, or Bhutanese friends to a celebration of a holiday. Christmas, Easter, or national or patriotic holidays offer great opportunities to share your own culture and the worldview behind it. Sing the songs, serve the foods (better, ask them to help you prepare the foods), play games, set up a booth for photographing families, present a drama (again, it's even better to involve them in the presentation), or teach a folk dance of your country. Explain that in most Western countries Christmas, Easter, (and in North America, Thanksgiving) celebrations are a combination of secular holiday and Christian celebration day. Help your Asian friends see which parts are which, since in our cultures we tend to send confusing and conflicting messages through mixing secular and sacred) [711] In your presentation about the holiday you can incorporate how it relates to your faith. Tibetan-style pictures of the Christmas and Easter stories are available for use.

2. Some of the many ways individuals, churches and groups have successfully assisted Tibetan Buddhist communities include launching a sports program, providing short-term

housing, tutoring children after school, helping with the writing of resumes and with preparation for job interviews, taking someone through the entire process of buying a home, going with parents to parent-teacher conferences, giving cooking instruction, teaching music classes (especially guitar lessons), giving driving instruction, offering classes in a national language (for example, English as a Second Language or ESL), citizenship preparation, or computer skills. Others have found that Tibetan or Mongol communities have appreciated summer camp programs for their young people. Just keep in mind that we must not go into the community aggressively offering to do things *for* them. Be a friend in the community first, listen to what they say are their needs, and offer to work *with* them in finding ways to meet those needs. Also, when you start a project be committed to carrying it through. Be certain, for example, that there are enough volunteers to do the after school tutoring before starting the project.

3. Tibetan Buddhists in diaspora have need of good counseling in areas like inter-personal relationships, success in the job situation, and financial planning. You might be able to offer workshops or one-day fairs in which people with expertise in these areas would sit with small groups answering their questions and suggesting ways of dealing with issues. You might work with a church or a Christian professional group to provide workshops on management of finances, on understanding and coping with the school systems, on youth and parent adaptation issues, on goal setting, on leadership skills, and on entrepreneurial skills or job skills training.[712]

4. It may be possible to enlist lawyers, accountants, and management professionals as consultants to aid the Tibetan community. Work with these professionals to determine the extent to which they might be able to help and set up appropriate communications channels (perhaps through a

volunteer who serves as gatekeeper) so that they are not overwhelmed with requests.

5. In North America the combination of long work hours that keep the Tibetans away from their home and families for extended periods and the new cross-cultural settings in which they are trying to raise their families means their children are now living their own "American" or "Canadian" lives, and may be in need of direction that their parents are unable to provide. Parents can't be physically present (because of the long work hours) and may not understand the needs and concerns of young people.[713] Many Tibetan young people are apathetic toward the culture preservation goals of their parents and have no thought about someday moving to Tibet. They are becoming acculturated into the countries in which they are living. The question of how we can pass on an appreciation for the values of the parents when our young people are exposed in school and through the media to values that may be of a different sort is one that is asked in our churches as well. A church might organize a workshop on the transmission of values in a family and invite members of a diaspora community to join in.

6. One worker who has spent many hours in the homes of Tibetan friends submitted the following as key items to remember:
   a. People are often more comfortable in their own homes. Be prepared to meet with them where they are at ease. This will inevitably mean a ringing phone and people coming in and out. The Tibetan community is close knit and they circulate freely in each others' homes. While there may be distractions this lends itself to meeting more people and having the opportunity to speak to and influence those who drop in.
   b. They always make tea. Learn to like butter tea. Take a snack to share — savory and spicy gets a better reception than sweet.

If you show yourself a faithful friend in a diaspora community, there may come a time when you can offer — the request sometimes even comes from the people themselves — to lead a study of the Bible. One person who has had such opportunities suggests:

1. You should first familiarize yourself with the basics of Buddhism and its development into Tibetan Buddhism. It is a complex religion but an understanding of key concepts will open the door to a way of thinking that is vastly different from the Western worldview. This may trigger topics of study or conversation that you will want to prepare or begin to think through. Some of these might include:
   a) An Understanding of Suffering
   b) The Concept of Forgiveness
   c) Animal Sacrifice
   d) Karma and the Death of Jesus

2. Find out what a Tibetan Buddhist is thinking when you speak of God, prayer, the Trinity, salvation, heaven, sin. As you prepare a study try to put yourself in their place to see if your teaching makes sense to one with a Tibetan Buddhist worldview. At the same time it's important you realize that no matter how much you have read or learned about Tibetan Buddhism, you are not an expert. Be a listener, a learner, open to hearing from your Tibetan friends and learning from them what their foundations for belief and action are.

3. Since English or other European languages are not their mother tongue (at least of the first generation immigrants) look for materials with simple wording. Some workers have made effective use of materials originally designed for children. An excellent Bible translation that uses an easily readable English vocabulary but is also an accurate translation is the Contemporary English Version (CEV) produced by the American Bible Society.

4. A didactic teaching approach is not very effective with Tibetans. They are less interested in the logical development of ideas and concepts and more interested in what happens in life. So storytelling is a good approach. They have good memories and can relate back to you in minute details the events of stories you tell them. This is helpful when one student is translating the teaching for another student with limited ability in English or other national language. During teaching sessions, they may forget you are there and start to speak in their own language to each other. Over time they will become more aware of your exclusion and translate for you or attempt to speak more of your language.

5. Resources and types of Bible study
   a) A Chronological Study: For those who are not Christians, you may ask if they are interested in knowing what is in the Bible. This is a non-threatening way to start an exploration of what it teaches. You may choose a study that starts with creation and moves through to Jesus. Discuss what the Bible contains. You are not defending or proving something, just simply relating what is taught in the Bible. They will be surprised by the moral teaching of the Bible since they suspect all westerners are Christians who subscribe to the decadent lifestyles they see in movies and on TV. As they study and as people are praying for them, they can flesh out a picture of Christ and the Christian faith. Your loving example over time will model what they are learning. Three good starting point resources are:

   i. *Firm Foundations*, which is published by New Tribes. It is a 50-week detailed study of the Bible from Creation to Christ.[714] Some of the editorial material is not relevant to the Tibetan Buddhist worldview, however.
   ii. *The Stranger on the Road to Emmaus* is a similar approach that is simplified into 15 lessons.[715] Some who have used it say the teachers' guide is excellent but the content of the studies is difficult for people for whom English is a second language.
   iii. *From Adam to Armageddon*[716] is another through-the-Bible study resource that some workers have recommended. This one is produced as a college-level textbook so may be more useful for the study leader's personal presentation.

iv. *God's Story*[17] is a VCD that has been used effectively among Tibetans in Nepal. It is available in English and in Central Tibetan as well as in Mongolian and Dzongkha.[718] It goes through the Bible, starting in Genesis.

b) There is a Christian *thanka* modeled after the Tibetan Buddhist Wheel of Existence. It is effective with Tibetans and comes in English and Tibetan script. The English text version is for the teacher. Feel free to have them read the script. They are keen to do so. Seeing the samsara (birth, death rebirth) broken is a wonder to them.

Ultimately, however, it will not be our videos or books or teaching that will open Tibetan Buddhist people to be interested in knowing the Lord Jesus Christ. It will be our sincere and loving interest in them, our committed offering of support and service, our openness to them as friend to friend that will enable them to see something of another dimension of spiritual truth from what they have known before. Can we do that? Apparently God intends to work through us in that way; that's why He has brought these Tibetan Buddhist peoples into our neighborhoods.

Peoples of the Tibetan Buddhist World

Summary

The table below summarizes the demographics of the Tibetan Buddhist world and offers a short list of Tibetan Buddhist peoples living in Inner Asia. Population figures are approximate, since reliable information is unavailable for several countries.

List of the Tibetan Buddhist Peoples

There are many ways of classifying people groups. Some authors (known in the vernacular as "lumpers") prefer to emphasize similarities, while others (known as "splitters") prefer to emphasize differences among peoples. "Splitters" tend to produce people group lists that are double or even triple the length of those produced by "lumpers." For reasons of space, the list below emphasizes similarities. To qualify as "Tibetan Buddhist," a people must have Tibetan Buddhist shrines, temples, village priests, monks or monasteries. Peoples are listed by country, and groups living in more than one country may be listed more than once. Some listed groups follow more than one religion and some may have only subpopulations who follow Tibetan Buddhism. There are unresolved questions about the status of several listed and unlisted groups. Principal group locations are listed in parentheses.

1. Russian Federation
  101. Buryats (Republic of Buryatia)
  102. Kalmyks (Republic of Kalmykia)
  103. Tuvans (Tuva)

2. Mongolia
  201. Mongols (entire country)
  202. Buryats (northern Mongolia)
  203. Ewenki (Selenge Aimag)
  204. Tuvans (Hovsgol and Hovd Aimags)

3. China
  301. Tibetans (Tibet, Sichuan, Yunnan, Qinghai, Gansu)
  302. Mongols (Inner Mongolia, Xinjiang, Liaoning, Jilin, Heilongjiang, Qinghai, Gansu)
  303. Yugurs (Xinjiang and Gansu)
  304. Tu (Qinghai)
  305. Daur (Heilongjiang, Xinjiang)
  306. Naxi — Mosuo subgroup (Yunnan)
  307. Monpa or Menpa (Tibet)
  308. Pumi (Yunnan)
  309. Jyarong (Sichuan)
  310. Nu (Yunnan)
  311. "Pingwu Tibetans" or Xifan (Sichuan)
  312. Qiang (Sichuan)
  313. Ewenki (Inner Mongolia)

4. Nepal
  401. Sherpas (Solu Khumbu)
  402. Lhomis (E. Nepal)
  403. Lopa (Mustang)
  404. Dolpopas (Dolpo)
  405. Larkepas (Larkye district)
  406. Tibetans
  407. Manangi Gurungs (Manang)
  408. Chuntel people (Central Nepal)
  409. Unclassified groups (living in Mustang, Manang, Humla, Olangchungola, Muktinath, etc.)
  410. Tamangs (mixed with Hinduism)
  411. Gurungs (certain subgroups only)
  412. Helambu "Sherpas" (Langtang valley)
  413. Thakalis (certain subgroups only)

5. Bhutan
501. Ngalops (western Bhutan)
502. Khengpas (central Bhutan)
503. Sharshops (eastern Bhutan)
504. Mangdipas (Tongsa district)
505. Gongdupas (Mongar district)
506. Tsalipa (Mongar district)
507. Bramis (near Tashigang)
508. Brokpas (near Tashigang)
509. Laya people (Laya)
510. Tibetans in Bhutan (Bumthang, Tongsa, others)
511. Sherpas (Chirang district)
512. Tamangs (Samchi district)
513. Lepchas (Samchi district)

6. India
601. Tibetans (widely distributed in camps)
602. Ladakhis (Jammu and Kashmir state)
603. Purikpas (Jammu and Kashmir state)
604. Lahulis (Himachal Pradesh)
605. Spitis (Himachal Pradesh)
606. Jads (northwestern Uttar Pradesh)
607. Garwhalis (northwestern Uttar Pradesh)
608. Lepchas (Sikkim, West Bengal)
609. Sherpas (West Bengal)
610. Drukpas (various subgroups)
611. Monpas (Arunachal Pradesh)
612. Sherdukpens (Arunachal Pradesh)
613. Membas (Arunachal Pradesh)
614. Khampas (Arunachal Pradesh)
615. Ngas (Arunachal Pradesh)
616. Tamangs (West Bengal, elsewhere)

Selected Peoples of the Tibetan Buddhist World

Entering a New Culture:
Key Questions

The following questions may help you begin to understand a new culture. Try to ask as many people as possible about as many areas as possible.

Cultural Questions

Architecture: How are homes and religious structures built?

Art: What forms are there? Is art used for religious teaching?

Body language: What is/is not acceptable for religious persons?

Business: How does the culture understand commerce? Who does business?

Communications: What mass media and traditional forms exist?

Customs: Eating, visiting, manners, superiors & inferiors, marriage, family

Decisions: How do local people make collective decisions?

Dress: Who wears what and why?

Economics: What are the culture's major economic activities?

Education: Who gets it? Who gives it? What's taught and how?

Entertainment: What forms are there? What do people do to relax?

Face and Shame: How is respect shown?

Family: Marriage, divorce rate, child raising practices, social networks

Food: What kind, made from what, how cooked, recipes?

History: How do people understand their history?

Language: Who speaks what and why; dialects; forms of written and spoken language

Leadership: How is this determined/exercised?

Literacy: What's the iteracy rate? Who can't read? Why can't they read?

Literature: What kinds are there? Who reads it or listens to it?

Media: Content, style of radio, TV, newspapers, etc.

Medicine: What happens when someone is sick?

Music: What instruments, popular music, songs

Nomads: Who are they, where are they, how do they fit into society?

Social Change: How fast is society modernizing/secularizing?

Social relationships: Social order, classes, ethnicity, in and out groups, social networks, boundaries

Sports and Games: Which ones played, can you learn them?

Technology: Level of development, traditional technologies

Urbanization: To what degree is the culture urbanized? What is the role of cities?

Ways of thinking: How do they process information?

Work: What occupations/trades are there, and how are they viewed?

Religious Questions

Attitudes: How do people feel about Tibetan Buddhism? Christianity? Conversion between faiths?

Buddhist Scriptures: What scriptures do they have, and how are these treated?

Church History: Has there been previous contact with the Gospel? When? How?

Demons and Spirits: How do people relate to them?

Folk Tibetan Buddhism: How does it influence people's lives?

Government: How does it relate to Tibetan Buddhists? Christians?

Holy Behavior: How is a religious person expected to behave? How do people act in front of monks?

Lamas: Who are they? How powerful are they in the local culture? How do they exercise this power?

Luck, Merit, Good Fortune: How do people keep bad things from happening to them?

Music: Is there religious music? Where can you go to hear it?

Other Religions: Are Christianity or Islam also present? How do people feel about them?

Religious Education: How do people receive their religious education?

Temples and Monasteries: Where? How big? Who goes there? Why?

Tibetan Buddhism: How strong is Tibetan Buddhism within the culture?

How to Learn About Spiritually Important Terms

A s discussed in the text, Christians and Tibetan Buddhists have very different concepts of important spiritual concepts such as mercy, love, and compassion. Christians who live and work in the Tibetan Buddhist world should be aware of these differences. This is a list of words whose meanings may differ markedly between one's own native language and a language spoken in Buddhist Inner Asia. To use this list most effectively, explore the meaning of each word in the list with a local Tibetan Buddhist (e.g. "Tell me about words in your language that might mean something similar to the English term love"). It may take several local words to cover the meaning expressed by one English term; rarely will meanings overlap completely. Looking at spiritually important terms in this way will help you to speak more clearly about Christ. See how many new words you can add to the list.

baptize	forgive	lord	repent
believe	gentiles	love	righteousness
bless	glory	mediator	sacrifice
body	God / god	meditation	Satan
Buddha	gospel	mercy	salvation / save
Christ	grace	miracle	scriptures
church	heart	parable	self
clean (physically, ritually)	heaven	path	sentient being
compassion	hell	peace	servant
create	holy	power	sin
cross	ignorance	praise	soul
die	jealousy	prayer	spirit
disciple	judge	priest	temple
evil spirit	justify	prophet	trust
faith	kingdom of God	reconcile	truth
fault	law	redeem	virtue
fellowship	liberation	refuge	wisdom
flesh	life	religion	world
			worship

Helpful Language Resources

Dictionaries

Das, Sarat Chandra, *A Tibetan-English Dictionary*, (Calcutta: Bengal Secretariat Book Depot, 1902; reprinted by Ratna Book Distributors, Kathmandu, 1985). This classic is still in print 100 years after its original publication; it is also available in electronic format. It is particularly strong on Buddhist terms.

Goldstein, Melvyn C., *English-Tibetan Dictionary of Modern Tibetan*, (Berkeley, USA: University of California, 1984). Very useful for modern terms not found in Das' dictionary.

Goldstein, Melvyn C. ed., *The New Tibetan-English Dictionary of Modern Tibetan*, (Berkeley: University of California, 2001). Very useful for modern terms.

Rigzin, Tsepag, *Tibetan-English Dictionary of Buddhist Terminology*, (Dharamsala, India: Library of Tibetan Works and Archives, 1986). Most useful for Buddhist meanings of spiritually significant terms.

Dzongkha Language

Dzongkha Development Commission, *Dzongkha Rabsel Lamzang*, (Bhutan: Dzongkha Development Commission, 1990). An introduction to Dzongkha, the national language of Bhutan.

Mongolian Language

Sanders, Alex JK, and Bat-Ireedui, *Mongolian Phrasebook*, (Victoria, Australia: Lonely Planet, 1995). Introduces the script, phonology, and grammar of Mongolian, plus useful phrases.

Tibetan Language

Bartee, Ellen, and Droma, Nyima, *A Beginning Textbook of Lhasa Tibetan*, (National Press for Tibetan Studies, 2000). A beginner-level introductory text.

Central Asia Fellowship, *How to Read Tibetan,* and *How to Read Tibetan: The Genesis Reader,* (CAF: 2004). Bible-centered lessons in reading Tibetan at the beginner level with an introduction to Tibetan grammar.

Goldstein, Melvyn C., *Essentials of Modern Literary Tibetan,* (Berkeley, USA: University of California, 1992). An excellent text introducing modern written Tibetan; available with a cassette tape.

Preston, Craig, *How to Read Classical Tibetan,* (Ithaca: Snow Lion, 2003). An intermediate text for those who already know Tibetan grammar.

Tournadre, Nicolas, and Dorje, Sangda, *Manual of Standard Tibetan: Language and Civilization,* (Ithaca: Snow Lion, 2003) Uses a linguistic approach to introduce the Lhasa dialect of Tibetan; available with compact disks.

Wilson, Joe, *Translating Buddhism From Tibetan,* (Ithaca, New York, USA: Snow Lion, 1992). Very helpful for learning Tibetan grammar and the vocabulary of Tibetan Buddhism.

A Tibetan Buddhist Timeline

Inner Asian Prehistory

B.C.

6000-2000	Neolithic Period in Inner Asia
	Pastoralists begin to replace hunter-gatherers on the steppes
	Stone and bone artifacts produced in Tibet
5000	Neolithic settlements in India
4000	Domestication of horses
3000	Indus Valley civilization in contact with Mesopotamia
	Pastoralism spreads widely across Central Asia
3000-1000	Bronze Age; Oasis cities appear in Central Asia
2600-2000	Indus Civilization (Harappan)
2500	Domestication of Bactrian camel
2200	Writing appears in the Indus Valley
	Abraham and the patriarchs
1523	Shang Dynasty begins in China
	Vedic Age
1500	Metal implements appear on the steppes
	Nomadic pastoralism in Mongolia
	Israel in Egypt
2000-1000	Ayran peoples enter India from the northwest
	Writing appears in China
1500	First urbanization of India
	Period of the Judges in Israel
1200	Composition of early Vedas
1027	Zhou Dynasty begins in China
1000	Urbanization of Ganges Valley
1000	Scythic Era in Central Asia (to 500 A.D.)
	Israel: United Monarchy
800-500	Later Vedic Period (*Upanishads*)
586	Fall of Jerusalem

Early Buddhism (mid 6th century B.C. - 500 A.D.)

c.563	Birth of Siddartha Gautama (later called Buddha)

291

Persian Empire
538   Jewish exiles begin to return from Mesopotamia
c. 528   Siddartha "enlightened" at Bodh-Gaya
c. 483   Death of Siddartha Gautama
c. 400   Approximate close of Old Testament Period
327   Alexander the Great invades northwest India
268   Birth of Ashoka (268-239)
      Buddhist missions to Sri Lanka
221   Qin Dynasty begins in China
206   Han Dynasty begins in China; capital at Changan
      (Xian)

A.D.
c.100   Buddhist city-states flourish along the Silk Road
      Rise of Mahayana Buddhism in India & spread
      across Central Asia
      End of New Testament Period
222   Six Dynasties Period Begins in China
c.300   Buddhism popular in China
c.500   Nestorian Christians in Central Asia

The First Tibetan Kingdoms (c. 600-866)
c.600   Tantra, Indian mystery religion
618   Tang Dynasty begins in China
c.627   Song Tsen Gampo becomes king of Tibet
      Tibet conquers the Buddhist city states of the Silk Road
      Thön Mi Sambhota standardizes Tibetan alphabet
635   Nestorian Christianity reaches China
670   Tibet and Tang Dynasty China at war
754   Ti Song De Tsen becomes king of Tibet
c.775   First Tibetan monastery founded at Samye
      Padma Sambhava in Tibet (?)
781   Tibetans occupy Dunhuang
c.792   Indian Buddhists win great debate at Samye
c.840   Persecution of Buddhism under Lang Darma
c. 842   Lang Darma assassinated; breakup of Tibetan kingdom

Tibet's Fragmentation (c. 978 - 1204)
958   Birth of Rinchen Sangpo (958-1055); first of the Great
      Translators
960   Song Dynasty begins in China
c.1000   Collapse of trade along the Silk Road

Early Buddhism begins to enter Mongolia
Buddhism declines in India
Nestorian Christianity among the Kerait Mongols

1042   Atisa (982-1052) comes to Tibet, reformation of Tibetan Buddhism begins

Marpa the Translator (1012-1096) active

1056   First Kadampa monastery founded

1073   First Sakya monastery founded

Milarepa (c.1040-1123) active

c.1162   Birth of Genghis Khan

Drukpa school begins to enter Bhutan

The Mongol Period (1207 - 1368)

1207   Tibetan chiefs submit to Ghengis Khan

1215   Peking captured by the Mongols

1215   Birth of Kublai Khan (d.1294)

1245   Carpini's mission to the Mongols

1260   Lamaism begins to enter Mongolia

1262   References to Christians appear in Chinese official documents

First visit of the Polo family to China

1271   Marco Polo leaves for China; Kublai Khan becomes emperor

1280   Yuan Dynasty begins in China

1330   Pu Tön (1290-1364) edits the *Tenjur* (Tibetan scriptures)

End of the era of the great translators

1357   Birth of Tsong Khapa (1357-1419), founder of Gelugpa school

1368   Fall of Mongol Dynasty frees Tibet; Ming Dynasty begins in China

Nestorian and Catholic churches begin rapid decline in China

Beginning of Ming Dynasty

Tibet's Theocracy: Rule by the Dalai Lamas (1391 - 1959)

1391   Birth of first Dalai Lama, Gedun Truppa (1391-1472)

1409   First Gelugpa monastery, Ganden, built near Lhasa

1416   Drepung monastery founded (Lhasa)

1419   Sera monastery founded (Lhasa)

1445	Tashilhunpo monastery in Shigatse begun
1475	Birth of second Dalai Lama, Gedun Gyatso (1475-1542)
1543	Birth of third Dalai Lama, Sonam Gyatso (1543-1588)
1570	First Panchen Lama born
1578	Sonam Gyatso given the title Dalai Lama by Altan Khan
1589	Birth of fourth Dalai Lama, Yonten Gyatso (d.1616)
1617	Birth of fifth Dalai Lama, Ngawang Gyatso (d.1682)
1620	Kalmyk Mongols migrate to European Russia
1624	Jesuit missionaries reach western Tibet
1626	Father Antonio d'Andrade's mission to Tsaparang, Tibet
1630	Visit of Fathers Cacella and Cabral to Bhutan and Tibet
1635	Collapse of mission at Tsaparang
1642	Gushri Khan makes Fifth Dalai Lama leader of Tibet Ladakh submits to Tibet; Construction of the Potala begins
1644	Qing Dynasty begins in China
1653	Fifth Dalai Lama visits Peking
1683	Birth of sixth Dalai Lama, Tsanyang Gyatso (d.1706)
1684	Tibet at war with Ladakh Drukpa sect established in Bhutan
1708	Birth of seventh Dalai Lama, Kalsang Gyatso (d.1757)
1716	Ippolito Desideri, Jesuit priest, arrives in Lhasa
1721	Desideri leaves Lhasa
1742	End of Christian mission at Lhasa
1758	Birth of eighth Dalai Lama, Jampal Gyatso (d.1804)
1765	Moravian mission to the Kalmyk (Kalmuck) Mongols
1793	William Carey arrives in India; modern era of Protestant missions begins
1797	William Carey visits Bhutan
1806	Birth of ninth Dalai Lama, Lungtok Gyatso (d.1815)
1816	Birth of tenth Dalai Lama, Tsultim Gyatso (d.1837)
1817	London Missionary Society begins work among the Buryat Mongols of Siberia
1838	Birth of eleventh Dalai Lama, Khedup Gyatso (d.1855)
1840	Mongolian version of the Old Testament published London Missionary Society's work among the Mongols ends
1846	London Missionary Society completes New Testament in Mongolian

1853   Moravian mission prevented from entering Tibet

1856   Birth of twelfth Dalai Lama, Tinley Gyatso (d.1875)

1865   American missionaries begin work among Mongols at Kalgan, China

1870   James Gilmour begins work among the Mongols

1876   Birth of Thirteenth Dalai Lama, Thubten Gyatso (d.1933)

1885   Moravians begin work in Leh, Ladakh

1890   London Missionary Society begins work among hill tribes of north India

China Inland Mission and others at work on the China-Tibet border

1892   Scandinavian Alliance Mission at work in Sikkim & Bhutan border

Roman Catholic missions in Mongolia

1893   Birth of Mao Tse Tung

1895   Scandinavian Alliance Mission begins work in Mongolia

1898   Swedish Mongolian Mission begins

Annie Taylor, Christian missionary at Yatung, Tibet

1898-1900   Boxer Rebellion

1904   Younghusband Expedition reaches Lhasa

Dalai Lama flees to Mongolia

1907   Aurel Stein discovers the Dunhuang library

1909   Dalai Lama returns to Lhasa

1910   Chinese expedition reaches Lhasa

Dalai Lama flees to India

1911   Chinese Revolution, beginning of Chinese Republic

1912   Dalai Lama returns to Lhasa

1921   Chinese Communist Party founded

1924   Communists seize power in Mongolia, repress Buddhism

1928   Soviet Government begins anti-Buddhist campaign

1933   Death of thirteenth Dalai Lama

1935   Birth of fourteenth Dalai Lama, Tenzin Gyatso

1950   Chinese attack Tibet

1951   Tibetan Government dissolved

Kalmyk Mongols move to United States

1953   Revision of Mongolian New Testament

Assertion of Chinese Control in Tibet (1959 - present)

1959   Tibetan uprising fails, Dalai Lama and followers flee to

India
1960   Tibetan government in exile established at Dharamsala,
        India
1963   First Tibetan Buddhist meditation center in the West
        founded in Scotland
1969   Tantric meditation center founded in Berkeley,
        California
1979   Dalai Lama visits Mongolia
1980s   Further spread of Tibetan Buddhism in Europe,
        North America, Australia
1989   Dalai Lama wins Nobel Peace Prize
1990   Democratic reforms in Mongolia
        Mongolian New Testament published
        Tuva declares Tibetan Buddhism official religion
1991   Breakup of Soviet Union, formation of Russian
        Federation
        Rebirth of Christianity in Mongolia
        Revival of Organized Tibetan Buddhism in Mongolia
        and Russia
1993   First Bön center established in North America
2000   Church growing rapidly in Mongolia

Glossary

Transliterations of Tibetan terms are given in parentheses.

Ashoka (268-239 B.C.) an Indian emperor and devout Buddhist who helped to spread Buddhism throughout south Asia.

Atisa (982-1052) Indian tantric sage who came to Tibet in 1042 in order to reform tantric Buddhism. He and his followers founded the Kadampa school of Tibetan Buddhism, which later became the dominant Gelugpa school.

Bhutan (*'brug yul*) a kingdom in the eastern Himalayas between India and China. The state religion is Tibetan Buddhism.

Boddhisattva (b*yang chub sems dpa*) a Mahayana Buddhist saint who postpones his own enlightenment in order to help others.

Bon (*bon*) see **Pün**

Bodh Gaya a town in the north Indian state of Bihar, scene of Siddartha Gautama's enlightenment.

Chan a Chinese form of Mahayana Buddhism, precursor of Zen.

Chenresi (*spyan ras gzigs*) a Buddha of mercy who is the patron saint of Tibet. The Dalai Lama is believed to be an incarnation of Chenresi.

Chö (*chos*) the Tibetan word for religion (and much else).

Chorten (*mchod rten*); also known by its Sanskrit name *stupa*. A large, round Tibetan Buddhist shrine, sometimes containing the remains of a famous lama. Walking around a chorten is a popular way of making merit.

Compassion (*snying rje*) a mental attitude that wishes others to be liberated from suffering.

Dalai Lama a Mongolian term meaning "ocean of wisdom." Head of the Gelugpa school of Tibetan Buddhism. The Tibetans usually refer to the Dalai Lama as Gyalwa Rinpoche (*rgyal ba rin po che*) or Kyap Gön (*skyab mgon*).

Desire (*'dod pa*) In its Buddhist sense, desire is the wish for ongoing personal existence, and is the chief cause of suffering.

Dharma (Tibetan *chos*) a Sanskrit term meaning religion.

Drepung (*'bras spungs*) constructed in 1416, Drepung is one of the large Gelugpa monasteries near Lhasa, Tibet.

Drukpa (*'brug pa*) the dominant school of Tibetan Buddhism in Bhutan; also used of the Tibetan Buddhist inhabitants of Bhutan.

Dunhuang (also Tunhuang) an oasis town on the ancient Silk Road, now in the northwestern part of China's Gansu province. Site of a famous ancient library discovered by Sir Aurel Stein in 1907.

Eightfold Path in Theravada Buddhism, the way by which self-effort leads to enlightenment and perfection.

Enlightenment the supreme experience by which Buddhists escape from rebirth and suffering.

Four Noble Truths (*bden pa bzhi*) are the basic propositions of Buddhism. They are: 1) that all life is suffering, 2) suffering arises from desire, 3) suffering is destroyed by eliminating desire, and 4) desire is eliminated by following the eightfold path.

Ganden (*dga' ldan*) 1) a famous Gelugpa monastery outside Lhasa, Tibet. It was extensively damaged during the Cultural Revolution (1966-1976). 2) a large Gelugpa temple in Ulaanbaatar, Mongolia.

Gelugpa (*dge lugs pa*) the dominant school of Tibetan Buddhism. The head of the Gelugpa order is the Dalai Lama.

Great Translators A series of Tibetan scholars who translated the major writings of Mahayana Buddhism into Tibetan.

Gu-ge (*gu ge*) a province in western Tibet visited by the Jesuit father Andrade in the seventeenth century.

Hinayana (*theg dman*) a Sanskrit term meaning "lesser vehicle"; applied by the Mahayana Buddhists to those who follow Theravada Buddhism. See also Theravada.

Incarnation see **Tulku**

Kadampa (*bka' gdams pa*) one of the major schools of Tibetan Buddhism.

Kalmyk (Kalmuck) A Mongol people group who settled in European Russia during the seventeenth century. Some of them were resettled in the United States in the 1950s.

Kangyur (*bka 'gyur*) also spelled *Kanjur;* a part of the Tibetan Buddhist scriptures, made up of 1,083 separate works.

Kargyupa (*bka' rgyud pa*) one of the major schools of Tibetan Buddhism.

Karma (*las*) in Hinduism and Buddhism, an impersonal principle that ensures that good actions are rewarded and bad actions punished in subsequent lives.

Kön Chok (*dkon mchog*) or *Kön Chok Sum:* a term used to refer to Buddha, his teachings, and the body of Tibetan Buddhist monks.

Kum Bum (*sku 'bum*): literally "hundred thousand images"; a large Gelugpa monastery in China.

Ladakh (*la dwags*) a province of Kashmir. Ladakh is predominantly Tibetan Buddhist, and it is home to several famous monasteries.

Lama (*bla ma*) a higher grade of monk. Often incorrectly used of all Tibetan Buddhist monks.

Lamaism see **Tibetan Buddhism**.

Lepcha an originally animist people who live in Sikkim.

Lha (*lha*) Tibetan for god or spirit.

Lhasa (*lha sa*) the capital of Tibet and former residence of the Dalai Lamas.

Mahayana (*theg chen*) a Sanskrit term meaning "great vehicle"; one of the major divisions of Buddhism.

Mandala Tibetan Buddhist version of a shamanist spirit trap, used in tantric rituals and as a meditational device.

Mantra (*sngags*) in tantrism, a mystical saying or magic spell that is believed to have coercive power over tantric deities.

Marpa (about 1012-1096) called the Translator. Marpa was a tantric monk whose disciples, including Milarepa, founded the Kargyupa school of Tibetan Buddhism.

Meditation (*sgom pa*) is generally of two types in Tibetan Buddhism: 1) analytical meditation employs rational thought in order to realize the fundamental precepts of Buddhism; 2) placement meditation seeks to empty the mind of rational thought in order to realize Buddhist truths intuitively.

Milarepa (*mi la ras pa*) (about 1052-1135) one of Tibetan Buddhism's most famous and beloved literary figures. A disciple of Marpa, he and his disciples were instrumental in founding the Kargyupa school of Tibetan Buddhism.

Mongolia a semidesert country located between China and Siberia. Under the Manchu Dynasty (1644-1912) Mongolia was a part of China and was called Outer Mongolia. Today Mongolia is an independent country; the so-called Inner Mongolia Autonomous Region is a part of China.

Monism a belief system that asserts that all things are fundamentally one. Vedism, Brahmanism, Hinduism, and Tibetan Buddhism are all monistic religions.

Mysticism the belief that religious truth can be found through inner realization without the use of rational thought. Mysticism is characteristic of Hinduism and Tibetan Buddhism.

Nepal an officially Hindu country located between India and China in the Himalayas. Nepal is home to several Tibetan Buddhist tribal groups, the most famous of which are the Sherpas.

Nestorian Christianity a form of Eastern Christianity which spread widely through Central Asia.

Nirvana (*myang 'das*) a metaphysical state that is the goal of Buddhist religious life.

Nyingma (*rnying ma*) the oldest school of Tibetan Buddhism, supposedly founded by **Padma Sambhava** in the eighth century A.D.

Padma Sambhava (also known as *Guru Rinpoche*) a legendary eighth century sorcerer who is credited with founding the Nyingma school of Tibetan Buddhism.

Potala (*po ta la*) a palace in Lhasa, Tibet; formerly home of the Dalai Lamas.

Preta a ghost; one of the six kinds of beings in Buddhism.

Pu Tön (*bu ston*) (1280-1364) last of the Great Translators, Pu Tön edited a vast quantity of Buddhist texts into a collection known as the *Tengyur,* a part of the Tibetan Buddhist scriptures.

Pün (*bon*) a religion combining elements of Inner Asian shamanism with tantric Buddhism.

Rinpoche (*rin po che*) literally "precious"; an honorific Tibetan title often used of high lamas.

Sakya (*sa skya*) one of the major schools of Tibetan Buddhism.

Sangha a Sanskrit term used of the body of Buddhist monks.

Sanskrit the classical language of India in which many early Hindu and Buddhist texts were written.

Scriptures The Tibetan Buddhist scriptures are in two parts, the 225 volume Tengyur and the 1,083 volume Kangyur.

Sera (*se ra*) a large Gelugpa monastery just north of Lhasa, Tibet. Constructed about 1419.

Shamanism the original religion of many peoples of Inner Asia and Siberia, as well as many American Indian tribes.

Sherpa (*shar pa*) a Tibetan Buddhist ethnic group living in Nepal and Tibet, famed for their mountaineering exploits in the Himalayas.

Siddartha Gautama (about 563-483 B.C.) the historical founder of Buddhism, was an Indian prince who became known by the title Buddha.

Sikkim a small Indian state lying between Tibet, Nepal, and Bhutan; home to a large Tibetan Buddhist population.

Silk Road ancient trade route which connected Europe and China. Both Christianity and Buddhism reached China via the Silk Road.

Song Tsen Gampo (*srong brtsan sgam po*) (about 609-650 A.D.) an early king of Tibet who is said to have introduced Buddhism to the country.

Stupa see **chorten**

Tantra (*rgyud*) a mystery religion which appeared in north India between the seventh and tenth centuries A.D. Tantra deeply influenced Tibetan Buddhism.

Tashilhunpo (*bkra shis lhun po*) a large Gelugpa monastery in Shigatse, Tibet's second city, and seat of the Panchen Lama.

Tengyur (*bsTan 'Gyur*) the 225 volume second part of the Tibetan Buddhist scriptures.

Theravada (see also **Hinayana**) the second school of Buddhism besides Mahayana.

Thön Mi Sambhota (*thon mi sam bho ta*) an early Tibetan government minister who devised the Tibetan alphabet.

Tibet (*bod*) a high plateau north of the Himalayas that is home to the Tibetan people. Before 1959, Tibet was much more extensive that the present Tibet Autonomous Region of the Peoples Republic of China.

Tibetan Buddhism a form of Mahayana Buddhism deeply influenced by animist, shamanist, and tantric beliefs.

Tibetan Buddhist World Asian countries and peoples whose cultures either are or have been influenced by Tibetan Buddhism.

Torma (*gtor ma*) a substitute offering often made of dough or rice.

Tsong Khapa (*tsong kha pa*) (about 1357-1419) tantric scholar who reformed the Kadampa school of Tibetan Buddhism into the Gelugpa school.

Tulku (*sprul sku*) a person who is believed to be a mystical emanation from a deity. The Dalai Lama is believed to be the tulku of the god Chenresi.

Tunhuang see **Dunhuang**

Vajrayana (*rdo rje theg pa*) (literally "diamond vehicle") see **tantra**.

Vedism an ancient Indian religion whose ideas are basic to Hinduism and Buddhism.

Wisdom (*shes rab*) refers to the means by which Tibetan Buddhists realize that all things are empty of inherent existence.

Yoga (*rnal 'byor*) an Indian cult which taught than man could achieve union with ultimate reality through psychological and physical training. Adopted by Mahayana Buddhists about 500 B.C.

Endnotes

Notes to Chapter One

1. This book uses the term "Inner Asia" to mean the Tibetan Plateau and its immediately adjacent mountains, the Gobi Desert, the Mongolian portion of the Central Asian steppes, and a small part of Siberia to the east and west of Lake Baikal.

2. The term "Tibetan Buddhist world" refers to the Inner Asian peoples whose lives and cultures have been shaped by both shamanism and the Tibetan form of Buddhism.

3. For an account of the British expedition, see Francis Younghusband's *India and Tibet* (Hong Kong: Oxford University Press, 1985).

4. The story of this ill-fated expedition is told in Melvyn Goldstein's *A History of Modern Tibet, 1913-1951: The Demise of the Lamaist State* (Berkeley: University of California, 1989).

5. On a journalistic assignment in Palestine during World War I, Thomas met the British Army officer T. E. Lawrence ("Lawrence of Arabia"). Thomas became famous when he made a film about Lawrence's exploits and toured the world narrating it.

6. See Hugh Richardson's *Tibet and Its History* (Boston: Shambhala, 1984) p. 14; Goldstein, p. 21, Thomas, p. 270.

7. This figure is the traditional population of the monastery given in N. Tsering's *A Tibetan Monk's Story* (Kathmandu: Samdan, 1995), p 1.

8. Thomas, p. 274.

9. Like many other Tibetans, "Tsering" uses only one name. The story that follows is based on the author's conversations with "Tsering," and on other sources.

10. This holiday is called "Turning the Wheel of the Dharma" or *chos 'khor dus chen* in Tibetan.

11. Isaiah 43:19

12. The history of this period is documented in Richardson, *Tibet and Its History.*

13. Gelugpa missionaries arrived in the United States in 1955, the Sakyapas in 1960, the Nyingmas in 1969, and the Kagyupas in 1970. For details, see Amy Lavine, *Tibetan Buddhism in America: The Development of American Vajrayana,* in Prebish, Charles S. and Tanaka, Kenneth K., *The Faces of Buddhism in America* (Berkeley: University of California Press, 1998).

14. Emma M. Layman's *Buddhism in America,* (Chicago: Nelson-Hall, 1976) p. 89-90, mentions Tibetan Buddhist missionary efforts in Switzerland, France, and the UK. This exposure to Tibetan Buddhism was further increased by the missionary efforts of American Buddhists on the Internet, beginning in the 1990s (Lavine, p. 113).

15. The shamanist and Buddhist *Yugur* people of Gansu Province, China, should not be confused with the Muslim *Uygur* people of neighboring Xinjiang Province.

16. Leviticus 4:3-12.

17. Numbers 31:3.

18 Exodus 4:14.
19 Exodus 20:5.
20 Matthew 26:3-4.
21 Hebrews 9:12.
22 For an example of these difficulties among Tibetan Buddhists in western Sichuan Province, China, see J. H. Jeffrey's *Khams* (Devon: Arthur H. Stockwell, 1974), p. 91-98.

Notes to Chapter Two

23 Lake Baikal is located in the Russian Republic of Buryatia. It is the deepest lake on earth, holding about 20% of the planet's fresh water. The peoples who live around its shores are traditionally shamanists and Tibetan Buddhists.
24 The Russian Republic of Kalmykia is culturally a part of this area, but its location on the northwest shore of the Caspian Sea is remote from the areas discussed in this chapter.
25 A number of historians have argued for the validity of Inner Asia as a distinct geographical and cultural region. See David Christian's *A History of Russia, Central Asia, and Mongolia, Volume I: Inner Eurasia from Prehistory to the Mongol Empire* (Oxford, Blackwell 1998).
26 Average precipitation in most of Inner Asia, including Xinjiang, Mongolia, and Tibet, is under 500 mm. per year, which is too dry for farming without irrigation (Christian p. 5).
27 In the Tarim Basin, some of these inward-draining streams watered the outposts of the ancient Silk Road, making possible the network of trade routes connecting India, China, Iran, Mesopotamia, and Europe.
28 Christian p. 7, and author's experience.
29 American University's *Area Handbook for Mongolia*, 1970, p. 16; and Liu Wulin, *Chang Thang*, (Beijing, China Forestry Publishing House, 1999) p. 36.
30 Lake Baikal lies north of the 50th parallel, and Ulaanbaatar above the 47th.
31 The average elevation of Mongolia is 1,580 meters above sea level (*Mongolia: Empire of the Steppes*, by Claire Sermier (New York, Norton, 2002) p. 69; and of Tibet greater than 4,000 meters (*Tibet*, China Intercontinental Press, 2002, p. 8).
32 For example, Lhasa lies at the same latitude as Cairo or northern Florida, while Ulaanbaatar is as far north as Paris or Vancouver.
33 In these choices the farmer is clearly the winner, because farming makes an acre of land produce enough food to feed 10-100 times more people than hunting and gathering of wild foods (Diamond p. 88).
34 Domestication in this sense means that certain animals were taken from the wild and selectively bred in order to produce characteristics useful to humans.
35 Christian, p. 48.
36 Raising livestock feeds more people than hunting-gathering by furnishing meat, milk, fertilizer, and transportation for goods / traction for plows (Diamond p. 88).
37 The approximate population densities of Tibetan Buddhist areas of Inner Asia are 3 persons per square kilometer in Buryatia, 2 in Tuva, 4 in Kalmykia, 19 in Inner Mongolia, 18 in Qinghai, and 45 in Bhutan. In 2002 the popu-

lation density of the Tibet Autonomous Region of China was 2.18 people per square kilometer (*Tibet* p. 30), and that of Mongolia 1.4 people per square kilometer (Lonely Planet *Mongolia* p. 33). By contrast, the present population density of China is 134 persons per square kilometer.

[38] Wild yak (*'brong* in Tibetan) are much larger than their domesticated relatives. In the early years of the 21st century, wild yak were an endangered species and the object of international conservation efforts.

[39] Diamond, p. 77.

[40] A Tibetan army sacked the Tang Dynasty capital at Chang An in the eighth century A.D.

[41] Diamond, p. 167.

[42] China is believed to have domesticated rice, millet, the pig and the silkworm by 7000 B.C., and domestic cattle, wheat, and barley were cultivated in the Indus Valley during the same period (Diamond p. 100).

[43] Cities appeared in the Indus Valley as early as 2000 B.C., and local monarchies existed in the Ganges basin as early as the 6th century B.C. (Burton Stein, *A History of India,* (Oxford, Blackwell 1998) p. 48, 60. Dynastic culture in the Yellow River valley appeared as early as the second millennium B.C. (Gernet p. 680).

[44] Writing appeared in the Indus Valley about 2200 B.C. (Diamond p. 231) and probably arose independently in China no later than 1300 B.C. (Diamond p. 218).

[45] By the third millennium B.C. China had entered the Bronze Age, and by 500 B.C. it had the earliest cast iron production in the world (Diamond p. 330).

[46] Even today, 40% of modern India's population lives on the Gangetic plain (Burton Stein, p. 9).

[47] These innovations were primarily philosophical and religious in the case of India, and technological in the case of China.

[48] Shared artifacts and trade goods show that the Indus Valley civilization was in contact with Mesopotamia from about 3000 B.C. onwards. See Stein, p. 6.

[49] The author is indebted to Professor David Christian for suggesting that the Inner / Outer Asia paradigm explains much of the history of what later became the Tibetan Buddhist World.

[50] A lifeway which sociologists call "pastoral nomadism."

[51] Christian, p. 87.

[52] Examples of artifacts from this era can be seen in the Tibet Museum in Lhasa.

[53] The Tungus were later known as the Ewenk.

[54] Classic Inner Asian shamanism is believed to have its roots in the hunting cultures of the Upper Paleolithic period (Christian, p. 64).

[55] Among the later Mongol tribes he was even named 'sky.' Belief in a high creator god is common in folk religions around the world.

[56] Christian p. 62.

[57] Compare with this belief the Biblical story of the Tower of Babel in Genesis 11.

[58] Eliade, p. 216.

[59] For a discussion of shamanist cosmology, see Eliade p. 259.

[60] The shamanic vocation is discussed at length in Eliade, chapter 3.

[61] This is the shamanist origin of the so-called "protector deities" in Tibetan Buddhism. See Rene de Nebesky-Wojkowitz, *Oracles and Demons of Tibet: The Cult and Iconography of the Tibetan Protective Deities* (New Delhi: Paljor, 1998).

[62] Sky spirits were called *tenger* or *endurs* in Mongolian; water spirits were called *lu* (in both Mongolian and Tibetan).

[63] Called *ongon* in Mongolian. Spirit houses or spirit traps are widespread in the modern Tibetan Buddhist World. In tantric Buddhism they take the form of mandalas.

[64] For the world-axis in shamanism, see Christian p. 62 or Eliade p. 259. Tibetan Buddhists venerate western Tibet's Mt. Kailash as the mystical axis (*ri rab lhun po*) of the Buddhist cosmos.

[65] Ritual repetitive drum-beating is still practiced by Tibetan monks and Himalayan shamans in modern times.

[66] Masks are another shamanic device still used in modern Tibetan Buddhism.

[67] From this symbolic archetype arose fantastic stories of Tibetan lamas being able to "fly." During the Soviet period, the secret police reportedly threw native Siberian shamans out of aircraft, telling them that if they really could fly, this was their chance (Reid p. 7).

[68] Such powers are claimed to this day by certain individuals in Tibetan culture who are called *delogs*. For an example, see Dawa Drolma's *Delog: Journey to Realms Beyond Death* (Junction City CA: Padma, 1995).

[69] Christian p. 41, 91ff.

[70] All of these are common themes of folk religions around the world (See Paul G. Hiebert's *Understanding Folk Religion*).

[71] Burning incense for purification is yet another shamanic practice which is found in modern Tibetan Buddhism.

[72] Shamanism eventually reached the New World, either across the Bering Strait or by cultural transmission among the peoples of the high Arctic.

[73] See for example, Larry Peters' *Tamang Shamans: An Ethnopsychiatric Study of Ecstasy and Healing in Nepal,* (New Delhi: Nirala 1998).

[74] Snellgrove, *Indo-Tibetan Buddhism*, p. 391.

[75] Artifacts from the Paleolithic and Neolithic periods can be seen in the Tibet Museum in Lhasa. They include stone and bone implements of various types, as well as examples of rock paintings found at Nagchu and Damshung. For photos, see Tibet Museum's *Tibet Museum* (Encyclopedia of China Publishing House, 2001).

[76] Carvings of the *khyung* bird dating to the 5th century B.C. have been found in western Tibet (Baumer, p. 30).

[77] Tibetan *gnod sbyin*

[78] Tibetan *'dre*

[79] For a more detailed description, see Baumer, p. 38.

[80] Tibetan *klu*

[81] Virtually all these beliefs were to enter Tibetan Buddhism intact.

[82] Indo-European is a family of over 400 languages spoken from Europe to India, all of which are thought to be descended from a common ancestor extant some 5,000 years ago.

83 See the "People" section in the *Encyclopedia Brittanica*'s article on Asia, p.155.
84 The religion of the Aryans is called Vedism, after these texts.
85 For a summary of this formative period of Indian philosophy, see David Burnett's *The Spirit of Hinduism* (Tunbridge Wells: Monarch, 1992).
86 See Christian, p. 215.
87 For a description of the Kushan Empire, see Christian, p. 210-218.
88 It was probably from this area that the Tibetans had their very first contact with Mahayana Buddhism. For the probable role of this contact in the formation of the Bon religion, see the next chapter, and David Snellgrove's *Indo-Tibetan Buddhism,* p. 390-391.
89 Gernet, p. 213.
90 Overpopulation, climate change, increased demand for products from Inner Asia, and the appearance of compound bows have all been suggested as causes for this increased level of conflict. See Christian, p. 124.
91 The Scythians inhabited the area around the Black Sea and were well known in Roman times. They are mentioned in the Bible in Colossians 3:11.
92 The Xiongnu (or Hsiung-nu) were a powerful confederation of Inner Asian nomadic tribes based in the Ordos Desert (now in the Chinese province of Inner Mongolia). They controlled a large area of the steppes from China to Siberia, and made repeated attacks on China during the second and third centuries B.C.
93 The Yueh Chih were a large group of Indo-European speaking peoples who in the second century B.C. occupied the oases of the Tarim and western Gobi deserts, areas now included in the Chinese provinces of Gansu and Xinjiang.
94 See Gernet, p. 120. Successive Chinese governments tried to pacify restive ethnic borderlands by settling them with large numbers of Han Chinese. This policy has continued intermittently from the Han Dynasty (206 B.C. - 221 A.D.) to the present.

Notes to Chapter Three

95 Quoted in Geshe Lhundup Sopa, *Lectures on Tibetan Religious Culture,* Volume 2, (Dharamsala: Library of Tibetan Works and Archives, 1983), p. 266.
96 For a more detailed discussion of the Upanishads, see David Burnett's *The Spirit of Hinduism* (Tunbridge Wells: Monarch, 1992), p. 60ff.
97 Whether brahma has any characteristics at all has been the subject of enduring debate in Indian philosophy (Burnett p. 64).
98 *Kena Upanishad,* Part IV, Juan Mascaro, translator, *The Upanishads* (London: Penguin Classics, 1965) p. 52-53ff.
99 The analogy with raindrops falling into the sea is found, for example, in the sixth question of the *Prasna Upanishad,* Mascaro, p. 74. It appears again in the *Mundaka Upanishad* (p. 81). David Snellgrove in his book *Indo-Tibetan Buddhism* claims that though the Upanishads were indeed teaching a doctrine of a 'soul' or *atman* which would ultimately unite with a "universal soul" or *brahman,* these ideas did not directly influence the first group of Sakyamuni's disciples (p.20). It is undeniable, however, that the monistic views described here formed the philosophical basis for Buddhism.

100 In Sanskrit the presence of *brahman* in individual people is called *atman*. The doctrine of *atman* is taught in the *Katha Upanishad* Part II, Mascaro, p. 59.

101 The *Mundaka Upanishad* expresses this by analogy with a fire that sends out thousands of sparks. *Mundaka Upanishad*, Part II, chapter 1, Mascaro, p. 77.

102 *Mandukya Upanishad*, Mascaro, p. 83.

103 *Katha Upanishad*, Part VI, Mascaro, p. 65.

104 In the twentieth century, another type of monism, materialistic monism, became influential because of the theories of Karl Marx and popular scientific writers such as H.G. Wells in the UK and Carl Sagan in the United States.

105 As the *Katha Upanishad* says, "Who sees the many and not the one, wanders on from death to death." *Katha Upanishad*, Part IV, Mascaro, p. 63.

106 In the words of the *Svetasvatara Upanishad*, Part I, "he is one with the one," Mascaro, p. 85.

107 This is referred to in the *Svetasvatara Upanishad*, Part I, as "the illusion which sees the one as two," Mascaro, p. 85.

108 This direct meditative experience was usually sought through ascetic meditation in the forest, as mentioned in Part II of the *Mundaka Upanishad*, Mascaro, p. 77.

109 The doctrines of rebirth and karma are taught in the *Svetasvatara Upanishad*, Part V, Mascaro, p. 94.

110 At least one Buddhist author (Snellgrove) claims that a belief in personal survival through the round of rebirths was taught by early Buddhists, citing the boddisattva ideal as an example. In view of the fact that those who are reborn can't remember their previous lives (except where there are religious or social incentives for doing so) this seems to stretch the sense of the term 'personal survival' beyond the breaking point.

111 Readers from a Western cultural background should note that the word "god" in this context has little to do with the Judeo-Christian concept of God. The fourteenth Dalai Lama has pointed out that belief in an independently existing creator God is not logical in Buddhist terms (Dalai Lama XIV, *A Flash of Lightning in the Dark of Night: A Guide to the Boddhisattva's Way of Life*, (Boston: Shambhala, 1994), p. 60-61.

112 Mascaro, p. 140.

113 The Dalai Lama, *Path to Bliss* (Ithaca: Snow Lion, 1991) p. 191.

114 *Path to Bliss* p. 127.

115 In early Buddhism the law of karma was unbreakable. In Mahayana Buddhism the law could be "bent" through faith in Boddhisattvas. In tantric Buddhism karmic effects can be manipulated by magic spells and occult rituals such as those described in the so-called Tibetan Book of the Dead, or *Bar Do Thos sGrol*.

116 These six possible states of rebirth are represented in the tutelary picture "The Wheel of Life" commonly seen on the walls of Tibetan Buddhist monasteries. The realms of gods, demigods, and humans are depicted in the top half of the wheel, and the realms of animals, hungry ghosts, and hell-beings are depicted in the bottom half.

117 Ascetic practices were common in the Vedic age, and may have represented a reaction to the ritualistic approach to religion practiced by the Vedic priests.

Ascetics sought spiritual power through fasting, self-torture, etc.

[118] There are many versions of the life of the Buddha. The reader is recommended to read John Davis' *The Path to Enlightenment: Introducing Buddhism* (London: Hodder and Stoughton, 1997). Other English language sources are Christmas Humphreys' *Buddhism* (London: Penguin, 1951, reprinted 1983; Nikkyo Niwano's *Shakyamuni Buddha: A Narrative Biography* (Tokyo: Kosei, 1980); and other brief accounts and traditions too numerous to list here.

[119] One chronology places Siddartha's birth in 563 B.C., another three years earlier. His life spanned the Babylonian captivity of the Jews, and his contemporaries included Confucius (551-479 B.C.) and the Hebrew prophet Zechariah.

[120] Niwano, p. 32.

[121] Niwano, p. 38.

[122] Niwano, p. 57.

[123] Dalai Lama XIV, *A Flash of Lightning in the Dark of Night: A Guide to the Boddhisattva's Way of Life* (Boston: Shambhala, 1994) p. 28.

[124] See Humphreys, p. 40; and Niwano, p. 116.

[125] The root word is used in modern languages of blowing out a candle, or turning off an electric light.

[126] For a more detailed discussion of nirvana, see the entry in *The Shambhala Dictionary of Buddhism and Zen* (Boston: Shambhala 1991).

[127] Tibetan Buddhists, writing centuries later, put Siddartha's Four Truths (Tibetan *bDen Pa bZhi*) in a somewhat different form: 1. Truths That are Suffering (*sDug bsNgal Gyi bDen Pa*); 2. Truths That are Sources (*Kun 'Byung Gi bDen Pa*); 3. Truths That Are Cessations (*'Gog Pa'i bDen Pa*); and 4. Truths That Are Paths (*Lam Gyi bDen Pa*).

[128] This mutual dependence between the monks and nuns on one hand and lay people on the other became a characteristic feature of Buddhist societies all across Asia. It was and is a vital feature of Tibetan Buddhism.

[129] Traditionally, there were 18 such schools, among which only the Theravadins have survived as a living tradition (Snellgrove, p. 26).

[130] For details on the spread of Theravada Buddhism into Southeast Asia, see Davis, p. 34.

[131] The Mahayanists taught that the Buddhas have three bodies, or *trikaya* in Sanskrit. These are: 1) a transcendent *dharmakaya* body identical with Buddhist teachings; 2) a *sambhogakaya* enjoyment body with which they reside in the Mahayana paradises; and 3) a *nirmanakaya* (Tibetan *sprul sku*) emanation body with which they appear in the human world.

[132] The Mahayanists professed belief in several different types of nirvana. In a Mahayana technical sense, the boddhisattva does not actually postpone or turn back from nirvana, but seeks the highest type of nirvana. See Paul Williams' *Mahayana Buddhism:The Doctrinal Foundations,* (London: Routledge, 1989) p. 53.

[133] Tibetan *byang chub sems dpa'*

[134] Gyatso, p. 104-5.

135 In the boddhisattva ideal, man takes God's place as ultimate redeemer (cf. Isaiah 14:13-14).

136 Mahayana and Hinayana are referred to in Tibetan as *theg chen* and *theg dman*, respectively.

137 Lamotte, Etienne, *Mahayana Buddhism*, in Heinz Bechert and Richard Gombrich, eds, *The World of Buddhism* (London: Thames and Hudson, 1984) p. 91.

138 Among the best known of these mythologies is the Jataka Tales, a set of stories about the previous lives of the Buddha. For an example in English, see Ethel Beswick, editor, *Jataka Tales: Birth Stories of the Buddha* (Delhi: Book Faith India, 1999).

139 Williams, p. 64.

140 Much of this teaching is attributed to the second or third century A.D. Indian Mahayana philosopher Nagarjuna.

141 Relative truth opened the door for relative morality, as Williams points out. See p. 144-145.

142 Williams, p. 143.

143 In the fifth and sixth centuries the Madhyamika school developed two subtraditions called *Suatantrika* and *Prasangika*. These spread from India to China and greatly influenced the form of Buddhism that entered Tibet.

144 For a more detailed discussion of the Madhyamika School, see the entry in *The Shambhala Dictionary of Buddhism and Zen* (Boston: Shambhala 1991).

145 This was the so-called Mauryan Empire, established by Ashoka's grandfather Chandragupta Maurya in 320 B.C. Legend connects Chandragupta with the defeat of the invading armies of Alexander the Great in the Punjab in 324 B.C. (See Stein, p. 75-76).

146 This area was part of the so-called Greco-Bactrian kingdoms left in the wake of Alexander the Great's invasion of India in 327 B.C. Greek was a living language in the area at that time. Aramaic was the administrative language of the Persian Empire, which had recently been defeated by Alexander. The Galilean dialect of Aramaic was probably the native language of Jesus.

147 For a description of the Kushan Empire, see Christian, p. 210ff.

148 In 781, a Tibetan army overran the Silk Road oasis town of Dunhuang (now in Gansu Province, China) and occupied this flourishing center of Buddhist civilization for the next 67 years. Written records from this period were placed in a local cave that remained sealed until 1907, when it was discovered by the British archaeologist Sir Marc Aurel Stein. Stein found a staggering treasure of over 3,000 complete manuscripts in half a dozen languages dating from as early as the fifth century A.D. One of these proved to be the world's earliest printed book, which, incredibly, bore its date of publication: May 11th, 868 A.D. Stein had also uncovered (though he did not realize it then) documents of the Nestorian Christians who once lived at Dunhuang. Among them were hymns, lists of books and saints, and a silken banner depicting a Nestorian bishop, which were evidence of the first contact between the Tibetans and Christianity.

149 In the great cities of the Silk Road, Mahayana Buddhism met another religion that was making its way eastward, Nestorian Christianity. Mahayana Buddhism first reached China during the first century A.D., fully 600 years before Christianity.

[150] See Raymond Dawson's *The Chinese Experience*, p. 116.

[151] Snellgrove, p. 390. Tasig (*ta zig* in Tibetan) is the Tibetan word for modern Iran or Persia.

[152] Snellgrove. p. 391. This theory accounts for the fact that the practitioners of the Bon religion continue to insist that their teachings came originally from Tazig, through Shangshung, and that all Buddhist teachings were originally theirs.

[153] What is described here is as much as is known of the content of original or *Lha Bon*, which may have existed as late as the first century A.D. From the first to the ninth centuries A.D. a second stage called *Dur Bon* appeared, which added an extensive set of rituals for the dead to the shamanic beliefs mentioned above. Some scholars mention a third stage, *Gyur Bon*, in which the beliefs of Bon were recorded in a set of scriptures. Bon declined during the introduction of tantric Buddhism into Tibet, but revived during the tenth century. The Lha Bon and Gyur Bon together are sometimes called Ancient, Eternal, or *Yungdrung* Bon. There is also a so-called "New Bon" which arose in the nineteenth century through influences from the Nyingma School of Tibetan Buddhism. Today, Bon believers are divided into followers of *Yungdrung* Bon and followers of New Bon.

[154] Historically, the pre-Buddhist religion of Tibet was shamanism, the source of so much of Tibet's present-day folk religion. If the historians of Bon are to be believed, elements of Buddhist teaching began to influence shamanism in western Tibet long before the arrival of Buddhism in Central Tibet. Only in an historical and temporal sense was Bon the pre-Buddhist religion of Tibet. For details of this argument, see Snellgrove, *Indo-Tibetan Buddhism*, p. 473.

[155] Most Western historians doubt that Tonpa Shenrab was an historical figure. Bon texts place him as early as 18,000 years ago, and as late as the time of the ninth Tibetan king, Pude Gungyal (Baumer, p. 86).

[156] Dawson, p. 116. In fact, China transformed Mahayana Buddhism into something uniquely Chinese, a process described on p. 131.

[157] Yogic practices are mentioned earlier than this, however. See Snellgrove, p. 124.

[158] Buddhists divide meditation into two types, *analytical* meditation and *placement* meditation. Analytical meditation uses conceptual thought, while placement meditation seeks to stop the action of thought in order to realize Buddhist truths directly, without the use of words or concepts.

[159] Snellgrove, p. 127.

[160] G.W. Farrow and I. Menon, *The Concealed Essence of the Hevajra Tantra* (Delhi: Motilal Banarsidass, 1992, reprinted 2001), p. 63.

[161] Panchen Sonam Dragpa, *Overview of Buddhist Tantra* (Dharamsala: Library of Tibetan Works and Archives, 1996), p. 72.

[162] This type of deity manipulation was also practiced by the shamans, as described in the previous chapter. The Kalachakra initiation of modern Tibetan Buddhism continues such rituals today. See Snellgrove, p. 130.

[163] Farrow and Menon, p. 32.

[164] Farrow and Menon, p. 29.

[165] Snellgrove, pp. 148, 235.

[166] Snellgrove, p. 143.

[167] The fourteenth Dalai Lama said that sexual practices persist in tantric Buddhist practice to the present day (Dalai Lama XIV, *The Dalai Lama at Harvard* (Ithaca: Snow Lion, 1988) p. 117. Berzin (p. 104, 112) agrees that the sexual element persists in modern tantric Buddhist practice.

[168] Berzin, p. 112.

[169] Snellgrove, p. 160.

[170] Berzin, p. 31. Revealing these secrets was accounted a cause for rebirth in the hell realms (Snellgrove p. 146).

[171] Farrow and Menon, p. 71.

[172] Mantras are sounds which are believed to have magical powers. Their use is described in the Upanishads, for example in the fifth question of the *Prasna Upanishad*, Mascaro, p. 73.

[173] See Snellgrove p. 219 for an example of a typical mantra.

[174] "Kalachakra" in *The Shambhala Dictionary of Buddhism and Zen* (Boston: Shambhala 1991).

[175] For a more detailed discussion of nirvana, see the entry in *The Shambhala Dictionary of Buddhism and Zen* (Boston: Shambhala, 1991).

[176] See Alexander Berzin's *Taking the Kalachakra Initiation* (Ithaca: Snow Lion, 1997) for a more detailed description.

[177] See Berzin p. 45, 46, 48. The reference to the Christian, Muslim, and Manichaean prophets establishes this tantra as historically late in composition. All these religions were well known in the Kushan Empire.

[178] Berzin, p. 49.

[179] Berzin, p. 32-33, 54.

[180] Berzin, p. 98, 143, and 103, 108, 112 respectively.

[181] Snellgrove, p. 161.

[182] Snellgrove, p. 456.

[183] Berzin, p. 32.

[184] In Tibetan the process is called *lha sgrub pa* or "god-realizing"; see Waddell, p. 153.

[185] See Gyatso, p. 121-2.

[186] Dawson, p. 118.

[187] The nineteen century period spans roughly 500 B.C. to 1400 A.D., from the completion of the Old Testament to the eve of the discovery of the New World.

[188] Sexual religious rituals were a prominent part of the pagan religions that surrounded Israel in Old Testament times (e.g. Genesis 38, Deuteronomy 23, 1 Kings 14, 15 and other passages mention their practice of shrine prostitution).

[189] The sixth Dalai Lama, a noted libertine, being a case in point.

Notes to Chapter Four

[190] This area lies about 5,000 meters above sea level, and it likely that the Rijnharts' baby perished from altitude sickness, symptoms of which may be difficult to detect in an infant. The region is now part of southern Qinghai Province, near the *rdza chu* (Mekong) River.

[191] With incredible courage, Dr. Susie Carson Rijnhart returned to medical mission work among the Tibetan Khampa tribes in 1903, but died shortly thereafter. She told the story of her travels in Tibet in *With the Tibetans in Tent and Temple*, (Chicago: Fleming H. Revell, 1901). An abridged version of her story can be found in Peter Hopkirk's *Trespassers on the Roof of the World* (Los Angeles: JP Tarcher, 1983).

[192] From the year 650 A.D., the Tibetan court maintained annals recording its foreign and domestic affairs (Snellgrove, p. 372).

[193] An alternative legend states that they descended to earth (and returned to the sky) via 6,636 meter Mt. Yarlhashampo, near the head of the Yarlung Valley in Lhokha Prefecture, Tibet.

[194] This myth was reintroduced at a later period in Tibetan history in the form of the death and "rebirth" of the Dalai Lama and other leaders of the Gelugpa sect of Tibetan Buddhism (Snellgrove, p. 382).

[195] David Snellgrove and Hugh Richardson, *A Cultural History of Tibet* (Boulder: Prajna Press, 1980) p. 25.

[196] They also invaded the area which they called Chiang (in modern Yunnan).

[197] David Snellgrove, *Indo-Tibetan Buddhism*, pp. 356, 385.

[198] At this time there were Buddhist civilizations in China and India, and in the Bactrian, Sogdian, and Kashmiri homelands of the old Kushan Empire. The tantric and magical practices that flourished in the latter areas deeply influenced Tibetan Buddhism.

[199] *Srong brtsan sgam po* in Tibetan.

[200] In fact, the Tibetans of this era were already familiar with the so-called Gupta scripts used by their Silk Road neighbors, and had adapted them to their own language. It is likely that Thon Mi's actual contribution was to standardize or systematize the use of these early types of written Tibetan. (See Snellgrove, p. 387.)

[201] Even today classical Tibetan is the language of Tibetan Buddhist monks and scholars, and it is being taught to a new generation of Tibetan Buddhist disciples in the West. The story of Thön Mi's mission to India is told in Chattopadhyaya, p. 198-211. A Tibetan source is *Thonmi Sambhota* (Xining: Qinghai Nationalities Publishing House, 1999).

[202] *Khri srong lde brtsan* in Tibetan.

[203] Tantric Mahayana Buddhism was popular in Bactria, Sogdiana, and Kashmir during this period.

[204] Snellgrove p. 404-405.

[205] See Snellgrove and Richardson, chapter 3.

[206] For a detailed description, see Baumer and de Nebesky-Wojkowitz.

[207] Waddell, p. 382, used by permission of Dover Publications.

[208] Snellgrove, p. 404-405.

[209] Bechert and Gombrich p. 263.

[210] Fields, p. 326.

[211] Five of Tibet's first ten kings were assassinated.

[212] Tsipon W.D. Shakabpa calls this "the period of Tibet's fragmentation" in his two-volume work *Political History of Tibet* (Dharamsala: Tibetan Cultural Printing Press, 1986), p. 235.

213 The so-called "First Diffusion of Buddhism" occurred during the time of the Tibetan kings in the seventh and eighth centuries.

214 Two centuries later, Marco Polo noted that the inhabitants of Kashmir were noted for their ability in black magic (Polo, p. 55). See also Baumer, p. 188.

215 Atisha is known as *rjo bo rje* in Tibetan and as *Dipamkara Srijnana* in Sanskrit.

216 Disciples must pay for religious teaching in many Tibetan Buddhist countries. The expense can be considerable, leading the famous Tibetan poet Milarepa to write: "Religion is forbidden to the poor."

217 See Stein, p. 71, and Geshe Lhundup Sopa's *Lectures on Tibetan Religious Culture,* Vol. 1, p. 160.

218 *bka' gdams pa* in Tibetan.

219 *dge lugs pa* in Tibetan. The Gelugpas eventually became the dominant school of Tibetan Buddhism, and the Gelugpa leader, the Dalai Lama, became the country's spiritual and temporal ruler.

220 For details of the historical period from the beginning of the Tibetan monarchy to the time of Atisha, see Alaka Chattopadhyaya.'s *Atisa and Tibet: The Life and Works of Dipamkara Srijnana in Relation to History and Religion of Tibet, With Tibetan Sources* (Delhi: Motilal Banarsidass,1981).

221 During the first millennium, a similar challenge from heretical beliefs led the Church to convene its great councils, whose statements of faith defined Western Christian orthodoxy.

222 Bechert and Gombrich, p. 269.

223 For details about Marpa, see Nalanda Translation Committee, *The Life of Marpa the Translator* (Boston: Shambhala, 1986).

224 The transformation of the dog into a spirit-being may seem bizarre to the modern reader. Recall, however, the shamanist belief that humans, spirits, and animals are equivalent and may change into each other at any time.

225 See Nalanda Translation Committee, p. xxxvii. Kukkuripa's biography appears in James B. Robinson, tr. *Buddha's Lions: The Lives of the Eighty Four Siddhas* (Berkeley, CA: Dharma Publishing, 1979) p. 128.

226 Lhalungpa (*The Life of Milarepa*) is an entertaining example in English.

227 *bka' brgyud pa* in Tibetan.

228 *Sa skya pa* in Tibetan.

229 For the history of the Sakyapas and their importance to Mongolia, see Snellgrove and Richardson, p. 115, 132; and Baabar's *History of Mongolia* (Mongolia and Inner Asia Studies Unit, University of Cambridge, 1999) p. 66.

230 For a classification of Tibetan Buddhist schools, see Snellgrove (table p. 488).

231 *Bu ston* in Tibetan.

232 *bstan 'gyur* in Tibetan.

233 *bka' 'gyur* in Tibetan.

234 The Mongol historian Batbayar Baterdene (known as Baabar) claims that this caused the majority of Tibetans to remain in ignorance and superstition while the lamas restricted learning to a few of the elite (p. 68).

235 Tucci, p. 37.

236 For an example, see Alexander Berzin's *Taking the Kalachakra Initiation* (cited elsewhere).

237 After Snellgrove, p. 488-9.

238 Richardson, p. 12.
239 Area Handbook for Mongolia, p. 185.
240 See Anna Reid's *The Shaman's Coat: A Native History of Siberia* (New York: Walker & Co. 2002) p. 79 for the figure for Buryatia.
241 Bechert and Gombrich, p. 257.
242 This was not always voluntary. See Melvyn Goldstein's *A History of Modern Tibet, 1913-1951: The Demise of the Lamaist State* (Berkeley: University of California, 1989) p. 21. The parents of one child recognized as an incarnate lama refused to hand him over, but were eventually compelled to do so by order of the Thirteenth Dalai Lama. (See Rene de Nebesky-Wojkowitz, *Oracles and Demons of Tibet: The Cult and Iconography of the Tibetan Protective Deities* (Delhi: Paljor 1998) p. viii.
243 For examples, see Melvyn Goldstein's *A History of Modern Tibet, 1913-1951: The Demise of the Lamaist State* (Delhi: Indian Book Company 1993).
244 Temuchin's mother, who helped him through this time of hardships, was said to have been a Christian. See Morton, p. 116; and the *Area Handbook for Mongolia*, p. 42.
245 Gernet, p. 384.
246 Marco Polo, p. 110. Marco Polo crossed the eastern borderlands of Tibet during his later travels. Here, too, he was impressed by their occult practices. "They perform the most potent enchantments and the greatest marvels to hear and to behold by diabolic arts . ." p. 173-174.
247 See Marco Polo's *The Travels of Marco Polo* (New York: Signet 2004) p. 102.
248 See Gernet, p. 417.
249 *Area Handbook for Mongolia*, p. 58.
250 Tucci p. 135. The idea of a line of continuously reincarnating monks dates back to the twelfth century, some 300 years before the Gelugpas applied it to the Dalai Lamas. Of course, the original source of this doctrine was the shamanist myth of Tibet's early kings, who descended from the sky to rule Tibet, only to return to the upper world by means of a magic cord, another form of the shamanist world-axis.
251 Mongol armies appeared in Lhasa again in 1705 and 1716 (Baabar, p. 85) during struggles over the Dalai Lamas' succession.
252 *spyan ras gzigs* in Tibetan.
253 As stated above, the spread of Tibetan Buddhism among the Mongols was encouraged by the Chinese in order to keep Mongolia militarily weak. Manchu emperors encouraged the printing and translation of Tibetan and Mongol Buddhist works, and in 1732 the emperor Yung Cheng even converted his palace in Peking into a Tibetan Buddhist temple. See Gernet, p. 477, and the *Area Handbook for Mongolia*, p. 61.
254 Baabar, p. 72.
255 Baabar, p. 99.
256 Baabar, p. 98-99.
257 See Anna Reid, *The Shaman's Coat* (New York: Walker and Company, 2002) p. 79. This book has worthwhile chapters on the history and culture of Siberia's native peoples, including the Buryats and the Tuvans.
258 Reid, p. 105.

259 This trade and its effects are documented in David J. Phillips' *Peoples on the Move: Introducing the Nomads of the World*, (Pasadena, William Carey, 2001) p. 359.

260 For details on the life of these peoples, see Bista.

261 For the history of Buddhism in Ladakh, see Rizvi.

262 Though this method of combining tantric Buddhism with local beliefs worked well in Tibet, among the Lepchas it produced a weak and superficial Buddhism that decayed rapidly. When Christian missionaries reached Sikkim in the nineteenth century, the nominally Buddhist Lepchas were among the groups most responsive to the Gospel. For details, see Foning p. 184-186; 304.

263 For a part of the history of Bhutan's relationship with Tibet, see Hugh Richardson's *Tibet and Its History* (Boston: Shambhala, 1984) p. 64.

264 See Melvyn Goldstein's *A History of Modern Tibet* (Los Angeles: University of California Press, 1989) p. 2. The monks called this arrangement *chos srid gnyis 'brel* or "religion and politics together."

265 This policy may have been encouraged by a previous Nepali invasion of Tibet, repulsed by a Chinese army in 1791. The presence of Chinese and Nepali armies on their soil gave the Tibetans reason to be concerned about the actions of their neighbors. It is also likely that the lamas were aware of the growing power of the British in India at the time. For the date of the declaration, see Snellgrove and Richardson's *A Cultural History of Tibet*, p. 289, and *Evangelicals in Central Tibet,* Tibet Information Network News Compilation, 22nd October, 1992.

266 For a description of Tibetan hermits in the last century, see L. Austine Waddell's *Lhasa and Its Mysteries* (New York: Dover 1988) p. 239ff.

267 Tibetan Buddhism is, as the anthropologist Sherry Ortner observed among the Sherpa people of Nepal, "a religion of anti-social individualism." See Sherry Ortner, *Sherpas Through Their Rituals*, (Cambridge: Cambridge University Press, 1978, p. 157).

268 The Tibetans classify all their traditional knowledge into ten subject areas: grammar, Buddhist logic, arts, medicine, Buddhist philosophy, rhetoric, composition, poetry, drama, and astrology.

269 Artists are still expected to conform to these norms. For visual arts, see Tsondu Rabgyal and Dorje Rinchen's *Bod kyi ri mo spyi'i rnam gzhag blo gsal 'jug sgo* (Beijing: Minorities Publishing House, 2001).

270 For a modern example of a dictionary of fixed metaphors, see Puchung's *mngon brjod tshig mdzod* (Lhasa: Tibet Peoples' Publishing House, 1997).

271 Only in the last few decades has creative artistic expression appeared in Tibet proper, much of it through Chinese influence. Contemporary writers and painters are either self-taught or trained in Chinese universities, and may work under official or foreign (grant-based) sponsorship.

272 See Snellgrove, p. 63. Tantric Buddhism is a gnostic religion in the sense that it has secret teachings which are disclosed only to initiates. Tantric Buddhism never became a truly popular movement in India or Tibet in the sense that all of its teachings were directed towards monks, who had to be initiated into secret knowledge in order to practice them. While the cult of various boddhisattvas (e.g. Avalokiteshvara and Tara — *Chenrezig* and *Dolma* in Ti-

betan) became enduringly popular, only by means of tantric practice, barred to the common people, could the ultimate enlightenment be achieved.

273 For a detailed description of shamanist practices at the folk Buddhist level in Tibet, see R. de Nebesky-Wojkowitz's *Oracles and Demons of Tibet.*

274 For details of the British action in Tibet, see Francis Younghusband, *India and Tibet* (reprinted Oxford University Press, 1985).

275 See Reid, p. 86-89.

276 See Saklani, p. 143.

277 By 1976 there were approximately 100 incarnate lamas, 5,000 monks, 600 lay priests, 400 nuns, and 109 monasteries in India, Nepal, and Bhutan, according to the statistics of the Dalai Lama's administration in India. See Saklani, p. 154.

278 See for example Robert Silverberg's *The Realm of Prester John* (London: Phoenix, 2001) or Hugh Kemp's *Steppe by Step* (London: Monarch, 2000) chapter 4.

279 The roots of the West's romantic fascination with Tibet are explored in Orville Schell's *Virtual Tibet* (New York: Holt, 2000).

280 *Kim* first appeared in serialized form in popular magazines in the United States and Britain. A complete British edition was published in October 1901. Interested readers are referred to Peter Hopkirk's *Quest for Kim: In Search of Kipling's Great Game* (London: John Murray, 1996).

281 His real name was Cyril Hoskins. His most famous book, *The Third Eye* (1956) told of his mystical adventures in Asia, but in reality he never left Europe.

282 See Emma M. Layman's *Buddhism in America* (Chicago: Nelson Hall, 1976) p. 234.

283 See Matthew 13:45. Like the merchant in Jesus' parable, the Tibetans gave every treasure they had for what they esteemed above all else.

284 For example, the lamas resisted modern education. By the 1940s, both India and China had hundreds of thousands of university graduates; Tibet had virtually none. Areas ruled by Tibetan Buddhist theocracies lacked elites with modern education, and did not have modern systems of commerce, finance, or transport; both the masses and many of the monks were functionally illiterate. See Dwight Perkins et al. *Economics of Development* (New York: Norton, 2001) p. 17.

285 Many aboriginal groups in Siberia, Australia, and the Americas can testify to this fact (or would be able to testify to it, if they still existed). For a discussion, see Diamond, p. 252-255.

Notes to Chapter Five

286 For details, see Rene de Nebesky-Wojkowitz's *Oracles and Demons of Tibet: The Cult and Iconography of the Tibetan Protective Deities* (New Delhi: Paljor, 1998).

287 For more about shamanism, see Mircea Eliade's *Shamanism: Archaic Techniques of Ecstasy* (Princeton: Princeton University Press, 1964, 1992). An excellent resource on the Mongolian form of shamanism is *Riding Windhorses*, by Sarangerel.

288 Called *lung rta* in Tibetan, and *hiimor* in Mongolian.

289 Tibetan *yung drung*, Mongolian *has temdeg.*
290 Tibetan *rdo spung*, Mongolian *oboo.*
291 Delogs are *'das log* in Tibetan. This and other shamanist beliefs have exercised a profound influence upon Tibetan Buddhism to the present day; for details see de Nebesky-Wojkowitz.
292 Paul G. Hiebert, *Understanding Folk Religions*, p. 80.
293 See Harrer, *Seven Years in Tibet*, p. 297.
294 Harrer, *Ladakh*, p. 128.
295 Waddell, p. 473.
296 The sociologist Robert Ekvall has described these behaviors in mediums in northeastern Tibet (p. 27). A similar description was given by Harrer (*Seven Years in Tibet*, p. 204-206).
297 von Furer-Haimendorf, p. 268.
298 Dorje, p. 29. Horoscopes are used in Tibet (Waddell p. 458); Sikkim (Chopra, p. 56ff); Bhutan (Mehra p. 28); and Ladakh (Harrer's *Ladakh*, p. 140), as well as in other parts of the Tibetan Buddhist world.
299 While the Tibetan Buddhist gods are generally detached and uninterested in worldly affairs, almost all of them have evil or malicious forms that are believed capable of causing great harm. See Ortner p. 92. The fourteenth Dalai Lama condemned the more grossly superstitious forms of spiritism. (*Path to Bliss*, p. 128)
300 Hiebert, p. 80.
301 Techniques from both shamanism and tantra are used in modern Tibetan Buddhism.
302 One of the cornerstones of Western logic is the law of non-contradiction, that is, a true statement excludes its opposite.
303 When Tibetan monks engage in monastic debates, they apply rules of logic which are similar to those of Western logic. But their goal in doing so is to prove Nagarjuna's Mahayana doctrine of so-called "absolute truth"; that is, that the truth lies beyond what can be put into words, and includes all opposites. (See chapter 3, and Perdue.)
304 For more on intuitional thinking, see David J. Hesselgrave's *Communicating Christ Cross-Culturally: An Introduction to Missionary Communication*, (Grand Rapids: Zondervan, 2nd. edition 1991).
305 Ekvall p. 70.
306 For details of the incident, see Fields p. 387. This kind of gullibility has been the source of many sensational reports about Tibet. Credulous Western travelers have reported tales of lamas who can fly, warm themselves without clothing, or make themselves invisible.
307 For example, even in the late twentieth century, astrologers selected the date for the public coronation of the present king of Bhutan. See Olschak, p. 36.
308 Harrer, *Seven Years in Tibet*, p. 191.
309 For details on the use of amulets and charms in Tibetan Buddhism, see de Nebesky-Wojkowitz, p. 503.
310 See Nalanda Translation Committee, *The Life of Marpa the Translator*, p. xlix.
311 See chapter 4.

312 The so-called "Great Proletarian Cultural Revolution" was a political campaign initiated by Mao Tse Tung during the period 1966 to 1976. It was characterized by arbitrary arrests, nationwide mob violence, and political murder.

313 Tibetan uses the same verb (*gsog*) for hoarding money and storing up merit.

314 The actual "workings" of merit and demerit in rebirth are somewhat more complicated than in this simplified example.

315 Waddell, p. 148.

316 Gyatso, p. 93.

317 The author has seen four monks doing this in a moderately wealthy Tibetan home. The figure of ten is from Harrer's *Ladakh,* p. 88.

318 Even in the early years of the twenty-first century, Tibetan families continued secretly setting apart sons for the monkhood, though the Chinese government allowed only a few each year to enter monasteries.

319 For an example of the relative priorities of merit making techniques in one Tibetan Buddhist society, see Ortner, p. 38.

320 Waddell, p. 149.

321 Fields, p. 380. This prayer wheel is driven by a system of automobile fan belts connected to an electric motor.

322 Prayer flags are another universally popular method of merit making in the Tibetan Buddhist world. For a description, see Waddell, p. 408.

323 Human body parts such as skulls, thigh bones, and blood are still used in modern Tibetan Buddhist rituals, however. (For details, see de Nebesky-Wojkowitz, p. 398). Skull and thigh bone implements were on sale in the Lhasa bazaar well into the twenty first century.

324 See Ortner, p. 91-127 for examples of substitute images in exorcisms; and p. 128-156 for examples of offerings using *torma*. Ekvall (p. 164ff) also explains the use of torma.

325 For details see de Nebesky-Wojkowitz. Instances of actual blood sacrifice are still said to occur occasionally, mainly in the form of self mutilation offerings (*dmar mchod* in Tibetan). Of these, self inflicted burns seem to be the most common. See Ekvall, p. 166.

326 The use of human flesh is described by Ekvall (p. 169). Its actual consumption by the Gelugpa order is denied by Norbu and Turnbull, but the use of human bones and other body parts in certain rituals is authentic. (See Norbu and Turnbull, p. 206, and de Nebesky-Wojkowitz).

327 For an example, see Harrer's *Seven Years in Tibet*, p. 191.

328 Traditional scapegoat rituals are described in de Nebesky Wojkowitz, p. 507 ff. The scapegoats in the Lhasa rituals were known as *glud 'gong rgyal po* in Tibetan.

329 For the details of scapegoat rituals in Lhasa and in Khalatse, Ladakh, see R.A. Stein, p. 217-220. For details of a similar ceremony at the Labrang monastery, see Waddell, p. 513.

330 The author once asked a Tibetan friend about the proper word for the love of children for parents. After thinking a minute, the Tibetan replied: "We would never say we *loved* our parents, only that we *respected* them."

331 Two sociologists who studied the Sherpa people found a 30% divorce rate (Ortner p. 46). Among the Bhutanese marriage and divorce are reported by

a sympathetic observer to be "matters of convenience" (Mehra, p. 29). Among the Mongols before the 1924 revolution "divorce was neither difficult nor rare" (*Area Handbook for Mongolia*, p. 105). Among the Tibetans themselves, divorce seems to be less common because of social pressures against it (Saklani p. 98-99).

[332] The author is aware of cases in which American or other Western converts to Tibetan Buddhism have offered their children to monasteries in Bhutan and Nepal.

[333] Melvyn Goldstein, *A History of Modern Tibet, 1913-1951: The Demise of the Lamaist State*, (Berkeley: University of California, 1989) p. 21.

[334] The figures for Tibet are from Saklani p. 141; for Mongolia from the *Area Handbook for Mongolia*, p. 185; and for Ladakh the figures are based on population statistics and the estimates quoted in Harrer's *Ladakh*, p. 25. Among Tibetan exiles in India, Nepal, and Bhutan, approximately 5% of the total population of 100,000 are monks or nuns (Saklani p. 154). Ten percent of the combined Bhotia-Lepcha population of Sikkim are monks. (Kotturan p. 112).

[335] Ekvall, p. 71.

[336] Ortner, p. 47.

[337] Waddell, p. 224.

[338] Goldstein, p. 23.

[339] Examples are vows of celibacy, abstinence from dancing, singing, music, use of alcoholic beverages, etc.

[340] For one example, see Gyatso, p. 73.

[341] Ortner, p. 157.

[342] Harrer, *Seven Years in Tibet*, p. 234.

[343] Snellgrove and Richardson, p. 184.

[344] Fleming, p. 202.

[345] Goldstein and Beall, p. 97.

[346] Ekvall, p. 76.

[347] Waddell, p. 213.

[348] Hiebert, p. 83.

[349] *chos rgyal* in Tibetan

[350] These kings were known collectively as the Shapdung Dynasty. Their line came to an end about 1905.

[351] For details, see Snellgrove and Richardson, p. 76; and Ekvall, p. 44.

[352] Tibetan *chos skad*.

[353] For Milarepa's position in Bhutan see Mehra p. 41; in Ladakh see Harrer's *Ladakh*, p. 141. Milarepa's biography is available in an English translation, but like many other works of its kind, it contains tales of magic and sorcery which some readers may find offensive.

[354] The spoken Tibetan language faces serious challenges from Chinese (in China) and English (in India). Chinese language dominates government offices, public facilities, and institutions to the extent that literacy in Tibetan may be of little practical use.

[355] An example of the attitude of the Buddhist priesthood to the laity is found in the doctrine of the "three individuals." The laity are "small individuals" (*skyes*

bu chung) while the "great individuals" (*skyes bu che*) are those who undertake to become boddhisattvas. See Geshe Lhundup Sopa's *Lectures on Tibetan Religious Culture*, Vol. 2, p. 222.

[356] Tibetan *dkon mchog.*

[357] Dalai Lama III, *Essence of Refined Gold*, p. 74.

[358] see Newland, p. 13.

[359] The ceremony is called the *Great Liberation Through Hearing in the Bardo*, detailed in the so-called *Tibetan Book of the Dead*. The "paradise" referred to is one of the many doctrines of Tibetan Buddhism added from later Hindu sources. For details on the Bardo rites, see Waddell, p. 488.

[360] Saklani, p. 130.

[361] For an explanation of the wheel of life, see Waddell, p. 108-119. For a discussion of Tibetan art in general, see Zwalf.

[362] For a discussion of musical instruments used in Tibetan Buddhist rituals, see de Nebesky Wojkowitz, p. 398 ff.

[363] The author has seen the wood block printing process at the Tibetan Medical College in Lhasa. A stack of blocks is inked by two or three printers, who make impressions on oblong strips of paper or cloth. When a text is completed, its leaves are bound together with endplates, numbered, and stored. Most Buddhists regard them as materially holy, and the texts themselves are treated with reverence to the point that some will crawl under tables on which scriptures are placed in order to gain merit.

[364] For details on these groups, see David J. Phillips' *Peoples on the Move: Introducing the Nomads of the World*, (Pasadena: William Carey, 2001) p. 300-344.

[365] Phillips, p. 9.

[366] Phillips, p. 17.

[367] Melvyn C. Goldstein and Cynthia M. Beall, *Nomads of Western Tibet*, (Berkeley: University of California, 1990.

[368] Phillips, p. 18, 21.

[369] Phillips, p. 27, 32, 358.

[370] Goldstein and Beall, p. 45, 80.

[371] Goldstein and Beall, p. 60.

[372] Sermier, p. 93.

[373] Baabar and R. Enkhbat, *Mongols*, (Ulaanbaatar: Monsudar, 2002), p. 56.

[374] Baabar and R. Enkhbat, p. 50.

Notes to Chapter Six

[375] The colossal Buddha images (55 and 37 meters tall) date from about the 4th century A.D.. They were defaced by the Mongols in 1222, and the defaced remains were blown up by the Taliban, a Muslim fundamentalist group, in 2001. The hypothetical first-century monk couldn't have seen the statues, but could have made the journey. For pictures of the statues as they appeared before they were blown up, see Bechert and Gombrich, p. 68.

[376] Matthew 2:1.

[377] Luke 2:1.

378 Stephen Neill, *A History of Christian Missions,* (Penguin, 1964; reprinted 1982) p. 26.

379 The early evangelists seem to have given special attention to the cities of the Roman Empire, probably because synagogues were already well established in major urban centers like Antioch, Alexandria, and Rome. The fact that Apostle Paul sent his letters to Rome, Corinth, Ephesus, Philippi, Colossae, and Thessalonica suggest that he realized the importance of cities for the growth of the Church.

380 1 Peter 2:12; for details, see Neill, chapter 2, and Hesselgrave, p. 405.

381 Acts 2:9.

382 Acts 11:26.

383 J. D. Douglas, ed., *New Bible Dictionary,* "Antioch," (Grand Rapids: Eerdmans, 1962) p. 40.

384 Christian, p. 179.

385 Neill, p. 48-49.

386 Ancient Armenia was considerably larger than its modern counterpart. It included much of what is now eastern Turkey.

387 Christian, p. 213.

388 For more about the Nestorian controversy, see Hugh Kemp's *Steppe by Step* (London: Monarch, 2000), chapter 1.

389 P. Y. Saeki, quoted in Young, p. 93. See also Moule.

390 The Nestorians consecrated a bishop of Tibet whose seat was probably in Tangut (modern Gansu Province, China). See Stewart, p. 161. Marco Polo met Christians in Tangut on his way through the kingdom in the thirteenth century.

391 Young, p. 2.

392 See Sir Henry Yule's *The Book of Ser Marco Polo* (London: John Murray, 1903), p. 13, and Marco Polo, p. 36. Broomhall (p. 7-8) states that this invitation is preserved in the French archives, but other sources have cast doubt on its authenticity.

393 The Catholic Church did later send missionaries to the Mongol Court at Peking. Most notable among them was John of Monte Corvino (1294) who was followed by a group of 50 fathers with John of Marignolli (1335). Unfortunately, these missions arrived just as the Mongol empire was about to collapse. For details, see Neill or Dawson (bibliography).

394 Kemp, p. 192

395 P. Y. Saeki, quoted in Young, p. 95. Young has an excellent chapter on the reasons for the Nestorians' decline.

396 For example, Tibetan and Christian manuscripts and paintings were found together in the sealed caves at Dunhuang. Nestorian Christians occupied other cities along the Silk Road, and the Tibetans must have met at least some of these Nestorians during their conquest of the Silk Road oases in the eighth century.

397 The Jesuit order was founded in the sixteenth century. It emphasized scholarship, education, flexibility, and obedience to the Pope. It was a major missionary arm of the Catholic church, especially in Asia.

[398] The foundation of this first church in Tibet was laid on April 12, 1626. See Wessels p. 71.

[399] For details of the Andrade mission, see Huc, p. 266ff; Allen, p. 33ff; Vannini, p. 27; and Snellgrove and Richardson, p. 203.

[400] For an account of Cacella and Cabral's visit to Bhutan, see Olschak, p. 150-155. The dates of the visit are variously given as 1627 (Olschak) or 1630 (Snellgrove and Richardson).

[401] The route of Desideri's harrowing journey was not retraced by Europeans again until 1904, when it was surveyed by two officers attached to the Younghusband Expedition. See Younghusband, p. 229 ff.

[402] Quoted in Allen, p. 52.

[403] See Daniel E. Perdue's *Debate in Tibetan Buddhism* (Ithaca: Snow Lion, 1992).

[404] The Capuchins were a Catholic order founded in Italy in 1525. Their rules emphasized extreme austerity, simplicity, and poverty; on these grounds they were probably well suited to life in 18th century Tibet.

[405] Details of the Catholic mission to Lhasa were taken from Allen, p. 41ff; Snellgrove and Richardson, p. 220; and Vannini. The bell was preserved in an upper storeroom of the Jokhang temple in Lhasa, where it was still to be seen at the beginning of the 21st century.

[406] See Drewery, p. 96.

[407] See Vannini, p. 437.

[408] For additional details, see Kemp, chapters 26 and 27.

[409] James Gilmour had a two-year furlough in Scotland in 1882-1884 during which he wrote an account of his work called *Among the Mongols*. The book focused attention on this remote Tibetan Buddhist people and inspired other 19th and 20th century efforts to evangelize them.

[410] The Tibetan language has a large number of dialects and regional variants. The written forms of the language differ significantly from the spoken forms. Linguists call this linguistic peculiarity *diglossia,* a trait which Tibetan shares with Arabic and certain other languages.

[411] Zangskar (Tibetan *zangs dkar*) is a region of India between Ladakh and Tibet; Baltistan is a Tibetan-speaking area of what is now northern Pakistan.

[412] The guesthouse was opened in 1939. In its first year it had 4,000 guests, but it gradually went into decline and had to be closed in the winter of 1948-9.

[413] Among the Alliance missionaries was the scholar Robert B. Ekvall, whose books on Tibet show a deep understanding of its language and culture, and remain well worth reading today.

[414] Apparently many of the converts were Han Chinese rather than Tibetan. Teichman (p. 226) states that most of the Catholic mission work was done among Chinese living in the border region. He adds that Catholic missions became identified with the repressive policies of the local Chinese government, and that the general attitude of the Tibetans towards Christianity in general was one of active hostility (p. 228).

[415] See Peter Hopkirk's *Trespassers on the Roof of the World* (New York: Kondasha, 1995).

[416] See Tony Lambert's *China's Christian Millions* (OMF Books).

[417] It is interesting to note that during the 20 centuries covered in this chapter, the Himalayas rose by almost 20 meters! Unseen geological forces push these great mountains skyward by about a centimeter a year, accentuating high, dry cold of Inner Asia and keeping this region distinct from its neighbors. Data from *The Himalayas: Two Continents Collide,* United States Geological Survey.

[418] See Baabar's *History of Mongolia,* (cited elsewhere) and Melvyn C. Goldstein's *A History of Modern Tibet: The Demise of the Lamaist State* (Berkeley: University of California, 1989).

Notes to Chapter Seven

[419] I am honoured to contribute this chapter on Mongolia to M. Tsering's new edition of this book. I was privileged to have lived in Mongolia between 1992 and 1997 and to have witnessed the tremendous political, social and spiritual changes that occurred during this time. My love for Mongolia and her people has not diminished since I left, and I still read about her avidly, and visit Mongolia periodically. I have consulted several of my colleagues, both foreign and Mongolian, to make sure my observations are valid. However, any bias, mistakes or illegitimate interpretations in this chapter are solely mine.

[420] For a fuller ethnography of the Mongols, refer to P. Hattaway's *Peoples of the Buddhist World: A Christian Prayer Guide* (Carlisle: Piquant, 2004).

[421] These numbers are attained from my own estimates, together with those of Kyo Seong Ahn, in "Christian Mission and Mongolian Identity: The Religious, Cultural and Political Context" *Studies in World Christianity* Vol. 9:1, 2003, 103-124.

[422] 'Ala-ad-Din 'Ata-Malik Juvaini, *The History of the World Conqueror,* trans. John Andrew Boyle (Manchester: Manchester University Press, 1958), 25.

[423] 'Ala-ad-Din 'Ata-Malik Juvaini, *The History of the World Conqueror,* trans. John Andrew Boyle (Manchester: Manchester University Press, 1958), 26.

[424] H. H. Howorth, *History of the Mongols: From the 9th to the 19th Century* (London: Burt Franklin, 1876), 3:558.

[425] *Ibid.*

[426] In June, 1989, thousands of Chinese youth gathered in Beijing's Tiananmen Square to demonstrate in favor of political reform. The Chinese army suppressed the demonstrators on June 4th, 1989; this was the so-called Tiananmen Square Incident.

[427] A similar demonstration by Mongolians occurred in 1990 in Ulaanbaatar's Sukhbaatar Square. The demonstrations were allowed to continue and were not suppressed by the army.

[428] Mongolian Bible Society brochure, 1995.

Notes to Chapter Eight

[429] Tibetan monks use a different form of this "different paths to the same goal" argument to explain the differences among the Hinayana, Mahayana, and Vajrayana schools of Buddhism.

[430] John 14:6.
[431] Dalai Lama III, with commentary by Dalai Lama XIV, *Essence of Refined Gold* (Ithaca: Snow Lion, 1982).
[432] Dalai Lama III, p. 78.
[433] Mark 12:30.
[434] Dalai Lama XIV, *The Dalai Lama at Harvard* (Ithaca: Snow Lion) p. 36.
[435] John 8:58; Genesis 1:1.
[436] For an example, see *The Dalai Lama at Harvard*, p. 22.
[437] The key word here is *ultimate*. In everyday life, Tibetan Buddhists have rules for good behavior just like anyone else. But in Tibetan Buddhism, these are only conventions, not categories with absolute meaning. Once a person reaches a certain stage of spiritual advancement, he or she is beyond conventional standards of right and wrong. For an example, see Ekvall, p. 70.
[438] For a history of how these ideas developed, see Guy Newland's *The Two Truths* (Ithaca: Snow Lion, 1992).
[439] Luke 18:19
[440] See Geshe Lhundup Sopa, Vol. 1, p. 106.
[441] This is generally referred to as the Buddhist doctrine of impermanence. To see how it is developed in the Tibetan tradition, see Geshe Kelsang Gyatso's *Buddhism in the Tibetan Tradition: A Guide* (London: Routledge and Kegan Paul, 1984) chapter 3.
[442] John 6:40.
[443] Recorded in the New Testament in 1 John 1:1. The early Christians insisted that God had come to earth not in some symbolic or mystical way, but in a real and tangible way. See the Apostle Paul's argument in 1 Corinthians 15:3-20, and Peter's statement in 2 Peter 1:16. Contrast this with Lama Thubten Jigme Norbu's belief that history and legend are two forms of the same thing. (see Norbu and Turnbull, p. 27).
[444] This doctrine, known as rebirth, is basic to Hinduism and Tibetan Buddhism. Reincarnation, in which a soul or personality enters another body after death, is a much later and different concept.
[445] Gyatso, p. 27.
[446] These five "proofs" are taken from Kelsang Gyatso, chapter 4.
[447] For an extensive treatment of the doctrines of rebirth and karma, see Albrecht.
[448] See, for instance, Norbu and Turnbull, p. 245.
[449] For a further discussion of rebirth, see the next chapter.
[450] John 11:25-26.
[451¹] See *Karma* in *The Dalai Lama at Harvard*, p. 127 ff.
[452] Gyatso, p. 34.
[453] See Lhalungpa, p. 58.
[454] I am indebted to Mark Albrecht for suggesting several of the lines of argument presented here.
[455] For an example from among the Sherpa people, see Ortner, p. 110-112.
[456] The story of the blind man is found in John 9:1-3, and the story of the tower of Siloam in Luke 13:1-5. That there is no connection between specific sins and subsequent suffering is also a theme of the book of Job. A discussion of the

Christian view of suffering and its causes is beyond the scope of this book, but it is an important topic for anyone who deals with Tibetan Buddhists.

[457] See Humphreys, p. 101. The lamas have created several rituals that will, in effect, let one escape from one's karma. The most famous of these is performed using the so called *Tibetan Book of the Dead*. (The Tibetan title is *The Great Liberation Through Hearing in the Bardo.*)

[458] The first quote is from Matthew 11:28.

[459] Jesus told a number of vivid stories about this, some of which may be found in Matthew 13:37-42 and 47-50, 18:23-35, 21:33-44, and the whole of Matthew 25.

[460] Ortner, p. 149.

[461] For a detailed description of these deities, see de Nebesky-Wojkowitz.

[462] Matthew 6:31-34.

[463] Ignorance of the true nature of the world is humanity's most serious problem, according to the Dalai Lama. See Dalai Lama XIV, *The Path to Bliss,* (Ithaca: Snow Lion, 1991) p. 144.

[464] Recounted in Humphreys, p. 81-82, and Niwano, p. 73.

[465] Luke 7:11-17

[466] Matthew 16:24-25

[467] Niwano, p. 79

[468] John 6:40

[468] John 11:25-26

[470] Matthew 22:37-39

[471] Luke 10

[472] John 5:39-40

[473] John 7:16-18

[474] Dalai Lama XIV, *Path to Bliss,* p. 175. In Tibetan, boddhisattva is *byang chub sems dpa'*

[475] See Kelsang Gyatso, chapter 11

[476] See Kensur Lekden's *Meditations of a Tantric Abbot* in Hopkins, p. 46-47.

[477] Matthew 9:36

[478] Matthew 14:14, 20:34, Mark 1:41

[479] Luke 7:13-14

[480] Matthew 15:32

[481] See Matthew 25

[482] 1 John 3:18

[483] See, for example, Newland, p. 26.

[484] Geshe Ngawang Dhargyey, *Kalachakra Tantra*, Library of Tibetan Works and Archives, New Delhi, 1985; marked "restricted sale" p. 159.

[485] John 8:31-32

[486] John 14:6

[487] For an example of the use of human bones in tantric rites, see Norbu and Turnbull, p. 206; for the use of other human body parts in the cult of Tibetan protector deities, see de Nebesky-Wojkowitz, p. 398 ff.

[488] John 1:4-5

[489] Revelation 20:15

[490] Revelation 21:4

491 Berzin, p. 35
492 Berzin, p. 127
493 Matthew 25:31-46
494 For an account of this process by an observer sympathetic to Tibetan Buddhism, see Heinrich Harrer's *Seven Years in Tibet*, p. 199.
495 See Burton Stein, p. 311-312.
496 See Saklani, p. 159.
497 See Baabar, p. 99.
498 For an interesting discussion of the effects of these ideas on the cultures of Asia, see Nakamura.
499 The categories "true" and "false" still retain a relative and conventional meaning, however, as in the statement, "A pot is not a dog." But Nagarjuna's essential argument was that *nothing* expressible in words can possibly be true in an ultimate sense.
500 The American philosopher Mortimer J. Adler discusses this point at some length in the appendix of his book *Truth in Religion* (New York: Collier, 1990).
501 e.g. in *The Times of India*, Friday, 26 January, 2001.
502 This is a common, if often mistaken, belief in Himalayan countries where conversions to Christ have followed Christian medical and social programs. For an Indian example of this point of view, see Awasty, p. 40, 42. For an articulate non-Christian view of the impact of Christian missions on the Tibetan Buddhist Lepcha culture of Sikkim, see Foning.

Notes to Chapter Nine

503 Graham Coleman, ed. *A Handbook of Tibetan Culture* (London: Rider, 1993).
504 Universities have played a key role in establishing Tibetan Buddhism internationally. Language programs and religious studies departments have trained many young Buddhists, who have produced popular English translations of Tibetan Buddhist literature.
505 For a detailed description of the content and procedure of such debates, see Perdue.
506 The medieval scholastic movement attempted to justify the beliefs of the Christian faith using logic. Its greatest figures included Anselm and Aquinas. For a description, see Latourette: *A History of Christianity.*
507 Because the Gelugpas are the dominant school of Tibetan Buddhism, and because their works are the most widely published in non-Tibetan languages, the discussion that follows will focus on the Gelugpa interpretation and defense of key doctrines.
508 For an example of the kind of "proofs" involved, see Hopkins: *Meditation on Emptiness.*
509 Dalai Lama: *Path to Bliss*, p. 202.
510 For a description of these exercises, see Hopkins: *Meditation on Emptiness.* This 1,000 page book describes the procedure one must endure to achieve a "realization of emptiness." The figure of six months for the "calm abiding" stage is taken from page 69.
511 Tibetan *bdag med*

512 Dalai Lama: *Path to Bliss*, p. 199.

513 For a Christian perspective on this view, see Weerasingha, p. 28 ff.

514 quoted in Newland, p. 15.

515 The consequences of such a view were appreciated by the Greek skeptic philosopher Cratylus, who believed that communication was impossible because the speaker, the words spoken, and the one hearing the words were constantly changing. When asked a question he would wiggle his finger to indicate that he had heard it, but would make no reply. (Geisler and Feinberg, p. 84) For another development of this argument, see C.S. Lewis, p. 132.

516 Identical twins, who have the same genes, are an exception to this rule.

517 DNA also carries the genes for the body's immune system. The immune system constantly patrols the body looking for foreign molecules brought in by viruses, bacteria, or other disease germs. When it finds these molecules, it has the remarkable ability to tell a molecule that came from its own body from one that came from a disease germ or from another person. In other words, the healthy immune system can tell "self" molecules from "non-self" molecules. Blood banks use this feature of the immune system every day to make sure that blood transfusions can be given safely.

518 Scientists are still learning about the relationship between human personality and the brain, but several facts show that our sense of self is closely related to how our brain cells function. For instance, some stroke patients lose the ability to identify parts of their bodies as belonging to themselves. The hand of such a patient can be held up in front of the patient's face and the patient would not recognize it as his own. In this case, the death of certain cells in the brain has caused a partial loss of the sense of "self."

519 Dharmasiri, p. 10.

520 If this is done in terms of the Christian concept of "soul," however, careful Bible study is in order! The existence of the soul is presumed but not explicitly discussed by the New Testament writers. Several Greek terms with overlapping meanings are used to describe all the functions of the English word "soul." Christians discussing the idea of "soul" with a Buddhist should be thoroughly familiar with these terms. Weerasingha (p. 30) points out that the idea of a soul existing from eternity is not Biblical, as a study of the Greek and Hebrew terms will show.

521 Willson, p. 10.

522 Dalai Lama: *The Dalai Lama at Harvard*, p. 138. The Dalai Lama was probably thinking of the universe in a Buddhist sense, which includes fantastic realms populated by the spiritual beings of ancient Indian mythology. Even so, given the central place of man in Buddhist cosmology, it is hard to see how the system of rebirth and karma could begin anywhere in the universe without man or a creature much like him.

523 Even one prominent Tibetan Buddhist has pointed out the logical flaws in attempting to prove that rebirths have occurred infinitely into the past. (Willson p. 66)

524 Dalai Lama: *Opening the Eye of New Awareness*, p. 37.

525 Willson, p. 55.

526 Willson, p. 20.

⁵²⁷ For example, there are drugs which can allow a surgical patient to feel pain but not to suffer from it.

⁵²⁸ Dalai Lama: *The Path to Bliss*, p. 191.

⁵²⁹ Newland, p. 40.

⁵³⁰ Newland, p. 17.

⁵³¹ Geshe Ngawang Dhargyey, *Kalachakra Tantra*, Library of Tibetan Works and Archives, New Delhi, 1985; marked "restricted sale," p. 159.

⁵³² Dalai Lama XIV, *The Dalai Lama at Harvard* (Ithaca: Snow Lion, 1988) p. 117. The Dalai Lama added that if higher tantric practices are not performed correctly, death can result (p. 118).

⁵³³ The statement was issued by the Northwest Dharma Umbrella in the Winter 1993 edition of the *Snow Lion Newsletter*, Ithaca, New York, USA, p. 10.

⁵³⁴ See, for instance, Geisler: *Christian Apologetics*, or C.S. Lewis: *The Problem of Pain*.

⁵³⁵ Dharmasiri, p. 23.

⁵³⁶ Dharmasiri, p. 56.

⁵³⁷ See, for instance, Geisler: *Christian Apologetics*, p. 218 ff.

⁵³⁸ Dharmasiri, p. 62.

⁵³⁹ Dharmasiri, chapter 6.

⁵⁴⁰ Newland, p. 20.

⁵⁴¹ Isaiah 55:8-9

⁵⁴² Willson, p. 77.

Notes to Chapter Ten

⁵⁴³ On December 10, 1948 the General Assembly of the United Nations adopted and proclaimed the Universal Declaration of Human Rights and urged its widespread promulgation.

⁵⁴⁴ One accusation against Christian missionaries is that they seek to change supposedly pristine indigenous cultures. The fallacy of this accusation is that human societies are always changing. Missions can help to equip cultures to deal with change on their own terms by providing education and literacy. Other change agents may not be so generous.

⁵⁴⁵ II Corinthians 5:19-20.

⁵⁴⁶ Acts 11:26-30.

⁵⁴⁷ Acts 13:3.

⁵⁴⁸ I Peter 3:15.

⁵⁴⁹ Tibetan Buddhism is a *gnostic* philosophy in the sense that the knowledge necessary for ultimate spiritual liberation (i.e. Highest Yoga Tantra) is secret, and shared only with initiates.

⁵⁵⁰ Colossians 2:8.

⁵⁵¹ Ephesians 6:18.

⁵⁵² James 5:16-18, Philippians 4:6.

⁵⁵³ John 4:9.

⁵⁵⁴ Acts 2:41.

⁵⁵⁵ Proverbs 9:1.

⁵⁵⁵ Ephesians 5:15-20.

⁵⁵⁷ James 3:17.

558 Luke 5:10. See Charles G. Martin's commentary on Proverbs in F.F. Bruce, General Editor, *The International Bible Commentary*, (Grand Rapids, Zondervan,1986), p. 667.

559 Matthew 10:16 *Revised Standard Version.*

560 Ephesians 6:12.

561 1 John 2:22

562 For the Christian, this idea is negated by the Bible's claim that Jesus Christ is the one way to God. In the book of John (14:6) Jesus declares: "I am the way and the truth and the life. No one comes to the Father except through me." Other Scriptures (such as Acts 4:12, 1 John 2:23) reinforce this claim to exclusive truth in terms that leave little room for compromise.

563 Jesus' claim that He alone is the way to God has been a stumbling block for many people, especially in these postmodern times. Religious modernists see any claim to absolute truth as exclusive and intolerant. Members of other faiths resent the implication that something is lacking in their religion. But obedience to Scripture leaves the Christian no room for choice. If Jesus Christ was who He claimed to be, then it indeed follows that there is "no other name under heaven given to men by which we must be saved."

564 Occult rituals, magic, astrology, worship of locality spirits, and worship of the head of state as divine are all features of Tibetan Buddhist culture, and in this respect the problems faced by modern evangelists are by no means new. For a discussion of these aspects of ancient Roman culture, see Harold H. Rowdon, "The Religious Background of the New Testament (Pagan)" in F.F. Bruce, General Editor, *The International Bible Commentary*, (Grand Rapids: Zondervan,1986) p. 1047.

565 Acts 17:22-31.

566 It was Dr. Saphir Athyal who suggested to the author that Paul's speech to the Athenians is a model for a Christian approach to Hindus and Buddhists.

567 Acts 17:34.

568 Acts 11

569 Acts 14

570 Acts 15

571 Acts 16

572 Acts 17:5-8

573 Acts 21:39

574 Acts 17:2

575 Matthew 28:19-20.

576 For example, Genesis 26:24, Deuteronomy 1:21, Psalms 23:4, Matthew 10:28, Romans 8:15, 2 Timothy 1:7.

577 Matthew 28:20

578 e.g. Mark 5:1-20.

579 e.g. Matthew 4:1-11.

580 For example, see Rene de Nebesky-Wojkowitz's *Oracles and Demons of Tibet.*

581 For example, Danish Public Television's documentary *The Art of Dying* (1992) or Elan Golomb's *Oracles of Ladakh* (1994).

582 For example, Isaiah 2:6, Malachi 3:5, Galatians 5:20, and Revelation 22:15.

583 Deuteronomy 18:10-12.

[584] For a clear discussion of spiritual warfare, folk religion and the occult in Asia, see Vivienne Stacey's *Christ Supreme Over Satan*, (Lahore: Masihi Isha'at Khana, 1986).

Notes to Chapter Eleven

[585] Many in recent times have published lists or catalogs of "people groups" who follow various religions. Users of such lists should be aware that the criteria for deciding what is or is not a people group vary, and are not consistent between sources. The figure of at least 60 people groups in the Tibetan Buddhist world represents a realistically minimum figure.

[586] Just as the criteria for people groups differ, so do the criteria for grouping dialects into languages. The figure of 80 languages is only an approximation.

[587] Taken from *Communicating Christ Cross-Culturally*, by David J. Hesselgrave. (page 99) Copyright 1978 by David J. Hesselgrave. Used by permission of Zondervan Publishing House. An updated edition of this valuable text was published in 1991.

[588] Philippians 2:6-8.

[589] For a general discussion of these points, see Hesselgrave, p. 130-141.

[590] For example, Paul's knowledge of Greek culture helped him to communicate the Gospel to the Athenian intellectuals in Acts 17.

[591] There was indeed an annual "scapegoat" ritual at Lhasa, practiced as late as the mid-twentieth century, but the custom is not now widely known. For a description, see de Nebesky-Wojkowitz, p. 508.

[592] See Duane Elmer's *Cross-Cultural Conflict: Building Relationships for Effective Ministry*, (Downer's Grove: Inter-Varsity, 1993).

[593] 1 Peter 2:17a

[594] At the worst of times, majority cultures have been responsible for the deaths of thousands of Tibetan Buddhist minority peoples, e.g. in Stalinist Russia.

[595] For further information on social research questions, see Shane Bennett and Kim Felder with Steve Hawthorne, *Exploring the Land: Discovering Ways for Unreached People to Follow Christ*, (Caleb Project, 2003).

[596] After Waddell, p. 176.

[597] Another problem area for foreign Christians is observing local customs related to food. For example, most non-Asians regard tea drinking as simple refreshment. In parts of Inner Asia, however, the serving and drinking of tea is governed by a set of social rules which foreigners should learn and obey.

[598] Related in Geoffrey Bull's *Tibetan Tales*, (Hodder & Stoughton, UK 1966) p. 43-44.

[599] See Hesselgrave, p. 404.

[600] Bull, p. 97, used by permission of Hodder and Stoughton Ltd. Religious debate is a standard educational tool in Tibetan monasteries. It is a highly stylized procedure complete with dramatic gestures and elaborate rules of logic. Anyone intending to debate a Tibetan Buddhist should be thoroughly familiar with the rules of Buddhist logic and with the forms of monastic debate. For details, see Perdue.

[601] Such careless gestures can have unfortunate consequences. One young Christian visitor to a church in Nepal shocked the local believers by placing his

Bible on the floor and sitting on it. In Inner Asian cultures, the Bible should always be treated with evident respect.

602 While a simple lifestyle has much to commend it, it may not always be possible, or even wise, for expatriates to live at the level of the local people. This is especially true where husbands and wives differ in their ability to adapt to local living standards, or where a adopting a slightly higher standard of living may help a family remain in a culture for a longer period of service.

603 See Matthew 25:31-46.

604 For the basic scheme of this classification, the author is indebted to the work of Professor Terry Muck.

605 See Acts 17:23-31. The pagan belief was the unknown god (verse 23), the Christian belief in the true God is expounded in verses 24-31, and the comparison showing that Christian belief is superior is implicit in verse 31.

606 figures from Compass Direct.

607 For details, see Thomas Hale, *Living Stones of the Himalayas* (Grand Rapids: Zondervan, 1993), chapter 13.

608 Romans 10:15.

609 John 1:41.

610 Mark 8:29.

611 Acts chapters 2 and 7.

612 Acts 5.

613 Acts 5:42.

614 Acts chapters 3, 5, 8.

615 John chapter 3.

616 Acts chapter 10.

617 1 Corinthians 3:6-7.

618 Bull p. 98, used by permission of Hodder and Stoughton, Ltd.

619 See Kelsang Gyatso's *Buddhism in the Tibetan Tradition: A Guide* (London: Routledge and Kegan Paul, 1984) p. 92.

620 For the Tibetan Buddhist sense of the word compassion, see Hopkins' *The Tantric Distinction* p. 67-72. Also see Hopkins' *Compassion in Tibetan Buddhism*, and Gyatso.

621 For one view of this complex subject, see Norbu and Turnbull's *Tibet*, p. 236.

622 For an example of this view, see Ekvall p. 70.

623 For example, see John 1:14. The New International Version reads: "The Word became flesh . .(and lived for a while among us)." In the 1970 version of the Tibetan New Testament this verse is translated: *bka' de sku lus ldan par sprul* This does not mean that the verse was poorly translated, but it does mean that Christians must be very careful to define the Christian meaning of words they use.

624 For example, see Christmas Humphreys' *A Popular Dictionary of Buddhism*, (London: Curzon, 1984) p. 204.

625 Alex G. Smith, *Strategy to Multiply Rural Churches*, p. 172-173.

626 For a detailed description see Waddell, p. 89-100.

627 This is not to say that Tibetan Buddhists know nothing of logic, only that most folk Tibetan Buddhists prefer an intuitive mode of thinking. For an introduction to Tibetan Buddhist logic, see Perdue.

628 I am indebted to the late Rev. Peter Rapgey for this illustration.

629 John 21:1-14

630 Matthew 14:16-21.

631 Exodus 23:12.

632 Genesis 18:30.

633 Deuteronomy 4:24.

634 Revelation 15:7.

635 Luke 14:25-33

Notes to Chapter Twelve

636 As used in current missions practice, "short-term" can mean anything from a week to two years.

637 Short-term mission trips can also be disasters that leave a trail of misunderstandings, problems, and hurt feelings! Such outcomes can be prevented by cooperating with long term workers or with the national church. A good orientation for the entire group before arrival in Inner Asia is essential, and can help make the trip a success for all concerned.

638 Short term visits are better made at some times than others. A group wanting to meet teachers in China may find this difficult during the spring or summer holidays. Crossing the northern plateau of Tibet by land in winter, or crossing the Himalayas by road in the summer monsoon, may be dangerous. (Expatriate travelers have lost their lives in both places due to cold and landslides.)

639 Including appropriate immunizations, medical and dental check-ups, advice about what's safe to eat and drink, and advice about altitude sickness (if visiting the Himalayas).

640 Orientations should cover appropriate conduct and dress for men (including local rules for interacting with women) and women (expectations for modesty, role of women in the local church, use of cosmetics, wearing of jewelry, etc.), local customs, body language, dealing with differences in wealth, use of alcohol and money, giving and receiving gifts, etc.

641 Some countries in the Tibetan Buddhist world are relatively free and open, while others are not. Security concerns include physical safety, crime prevention, and most importantly, protecting local Christians from unintended harm.

642 Ill-advised attempts at evangelism, especially through indiscriminate distribution of literature, can do serious harm to local Christians (who may be interrogated by the police), long-term workers (who may be told to leave the country), and other innocent people.

643 In some areas of Inner Asia, trying to find, meet, or photograph local believers can cause unintended harm.

644 See Neill p. 215. The history of Bible translation among the Kalmyks is given in Kemp, p. 252 ff.

645 The population density of the Tibet Autonomous Region of China is 2.18 people per square kilometer (Information Office of the Peoples Government

of the Tibet Autonomous Region, *Tibet*, (China Intercontinental Press, 2002, p. 30), and that of Mongolia is only a little more than one person per square kilometer.

646 The fact that cities offer anonymity and space for religious change may have been one of several reasons that the Apostle Paul and other evangelists concentrated their preaching in the cities of the Roman Empire.

647 One of the exceptions to this statement would be the Lepcha people of Sikkim. See Awasty and Foning for details. As Alex Smith has observed: "Three main causes account for the lack of permanent self perpetuating Christian communities among Buddhist peoples. First is persecution, second is syncretism, and third the failure of the Church to break through the social solidarity of Buddhist communities." (from *The Gospel Facing Buddhist Cultures*, Taichung, Taiwan: Asia Theological Association, 1980), p. 3.

648 Notably in eastern Tibet and Inner Mongolia.

649 In many cases this was regardless of their wishes or inclinations. See Melvyn Goldstein, *A History of Modern Tibet, 1913-1951: The Demise of the Lamaist State*, (Berkeley: University of California, 1989) p. 21.

650 The figure for Mongolia is from the *Area Handbook for Mongolia*, p. 185.

651 Goldstein, *A History of Modern Tibet*, p. 21.

652 For Ladakh the figures are based on population statistics and the estimates quoted in Harrer's *Ladakh*, p. 25. Among Tibetan exiles in India, Nepal, and Bhutan, approximately 5 per cent of the total population of 100,000 are monks or nuns (Saklani p. 154). Ten percent of the combined Bhotia-Lepcha population of Sikkim are monks. (Kotturan p. 112).

653 Melvyn Goldstein, *A History of Modern Tibet, 1913-1951* p. 816. The arguments cited by Goldstein are also applicable to the history of Mongolia, as documented by Baabar.

654 Marco Polo, p. 102.

655 Liao, p. 135.

656 Matthew 10:5-6.

657 See SIL's *Ethnologue* for the number of languages in Nepal. For ethnic groups see: Central Bureau of Statistics, *Statistical Pocket Book - Nepal 1984*, (Kathmandu: Gorkhapatra, 1984), p. 28; language statistic taken from the *Area Handbook for Nepal, Bhutan, and Sikkim*, p. 51 (see bibliography).

658 The author has seen lay Tibetans crawling under the wooden racks that hold the Buddhist scriptures in monasteries; they do this in order to rid themselves of any demons which might be following them and causing bad luck.

659 This was one of the points of contention between the Moravian editions of the Tibetan New Testament and the 1903 or "Shanghai" edition.

660 The Kangding missionary press is mentioned in *The Christian Occupation of China*, a work compiled in the 1920s for which the author has no bibliographical information. Geoffrey Bull was the missionary who commented on low literacy in the area some 30 years later. Literacy rates in the six countries of the Tibetan Buddhist world in the late 1980s were: Soviet Union 99.8%; Mongolia 80%; China 76% (Tibet 30%); Nepal 23%; Bhutan 12%; and India 36%.

661 In 2002 a leading monk in a monastery in Mongolia complained bitterly to the author about Christians who had distributed in his monastery some literature containing derogatory statements about Buddhism. Christians should remember that literature is used best in the context of personal relationships, and that the Church does not grow by giving unnecessary offense to Buddhists or anyone else.

662 Just as the Apostle Paul did when he preached in Athens (Acts 17).

663 A Tibetan pastor informed the author that Christian literature should be well printed and pleasing in appearance. It should be treated with outward respect. Bibles especially should be wrapped in cloth before they are given to Tibetans.

664 For details, see Rene de Nebesky-Wojkowitz' *Oracles and Demons of Tibet: The Cult and Iconography of the Tibetan Protective Deities* (New Delhi: Paljor, 1998).

665 Mark 4:3-20.

666 See Phill Butler's Lausanne Paper, *Mongolia: A Case History in the Power of Partnership.*

667 O'Connor, p. 124 and 152.

668 See Alex G. Smith, *Strategy to Multiply Rural Churches*, p. 171-173.

669 In one survey, 14,000 people were asked what method God used to bring them to Christ. Over 75% indicated that a friend or relative was the means God used to convert them. Only half of one percent indicated that they had been won to Christ through an evangelistic campaign. See Arn, McGavran and Arn, *Growth: A Vision for the Sunday School* (Pasadena: Church Growth Press, 1980), p. 75-76.

670 Matthew 10:5.

671 Foreign Christians should be very careful not to subvert the local churches by hiring away their leadership or offering exclusive training opportunities to those who happen to have good English. Such activities can create resentment and problems among local believers.

672 Nepal and Ladakh would be examples.

673 For an example what can happen to church growth when institutional work is emphasized to the detriment of evangelism, see Alex G. Smith's *Siamese Gold: A History of Church Growth in Thailand*, p. 159-169.

674 See McGavran's *A Church in Every People: Plain Talk About a Difficult Subject*, in Winter and Hawthorne, p. 626.

675 The strategy of family and group conversion is discussed at length in Hesselgrave, p. 344 ff, and in Winter and Hawthorne, p. 617.

676 Alex Smith, *Strategy to Multiply Rural Churches*, p. 193.

677 Foning, p. 294. Foning notes that missionary influence is not all anti-cultural, citing good works like education, sanitation, and the preservation of the Lepcha language.

678 A list of principles for Christians working in totalitarian societies is given in Hesselgrave, p. 376.

679 See Matthew 8:4; 9:30.

680 Both have happened in church history. Armenia was won through the conversion of its king and nobility, after which the common people followed. In India, members of the lowest castes have been more responsive to the Gospel than people from higher castes.

681 Concentrating resources on responsive people (while not neglecting "resistant" ones) is consistent with Scripture. When Jesus sent his 12 disciples to preach in the towns of Israel, he told them to leave any town where they were not received or where people would not listen to their preaching (see Matthew 10:14). Again, in Jesus' parable of the great banquet, a king sends his servants to summon invited guests to a feast. When those who had been invited refused to come, the servants were told to find others who would attend (Luke 14:16-24).

682 Acts 18:11; 19:10.

683 Acts 14:23, Titus 1:5.

684 John 3:8.

Notes to Special Supplement

685 *The American Heritage® Dictionary of the English Language, Fourth Edition.* Houghton Mifflin Company, 2004.

686 We recommend two web sources for additional information on the Mongolian diaspora: *An Introduction to the Mongolian Community in India* available at http://intermongol.net/diaspora/ and *Social and Cultural Change in the Mongol-American Community* http://condor.depaul.edu/~rrotenbe/aeer/v17n2/Baatar.pdf

687 1921-1989.

688 http://intermongol.net/diaspora/stories/gombjab.html

689 http://www.maca-usa.org

690 http://www.arjiagegeen.com/foundation.html

691 Sikkim was at that time an independent nation.

692 Jessica Johnson, *Tibetans,* Paper presented in ISTD 5950: Transnational Migration and Global Diaspora Communities, Fall 2002 at Hamline University, St. Paul, Minnesota. Available on the Internet at http://www.hamline.edu/cla/academics/international_studies/diaspora2002/Tibetans/paper.htm

693 James Mullins & Tsering Dolma Mullins, "Community Leader Survey Report," *North American Tibetan Community Needs Assessment Project.* Washington, DC: Conservancy for Tibetan Art and Culture, p. 12.

694 The original cities chosen for the Resettlement Project were Seattle, Washington; Portland, Oregon; Missoula, Montana; Boise, Idaho; Salt Lake City, Utah; San Francisco, California; Los Angeles, California; Boulder, Colorado; Denver, Colorado; Burlington, Vermont; Amherst, Massachusetts; various places in Connecticut; Santa Fe, New Mexico; Albuquerque, New Mexico; Austin, Texas; Minneapolis, Minnesota; Madison, Wisconsin; Chicago, Illinois; St. Louis, Missouri; Bloomington, Indiana; Charlottesville, Virginia; Boston, Massachusetts; New York City, New York; and Ithaca, New York.

695 Tibetan Demographic Survey of 1998, Planning Council, Dharamsala

696 See Deuteronomy 10:18-19

697 See Matthew 25:35

698 Though they also accept practitioners of *Bon* as valid members of the community, recognizing its strong link the land.

699 See the discussion of this issue in Mullins & Mullins, p.

700 Mullins & Mullins, p. 6.

701 "Bollywood" is the nickname for the film studios in Mumbai, India.

702 Thirumalai, p. 17

703 Mullins & Mullins, p. 13.

704 Though it should be remembered that "religion" is not a separate category in their thinking as it is for many western peoples.

705 Thirumalai, p. 27.

706 In the section which follows, this writer draws heavily on suggestions and comments submitted by people currently working among Tibetans in western countries.

707 Be aware these names are found in other people groups as well, but they can be a clue to the presence of a community of Tibetans. In the absence of a pre-existing personal relationship, actually ringing up such people on the telephone is likely to generate antagonism and is definitely not recommended!

708 Thirumalai, p. 14.

709 Remember it is more effective to do things *with* them than to do things *for* them. Teach them how to make blueberry pancakes; ask them to teach you how to make *momos*.

710 M.S. Thirumali (2004). *Evangelism among the Tibetan Buddhists.* Bloomington, MN: Bethany College of Missions.

711 This dichotomy of secular and sacred is more typically a western pattern. In Asian cultures there is no such sharp division.

712 Mullins & Mullins, p. 10.

713 Mullins & Mullins, p. 9.

714 For information and to see samples of the adult and children's versions go to http://www.ntm.org/books/ffless.html

715 By John R. Cross, published by Good Seed International. The current edition is the third edition (2000). For information see http://www.goodseed.com/usa/stranger/english.aspx

716 J. Benton White & Walter T. Wilson, *From Adam to Armageddon: A Survey of the Bible.* Wadsworth Publishing, 1994.

717 Details available at http://www.gods-story.org/default.htm

718 Spoken in Bhutan.

Sources

Adler, Mortimer J., *Truth in Religion*, (New York: Collier, 1990).

Ahn, Kyo Seong, in "Christian Mission and Mongolian Identity: The Religious, Cultural and Political Context," *Studies in World Christianity* Vol 9:1, 2003.

Albrecht, Mark, *Reincarnation: A Christian Appraisal*, (Downers Grove, Illinois: Inter Varsity Press, 1982).

Allen, Charles, *A Mountain in Tibet*, (London: Futura, 1982).

American University, *Area Handbook for Mongolia*, (Washington: U.S. Government Printing Office, 1970).

"   " *Area Handbook for Nepal, Bhutan, and Sikkim*, (Washington: U.S. Government Printing Office, 1973).

Awasty, Indira, *Between Sikkim and Bhutan*, (Delhi: B.R. Publishing Corporation, 1978).

Batbayar Baterdene (Baabar), *History of Mongolia*, (Mongolia and Inner Asia Studies Unit, University of Cambridge, 1999).

Batbayar Baterdene (Baabar), and Enkhbat, R., *Mongols*, (Ulaanbaatar: Monsudar, 2002).

Baumer, Christoph, *Tibet's Ancient Religion, Bon*, (Bangkok: Orchid Press, 2002).

Bawden, C., *Shamans, Lamas, and Evangelicals: The English Missionaries in Siberia*. London: Routledge and Kegan Paul, 1985.

Bawden, C., *The Modern History of Mongolia*. London and New York: Kegan Paul International, 1989.

Bechert, Heinz, and Gombrich, Richard, eds, *The World of Buddhism*, (London: Thames and Hudson, 1984).

Bennett, Shane and Felder, Kim, with Hawthorne, Steve, *Exploring the Land: Discovering Ways for Unreached People to Follow Christ*, (Caleb Project, 2003).

Berzin, Alexander, *Taking the Kalachakra Initiation*, (Ithaca: Snow Lion, 1997).

Beswick, Ethel, editor, *Jataka Tales: Birth Stories of the Buddha*, (Delhi: Book Faith India, 1999).

Bista, Dor Bahadur, *People of Nepal*, (Kathmandu: Ratna Pustak Bhandar, 1987).

Broomhall, Marshall, ed., *The Chinese Empire: A General and Missionary Survey*, (London: China Inland Mission, 1907).

Bruce, F.F., General Editor, *The International Bible Commentary*, (Grand Rapids, Zondervan, 1986).

Bull, Geoffrey, *Tibetan Tales,* (Hodder & Stoughton, UK 1966).

Burnett, David, *The Spirit of Hinduism,* (Tunbridge Wells: Monarch, 1992).

Central Bureau of Statistics, *Statistical Pocket Book—Nepal 1984,* (Kathmandu: Gorkhapatra, 1984).

Chattopadhyaya, Alaka, *Atisa and Tibet: The Life and Works of Dipamkara Srijnana in Relation to History and Religion of Tibet, With Tibetan Sources,* (Delhi: Motilal Banarsidass, 1967, reprinted 1981).

Chopra, P.N., *Sikkim,* (New Delhi: S. Chand, 1979).

Christian, David, *A History of Russia, Central Asia, and Mongolia, Volume I: Inner Eurasia from Prehistory to the Mongol Empire,* (Oxford, Blackwell 1998).

Coleman, Graham, ed. *A Handbook of Tibetan Culture,* (London: Rider, 1993).

Dalai Lama III, with commentary by Dalai Lama XIV, *Essence of Refined Gold,* (Ithaca: Snow Lion, 1982).

Dalai Lama XIV, *A Flash of Lightning in the Dark of Night: A Guide to the Boddhisattva's Way of Life,* (Boston: Shambhala, 1994).

Dalai Lama XIV, *The Dalai Lama at Harvard,* (Ithaca: Snow Lion, 1988).

Dalai Lama XIV, *Opening the Eye of New Awareness,* (Boston: Wisdom, 1990).

Dalai Lama XIV, *Path to Bliss,* (Ithaca: Snow Lion, 1991).

Dhargyey, Geshe Ngawang, *Kalachakra Tantra,* (New Delhi: Library of Tibetan Works and Archives, 1985, marked "restricted sale").

David-Neel, Alexandra, *With Mystics and Magicians in Tibet,* (London, 1931).

Davis, John, *The Path to Enlightenment: Introducing Buddhism,* (London: Hodder and Stoughton, 1997).

Dawson, C. (ed.) *Mission to Asia; Narratives and Letters of the Franciscan Missionaries in Mongolia and China in the 13th and 14th Centuries.* Translated by a nun of Stanbrook Abbey. NY: Harper & Row, 1966.

Dawson, Raymond, *The Chinese Experience,* (London: Phoenix, 1978).

de Nebesky-Wojkowitz, Rene, *Oracles and Demons of Tibet: The Cult and Iconography of the Tibetan Protective Deities,* (New Delhi: Paljor, 1998).

Dharmasiri, Gunapala, *A Buddhist Critique of the Christian Concept of God,* (Antioch, California, USA: Golden Leaves, 1988).

Diamond, Jared, *Guns, Germs, and Steel: A Short History of Everybody for the Last 13,000 Years,* (London: Random House, 1998).

Dorje, Rinjing, *Food in Tibetan Life*, (London: Prospect Books, 1985).

Douglas, J. D., ed., *New Bible Dictionary*, (Grand Rapids: Eerdmans, 1962).

Dragpa, Panchen Sonam, *Overview of Buddhist Tantra*, (Dharamsala: Library of Tibetan Works and Archives, 1996).

Drewery, Mary, *William Carey*, (Grand Rapids: Zondervan, 1979).

Drolma, Dawa, *Delog: Journey to Realms Beyond Death*, (Junction City CA: Padma, 1995).

Ekvall, Robert, *Religious Observances in Tibet*, (Chicago: University of Chicago, 1964).

Eliade, Mircea, *Shamanism: Archaic Techniques of Ecstasy*, (Princeton: Princeton University Press, 1964, 1992).

Elmer, Duane *Cross-Cultural Conflict: Building Relationships for Effective Ministry*, (Downer's Grove: Inter-Varsity, 1993).

Farrow, G. W. and Menon, I., *The Concealed Essence of the Hevajra Tantra*, (Delhi: Motilal Banarsidass, 1992, reprinted 2001).

Fields, Rick, *How the Swans Came to the Lake*, (Boston: Shambhala, 1986).

Fischer-Schreiber, Ingrid, Ehrhard, Franz-Karl, and Diener, Michael S., *The Shambhala Dictionary of Buddhism and Zen*, (Boston: Shambhala 1991).

Fleming, Peter, *Bayonets to Lhasa*, (Hong Kong: Oxford, 1961; reissued 1986).

Foning, A.R., *Lepcha My Vanishing Tribe*, (New Delhi, Sterling, 1987).

Geisler, Norman L., *Christian Apologetics*, (Grand Rapids, Michigan, USA: Baker, 1988).

"   " and Feinberg, Paul D., *Introduction to Philosophy*, (Grand Rapids, Michigan, USA: Baker, 1980).

Gernet, Jacques, *A History of Chinese Civilization*, (Cambridge: Cambridge University Press, 1982).

Gilmour, J., *Among the Mongols*. London: The Religious Tract Society, [1885].

Goldstein, Melvyn, *A History of Modern Tibet, 1913-1951: The Demise of the Lamaist State*, (Berkeley: University of California, 1989).

Goldstein, Melvyn and Beall, Cynthia M., *Nomads of Western Tibet*, (Berkeley: University of California, 1990).

Goldstein, Melvyn and Beall, Cynthia M., *The Changing World of Mongolia's Nomads*, (Berkeley: University of California, 1994).

Grousset, R., *The Empire of the Steppes: A History of Central Asia*. Translated by Naomi Walford. USA: Rutgers University Press, 1970.

341

Gyatso, Geshe Kelsang, *Buddhism in the Tibetan Tradition: A Guide,* (London: Routledge and Kegan Paul, 1984).

Hale, Thomas, *Living Stones of the Himalayas,* (Grand Rapids: Zondervan, 1993).

Harrer, Heinrich, *Ladakh,* (Innsbruck: Pinguin Verlag, 1978).

" ", *Seven Years in Tibet,* (Los Angeles: J.P. Tarcher, 1981).

Hattaway, Paul, *Peoples of the Buddhist World: A Christian Prayer Guide,* (Carlisle: Piquant, 2004).

Heissig, W., *The Religions of Mongolia.* Translated by G. Small. London: Routledge & Kegan Paul, 1980; and USA: University of California, 1980.

Hesselgrave, David J., *Communicating Christ Cross-Culturally: An Introduction to Missionary Communication,* (Grand Rapids: Zondervan, first ed. 1978, second ed. 1991).

Hiebert, Paul G, Shaw, R. Daniel, and Tienou, Tite, *Understanding Folk Religion: A Christian Response to Popular Beliefs and Practices,* (Grand Rapids, Baker, 1999).

Hopkirk, Peter, *Trespassers on the Roof of the World,* (Los Angeles: JP Tarcher, 1983; also New York: Kondasha, 1995).

Hopkins, Jeffrey, ed., *Compassion in Tibetan Buddhism,* (Ithaca: Snow Lion, 1980, reprinted 1985).

" ", *Meditation on Emptiness,* (London: Wisdom, 1983).

" ", *The Tantric Distinction,* (London: Wisdom Publications, 1984).

Hopkirk, Peter, *Quest for Kim: In Search of Kipling's Great Game,* (London: John Murray, 1996).

Howorth, H.H., *History of the Mongols: From the 9th to the 19th Century,* (London: Burt Franklin, 1876).

Huc, Abbe, *Christianity in China, Tartary, and Thibet,* (London: Brown, Green, Longmans, and Roberts, 1857).

Humphreys, Christmas, *A Popular Dictionary of Buddhism,* (London:Curzon, 1984).

Humphreys, Christmas, *Buddhism,* (London: Penguin, 1951, reprinted 1983).

J.H. Jeffrey's *Khams,* (Devon: Arthur H. Stockwell, 1974).

Jagchid, S. and P. Hyer, *Mongolia's Society and Culture.* USA: Frederick A Praeger, 1979; UK: William Dawson and Sons Ltd, 1979.

Juvaini, 'Ala-ad-Din 'Ata-Malik, *The History of the World Conqueror,* trans. John Andrew Boyle (Manchester: Manchester University Press, 1958).

Kemp, Hugh, *Steppe by Step,* (London: Monarch, 2000).

Kotturan, George, *The Himalayan Gateway: History and Culture of Sikkim,* (New Delhi: Sterling, 1983).

Latourette, Kenneth Scott, *A History of Christian Missions in China,* (New York: Macmillan, 1929).

" " *A History of Christianity,* (New York, USA: Harper and Row, 1975).

Lavine, Amy, *Tibetan Buddhism in America: The Development of American Vajrayana,* in Prebish, Charles S. and Tanaka, Kenneth K., *The Faces of Buddhism in America,* (Berkeley: University of California Press, 1998).

Layman, Emma M., *Buddhism in America,* (Chicago: Nelson Hall, 1976).

Lewis, C.S., *The Problem of Pain,* (New York: Macmillan, 1962).

Lhalungpa, Lobsang P., *The Life of Milarepa,* (New York: Granada, 1979).

Liao, David C., *The Unresponsive: Resistant or Neglected?,* (Pasadena: William Carey Library, 1972).

Mascaro, Juan, translator, *The Upanishads,* (London: Penguin Classics, 1965).

Mayhew, Bradley, *Mongolia,* third ed. (Melbourne: Lonely Planet, 2001).

Mehra, G.N., *Bhutan,* (New Delhi: Vikas, 1974).

Moffett, S.H., *A History of Christianity in Asia. Vol. 1: Beginnings to 1500.* NY: Harper Collins, 1992.

Morton, W. Scott, *China: Its History and Culture,* (New York: McGraw Hill, 1980).

Moule, A.C., *Christians in China Before the Year 1550,* (London: Society for Promoting Christian Knowledge, 1930).

Nakamura, Hajime, *Ways of Thinking of Eastern Peoples,* (Honolulu: University of Hawaii Press, 1985).

Nalanda Translation Committee, *The Life of Marpa the Translator,* (Boston: Shambhala, 1986).

Namgyal, Tenzin, ed. *Tibet Museum* (Encyclopedia of China Publishing House, 2001).

Neill, Stephen, *A History of Christian Missions,* (Penguin, 1964; reprinted 1982).

Newland, Guy, *The Two Truths,* (Ithaca, New York, USA: Snow Lion, 1992).

Niwano, Nikkyo, *Shakyamuni Buddha: A Narrative Biography* (Tokyo: Kosei, 1980).

Norbu, Thubten Jigme, and Turnbull, Colin, *Tibet*, (New York: Penguin Books, 1972, reprinted 1983).

O'Connor, Patrick, *Buddhists Find Christ*, (Tokyo: Charles E. Tuttle, 1975).
Olschak, Blanche C., *Ancient Bhutan*, (Zurich: Swiss Foundation for Alpine Research, 1979).
Ortner, Sherry, *Sherpas Through Their Rituals*, (Cambridge: Cambridge University Press, 1978).

Pegg, Carole, *Mongolian Music, Dance, and Oral Narrative*, (Seattle and London: University of Washington Press, 2001).
Perdue, Daniel, *Debate in Tibetan Buddhism*, (Ithaca, New York: Snow Lion, 1992).
Peters, Larry, *Tamang Shamans: An Ethnopsychiatric Study of Ecstasy and Healing in Nepal*, (New Delhi: Nirala 1998).
Phillips, David J., *Peoples on the Move: Introducing the Nomads of the World*, (Pasadena, William Carey, 2001).
Polo, Marco, *The Travels of Marco Polo*, (New York: Signet 2004).
Puchung, *mNgon brJod Tshig mDzod*, (Lhasa: Tibet Peoples' Publishing House, 1997).

Rabgyal, Tsondu, and Rinchen Dorje, *Bod Kyi Ri Mo sPyi'i rNam gZhag Blo gSal 'Jug sGo*, (Beijing: Minorities Publishing House, 2001).
Reid, Anna, *The Shaman's Coat: A Native History of Siberia*, (New York: Walker & Co. 2002).
Richardson, Hugh E., *Tibet and Its History*, (Boston: Shambhala, 1984).
Rijnhart, Dr. Susie Carson, *With the Tibetans in Tent and Temple*, (Chicago: Fleming H. Revell, 1901).
Rizvi, Janet, *Ladakh: Crossroads of High Asia*, (Delhi, Oxford, 1983).
Robinson, James B., tr. *Buddha's Lions: The Lives of the Eighty-Four Siddhas*, (Berkeley, CA: Dharma Publishing, 1979).

Saklani, Girija, *The Uprooted Tibetans in India*, (New Delhi: Cosmo, 1984).
Sarangerel, *Riding Windhorses: A Journey into the Heart of Mongolian Shamanism*, (Rochester, Vermont: Destiny Books, 2000).
Schell, Orville, *Virtual Tibet*, (New York: Holt, 2000).
Sermier, Claire, *Mongolia: Empire of the Steppes*, (New York, Norton, 2002).
Shakabpa, Tsipon W.D., *Political History of Tibet*, (Dharamsala: Tibetan Cultural Printing Press, 1986).

Silverberg, Robert, *The Realm of Prester John,* (London: Phoenix, 2001).
Smith, Alex G., *The Gospel Facing Buddhist Cultures,* (Taichung, Taiwan: Asia Theological Association, 1980).
" " *Strategy to Multiply Rural Churches,* (Bangkok: OMF Publishers, 1977).
Snellgrove, David, *Indo-Tibetan Buddhism,* (Bangkok: Orchid, 2004).
Snellgrove, David, and Richardson, Hugh, *A Cultural History of Tibet,* (Boulder: Prajna Press, 1980).
Sopa, Geshe Lhundup, *Lectures on Tibetan Religious Culture,* (Dharamsala: Library of Tibetan Works and Archives, 1983), 2 volumes.
Stacey, Vivienne, *Christ Supreme Over Satan,* (Lahore: Masihi Isha'at Khana, 1986).
Stein, Burton, *A History of India,* (Oxford, Blackwell 1998).
Stein, R. A., *Tibetan Civilization,* (London: Faber and Faber, 1972).
Stewart, John, *Nestorian Missionary Enterprise,* (Edinburgh: T and T Clark, 1928).

Teichman, Eric, *Travels of a Consular Officer in Eastern Tibet,* (London: Cambridge University Press, 1922).
Thomas, Lowell Jr., *Out of This World,* (New York: Greystone Press, 1950).
Thonmi Sambhota, (Xining: Qinghai Nationalities Publishing House, 1999).
Tibet, China Intercontinental Press, 2002.
Tsering, N., *A Tibetan Monk's Story,* (Kathmandu: Samdan, 1995).
Tucci, Giuseppe, *The Religions of Tibet,* (London: Routledge and Kegan Paul, 1980).

United States Geological Survey website: *The Himalayas: Two Continents Collide.*

Vannini, Fr. Fulgentius, *The Bell of Lhasa,* (New Delhi: Devarsons [Stylish Printing Press], 1976).
von Fürer-Haimendorf, Christoph, *The Sherpas of Nepal,* (London: John Murray, 1964).

Waddell, L. Austine, *The Buddhism and Lamaism of Tibet,* (New Delhi: Heritage Publishers, 1979).
Waddell, L. Austine, *Lhasa and Its Mysteries,* (New York: Dover 1988).
Weerasingha, Tissa, *The Cross and the Bo Tree,* (Taichung, Taiwan: Asia Theological Association, 1989).

Wessels, C., *Early Jesuit Travellers in Central Asia 1603-1721*, (The Hague: Martinus Nijhoff, 1924).

Williams, Paul, *Mahayana Buddhism: The Doctrinal Foundations*, (London: Routledge, 1989).

Willson, Martin, *Rebirth and the Western Buddhist*, (London: Wisdom, 1987).

Winter, Ralph D., and Hawthorne, Stephen C., *Perspectives on the World Christian Movement*, (Pasadena: William Carey Library, 1981, reprinted 1999).

Wulin, Liu, *Chang Thang*, (Beijing, China Forestry Publishing House, 1999).

Young, John M.L., *By Foot to China: Mission of the Church of the East*, (Tokyo: Radio Press, 1984).

Younghusband, Sir Francis, *India and Tibet*, (London: John Murray, 1910, reprinted Hong Kong: Oxford University Press, 1985).

Zwalf, W., *Heritage of Tibet*, (London: British Museum Publications, 1981).

Index

philosophical changes 39-42
spread across Asia 42-44
tantra and 50-51
truth, view of 41, 42, 48, 51,
52, 89, 151, 153, 162-
163, 165, 169, 237
absolute 41, 46, 151,
162, 163, 183, 238
relative 41, 162, 183-184
view of reality 88, 153, 165
Theravada (Hinayana) chart p.
47, 236, 297, 298, 300,
309
Tibetan: see Tibetan Buddhism
Buryat Mongols of Siberia 8, 9, 69,
74, 75, 104, 117, 128,
212, 244, 261, 282, 294
language of 131, table p. 213
Buryatia 49, 127, 129, 130, 147, 282,
304, 305, 315
Buddhism in 63, 69, 74, 122
map p. xiv

C

camels, Bactrian 17, 43, 107, 291
Carey, William 116-117, 294, 316,
321, 341
Catholic missions 108-109, 111-116,
121 - 122, 124, 129-130,
131, 132, 145, 228, 242,
244, 251, 295
Andrade at Tsaparang 112-113,
115, 116, 294
Cacella and Cabral in Bhutan and
Tibet 113, 170, 294, 323
Lhasa 113-115, 116, 249, 294,
323
Peking 322
Sichuan-Tibet border 228
chan Buddhism 55, 297
Chenresi 235, 297, 301
China
and Inner Asia 13, 68, 124
and Outer Asia 17-18
Buddhism in 19, 28, 43, 44, 49,
99,
Catholic missions in 112, 130,
228
languages 213
modern 75, 123, 124, 131, 166

Mongolia and 68, 69, 127-128
Nestorian Christianity in 19, 108,
109, 110
Protestant missions in 121-122
tantra and 49
Tibet and 54, 69, 104, 272
Tibetan Buddhism in 8
Tibetan Buddhist peoples of 282
China Inland Mission 121, 295
chorten 2, 224, 297, 300
Christ: see Jesus Christ
Christian and Missionary Alliance 118,
121
Christian literature 114-115, 118, 121,
147, 224, 242, 248, 249 -
250, 335
Christian missions (see also individual
countries, churches, and
mission groups)
early Catholic and Nestorian, to
Asia 108-116
holiness in 196, 197, 210, 221,
222
incarnational 201, 205-207, 210,
227
magic key, nonexistence of 229
methods of 223
ministry, approaches in 170
preparation for 247-248
Protestant 116-122, 130
relationships in 212, 218, 221,
table p. 231, 232-233,
240, 253, 275, 286
short-term trips 241-242
strategy 141, 170, 223, 332,
252-259
Christian professionals 242-243
Christian workers
as ambassadors 193, 194, 197,
202, 208, 210
cooperation and 143, 145
cultures, and other 258
death of 118
development, in 223
evangelism and 251
language learning 247
lifestyle of 257
long-term 242, 243, 333
strategy and, see Strategy
tourism and 223, 258

348